American History/American Television

Ungar Film Library

Stanley Hochman, GENERAL EDITOR

American History American Television

Interpreting the Video Past

Edited by John E. O'Connor

Foreword by Erik Barnouw

Frederick Ungar Publishing Co.

NEW YORK

Copyright © 1983 by John E. O'Connor
Printed in the United States of America

Library of Congress Cataloging in Publication Data
Main entry under title:

American history, American television.

  (Ungar film library)
  Bibliography: p.
  Includes index.
  1. Television broadcasting—United States—Addresses,
essays, lectures. 2. United States—Popular culture—
Addresses, essays, lectures. I. O'Connor, John E.
II. Series.
PN1992.3.U5A48   1983   791.45'09   83-4954
ISBN 0-8044-2668-6
ISBN 0-8044-6621-1 (pbk.)

For Alice

Contents

CONTENTS

Preface

This volume seeks to demonstrate some of the ways in which political, social, cultural, and other historians are beginning to study television both as a force in recent history and as a medium for scholarly research. The essays published here have all been conceived and written expressly for this volume, and they all reflect the experience of a unique association. Over a twelve-month period in 1981 and 1982 the Columbia University Seminar on Cinema and Interdisciplinary Interpretation devoted itself to the presentation and formal discussion of drafts of each of these fourteen essays. Those sessions, which took place at the Museum of Modern Art in New York City, provided opportunities for participants in the project as well as the general membership of the seminar to benefit from each other's insight and experience in working with what, for many, was a new medium for research. The overall project was carried on with the support of a grant from the Rockefeller Foundation. Abstracts of those seminar presentations and transcripts of most of the discussions are preserved in the Film Study Center of the Museum of Modern Art and in the archives of the University Seminars, 606 Dodge Hall, Columbia University, New York, N.Y. 10027. Perhaps in the future scholars will be interested in this record of how historians tried to come to grips with these new media materials.

Thanks are due to the entire membership of the seminar and especially to its cochairman Daniel J. Leab. In providing the forum for our interchange and the administrative support necessary for the project, the University Seminars program and its director, Dean Aaron Warner, have reaffirmed the program's nearly four decades of commitment to the encouragement of interdisciplinary scholarship. I also wish to thank Eileen Bowser, John Gartenberg, and the other staff of the Museum of Modern Art. Thanks, of course, are due to the Rockefeller Foundation for providing the necessary financial support. For arranging to make special compilations of television news materials available to teachers and researchers using this book, thanks to James Pilkington of the Vanderbilt University Television News Archive. In addition to serving as secretary of the seminar and writing an essay of his own for this volume, Gregory Bush was of special assistance in preparing the chronology. Thanks, too, to Mary White, secretary to the Man and Technology Degree Program at New Jersey Institute of Technology and to William F. X. Reynolds and John Dempsey of NJIT's Instructional Media Center, who have been unstinting in their assistance. For other various forms of input I also want to thank my colleagues Jeffrey Sturchio and Robert Lynch of the humanities department at the Institute.

Of course, any errors of fact or interpretation are the responsibility of myself and the authors.

JOHN E. O'CONNOR
Bloomfield, N.J.
January 1983

Foreword

ERIK BARNOUW

Some years ago I attended a number of meetings at which the need for television archives was fervently argued. At one meeting, sponsored by the Ford Foundation, I was asked to assemble a committee that would draw up a statement of the kinds of programming that should be included in an American television archive. What should be its selection policies? What programs should be preserved?

I duly assembled historians and others for an all-day meeting in Washington and posed the question: "Just what should a historian or other scholar, forty or fifty years from now, be able to find in such an archive?"

Not surprisingly, they wanted network news programs as well as all network documentaries and special events. But their list went much further. They wanted all drama specials and samples of continuing drama series—not just of the first season but intermittent samples of an entire run, so that the subtle shifts in stereotypes and other clichés could be traced and studied. They wanted talk shows of all kinds: would not the selection of guests, they argued, be an indicator of our society's priorities, tastes, prejudices, and evasions—as would the talk itself? And they wanted quiz programs: again, the questions asked—and not asked—would provide a gold mine of clues to currents of our time. And they wanted the game shows in which people win motor boats, trips to Tahiti, fur coats, microwave ovens, and king-size beds and know exactly how to scream, jump up and down, and hug and kiss the master of ceremonies when their winnings are announced. Had this not become a standardized tribal dance of the culture? The committee also wanted promotional spots and copious commercials, and they wanted them in context. Typical days should occasionally be recorded in full, they urged, so that a researcher would be able to taste the total experience of those whose lives—as the polls tell us—are accompanied six hours a day by television images and sounds. The committee also wanted a sampling of local and regional programming. It was saying, in effect: these are all parts of our social history. All reflect, in one way or another, pressures and impulses at work. And while our society shapes these programs, they are presumably helping to shape us.

We had no inkling that a year or two after that meeting there would be, in the copyright revision of 1976, a mandate to the Library of Congress to create a television and radio archive to preserve the broadcasting "heritage" of the American people, and to provide access to "historians and scholars" for research purposes. It was to include programs that were of "present or potential public or cultural interest, historical significance, cognitive value, or [that were] otherwise worthy of preservation." Apparently it was an idea whose time had come. In addition to the Library of Congress archive, other valuable research collections were taking shape.

The Library collection was launched in 1978 as part of a newly formed Motion Picture, Broadcasting, and Recorded Sound Division. For its first three years I had the privilege of serving as its chief, and the half-forgotten committee meeting often came to mind. I felt I had some notion of what scholars of a future day might hope to find. In the context of the Library of Congress and its history, those hopes did not seem unreasonable. Among the diverse treasures of its rare book room one finds surviving copies of dime novels—now considered an important link in our social and political history, but once regarded as so ephemeral in value that most people felt they could be thrown on the trash heap. Who can tell what information historians will glean from our broadcasting ephemera as well as from our more "important" programming?

In the present volume, a group of historians probes the long-range historical meanings of our television fare. Each has selected a specific series or genre or phenomenon. I am delighted (and not surprised) to find that they are concerned not only with news, documentaries, and special events, but also with those items of popular culture that are generally regarded as "mere" entertainment but that may be as influential—or more so—in the complex struggle of ideas. I find both fascinating and meaningful the collection that has been assembled under the able editorship of John E. O'Connor. I hope this volume, a logical successor to the highly regarded *American History/American Film*, will be followed by more such studies and compilations and lead to a greater awareness of the many ramifications—social and political, economic and psychological, conscious and unconscious—of our television fare.

Introduction: Television and the Historian

JOHN E. O'CONNOR

One of the special highlights of a typical tourist's visit to Southern California is a tour of the NBC studios in Burbank. Amiable guides lead groups of thirty or more wide-eyed visitors through a series of sound stages identified with various programs—*Real People*, perhaps, or the David Horowitz's *Fight Back!*, a syndicated consumer program. They walk through "Costume," where dozens of seamstresses scurry amid cutting tables and sewing machines; through huge prop rooms where they might find the backdrops to last year's favorite game shows; past Floyd Jackson's shoeshine stand where, since the studio opened in 1952, numberless stars have tried to out-tip one another and left their autographs on the walls. Finally the main attraction, the set of Johnny Carson's *Tonight Show*. For ten or fifteen minutes people sit in an empty theater gaping at the place where Johnny and Ed McMahon perform. The guide points out the booth where Doc Severinsen sits and demonstrates how little footstools automatically slide out from beneath the guests' chairs to make them more comfortable. People are told that if they queue up at 7:00 or 7:30 the next morning they will stand a good chance of getting tickets for an actual performance. Then it's off again to the souvenir shop and the parking lot. NBC reports that two hundred thousand people each year take the tour.

What can it be that attracts so many to these hallowed halls? One answer may be that, in a very real sense, *television is American Culture*, and the personalities of television (be they actors, comedians, politicians, or news commentators) are those with whom the society most readily identifies. At least for the vast majority of Americans— people who may never attend a play or a concert, visit a museum, or read a book—TV is all there is. Elite bias aside, there is considerable truth to former FCC Commissioner Lee Lovinger's 1966 description of television as "the literature of the illiterate, the culture of the low-brow, the wealth of the poor, the privilege of the underprivileged and the executive club of the excluded masses."[1]

TV has become a significant part of American life, with 98 percent of American homes having at least one set and with the average set turned on six hours each day. Not everyone watches intently, to be sure. For some the TV is a babysitter, an alarm clock, a night light. In the wake of the New York blackout of 1966, some even noted its significance as a birth-control device. Two million people live alone in New York City. For many of them (the aged, infirm, or otherwise housebound) the television serves as a lifeline, their only link with the outside world. For others, reliance on the tube may be more purely psychological. They may use it to keep them company as they cook dinner or as therapy when they feel depressed. In one way or another every American household is identified by its television habits, those without a TV set perhaps more than all the rest.

Literally thousands of studies of television and its impact on human behavior have appeared since the 1960s. Yet the tendency has been for humanists to tread lightly. Refusing to admit that they too may have been TV sports junkies or closet soap opera fans, scholars argued, for example, that the medium was too young to warrant refined critical approaches; that the process of television production was such a corporate effort and its intent so blatantly commercial that criticizing it as art seemed inappropriate; that American television was, to use Newton Minow's famous phrase, "a vast wasteland" that mocked serious analysis.

In the last few years this situation has been changing. Recognizing that not all television is unredeemable and that even the aesthetically indefensible cannot be ignored if it so obviously influences the world around us, scholars of American studies, popular culture, political science, and history have come to study seriously the role of television in American culture. This book is intended to demonstrate several approaches undertaken by American historians in this new field.

Television as a Force in American Life

One of the first American historians to write about the significance of television for an understanding of American culture was also one of the most perceptive. In 1953 David M. Potter published his widely read and still often cited book, *People of Plenty: Economic Abundance and the American Character.* In it Potter recognized television as in some ways the ultimate American institution, a creature of the advertising industry, which was already using the new medium as its most effective tool. As he made clear in an article some years later, Potter saw in television the culmination of America's long evolution toward a mass society. Though control by advertisers was clearly at the heart of the undistinguished quality of most television, he traced the roots of this problem deeper into the culture. Unlike other societies in which the public had traditionally accepted standards of taste imposed from above, Americans had rejected such authority (and the more refined intellectual and aesthetic values associated with it) as undemocratic. In the process, the broad sweep of American culture had been shackled to the popular taste, in all its mediocrity. "Even without advertising," Potter predicted, "the mass society would show in the realm of television the same preferences which it had shown in motion pictures, drugstore paperback fiction, and tabloid newspapers."[2]

Another early perspective on television was offered by Daniel Boorstin. Whereas Potter viewed it as an expression of the broader American mass culture, Boorstin showed how media technology had twisted that culture in unfortunate ways. In his 1962 book, *The Image: Or What Happened to the American Dream*, Boorstin employed the term "pseudo event" for those artificial "realities" such as press conferences and publicity stunts designed to orchestrate the media and, thereby, to influence the public mind. Modern-day journalists, forced by pressure to deliver stories with both drama and immediacy, had turned from gathering news to creating it. Goading public officials to make controversial statements, Boorstin explained, was just one of the journalistic techniques developed in response to the demands of the technology for a new and exciting story every morning for the front page and every evening for the network newscast. Similarly, he argued, the heroes of yesterday have been replaced by the celebrities of today, "human pseudo events" who are recognized for their "well-knownness" rather than highly regarded for their accomplishments. Whereas in the past it was a mark of dignity to stay out of the news, today's celebrities hire press agents to assure that they stay in the public eye. Boorstin saw this manipulation as having a negative impact on the national consciousness. The news media in general and television in particular had jaded us as a people into expecting exciting news or spectacular entertainment whenever we turned on our sets. Writing more generally a few years later in *The Americans: The Democratic Experience*, Boorstin held that "just as the printing press five centuries before had begun to democratize learning, now the television would democratize experience." Unfortunately, he concluded, those shared images perceived through the tube were far removed from reality.[3]

Potter's and Boorstin's ideas are especially interesting because they were expressed so early in the nation's television experience. A decade later, in 1970, Erik Barnouw's landmark *The Image Empire*, the third volume of his *History of Broadcasting in the United States*, went deeper. By focusing, for example, on the role of broadcasting in the history of McCarthyism, both for the industry's own experience with blacklisting and for the long-credited role of television in the public's disaffection with McCarthy, he placed in sharp relief the interplay of television and other trends in modern American culture.[4] In this model of scholarship, Barnouw exemplifies for us what one real contribution of the historian can be to the study of television—the filling out of the historical and cultural context. Television has, after all, become an integral part of the American cultural environment at the same time as our culture has undergone some other notable changes. All cultures evolve and—TV or no TV—a society such as ours could never remain static. There is, however, considerable evidence to suggest that at least a few recent cultural trends have been influenced by television. Consider the following selective survey.

Leisure and Entertainment. In the twentieth century, as their available leisure time has expanded, Americans have dramatically changed the ways in which they entertain themselves. Access to professional entertainment once depended on whether or not one lived in the city and could afford both the time and the expense involved in attending a play or a concert. Nineteenth-century vaudeville changed some of that, and soon after 1900 the proliferation of nickelodeons and movie theaters in working-class neighborhoods made world-famous entertainers available to anyone who had some small change and a free hour after work. Then radio and TV brought the best actors, comics, and musicians right "into our living rooms." Today, with cable television sweeping the country, we have come to expect enthralling diversion twenty-four hours a day at the twist of a knob. There was a time when people of wealth and breeding would not dream of frequenting theaters and concert halls where more "common folk" were likely to be found. Today, it would not be surprising to find the unemployed auto worker watching the same soap opera or *Masterpiece Theater* episode as a Park Avenue lady of leisure or a prep school coed. In entertainment, at least, there has been a great democratization.

Exposure to television has not made the masses more discriminating, but now that the novelty of TV is gone, we are certainly more aware of technical quality, narrative structure, and general acting ability. We have come to demand in everything we watch the slickness and technical pizzazz originally developed for commercials and sports spectaculars. As a result old (even "classic") movies may seem to drag on, and audiovisual aids hold less student interest if they lack the punch of a TV commercial.

Another major shift in entertainment patterns is that fewer people go out at night. More and more the home has become the family "entertainment center," with the TV set at the heart of it. Since 1950 movie theaters, skating rinks, and neighborhood taverns have closed by the thousands—victims of this entertainment revolution. It is telling that the newest football stadiums (football, by the way, is a sport peculiarly well suited to television) are equipped with huge screens above the scoreboard so that the people who took the trouble to come out in the cold and paid $20 for the privilege will not feel that they have "missed out" on the instant replay they might have seen at home.

A homogenized national culture. The mass society that began to develop in congested industrial cities at the turn of the century has been fulfilled, and television, through its advertising and its reduction of taste to whatever may be nationally acceptable, is an integral part of it. America used to be a collection of regions. Each had its distinctive turn of phrase, its own folk tradition, its peculiar taste in music, architecture, and food. The experience of first radio, and later, television has served to reinforce the trend to sameness that has overtaken us. Pressures are increased for young people with regional accents to "correct" their speech patterns and adopt "proper" pronunciation—like the announcers on TV. Children of today are more likely to be steeped in the lore of *Sesame Street* than in their regional folk tradition, to be more familiar with *Mr. Rogers' Neighborhood* than with their own. The movement toward a national culture can be traced back to the late nineteenth century and beyond, but over the last thirty years TV has been the single most influential force in that direction.

This unifying of the culture is important with regard to news as well as entertainment. The development of network television has provided a common base of information that is shared by viewers in every corner of the nation. Some of the more than 70 percent of Americans who say that they get most of their news from television may have stopped reading newspapers, but it is likely that others of them (except perhaps for radio) got no news at all before TV. Thanks to television they have become part of the cultural mainstream. Along with the demise of major city and regional newspapers, we have lost the variety of editorial perspectives on national issues they used to provide. Today, if there is a bias in the way news is presented, it is presented that way to viewers everywhere. For example, Edward Jay Epstein argues that, since international news is thought to be of little interest to viewers outside the Washington-New York axis, it is given less than it appropriate share of network coverage.[5] The ratings-conscious network news understandably puts heavy weight on stories that will have meaning for any and all viewers—hence stories of "national significance." Local radio, TV, and newspapers are left to cover stories of local importance, but regional news often goes unreported. To some extent we have come to think of regions of the country according to when our favorite shows come on there; they're either an hour ahead or two hours behind.

Social and cultural values. In any society, social and moral values evolve over time. As a society becomes more complex, such changes tend to happen more quickly. In America attitudes toward sex, for example, have been transformed dramatically in the last generation or so. Some who are committed to the older ways (and who prefer simple explanations for complex phenomena) blame TV. In a 1982 PBS special about TV and its critics, Hodding Carter wondered whether the "vast wasteland" might not better be thought of as a "moral swamp."

As early as 1952 hearings took place in the House of Representatives on charges of excessive sex and violence on commercial television, and in the late 1960s two special government commissions reported on television violence and its social impact. In its 1982 report, *Television and Behavior: Ten Years of Scientific Progress and Implications for the Eighties*, the National Institute for Mental Health (NIMH) reaffirms these earlier findings. The incidence of television violence has remained about the same since 1967 (with small variations from year to year). In addition, despite a few studies to the contrary, numerous laboratory and field tests have demonstrated that there is a positive correlation between children's exposure to television violence and the development of their own aggressive behavior.[6]

During the 1950s and early 1960s vigorous self-regulation made the world of television a sexless place where double beds were unknown. When Elvis Presley appeared on the *Ed Sullivan Show* in 1956, he was photographed above the waist to avoid what were thought to be sexually suggestive gyrations, and Jack Paar walked off in a huff when NBC would not allow him to use the words "water closet" on the air. Gradually, in the 1960s and early 1970s programs such as *Laugh-In* and *The Smothers Brothers Comedy Hour* began to introduce sexual references for their shock value, and soon they became routine. Commercials for the most intimate personal care products found their way to the screen, something inconceivable ten years before. All sorts of vehicles were used to present bevies of buxom beauties jiggling their charms to titillate us. Therefore, when extramarital sex and recreational drug use became more socially accepted and divorce figures soared, TV was singled out for blame. Crusades have been mounted by the so-called Moral Majority to force networks to cancel shows its members found objectionable and to boycott the products of the shows' sponsors.

Researchers have been unable to establish causal links between television and sexual behavior as they have with violence and aggression, but it seems inevitable that some correlation exists between changing social values and the evolving television images of them. Other studies have suggested that personal interaction and interpersonal relationships of family members, for example, have been shaped by the social context of viewing. Many families, if they do nothing else as a unit, gather around the television with some regularity. It is socially significant that a large percentage of adult entertainment has therefore become children's entertainment as well. For this reason much television humor today is quite consciously designed to be understood on several levels. Parents have perfected the knack of glancing inconspicuously in little Johnny's or Lucy's direction in hope that such remarks have gone "over their heads." But as Neil Postman posits in his suggestively titled new book, the role of television in introducing children at an early age to sex, alcohol, and the other accoutrements of adult life may be the single most important force in bringing about *The End of Childhood*. [7]

Learning and emotional development. It has long been argued that television is a passive medium, that by spending hours in an almost hypnotic trance before the set, children surely stunt their emotional and intellectual growth. Over the past thirty years, as students did less reading and more watching, the correlation in the public's mind between increased television viewing and falling test scores was inevitable.

Research into these questions has given us more information, but has not provided solid answers. The National Institute of Mental Health (NIMH) confirms that children who watch a great deal of television are also likely to have lower IQ scores and reading comprehension levels. It has not been determined, however, if there is a cause-and-effect relationship, or if both phenomena are the result of larger underlying causes. Research has found that television may enhance materials for creative and imaginative play for some children, but according to NIMH, "the predominant evidence suggests that heavy viewing is associated with lower imagination and less creativity." [8] In addition, habituation to the frantic pace and dynamic movements of television may make it difficult for children to think reflectively. The pace of television may be important for emotional development too. It has been established that when programs set out to instill pro-social or altruistic attitudes in youngsters, a more leisurely pace is much more effective. Tendencies toward violence and aggressive behavior, in fact, may be as much due to the fast-paced and disorienting structure of a program as to its violent content. If, as statistics suggest, the emotional and educational problems of today's children differ from those of thirty years ago, television cannot be ignored as a factor.

Television and Politics. A great deal has been written about the way American political processes have changed because of television. Franklin D. Roosevelt distinguished himself as a master of the media in his own day, but every politician today has either become a media specialist or hired one. As David Broder states in *The Changing of the Guard*: "If there is one institution that has changed American politics since World War II—and changed both the politicians' and the voters' perceptions of reality—it is television."[9] The experience of almost any recent political campaign confirms Broder's charge.

Presidential nominating conventions are now media events. In a government traditionally bound to a party structure, congressional leaders complain of losing their ability to maintain order. Even freshman legislators can afford to ignore the pressure of the party caucus if they know that their reelection is less dependent on party loyalty than it is on their personal image and on the slogans that can be created in a series of two-minute TV spots next fall. Television advertising has become the largest item in the average political campaign budget; the media consultant has become the most important staff member. Another change is the greatly increased stature of the presidency. The White House is assured coverage on almost every nightly news broadcast, while members of Congress or senators have to stand on their heads.

Joel Swerdlow cautions us that while television has transformed American politics, "its influence is like a *pointilist* painting; easy to trace from a distance, but less so the closer one gets."[10] Still the temptation to suggest relationships is great. Since the 1950s, as voter turnout in non-presidential years has slipped into the 40 percent range, it has become increasingly difficult to speak of our system as a "participatory democracy." Could this deepening apathy have something to do with television? The drawn-out disclosures about Watergate brought nightly into our homes and the repeated broadcasts of the Abscam videotapes of congressmen stuffing money into their pockets could not help but diminish public trust in political leaders. As television news of elections involves viewers more and more in the campaign strategy and lays bare more efforts at voter manipulation, should it be surprising that people "tune out"? This is not to suggest that reporters turn their backs, only that scholars should become more sensitive to the ways that media technology may come to shape our history.

There have been many more connections suggested between television and society, but there is not room to explore all of them here. For a more complete survey of research to date readers should turn to the NIMH report, *Television and Behavior* (1982), and to George Comstock, et al., *Television and Human Behavior* (1978).[11] Research of the 1970s has supported the general conclusions of historians such as Potter, Boorstin, and Barnouw. While specific or categorical conclusions on many questions, especially those concerning cause and effect, have thus far eluded students of television, one overall judgment appears sound: television certainly has come to be a significant factor in American life.

Four Approaches to Television as Historical Artifact

To focus more closely on the purposes of this volume, let us consider four ways in which television opens possibilities for productive historical scholarship. These four categories are not perfect by any means. For one thing, there is considerable overlap among them. Another effective breakdown might very well have been based upon different principles. One approach others have tried, for example, is to stress the difference between entertainment and news (or information) programming. As several of the essays to follow demonstrate, this distinction can be very fuzzy indeed. A program such as *60 Minutes*, like much of television news today, is produced with a very careful eye to entertainment values. Instead, these four problem areas have been conceived according to the types of questions historians are likely to ask, and they represent the themes that have been developed in various ways by the scholars represented in this volume.

Television news and documentary as primary evidence for historical events.

On the most obvious level, television news is a visual record of historical events. Some of the most memorable happenings (a word coined by the TV generation) of recent American history are remembered because there was a camera present. While the death of FDR stunned the nation, it was television that made the four days following John F. Kennedy's tragic killing such a poignant experience for the average American. In the midst of that came another tragedy, Jack Ruby's shooting of Lee Harvey Oswald, for the world to see. People remember where they were when they heard the news of Pearl Harbor—a church, or watching a football game perhaps. In 1969, when Neil Armstrong stepped out of his lunar module for the first time, the American people were there on the moon with him. A significant (even pivotal) historical event in its own right, television's live coverage of Armstrong's moon walk was an unforgettable experience for millions.

It is evident that television can help to shape events as well as report them. There can be no doubt that the expected TV coverage of the Democratic Convention in Chicago in 1968 helped the protesters to decide how and when to stage their demonstrations. During the convention coverage at least one network aired pictures of the same incident of street violence twice (pictures taken by different cameras and at different angles) without explanation. Unsuspecting viewers could only assume that they were seeing two incidents instead of one. Another often cited example of television shaping events involved a CBS News special report from Vietnam in February 1968, in which Walter Cronkite came out against deepening U.S. involvement there, and Lyndon Johnson's decision not to seek renomination to another term in the White House. According to David Halberstam, Johnson reasoned that "if he had lost Walter Cronkite he had lost Mr. Average Citizen." More recent scholars have disagreed.[12]

Used cautiously, television news can add intriguing new insights to our understanding of popular history, but the caution must be emphasized. Imagine a world in which the only sources a historian might have to study a period or an event were old newsreels or television news programs. In fact, there are some cases in which this situation exists. Much of the archival record of the breaking of the sound barrier, a particularly important chapter in the history of aviation, was lost in a fire some years ago. Some of the best remaining sources which document that event are the movies of test flights routinely taken by government camera operators. Except for such unusual cases, however, the film or television record is just one of the many types of documents to which the historian should refer.

At first glance it might seem that such a direct visual record would be the best form of evidence. What Lincoln scholar would not trade a new word processor for ten minutes of videotape of what went on in Ford's Theater that April night in 1865? For many events in the twentieth century we have that visual and aural record. But its value is not always clear-cut. The television news film of John Hinkley's attempt to assassinate President Ronald Reagan in 1981 helps to illustrate some of the limitations of the "electronic eyewitness" to a historical event. The camera caught very effectively the instant confusion that the sound of a gunshot sets off in the presence of a world leader. Secret Service agents jumped to protect the president and seized the gunman. We saw Press Secretary James Brady collapse to the pavement. Another camera captured the expression of pained surprise on Reagan's face as he was pushed down into the waiting car. As quickly as possible the networks suspended regular programming and turned to a minute-by-minute account of the events as they transpired in Washington. The result was one of the most exciting half-hours of television in recent years.

Dramatic and unusual as such images are, however, how well can they serve the historian, who should be more interested in analyzing events in context than in simply recounting the electricity of a split-second experience? Certainly the court records of Hinkley's trial and the studies of his background and personality will provide more information about his motives than a picture of the gun being wrenched away. Surely the medical records of those wounded will provide fuller and more reliable evidence concerning the direct results of the attack. For more searching analysis one would expect scholars to refer to the heated (if unproductive) debate on gun control that ensued in Congress, to the public opinion polls that showed how the popularity of the stricken president had been bolstered, or to the flurry of editorials following Hinkley's acquittal that questioned the justice of the insanity defense in American law. The videotape of the shooting itself provides precious little information with regard to these larger questions.

Even in the information that the camera does capture and the network or local station broadcasts, however, there are problems. Which stories are covered, and how they are treated, depends upon numerous factors. Since 1963, for example, when the networks' evening newscasts were expanded from fifteen to thirty minutes, all the news of the day has had to be compressed into about twenty-two minutes (leaving time for commericals). Thus there are serious temporal limitations. Recently expanded late-night news programming provides opportunities for in-depth coverage, but even those shows must be designed to have audience appeal. In his book *Deciding What's News*, Herbert Gans suggests some of the "enduring values" among news personnel (altruistic democracy, responsible capitalism, moderatism, etc.) that he sees influencing decisions about what gets reported and how. Edward Jay Epstein in his earlier *News from Nowhere* suggested that such decisions had more to do with technological and institutional constraints within the industry.[13] In recent years much has been written (and reported on television) about the various efforts of news producers to find new ways to appeal to an audience—for example, by making the news fun. A few dozen media consultants around the country have made a fortune in the process, and one criterion for broadcasting a news story has become its entertainment value.[14]

TV news organizations expend much of their efforts in covering events on which they have advance information. This makes it possible for an assignment editor to use the reporting staff efficiently. Unlike the 1968 Chicago demonstrations discussed above, however, even for a planned event there is usually only one camera sent to record it. This means that the viewer can achieve only one limited perspective on what happened there. As much as the Zapruder home-movie film of the Kennedy assassination told (or confirmed for) investigators about the second-by-second sequence of events that day, Mr. Zapruder did not point his camera at the famous grassy knoll from which another assassin was said to have fled. Just as important, before we see film of a TV news story it has been carefully edited, consolidating its point of view and limiting still further its reliability as a record of events. Historians may by nature be more comfortable in working with "actuality" footage of real events than with a theatrical film contrived by actors and such, but the editing of news film (or videotape) can be every bit as contrived. Usually such editing means deleting all but the passages that can be fitted into the limited time allowed and that fit best within the framework of the news story as written. In the process people's statements are often presented out of context, and the order of events is sometimes confused. In trying to present as technically polished a product as possible, editors often use visual "cutaways" or reaction shots to hide the splices made in the edited audio track. As unintentional as it may be, the result is often to misrepresent (or invite viewers to misconstrue) what people actually said before the camera. Garth Jowett's essay on *The Selling of the Pentagon* in this volume analyzes one of the most controversial examples of this problem where TV editing techniques became the focus of congressional inquiry. Newspapers may not be any better than TV news at accuracy in reporting, but the technical and institutional restraints they face are less limiting than the demands of broadcasting.

The value of television news to the historian, then, is less in documenting the news events themselves than it is in understanding what the public may have thought of them. In an important sense it really does not matter how well television reports on actuality. For the vast majority of viewers, *television is actuality*. What, after all, was really important about the events in the streets of Chicago in 1968? The actual happenings were of primary importance in the federal conspiracy trial that dragged on for the next few years, but in the court of public opinion what was reported meant much more—whether or not it was accurate. Volumes have been written about how well (or how poorly) television portrays reality. But the fact that an event gets reported on television at all is what makes it real for the mass of the American people. No matter how contrived a press conference or how artificial a publicity stunt, if it makes the eleven o'clock newscast it has been impressed upon the public consciousness. In the media-dominated environment of modern America, to be reported is to be.

Using the news in this way to comprehend more fully the public's response to events is especially complex. Consider one factor, for example—the social or psychological context in which the information is received. Media expert Tony Schwartz points out that the relative impact of a news story (or a commercial, for that matter) may depend on the way it resonates with the rest of the culture. Will the story fit the viewers' expectations or run counter to them either in context or in mode of presentation?[15] These expectations can and do change on a day-by-day basis. The impact of *Harvest of Shame* (1960), a CBS documentary on the plight of migrant farm workers, was increased immeasurably because it was originally broadcast late in the afternoon of Thanksgiving Day. Images of starving migrant children were especially effective among viewers who had just pushed themselves away from the holiday table. Religious, ethnic, and occupational groups are likely to respond differently to particular stories as well. One would expect viewers in Chicago, for example, where there is a large Roman Catholic Polish-American population, to have responded in a special way to the news of the assassination attempt on the Pope. On the other hand, as Robert Allen describes in his essay on *The Guiding Light*, many soap opera viewers objected to having their favorite serial interrupted with live "breaking" news of that same story.

There may be long-term effects of the treatment of the news on the public mind. By covering a story on the news, television elevates it to the same level of importance as every other story. Placing it last and introducing it with a chuckle is not enough to diminish the significance of an item being covered on the same broadcast as a presidential press conference and an overseas war. The more troublesome result may, however, be the trivializing of the really important news stories, which, in the unconscious response of the public, may seem no more important than the beauty contest or the cat up a tree.

Television news, then, offers significant opportunities for studying the public perception of issues and events over time, but the myriad technological, institutional, and psychological factors involved make such study a fascinating challenge. Historians always want to know all they can about the conditions under which their primary sources took shape. With television as a primary document, this requires that they begin to understand the inner workings of a complex industry.

Television as social and cultural history. Using this second approach, historians can find in television a rich mine of sources for studying social and cultural history. Sociologists, psychologists, and other behavioral scientists have begun to establish correlations between television content and the attitudes of TV viewers. These experiments were easier to mount twenty or thirty years ago when viewers could be compared with nonviewers or when people could be studied before and after television entered their lives; today virtually everyone has had exposure to the medium. Laboratory experiments and poll taking, however, are not the techniques of the historian, who is more likely to concentrate on studying the transformation of either the television content or the changing social attitudes (or both) over time.

The claims of many groups about the way television has affected their image in society are rather impressionistic, but interesting nonetheless. Take, for example, the change that television courtroom dramas such as *Perry Mason* have made people come to expect the same level of edge-of-the-seat suspense in the real-life judicial process, expectations lawyers cannot fulfill. This can be of special significance when TV viewers become jurors (note that a relatively high percentage of jurors are old people, and that old people are also known to be among the heaviest television viwers). At least one county attorney has claimed that his work was affected; if the prosecutor "doesn't resort to theatrics, as the TV prosecutors do, they [jurors] are inclined to bring in an innocent verdict."[16]

There is considerably more evidence to suggest that relevance of television for an understanding of the dynamics of American racism. At least one chapter in the history of American racial attitudes since World War II should focus on the changing role of blacks in American commercial television (on entertainment shows, as news commentators, and in commercials). Although the roles of George and Louise Jefferson still admit to the stereotype, they are considerably different from characters such as Beulah from the early 1950s. The marshaling of minority pressure to change that image is historically significant. The increasing presence of black actors and reporters since the mid-1960s clearly marks the demise (or at least the readjustment) of the color line in one more industry, but in subtler ways it also encourages the broader culture to adapt to change. Unfortunately, racism dies hard. Patterns of unemployment and feelings of interracial brotherhood have changed less quickly. In a way that may be far more important to future generations, however, television has integrated the experience of every American child who watches it.

Those images that find their way into our homes (and presumably influence our view of the world) have become important to all sorts of groups in the society who worry about how they are represented. Two such groups that are interesting because of the seemingly contradictory cases they argue are the corporations and the labor unions. The Mobil Oil Company focused on one side in a May 1981 op-ed page ad in the *New York Times*. Headlined "Does the TV Camera Distort Society?"

the ad argued that business executives as a group were discriminated against on television. Evidence was drawn from a Media Institute content analysis of the 1979–1980 season. "If J. R. Ewing were a woman or a member of a racial or ethnic minority," Mobil asked, "would the person who shot him go unprosecuted?"[17] On the other side, a Union Media Monitoring Project sponsored by three national union organizations published a sixteen-page tabloid entitled "Television: Corporate America's Game," which detailed the results of an impressively broad content analysis they had performed themselves. In it all three network news operations were criticized for presenting pro-corporate rather than a pro-labor bias (in proportion of news stories, NBC was 3 to 1 pro-corporate, ABC 5 to 1, and CBS 6 to 1). For entertainment shows studied (fifty television series in all), the union members who did the monitoring itemized the occupations of all major and all background characters and worked out the percentage that were in typically unionized occupations. The series that ranked highest were those such as *Lou Grant*, which in addition to representing many union trades also developed occasional scripts around labor/management issues.[18] Are the unions right or is Mobil? The likely answer is that both are correct, for a proportion of the viewers. Remembering the importance of the psychological, social, and (perhaps) occupational context of those who watch a program, contradictory messages are possible. Studies showed that the same thing happened with *All in the Family*. While a few viewers may have identified themselves with Archie's position on most social issues, others saw his character as a sarcastic critique of those very same attitudes. All American commercial television, of course, whether it portrays liberals or conservatives, business or labor, presumes support for the capitalist system that produces it.

While researchers have established correlations between certain social trends and television, they have been less successful in *proving* cause and effect. In one sense this is because the tools are not at hand to demonstrate clinically how one set of perceived images (among many external factors) becomes translated into individual attitudes and personality traits. On the other hand, for those who would argue that TV *reflects* more than it shapes values, little attention has been paid to systematically understanding the process that decides how attitudes or values are portrayed. Here the historian can make a significant contribution.

Mobil's presumptive explanation for television's supposedly negative view of business people was that a majority of "the handful of Hollywood producers responsible for what the rest of us see" are "admittedly anti-business." Incongruous at face value, the other problem with such logic is that nothing in modern corporate television happens so casually. The industry today is so bound by complex institutional limitations that it borders on the ridiculous to suggest that a few people's prejudices might be allowed to shape TV content over a long period of time. As historians achieve access to the manuscript records of the industry and as the principals in the earlier history of the medium have their insights drawn out, we can come to understand much more about the ways in which images reach the screen.

Several of these factors are made evident in the essays to follow. For example, there are dramatic considerations in producing for television that limit the choices producers can make. On this point see especially Kenneth Hey's essay on the evolution of early television drama and Robert Allen's on the dramatic structure of soap operas and the ways in which form shapes content. Political pressures become involved. Bert Spector raises such issues in analyzing the troubles between the Smothers Brothers and CBS in the late 1960s; and Thomas Cripps analyzes the political pressures brought to bear on the producers of *Amos 'n' Andy* by the NAACP. Commercial considerations in television characteristically prevail over all the rest. Not only do programs have to attract the largest possible audience, they must also appeal to their advertisers. This factor was more important in the 1950s than it is today, as pointed out in Peter Rollins's discussion of the difficulties the *Project 20* team had with their sponsors and by Daniel Leab's recognition of the importance of the support of the Alcoa corporation to Edward R. Murrow's efforts at CBS. Although technological advances seem to be opening up new opportunities all the time, the historian must also remain aware of what was technically possible at different times in the past. Surely, as David Culbert notes, even with then-current technology a more effective job could have been done in staging and televising the 1960 presidential debates. By documenting such dramatic, political, commercial, and technical considerations and evaluating their impact on production, historians can help to define the complex relationships between television and society.

Faced with the question of which caused which, the TV image or the social reality, historians have understandably been cautious. Lawrence Lichty's essay on the charges of news bias affecting the 1972 election provides several interesting examples. Progressively, TV has been seen as an "agenda setter" that may help to focus the public's attention on an issue, but does not really shape the public's response. In general, serious scholars in various disciplines have suggested that, rather than creating new social values out of thin air, TV images serve more to direct and reinforce attitudes that have their roots in many other aspects of the culture.

Historian Paula S. Fass has written, "Television programs can do what very few other historical documents can: provide a focus for studying the slow process by which common images evolve within a recognizable context."[19] As the sources open up (see the guide to archival sources on television in the appendix to this volume) the methodological and conceptual tools of the historian will offer important insights into a field which, until now, has had to rely on at least some guesswork.

The history of television as industry and as art form. As noted above, Erik Barnouw's *Image Empire* (later updated as *Tube of Plenty*) serves as a general model for others, but there are numberless opportunities for more closely defined study. As business-history television has all the drama and lore of other tales of entrepreneurial heroism—William Paley turning the inheritance from his father's cigar business into a huge media empire over which he personally presided for over fifty years—but it also represents some intriguing economic and financial trends. The expansion of the TV marketplace in the early years was phenomenal. In 1949 there were fewer than 1 million TV households in America. Even with a federal freeze on the licensing of new stations (in place from 1948 to 1952) this figure grew to 15 million by 1952. After the freeze was lifted in April of that year, viewership rose again to 30 million by 1955. By the end of the first TV decade in 1960, almost 46 million homes—87.1 percent of all American households—had television.[20] As viewership soared, so did advertising revenue.

Television has proven itself one of the most predictably profitable American businesses. Apparently inflation proof, it has passed through economic hard times without serious financial trouble. For investors, managers, and advertising salespeople on commission, television has proven a gold mine. Even the moving picture companies that shied away in fear for most of the first decade of television's growth soon realized that there was big money to be made in compromising with the beast. Douglas Gomery's essay on *Brian's Song* includes a persuasive analysis of this shift, as the studios first sold off their old movie archives to television and then began producing especially for the small screen.

Personalities and programming have been the focus of much of what has been published on the so-called golden age of television. One of those larger-than-life figures treated most often is Milton Berle, "Mr. Television." His special popularity did give Berle an unusual level of control over his show in its heyday, as Arthur Wertheim notes in his essay, but this situation did not last long. A look at one of the old *Texaco Star Theater* shows quickly indicates that Berle's humor has not survived well, but there are other programs that might be classed as more enduring artistic successes. Such shows rise over the bland sort of corporate decision making that colors most productions. *Marty* is one example. Ironically, as the technology has become less expensive, and independent video artists have proposed to use the medium more creatively, much of their work has involved borrowing the commercial image in order to comment on it.

The most significant factor in the history of television programming is that from the beginning (from the days of radio, in fact) it has been chained to the ratings system and to the advertiser's control. The result has been to keep certain types of programming, in the fine arts for example, to a minimum. The Public Broadcasting System (PBS) has to its credit some fine productions, but it has never been able to make substantial inroads into the larger commercial marketplace. At least one reason for this may be historical. In Britain, Japan, Canada, and elsewhere, where state-sponsored efforts have garnered a larger percentage of total viewership, public networks were able to get a head start before commercial broadcasters entered the field. In America the commercial networks fully dominated the market before public efforts even got off the ground. Some critics suggest that (especially since the introduction of cable) more and better cultural programming should result from the trend toward "narrow casting." But others such as Todd Gitlin argue that cable and the structural changes in the industry that are bound to come with it will not of themselves improve programming unless individuals and communities insist.[21]

For those scholars interested in studying business regulation, television offers ripe ground. Here is an industry founded and nurtured in a regulatory environment already established around radio. Unlike some other industries where the regulation focuses solely on the product (auto safety, for example), in TV the process is regulated as well. The "equal time" provisions of the Federal Communications Act, as long as they continue to stand, must be considered whenever a TV news team covers a political candidate. The article by Gregory Bush on the role of television in Edward Kennedy's unsuccessful campaign for the 1980 nomination demonstrates how such matters helped to determine the early scheduling of a broadcast that may have done real damage to Kennedy's chances even before he announced his candidacy. The regulatory debate continues in Congress as committees continue to study proposed revisions of the still-operative Communications Act of 1934.

There are also interesting chapters to be written on the history of the technology of television. The earliest developments took place in the mid-1870s as mechanical devices were designed to take advantage of the newly discovered qualities of the element silenium—its electrical resistance would vary according to the intensity of the light shined upon it. Gradually electronic scanning devices replaced the mechanical ones, but research dragged on for decades before RCA's famous demonstration of broadcast television at the 1939 New York World's Fair. The developing process of technical standard setting within the industry invites historical analysis, as does the role of corporate decision making in technical innovation. For example, NBC's decision to lead the other two networks in its willingness to broadcast color movies and specials was tied to the efforts of RCA (the network's parent company) to market its newly developed color receivers. Most recently the technology of interactive cable television has made dramatic new applications possible. Advertisers have already begun to use such systems as more reliable and convenient ways to gauge the effectiveness of their commericals or to evaluate products newly introduced into test markets. In terms of impact on the broader society, no technology has been more clearly associated with changes in popular values and belief systems than television.

Television as interpreter of history. Scholars must take note of the ways in which TV docudrama, historical compilations, and entertainment shows placed in historical settings may influence the public's view of its past.

The most subtle and unintended such impact is through the entertainment series.

What a series such as *The Waltons* has to say about life in the Depression is likely to have a far more penetrating and long-lasting effect on the nation's historical consciousness than any number of carefully researched scholarly articles or books. Such a production does not begin without some research, to be sure, but typically it is research to try to identify a series of characteristics (for example, of rural life in the Depression) that can be portrayed simply and visually without distracting the audience from the really important thing—the development of the characters and the situations (often very modern, in contrast to the setting) that make the show entertaining and bring people back week after week. Earl Hamner, Jr., author of the novel *Spencer's Mountain* (1962) and creator of *The Waltons* series which grew out of it, had in fact grown up in Depression Appalachia and thus had a special sensitivity for the material. Here too, however, as might be expected in any series which goes beyond a season or two and requires multiple writers, characters and plot conventions are transformed into stereotypes with which the audience can easily relate. This is why such images of the past are so compelling to the average viewer: they are repeated and reinforced every week, and the characters in them become the viewer's friends. The same might be said about *Little House on the Prairie* or dozens of other historical locales. Is there anywhere a historian who has done as much to influence the public's view of the Korean conflict as have the producers of *M*A*S*H*?

In the early days of television, producers clearly perceived the value of history as a source of both background and subject matter. One form that resulted was the historical compilation film made for television, a technique similar to that used to make compilation propaganda and training fims such as the *Why We Fight* series during World War II. But, as Peter Rollins explains, the productions for television tended to put much more emphasis on entertainment values—values that twisted the history. Another early effort at historical programming was *You Are There*. As Robert Horowitz notes, this series, like much of the earliest TV programming, grew out of radio. Some of the *You Are There* programs appear terribly contrived today because of their artificial situations and their interposition of modern newscasters with historical characters, but Horowitz finds that the series does stand up to historiographical analysis. While *You Are There* may have succeeded at preserving historical values in the production process, however, such concern has not been common in the years since. Consider for example the new series offered on NBC in the fall of 1982 entitled *The Voyagers*. Its stars are two young men who use a hand-held jewellike "omni" to enable themselves to move backward in time to any point in history. Once there they proceed to "give history a shove in the right direction." On one program, for example, they helped Cleopatra escape from Caesar's assassins, suggested to Sir Isaac Newton that he might find it more comfortable to sit under an apple tree while he theorized about the nature of gravity, and convinced Babe Ruth that he had more of a future as a hitter than as a pitcher in the big leagues. Some of the docudramas of the 1970s and 1980s provide equally distressing examples.

As a genre, docudrama has not fared well among historians. The word itself, a convenient composite of "documentary" and "drama," points to the problem. Producers may see themselves (they certainly advertise themselves) as bringing life to the documented actuality—a very misleading idea for the audience. Even the presumption that "documentary" represents truth is palpably, untrue, especially in the hands of a creative editor. Moreover, it is the form and pacing of the drama that gives each production its structure and direction; the history is almost never seen as a limitation. Consider, for example, the docudramas that have been based on the fictionalized trials of both General Custer and Lee Harvey Oswald. As Mark Harris put it in a *TV Guide* article: "The docudrama is routine television dressed up to look serious." Continuing, he quite rightly stressed the overwhelming concern with entertainment values: "The docudrama neither dramatizes nor documents history. We are not seeing the world out there. We are seeing ourselves, watching our own fantasies of life in high places. We are not being illuminated. Rather, we are being in the simplest sense, entertained, immersed in a psychological bath that is painless, soothing fun."[22] Could more be realistically expected from well-trained commercial television producers who take on a docudrama as one more assignment? There is an interesting contrast in the few docudramas that have been produced by teams of historians and producers working hand in hand, usually with grant funds. The unusual control that this allows to the historian has resulted in more historically perceptive productions such as Daniel Walkowitz's *Moulders of Troy* (1979) on the iron workers of upstate New York and Robert Brent Toplin's *Denmark Vesey's Rebellion* (1981), both aired on PBS.

Leslie Fishbein's analysis of *Roots* in this volume finds it to have been a basically well-balanced and responsible portrayal of slavery. As she explains, however, *Roots* had something unique among such historical productions—twelve hours to make its point. In such a situation, especially in the night-after-night miniseries format that *Roots* pioneered, there is room to fill in some of the historical complexity and allow characters to develop some depth as human beings. In contrast, the press kit put out to publicize *The Mayflower*, first broadcast on Thanksgiving eve in 1979, claimed that the show broke "new ground" in historical understanding about the founders of the colonies. How many viewers accepted that ninety-minute popularized image as the last word on the subject, with no idea of the lifetimes of scholarship that have gone into studying colonial New England or how little such research really meant in the design of the production they watched?

As unsatisfactory as most docudramas have proven to be, however, historians cannot afford to turn their backs. It is particularly important that we study television's portrayal of history in general and the docudrama in particular because of the impact they threaten to have on the nation's historical consciousness. In a recent book on feature films that seek to "restage the past," Pierre Sorlin has drawn some generalizations that we should consider for the history of television as well. He notes, for example, that the historical film differs from the work of the historian in that rather than questioning its subject, it simply "establishes relationships between the facts and offers a more or less superficial view of them."[23] The same could obviously be said for docudrama. But the more important point Sorlin makes is that in the media-dominated world of the twentieth century one cannot really understand a nation's sense of itself without understanding these most popular and compelling of historical images. If we are concerned with the popular image of FDR in the country today, there have been several docudramas that are likely to have had far more impact on the public mind than all of the scholarhship since the 1930s put together.

Docudramas, historical compilations, and series such as *The Waltons* or *The Voyagers*, programs that characteristically use or abuse history in fulfilling their real interest in entertainment, represent another perhaps more serious level of concern. In addition to often misrepresenting the events and characters they portray, such programs as a regular diet may have the long-term effect of trivializing the work of the historical profession. Rather than plumb the complexities of issues, analyze the contraditions of human motivation, and interpret events from various perspectives in the context of their own time, film and television producers work to reduce complex issues and motives to simple ones and to present one view of events in a context with which the audience will feel immediately at ease. Moreover, unlike the historical monograph that invites response and rebuttal, the completed film or broadcast docudrama has a more powerful presence—the quality of a more final statement. This is true on several levels. Not only is the film or television production likely to live on itself, either in syndicated reruns or in 16mm classroom screenings, but average viewers are likely to have the feeling that they have actually absorbed and understood the history. Such a response is even more likely in the miniseries format. The viewers who came back three evenings in one week to watch all eight hours of *The Blue and the Gray*, for example, may have felt that they had completed a sort of painless minicourse on the Civil War. CBS went to considerable expense to provide teachers with study guides to the programs, and each episode ended with the injunction that those who wanted to know more should visit their libraries. The promotion of the miniseries, however, as "an American epic," years in the making, "meticulously researched," and based on the work of Bruce Catton, could only encourage the average viewer unquestioningly to accept the program's point of view. There was no effort, even in the materials for teachers, to indicate that other interpretations were possible.

In summarizing the impact of television on the nation's historical consciousness, Daniel Boorstin argued that by focusing people so dynamically on the drama of the present, "television dulled the American's sense of his past."[24] If historians fail to take seriously the television view of American history as absorbed by the culture week after week, the popular definition of the profession itself may be in even deeper jeopardy. Historical scholars may come to be seen even more broadly than they are today as no more than storytellers, moving historical charactes around like actors on the set of *Eleanor and Franklin*.

The purpose of this volume is to demonstrate some of the approaches outlined above through the detailed work of individual scholars. The essays that follow were written expressly for this volume, but they were not intended to be carbon copies of one another. Some deal with specific programs or series of programs, some with different genres of television, some with news, still others with personalities. The fourteen authors have applied varying analytical techniques and have used different types of sources to illuminate their subjects. There are, however, elements that all the essays do share by design. Each author was asked to concentrate on at least one discrete example of what appeared on the screen, and to analyze that material as historical artifact. Each author was also asked to integrate his/her insights into the history of television with our understanding of the broader contemporary culture.

There has been an effort in the choice of topics to span the entire thirty-year period of commercial television's history; the intent is not, however, to draw generalizations about that overall history. Instead, subjects have been kept specific so that the focus would remain on applying both traditional and some relatively new methodologies to the study of television materials. Neither is it the intention here to cover all aspects of television. If it were, the absence of articles on TV commercials, sports, and PBS (to name only three) would be glaring omissions. Rather it is hoped that, in addition to filling out a few interesting chapters in the history of an important American institution, these essays will provide models that others will follow in delving still deeper into the video culture.

Focusing on an analysis of two of the most famous *See It Now* broadcasts, Daniel Leab reevaluates Edward R. Murrow's contribution to broadcast journalism and the television documentary. Though he made protestations of detatched objectivity, Murrow's best shows were those in which he and his team took a stand on an issue. Through careful analysis of such programs and in-depth interviews with Murrow's associates, Leab reevaluates the Murrow legend and finds it sound.

Thomas Cripps's essay on *Amos 'n' Andy* cites extensive manuscript sources as it delves into the controversy between those who brought the show from radio to television and the NAACP, which was particularly concerned about the impact of this show on the public mind. The context of special importance here was the timing of the decision to bring the show to television, and the growing political awareness of the black bourgeoisie who had particular objections to the show. Analysis of the shows themselves indicates considerable effort to present precisely that solid middle-class image that the NAACP wanted. The controversy did die out, but not before it opened fissures in the black leadership community that had significance far beyond the question of what would or would not get on TV.

Why was Milton Berle such a cultural institution in the early years of television, and why did he disappear so quickly? Arthur Frank Wertheim seeks answers to these questions, paying special attention both to the analysis of Berle's comic persona and the technical/commercial pressures of the first years of mass-consumption television. In fact, Wertheim argues, Berle's appeal was quite narrow, limited by the urban concentration of the broadcasting audience in the early 1950s. As the audience grew into the American hinterland, its passion for Berle passed almost overnight.

When Walter Cronkite became host of *You Are There*, there was no way to predict the impact that his career would have on American newswatchers. Neither was it clear how long a life these basically low-budget programs would have, or how well they would stand the test of time and evolving historical interpretation. As Robert Horowitz points out, *You Are There* has had a long life in the history classroom where 16mm prints still find use. Analysis of the programs in light of then-current historiography indicates that the historical research that went into them was substantial.

Between 1945 and the mid-1950s the form of television drama gradually evolved out of a combination of basic dramatic structures, the influential traditions and personalities of the New York City stage, and the commercial and technical imperatives of the new medium. By the time Paddy Chayevsky's *Marty* was produced in 1953, the form had developed an aesthetic all its own. Kenneth Hey analyzes this production in the light of both theater history and the evolving television medium.

Relying on extensive personal interviews with the creative minds responsible for the *Project 20* series, Peter Rollins seeks to understand *Nightmare in Red* as both a political document and an example of 1950s television documentary. An award-winning filmmaker in his own right, Rollins gives special attention to the structure of the compilation film and the difficulties involved in presenting historical subjects in such dramatic forms. The educational objectives of the *Project 20* team,

Rollins argues, were overwhelmed by the prevailing attitudes of the producers' own time in history and by the way they interpreted the requirement that their program also entertain.

Week after week the Smothers Brothers challenged the CBS censors and gradually pushed back the limits on what was acceptable for network TV. Bert Spector concentrates on one of their small victories over the corporate decision makers, the 1968 appearance of folksinger Pete Seeger singing his antiwar tune "Waist Deep in the Big Muddy." The Smothers Brothers, Spector maintains, were in no way radical activists, and the themes presented in their show were already well established in the broader culture. In this context, the resistence of the network is all the more interesting.

If the career of any one politician can be seen as representative of the developing role of television in American politics, that career would be Richard Nixon's. David Culbert's essay draws heavily on manuscript sources and concentrates on the visual texture of Nixon's television image at two critical points in his political life—his 1952 "Checkers" speech and the 1960 presidential debates. Culbert's extensive research in the papers of the political parties and in Nixon's personal papers raises some interesting questions about how politicians may use TV or be used by it.

In his essay on *Brian's Song* Douglas Gomery analyzes the complex and evolving relationship between the Hollywood movie makers and the television industry from 1945 until 1971. Then he analyzes what industry ratings have identified as the most successful movie made for TV. Set out in the formulaic style typical of dozens of Hollywood sports dramas, the success of *Brian's Song* is explained in part by its seemingly sensitive but not too challenging treatment of the race issue.

Through detailed content analysis Lawrence Lichty studies the reporting of the Watergate break-in and its impact on the coverage of the 1972 elections. Historians can learn much from these techniques, developed by communications scholars over the past two decades. Lichty takes the statistical results of his analysis and uses them to focus on such questions as how well TV news covered the break-in and investigation before November 1972, and whether or not it influenced voter behavior.

Challenged by the military and the Congress on *The Selling of the Pentagon*, CBS defended its controversial 1970 documentary on First

Amendment grounds. Relying on extensive personal interviews with the principals and close analysis of the congressional investigation, Garth Jowett considers the merits of the case and its impact on the future of documentary television. Do TV reporters have the same consitutional protections as print journalists? Jowett finds that this important question still remains to be tested in the law.

The most famous and most commercially successful of the 1970s docudramas, *Roots*, garnered huge audiences despite the controversy surrounding Alex Haley's best-selling book, which was criticized for its sketchy research and ultimately for plagiarism. Fishbein analyzes the conversion from the book to the teleplay with which ABC gambled on the new miniseries format. *Roots* was widely credited with having sensitized millions of Americans, black and white, to the historical issues of slavery and racism. Although the series did offer a basically well-balanced and responsible portrayal of slave life, it was based on highly flawed genealogy and on several other questionable assumptions. For example, while current scholarship does demonstrate the continued vitality of the black family under slavery, as book and even more as teleplay *Roots* exaggerated its ability and that of the preservation of the African heritage to shelter blacks from the oppressive and debasing nature of the "peculiar institution."

Perhaps more obviously than any other television form, soap operas can reflect the changes over time in cultural values portrayed on the screen. Robert Allen's essay on *The Guiding Light*, the longest continually running daytime serial (first on radio and then TV), concentrates on how the dramatic structure of such presentations may help to shape their tone and content. Specifically, he spells out some of the basic elements of semiotic analysis and examines how some of the various codes or message systems of the soap opera form help such programs to communicate.

Finally, Gregory Bush studies the role of television in Edward Kennedy's abortive bid for the 1980 presidential nomination. His essay considers television as just one of the important elements in a much-watched campaign, and seeks to establish how and why its influence was felt. Bush sees in television the technological facilitator for the fulfillment of the "cult of personality" in American politics—a theme he traces back to the beginning of the century.

In various ways each of these essays demonstrates the contributions that historians can make to a better understanding of television as an institution by filling out the historical background and analyzing individual television artifacts in terms of their specific historical context: *Marty* in the context of theater history, for example; Milton Berle in the context of the rapidly changing nature of the television audience in the early 1950s; *Project 20* in terms of the pressures within the industry in the midst of the cold war and the personal attitudes the producers had drawn from their wartime experiences of the previous decade; *Brian's Song* in the context of the Hollywood movie industry's evolving relationship with television; *The Selling of the Pentagon* in the context of the history of journalism and the U.S. Constitution. Equally significant, these essays also illustrate the relevance of the study of television for a broader understanding of American culture: its tastes in entertainment, its social and cultural values, its politics, its understanding of its own history, and its more general sense of what is involved in historical scholarship. As recent textbooks have shown, the study of American social, cultural, and political history since 1950 can no longer ignore the influence of TV.[25] In apparent recognition of this fact, besides the exhibits of Lindbergh's plane and the earliest space capsules, the Smithsonian Institution now displays two television props—the original easy chairs from Archie and Edith Bunker's living room.

The tourists who line up in Washington, like those who gawk at *The Tonight Show* set at the NBC studios in Burbank, offer striking testimony about the continuing interest television holds for the American people. The challenge to scholars is to improve our understanding of that relationship.

NOTES

1. Quoted in Martin Mayer, *About Television* (New York, 1972), p. 382.

2. David M. Potter, "The Historical Perspective," in *The Meaning of Commercial Television* (Austin, Tex., 1967), p. 65.

3. Daniel Boorstin, *The Americans: The Democratic Experience* (New York, 1973), p. 393. See also *The Image: Or What Hapened to the American Dream* (New York, 1962).

4. Erik Barnouw, *History of Broadcasting in the United States*, vol. 3, *The Image Empire* (New York, 1970).

5. Edward Jay Epstein, *News from Nowhere: Television and the News* (New York, 1973). For a recent observation on the impact of TV news which challenges the seventy percent Roper poll statistics, see Lawrence Lichty, "Video vs. Print," *The Wilson Quarterly* 6 (winter 1982): 49–57.

6. National Institute of Mental Health, *Television and Behavior: Ten Years of Scientific Progress and Implications for the Eighties*, vol. 1, *Summary Report* (Washington, D.C., 1982).

7. Neil Postman, *The Disappearance of Childhood* (New York, 1982).

8. National Institute of Mental Health, *Television and Behavior*, p. 48.

9. David S. Broder, *Changing of the Guard: Power and Leadership in America* (New York, 1980), p. 386.

10. Joel Swerdlow, "A Question of Impact," *The Wilson Quarterly* 5 (Winter 1981): 89.

11. George Comstock, Steven Chaffee, Natan Katzman, Maxwell McCombs, and Donald Roberts, *Television and Human Behavior* (New York, 1978).

12. David Halberstam, *The Powers That Be* (New York, 1979), p. 514. Elsewhere, David Culbert has challenged the idea that Johnson even saw the program as broadcast; see his "Johnson and the Media" in Robert A. Devine, ed., *Exploring the Johnson Years* (Austin, Tex., 1981), pp. 223–227.

13. See Epstein, *News from Nowhere*, and Herbert Gans, *Deciding What's News* (New York, 1979).

14. On entertainment values in news programs see Ron Powers, *The Newscasters* (New York, 1978).

15. See Tony Schwartz, *The Responsive Chord* (New York, 1973).

16. Harry Castleman and Walter J. Podrazik, *Watching TV: Four Decades of American Television* (New York, 1982), p. 122. Also on *Perry Mason* see Horace Newcomb, *TV: The Most Popular Art* (New York, 1974, pp. 94–100.

17. *New York Times*, 17 May 1981.

18. The Union Media Monitoring Project was sponsored by the International Association of Machinists and Aerospace Workers, the International Union of Operating Engineers, and the Bakery, Confectionery and Tobacco Workers International Union.

19. Paula S. Fass, "Television as Cultural Document: Promises and Problems," in Richard Adler and Douglas Cater, eds., *Television as a Cultural Force* (New York, 1976), p. 56.

20. Christopher H. Sterling and John M. Kitross, *Stay Tuned: A Concise History of American Broadcasting* (Belmont, Calif., 1978), pp. 515, 535.

21. See Todd Gitlin, "New Video Technology: Pluralism or Banality," *Democracy* 1 (October 1981): 60–76.

22. Marc Harris, "Docudramas Unmasked," *TV Guide*, 4 March 1978.

23. Pierre Sorlin, *The Film in History: Restaging the Past* (Oxford, 1980), p. 21.

24. Boorstin, *The Americans*, p. 387.

25. See, for example, James Gilbert, *Another Chance: Postwar America, 1945–1968* (New York, 1981).

1

See It Now: A Legend Reassessed

DANIEL J. LEAB

"Banal, "meretricious," "mediocre," "a vast wasteland"—these phrases are but some of the many negative judgments passed on the general runs of American commercial television programming since the end of World War II. With startling unanimity a surprising number of disparate critics have attacked the great mass of such programming—which, according to one understandably concerned viewer, "now constitutes a major source of behavior . . . for the American people."[1]

These same critics, however, have had a very different reaction to the series *See It Now*, both during its heyday in the mid-1950s and since then. Moreover, this positive response does not arise just because these critics have a tendency (in the words of one concerned viewer) "to disdain the world of television [as] popular culture." They have found *See It Now* better, have argued that its producers had "the simplicity of mind and the sweep of imagination to understand what television can do best in the news field, and "have maintained that it must be numbered among television's "hours of greatness."[2]

What was *See It Now*? There are many answers to that question. A simple (and certainly not incorrect) answer is to describe it as does one current guide to American TV as "the prototype of the in-depth quality television documentary." A veteran network news executive has aptly characterized *See It Now* as a "brilliant" example of "informational programming." A media historian has perceptively lauded the series for "its recognition of television's intrinsic characteristics of intimacy and immediacy in presentation" and for its "probing controversial treatment of . . . events and conditions of our existence." A media critic probably summed up its characteristics best when, in reviewing the history of *See It Now*, he noted that the series examined important subjects "sensibly, critically, fearlessly . . . employed the best of pictures with powerful prose [and] called on the top experts who could add information or opinion."[3]

Such a complex effort did not, like Athena, spring full-grown from the head of Zeus. *See It Now*, throughout its history, was very much the product of the intense and unceasing efforts of a dedicated, hardworking group of people, headed by the series' creators and coproducers, Edward R. Murrow and Fred W. Friendly. The better known of the two men was, is, and probably always will be Murrow. To state that is not to slight Friendly but simply to accept a fact pointed out in 1959 by a newspaper correspondent dealing with their efforts at CBS (the Columbia Broadcasting System): "Murrow's . . . personal prestige overshadows the network and every other figure at the network. A documentary turned out by the team of Murrow . . . and Friendly is, in the public mind, not a CBS documentary or a Murrow-Friendly documentary. It is a Murrow program." And Murrow's prestige and reputation have not diminished over the years. On the contrary, he has become even more respected and revered. In 1975, on the tenth anniversary of Murrow's death, Sir Hugh Greene (then director of the British Broadcasting Corporation) called him "the patron saint of the broadcasting profession." Murrow, as one history of CBS News puts it, "has become the stuff of legend, a figure of Olympian stature."[4]

That legendary stature was hard won. Born in 1908, in modest circumstances, Murrow was graduated from Washington State College in the Depression year 1930. After stints with student and education organizations, he joined CBS in 1935 as director of talks, a low-level job whose main responsibility was to secure important figures for various broadcasts over the fledgling network. Two years later CBS sent him overseas as its European director, them a relatively humble job. As Murrow's biographer points out, he was sent overseas as "an arranger of talks and musical events," not as a correspondent. Adapting to the changing circumstances caused by World War II, however, he did a superb job for the network. By war's end in 1945, he had played a significant role in transforming CBS's one-man European show (himself) into a highly professional, outstanding news operation staffed by correspondents imbued with his zeal and dedication. "Murrow's boys," as they inevitably came to be known, for decades served as the backbone of CBS news and public affairs programming.[5]

His accomplishments as an administrator notwithstanding, Murrow made his public mark as a broadcaster. The rush of Nazi aggression gave him the opportunity. When Hitler marched into Austria in 1938, Murrow—then in Poland—chartered a twenty-four passenger German airliner for himself, flew to Vienna, and broadcast from there and subsequently from London about what had befallen Austria. His broadcasts to the United States during the next months, as diplomatic crisis followed diplomatic crisis and then after hostilities commenced in September 1939, had what has been described as "the special quality of excellence."[6]

As Friendly noted years later: "Whether speaking from the rooftops of London during the Blitz [the massive German air raids on London in 1940-1941] or on a bombing raid over Berlin or from [the concentration camp] Buchenwald on the day it was liberated, Murrow became one of the most identifiable and trusted voices of the war." Although not trained as a print journalist, he had a way with words; his peers were, as one said, "keenly aware of his excellence as a reporter." And these verbal abilities were coupled with a superb and dramatic sense of delivery as well as with a breadth and humanity of thought. Murrow, as one scholar has perceptively and correctly indicated, "in effect sought to become the radio listener's surrogate, speaking in terms he could understand or developing images he could sympathize with." The poet Archibald MacLeish, in discussing Murrow's Blitz broadcasts, said that he "burned the city of London in our houses and we felt that flame . . . [he] laid the dead of London at our doors." Indeed, some of these broacasts have been described as "metallic poetry."[7]

Morever, Murrow had no hesitation about making his views known. He did not believe in objectivity for its own sake. He saw no value in balancing Hitler evenly against Churchill. Murrow, as one observer has said, compared "artificial fairness . . . with balancing the views of Jesus

Christ with those of Judas Iscariot." The broadcaster, as his wife once stated, was a "sufferer," and his wartime broadcasts reflected that aspect of his character, but they also reflected something more—what William Paley (the long-time CBS head and for a while a close personal friend of Murrow) recalls as "some higher mission that overrode his inherent gloom." One of Murrow's boys, Charles Collingwood, has asserted that Murrow's broadcast career was influenced by his belief "that we lived in a perfectible world."[8]

Murrow returned to the United States in 1946 an extremely popular figure and a vice-president of CBS (in charge of news and public affairs). Like many of his peers in the media business, and like many other Americans in general, he hoped the media that "had helped defeat external enemies would now be useful in fighting subtler battles against injustice and ignorance." But within a few years the euphoric idealism of the postwar months had given way to a rancid climate of fear as the cold war fastened its grip on American soceity. Already in 1947, before McCarthyism had become rampant in the media, a disquieted Murrow—obviously uncomfortable as a network executive—resigned his administrative position to return to broadcasting full time. He was happy to do so: "The administrative end has ridden me like a piano on my back." And truth be known, the essentially shy and private Murrow had not done well as a CBS executive.[9]

It was at this time that Murrow met Friendly. Born Ferdinand Wachenheimer in 1915, Friendly grew up in petit-bourgeois circumstances in Providence, Rhode Island. In the mid-1930s, after finishing his education, he entered radio work in Providence, changing his name to Fred Friendly (the surname is a family name of his mother's side of the family). He had some success in Providence, especially with a program series of dramatized biographies of important historical figures, such as Edison and Marconi. Known as *Footprints in the Sands of Time*, the series was later bought from Friendly by a recording company.[10]

World War II was for Friendly—in his own words—"a relatively soft war." After being inducted in 1941, he was involved in the development of a panel competition, "Sergeant Quiz," used for testing GIs on knowledge acquired in basic training. He traveled for the army's Information and Education Section, setting up the quiz at various camps and lecturing to soldiers about the war's background. In 1943 he became overseas correspondent for the *CBI Roundup*, the army daily for the China-Burma-India theater of operations (a sort of Asian equivalent of *Stars and Stripes*). Friendly reported from all over the world on such events as the D-Day landings in France and the atomic bombings of Hiroshima and Nagasaki. After the war he spent the next few years, as one history puts it, "making the rounds of networks and agencies trying to sell program ideas." He sold to the National Broadcasting System in 1948 a panel quiz show called *Who Said That?* It was well received, with one influential media critic calling the program "one of the happier of recent inspirations in radio."[11]

Most commentary about Murrow verges on hagiography, and I could find little serious writing about him or his efforts that did not incline to the adulatory. There is no such unanimity of opinion about Friendly. There is general agreement about his "enormous energy," "superb technical skills," "superior taste." He has been dubbed affectionately by his colleagues "Big Moose," and has been less warmly styled "Brilliant Monster." A man of great passion, Friendly has been known to be extravagant in praise of his associates; he also, when dissatisfied, expressed his displeasure in no uncertain ways—shouting loudly and at times abusively, and even flying "into tantrums" now and then. The story is probably apocryphal, but it is reported that once he "picked up a table and threw it at the head of a young assistant." But this passion, inspired by very high standards, also enabled him to do things that supposedly couldn't be done. Fellow producers, who were not particularly enamored of him, remember Friendly as "a gutsy guy" and as someone who "went ahead and did what everybody who knew better knew you couldn't do. He broke the rules." In so doing Friendly made basic, lasting contributions to the art of TV documentary. As for *See It Now*, a close observer of its operations recounted at the time that "Friendly's vitality . . . permeates the offices. . . . Murrow is held in awe."[12]

Such distinctions aside—and the different personalities of the men account for them as much as anything—their collaboration was close and effective (years later a veteran of the series emphasized that it "*was* Fred Friendly as much as it was Ed Murrow"). As in any joint creative relationship involving people of intelligence, passion, and energy, there were occasional tensions between Murrow and Friendly, but nothing lasting or serious. Murrow's biographer has found only "a sole major occasion" in their long association when Friendly was seriously reproached by his associate, and that was when their active collaboration had been over for some years. In the main, they worked extremely well in tandem, especially given the divergent backgrounds of the two men. The working marriage of their great, if diverse, skills produced enviable offspring both before and after *See It Now*.[13]

The collaboration began with production of a record album, *I Can Hear It Now*, "the history of an era spoken by the men who made it and narrated by Edward R. Murrow." This forty-five minute "scrapbook in sound" began with Will Rogers discussing the Depression in 1932 and ended with General Douglas MacArthur accepting the surrender of the Japanese aboard the battleship *Missouri* in 1945. Chance played a role in the making of this album and the birth of the Murrow-Friendly team. Facilities were available because the musicians' union had for the moment banned its members from playing recording sessions, and as Friendly recalls, CBS "wanted material to keep the idle recording facilities busy."[14]

I Can Hear It Now, released toward the end of 1949, was a phenomenal success both critically and commercially. It won many awards including the Newspaper Guild Page One Award for its "stirring presentation of contemporary history." Selling approximately 250,000 copies within a year of its release, *I Can Hear It Now* was, by all accounts, "the first non-musical album to be a financial success." Murrow and Friendly collaborated on other such records over the next few years (including an *I Can Hear It Now* for the years 1945-1949, which was released in 1950, and a collection of Winston Churchill's speeches).[15]

The Murrow-Friendly partnership then put together for broadcast over the CBS radio network a weekly program, *Hear It Now*, which made its debut toward the end of 1950. Described as a "document for the era," "a new magazine of the air," "a current history set forth in the voice of the people who make it," *Hear It Now* was produced with verve, imagination, and intelligence. The hour-long program did well in the ratings and was a critical success (the prestigous Peabody Award was but one of several it earned). Designed to deal both with important and not-so-important issues and events of the week past, *Hear It Now* was kaleidoscopic in content. Thus the first show included commentary on the war in Korea from the perspective of Marine recruits, Carl

Sandburg reading poetry, and Thomas Dewey and Bernard Baruch discussing the state of the economy.[16]

See It Now initially was a half-hour television version of the Murrow-Friendly radio series. It premiered Sunday afternoon, November 18, 1951, on the CBS-TV network. During the 1951–1952 season, *See It Now* was presented from 3:30 to 4:00 in the afternoon, thus making it part of what Murrow aptly called "that intellectual ghetto" of Sunday afternoon programming. *See It Now* inched its way to the fringes of prime time during the 1952–1953 season, when it was presented Sundays between 6:30 and 7:00 in the evening. The series had a regular half-hour slot on Tuesday night at 10:30 during the 1953–1954 and 1954–1955 seasons. Thereafter, until July 1958, when the program went off the air, *See It Now* was an irregularly scheduled program presented about eight times a season, usually for an hour but occasionally for ninety minutes. At this point, jaundiced spectators dubbed the series "See It Now and Then."[17]

The first telecast in 1951 utilized a familiar magazine-style format, one that would define the series for its first two seasons. It included Murrow talking either live or on film with CBS correspondents about purported atrocities taking place during the Korean War and about United Nations efforts toward achieving disarmament; the telecast also included a very moving filmed visit in Korea with Fox Company's Second Platoon, United States 19th Infantry, a visit that emphasized the men rather than hardware of issues. This segment caught the soldiers (to use a critic's description) "as they ate and slept and gambled and groused and joked, catching the tedium of warfare, the waiting, the humor of an essentially unhumorous profession."[18]

For all the pungency of this segment, *See It Now*, as one media historian correctly points out, "in content . . . made a cautious start." And the format remained cautious for some time. Murrow and Friendly dealt and quite well (winning various prestigious awards) with a potpourri of topics, none really controversial. One student has described the bulk of the subjects covered during the 1951-1952 and 1952-1953 TV seasons as "current events of interest to the nation as a whole . . . such as speeches of national significance, disasters, and international happenings" as well as features "which added more of a note of sheer entertainment." These topics—whose treatment in each case seldom exceeded ten minutes—included floods in the United States and England, Winston Churchill speaking at a British political rally, a visit to a West Virginia coal mine, an interview with historian Arnold Toynbee, and a trip on the Orient Express. Some topics were dealt with live; more were filmed (as would be true throughout the history of the series); all were held together by Murrow's incisive and urbane commentary. At the time Murrow told an interviewer that "we try to handle stories differently from the way they were presented earlier," but he also declared, in response to the many critical garlands gathered by *See It Now* during its first two broadcast seasons, that "everyone yelled genius. . . . We only did the obvious." And these early *See It Now* programs, although they ran somewhat longer, differed little in concept or style from the traditional movie newsreel.[19]

From the start Murrow and Friendly seem to have been clearly aware of what TV could do. The first *See It Now* program presented a startling innovation, one that highlighted the potential of the medium. Making use of the just-developed coast-to-coast broadcasting facilities (a combination of coaxial cable and microwave relay), Murrow sat on a swivel chair before two TV monitors that could be viewed by his live audience and called on Camera One to "bring in the Atlantic Ocean." Then he called for a picture of the Pacific Ocean on the other monitor, and these live pictures of the oceans were followed by simultaneous live views of the Brooklyn and Golden Gate bridges and the New York and San Francisco skylines. A gimmick? Yes. But an extraordinarily effective gimmick, for, as Murrow told his audience, the telecast allowed "a man sitting in his living room . . . for *the first time* to look at two oceans at once."[20]

Such mechanical wizardry aside, Murrow and Friendly well understood, as the newsman told their viewers that night, that "this is an old team trying to learn a new trade." It took time to do that; it also took an understanding of the need to change *See It Now's* format, so that often the bulk of the half-hour broadcast time would be devoted to one subject, and it took a willingness to incorporate in various programs what Friendly has succinctly described as "the missing ingredients . . . conviction, controversy, and a point of view." By the beginning of the 1953–1954 season the *See It Now* team (not only Murrow and Friendly, but also the staff they had put together) had learned the new trade and were willing to put their new learning to use.[21]

During this season and the next, *See It Now* hit its stride, dealing with a wide range of subjects: programs were devoted to Senator Joe McCarthy, the New York Philharmonic, the Las Vegas boom, the fight against polio, and the "Stockmobile" (a Merrill, Lynch office on wheels that serviced various Massachusetts towns). The majority of the programs were not controversial muckraking exercises; many were pleasant, entertaining visual essays (such as *A Visit to Flat Rock—Carl Sandburg*, in which the poet talked about Lincoln, Ty Cobb, "bad poetry," and goat's milk and goober peas). Some shows were obviously better than others, yet almost none lacked interest. But it was a transformed *See It Now's* treatment of McCarthyism and other provocative subjects such as the relationshp between cigarette smoking and lung cancer that helped to make television an indispensable medium. So said Erik Barnouw, claiming that "few people now dared to be without a television set."[22]

When Murrow and Friendly zeroed in on a subject, they did so in an innovative manner that differed considerably from previous documentary filmmakers and from contemporary TV practice. They were interested neither in the "innocent eye" of a Robert Flaherty nor in "the poetic propaganda" of a John Grierson—to mention just two of the dozens of modern documentary. Nor were Murrow and Friendly interested in evenhanded, objective analysis—despite protestations to the contrary. (Murrow at one point stated on the air that "this program [*See It Now*] is not a place where personal opinion should be mixed up with ascertainable fact. We shall do our best . . . to resist the temptation to use this microphone as a privileged platform from which to advocate action.") For both Murrow and Friendly, however, the temptation often proved too great. As C. M. Hammond, Jr., perceptively points out, they "did for documentary what the progenitors of earlier linkups between film and news failed to do; namely, they reported not only what was happening, but also *what was wrong with what was happening*." Murrow and Friendly had a sense of justice, and they believed that where injustice existed, "then proper attention must be paid via public exposure to redressing or eliminating" such injustice. For them, as they said, television was an "entirely new weapon in journalism."[23]

This weapon was first unsheathed the evening of October 20, 1953, with the airing of *The Case of Lt. Milo Radulovich A0589839*. This program dealt with a twenty-six year-old University of Michigan student who lost his Air Force Reserve commission and was separated from the service as a security risk. As the articulate and attractive Radulovich explained on camera:

> The Air Force does not question my loyalty in the least. . . . They have presented me with allegations . . . to the effect that my sister and dad . . . have read what we now called subversive newspapers, and that my sister and father's activities are questionable . . . Against me, the actual charge . . . is that I had maintained a close and continuing relationship with my dad and my sister over the years.

Radulovich was not discharged for being disloyal; he was discharged because the Air Force considered him a potential security risk if he continued associating with his father and sister.[24]

No matter how absurd the charges against Radulovich may now seem, it took courage for Murrow and Friendly to deal with such a subject in the chilling political and social climate of the early 1950s. At that time in the United States to invoke the Fifth Amendment before a congressional committee investigating subversion was considered tantamount to an admission of guilt. In at least one community it meant being denied a license to sell secondhand furniture. Professional wrestlers who wished to perform in the state of Indiana were required to take a loyalty oath. So too were CBS employees, including Murrow and Friendly, when the network decided to appease those who because of its less than rabidly patriotic news orientation had dubbed CBS the "Communist Broadcasting System." The early 1950s were, as journalist Fred Cook asserts, a "time of national paranoia . . . in which millions of average Americans looked fearfully over their shoulders wondering whether *they* would be tapped next to explain themselves."[25]

However the period has been labeled, be it the Age of Fear or the Era of Anxiety, a key figure was the junior senator from Wisconsin, Joseph R. McCarthy, who gained notoriety as a recklessly zealous, indefatigable hunter of Communists and subversives in American public and private life. One problem with the senator's zealousness was that it was tempered only rarely with sound judgment and that just about everybody who disagreed with him could be designated "subversive." The senator gave his name to the era, and "McCarthyism" has become part of the American language. But it must be remembered that the process McCarthy symbolized ("personal attacks on individuals by means of widely publicized indiscriminate allegations esp. on the basis of unsubstantiated charges") had begun in post-World War II America, before he gained prominence, and unfortunately continued well into the decade, even after McCarthy's powers waned in the mid-1950s. What one historian has dubbed "The Great Fear" had many aspects; nonetheless "the key notion was guilt by association." And, in effect, it was that with which Radulovich was being charged by the Air Force, on the basis of evidence presented by witnesses he could not confront.[26]

See It Now's treatment of the Radulovich case is a first-rate example of advocacy reporting and a good indication of how the Friendly-Murrow team dealt with controversial subjects. The program opened with a subdued statement by Murrow that set the tone for what followed:

> Good evening. A few weeks ago there occurred a few obscure notices in the newspaper about a Lt. Milo Radulovich, a lieutenant in the Air Force Reserve, and also something about Air Force regulation 35-62. That is a regulation which states that a man may be regarded as a security risk if he has close and continuing association with Communists or people believed to have Communist sympathies. Lt. Radulovich was asked to resign. He declined. A Board was called and heard his case. At the end it was recommended that he be severed from the Air Force, although it was also stated that there was no question whatever as to Lt. Radulovich's loyalty. We propose to examine insofar as we can, the case of Lt. Radulovich.[27]

Murrow referred to Radulovich as "no special hero—no martyr" and allowed him to explain eloquently that the basis for the Air Force's concern was the relationship with his father and sister. There followed statements from various people in Dexter, Michigan, where Radulovich lived, all of whom supported him. His lawyer, the town marshal, the proprietor of a local dry-cleaning establishment, a former mayor, a gas-station owner, the commander of the local American Legion post— some of these people did not know Radulovich personally, but in effect all served as character witnesses, as they expressed disagreement with the Air Force's policy and actions. The lawyer declared that in more than thirty years of practice he had "never witnessed such a farce and travesty." The Legionnaire said he would not know Radulovich "if he came down the middle of the street," but he felt that was "beside the point." He believed that if the people "purging" this man "get away with it, they are entitled to do it to anybody. You or me or anybody else . . . then we all had better head for cover." Each of these people was filmed in what are known as "shoulder shots," that is, just the head and shoulders visible. All were filmed in a manner that emphasized the serious, positive tenor of their remarks. The TV camera, as is well known, can play tricks, making a subject seem honest and straightforward or quite the reverse. Radulovich's supporters were filmed in such a way as to underline their remarks, not to undercut them.[28]

The program then turned to the cause of Radulovich's problem—his father, John, and his sister, Margaret. A United Auto Workers local officer and co-worker with the father asserted that the union "don't want any part" of the Communists, but "I would never classify John Radulovich as subversive in any way, shape, or form." In introducing the father, Murrow pointed out that John Radulovich "denied subscribing to the *Daily Worker* and said he subscribed to the Serbian language newspaper, which was pro-Tito, because he liked their Christmas calendars." The father, in a touching sequence, read in a thick accent a letter he had written to the president asking for "justice for my boy." The sister made a short statement in which she did not commit herself politically in any way, except to assert, "My political beliefs are my own private affair." There was no probing of the sister, who indicated that she felt that her brother was "being forced to undergo a strain for a very unjust cause."[29]

The filmed portion of the program ended with responses by Milo Radulovich and his wife, Nancy, to questions asked by *See It Now* staffer Joseph Wershba. They were filmed in their modest but comfortable living room, which, as one critic said, exuded "the atmosphere of the average American home." Nancy Radulovich said she did not "regret anything. . . . I wouldn't want him to take it lying down. If he did, he would be admitting to something we aren't guilty of." Milo Radulovich asked "if I am being judged on my relatives, are my children going to be asked to denounce me?" And he again asserted that he did not believe that "this procedure that I have been subjected to by the Air Force is in that democratic tradition."[30]

What Friendly has described as the "tail piece"—the last few minutes in the program—were given over to Murrow's stirring and thought-provoking live commentary. He read from parts of the transcript of the hearing, demonstrating its essential unfairness (e.g., the evidence was in a closed envelope that could not be examined by Radulovich or by his attorney). Murrow said:

We are unable to judge the claims against the Lieutenant's father or sister because neither we, nor you, nor they, nor the lieutenant, nor the lawyers know precisely what was contained in that manila envelope. Was it hearsay, rumor, gossip, slander, or was it hard ascertainable fact that could be backed by creditable witnesses. We do not know.

. . . Security officers will tell you that a man who had a sister in Warsaw, for example, might be entirely loyal, but would be subjected to pressure as a result of threats that might be made against his sister. . . . They contend that a man who has a sister in the Communist Party in this country might be subjected to the same kind of pressure, but here again no evidence was adduced to prove that Radulovich's sister is a member of the party and the case against his father was certainly not made.

We believe that "the son shall not bear the iniquity of the father," even though that iniquity be proved; and in this case it was not. But we believe, too, that this case illustrates the urgent need for the Armed Forces to communicate more fully than they have so far done, the procedures and regulations to be followed in attempting to protect the national security and the rights of the individual at the same time. Whatever happens in the whole area of the relationship between the individual and the state, we will do it ourselves. . . . And it seems to Fred Friendly and myself . . . that that is a subject that should be argued about endlessly.[31]

The response to this program was remarkable. Friendly recalls that the reaction was "more than Ed had hoped for" and that CBS received "hundreds of phone calls, most of them favorable, but some bitter denunciations of Murrow and CBS." The mail response, according to a contemporary report, "rather surprised the staff." Approximately eight thousand letters were received, with the bias aout 100 to 1 in favor of Radulovich. Media historian Erik Barnouw reports that "a few newspaper columnists denounced the program, but there were many paeans of praise." Typical were the hosannahs offered by *New York Times* staffer Jack Gould, then perhaps the nation's most influential media critic, who called the Radulovich program "a long step forward in television journalism." Years later CBS head William Paley nostalgically wrote of the program's "impact," but Friendly remembers that he "never heard a word from company executives about the Radulovich broadcast other than about the mail count." Perhaps the most gratifying response came from the Air Force. Five weeks after the broadcast of the Radulovich program the secretary of the Air Force appeared on *See It Now* and announced that he had "decided . . . it is consistent with the interests of the national security to retain Lt. Radulovich in the United States Air Force Reserve . . . .The question . . . raised as to security has thus been resolved in Lt. Radulovich's favor." *See It Now* cannot take sole credit for this decision, but its airing of Radulovich's plight did result in the necessary "public exposure," and did alert the nation's media, an essential portion of which took up the case.[32]

The putting together of the Radulovich program was typical of the way *See It Now* worked, even though the routine did vary from subject to subject. A story about Radulovich caught Murrow's eye in one of the various out-of-town newspapers that he regularly perused. He clipped it and asked Friendly to follow up. At other times the initiative would come from Friendly; both agreed that seldom could "an idea's organization . . . be actually attributed to either one of them specifically." Murrow at one time said that many of the program's topics were chosen "on anticipatory news judgment."[33]

To check out the Radulovich story a staff member, Joseph Wershba, was sent to Michigan. The story seemed to be a promising enough feature for him to request a camera crew, and one was sent. Altogether about five hours of film was shot, even though less than twenty-five minutes was used. Such a ratio of footage shot or compiled to film used was not unusual; for the McCarthy program the staff put together over fifteen times as much footage as was finally utilized. Filming the interviews was, on the whole, a standard procedure. As described by a staff cameraman at the time:

> . . . Two cameras are used, both . . . start off at the same time. The first . . . takes a closeup picture of the person being interviewed. The . . . other takes a long shot—or a picture encompassing possibly both interviewer and interviewee with some of the surrounding scene. . . . This second camera films approximately 3 minutes and stops. As the first camera begins to run out of film, the second takes over shooting closeups while the first reloads. When reloaded, the first camera resumes the closeup filming. . . . Cameras are always trained on the person being interviewed throughout the interview period. . . . After the interview, pictures are taken of the interviewer repeating the questions as if he were actually asking them . . . for the first time. . . . Extra pictures are taken . . . for the sake of visual variety and editing purposes.

Most scenes, whether interviews or not, were shot several times from different angles and in different ways (close-ups, medium shots, long views, etc.).[34]

Once shot, the film was rushed to New York City, where Friendly would assign segments of the program being prepared to various staff members. Often the footage would just keep coming in, and there would be constant reevaluation and reediting. "The circumstances under which *See It Now* was assembled . . . and telecast" were, as Barnouw accurately points out, "primitive." Friendly recalls that for the Radulovich program

> the film shot in Dexter, Michigan, was developed and printed in a laboratory on Ninth Avenue. The screening and editing were done at the Fifth Avenue facilities near Forty Fifth Street. The Murrow off-camera narration was recorded in a studio near his office, piped over to the mixing facility on Fifth Avenue and thence would be sent by telephone circuit to . . . Master Control at Grand Central.[35]

Often the results that came out of this semiorganized chaos, as with the Radulovich program, were splendid, but there could unfortunately also be stumbles. Staff member Palmer Williams recalled that the first program of the 1954-1955 season (which dealt with Berlin's role in the cold war) was the "biggest stumble" because of a lack of cohesion as the film "poured in."[36]

See It Now was produced in what Friendly describes as "a pressure cooker atmosphere." To keep the series topical, especially while it still was a half hour, a program often had to be put together on very short notice. The Radulovich program, from conception to broadcast, was put together in less than three weeks. The lack of sophisticated technology (*See It Now* did not, for example, have the benefit of "live on tape," or minicameras, or computer-assisted editing) meant that often the ninety-six hours prior to broadcast time were extremely hectic. Friendly believes much of the success of the series was due to the willingness of the staff to put in long hours under almost impossible conditions: "We had a hardy bunch of guys who were a band of brothers under Ed."[37]

For the Radulovich program, like many others, the final editing work began on the Friday before the Tuesday night broadcast. Editing continued through the weekend, and on Monday work went on around the clock and through the night. Murrow, whose final commentary usually was live, looked at the editing on Monday but was still concerned with writing a strong conclusion to the program. Because the Radulovich program had not been finalized by late Tuesday afternoon (a not unusual occurrence), it was impossible to put together a composite print (*See It Now* was what was then called a "three-track production"—the picture was printed on one track, the sound printed on another, and on the third Murrow's narration was recorded); the three tracks had to be synchronized—put "in sync"). When the show ran weekly, it was not always possible to make up a composite print of the whole program. The Radulovich program did not even have a complete run-through prior to air time, but it had very much impressed staff who had seen just parts of it. Friendly recalls that *See It Now's* on-the-air director, Don Hewitt, "told the crew he'd murder someone if we lost 'sync' that night, as we had a few weeks ago."[38]

Just before the Radulovich program went on the air Murrow told Friendly, "Things will never be the same around here after tonight." And he was right: the implications of the broadcast were inescapable. It was quite clear, as media historian Barnouw points out, that *See It Now* "was not merely probing the judicial processes of the Air Force and Pentagon—a quixotic venture few broadcasters would have undertaken at this time—but was examining the whole syndrome of McCarthyism with its secret denunciations and guilt by association." This program was followed by others that dealt with McCarthyism— one program concerned the denial of an Indianapolis public auditorium to the American Civil Liberties Union for an organizational meeting in that city. Making use of splendid editing, *See It Now*, through vivid if not always fair intercutting, in effect created a debate between what was said at the ACLU meeting—which was held in a church hall—and an American Legion assembly called to denounce the ACLU meeting. Murrow forwent his usual tail piece and gave the last word to Father Victor L. Goosens, pastor of St. Mary's Roman Catholic Church, who had made the church's social center available to the ACLU.

> When the climate is such that so many people are so quick to . . . ignore the law and to deny to others the right to peaceful assembly and free speech—then somebody certainly has to take a stand. . . . And it's up to us . . . to lead the way, because we know that . . . the American freedoms . . . are all based upon the rights which God has given us. And if the church and religion do not uphold those basic principles which come from God, then who will?[39]

Having taken on the "ism," Murrow and Friendly, in the colorful but accurate words of a media critic, now "decided to lunge for the heart of the beast." Since the spring of 1953 the *See It Now* staff had collected a film record of Senator McCarthy in action. A considerable amount of footage had been amassed, but a kind of equivocation delayed use of this material. Each week the staff would update the material, and each week, as Murrow's biographer reports, "Friendly would consult [with his partner] and then say 'No, let's hold for another week.'" Finally, Murrow and Friendly decided that the time was ripe for such a program, and it was scheduled for March 9, 1954.[40]

Unhappy comments on the tenor of the times in which this broadcast was scheduled are evidenced by the fact that Murrow had come to believe his telephone was being tapped and that Friendly felt it was necessary for the unit putting the McCarthy program together to meet and discuss their personal lives and backgrounds. As Friendly put it candidly to his partner (and perhaps not unreasonably in the context of the 1950s), "It would not be fair to CBS to enter into this battle if we had an Achilles heel." Murrow agreed. The unit was called together; they discussed (as Friendly remembers) not only the quality of the program, but also the question of whether there was "anything in their own backgrounds that would give the Senator a club to beat us with, because if the broadcast was successful, he and his supporters would certainly be looking for one."[41]

Whether or not the program could be judged a success depended on the political beliefs of the viewer and the critics, but the program certainly achieved its purpose—which, as a contemporay critic saw it, was "to show McCarthy as Murrow and Friendly believed him to be." The "report on Senator Joseph R. McCarthy told mainly in his own words and pictures" remains understandably the most famous of all the *See It Now* broadcasts—not the most typical, not the best in terms of style or format by any means, and certainly not the most objective. Murrow and Friendly believed it really important to show Senator McCarthy in action browbeating witnesses at congressional committee hearings, contradicting himself without any regard to truth, resorting to innuendo and slander, playing the bully. And this they did.[42]

Viewers could see and hear McCarthy assert, "Those who wear the label 'Democrat' wear it with the stain of a historic betrayal . . . twenty years of treason"; refer to that party's 1952 presidential candidate as "Alger, I mean Adlai" Stevenson (a reference to Alger Hiss, who had been convicted of perjury but really had been tried for his 1930s associations); place himself above the nation's chief executive and promise "to continue to call them as I see them regardless of who happens to be President." And how did Senator McCarthy see them? According to *See It Now* his vision was bleak: "When the shouting and the tumult dies the American people and the President shall realize that this unprecedented mud-slinging against my Committee by the extreme left-wing elements of the press and radio were caused solely because another Fifth Amendment Communist was finally dug out of the dark recesses and exposed to the public view."[43]

See It Now included footage from what was referred to as "a sample investigation" with commentary by Murrow on the senator's statements. The witness was Reed Harris, an employee of the United States Information Agency, who had been suspended from Columbia University some twenty years earlier and then had accepted legal counsel provided by the ACLU. The footage showed Senator McCarthy at his "browbeating worst," as this excerpt from the program demonstrates:

McCarthy: The question is did the Civil Liberties Union supply you with an attorney?

Harris: They did supply an attorney.

McCarthy: The answer is yes?

Harris: The answer is yes.

McCarthy: You know the Civil Liberties Union has been listed as a front for and doing the work of the Communist Party.

Harris: Mr. Chairman, this was 1932.

McCarthy: I know it was 1932. Do you know they since have been listed as front for and doing the work of the Communist Party?

Harris: I do not know they have been listed so, sir.

McCarthy: You don't know they have been so listed?

Harris: I have heard that mentioned or read that mentioned. . . .

Murrow: The Reed Harris hearing demonstrated some of the Senator's techniques. Twice he said that the American Civil Liberties Union was listed as a subversive front. The Attorney General's list does not and never has listed the ACLU as subversive, nor does the FBI or any other government agency.

Overall this *See It Now* program portrayed Senator McCarthy in what one writer recently cogently described as "his full, foul glory. . . . remoreslessly revealing his shabby practices and demeanor."[44]

On camera, Murrow cannot be said to have paid even lip service to objectivity. His comments may not have been fair, but they were sincere, and he left no doubt that intense conviction motivated him. The usually urbane and cool Murrow seemed strained, concerned, moved. Indeed, Joe Wershba remembers that "for the first and last time," prior to the airing of a program, Murrow "made an ideological preachment" to the staff. And Murrow's eloquent summation at the end of the program had just the right touch. Turning to the camera, he said:

> No one familiar with the history of this country can deny that congressional committees are useful . . . but the line between investigation and persecution is a very fine one and the junior Senator from Wisconsin has stepped over it repeatedly. . . .
>
> This is no time for men who oppose Senator McCarthy's methods to keep silent, or for those who approve. We can deny our heritage and our history, but we cannot escape responsibility for the result. There is no way for a citizen of the republic to abdicate his responsibilities. As a nation we have come into our full inheritance at a tender age. We proclaim ourselves—as indeed—we are—the defenders of freedom, what's left of it, but we cannot defend freedom abroad by deserting it at home. The actions of the junior Senator from Wisconsin have caused alarm and dismay amongst our allies abroad and given considerable comfort to our enemies, and whose fault is that? Not really his. He didn't create the situation of fear; he merely exploited it, and rather successfully. Cassius was right: "The fault, dear Brutus, is not in our stars but in ourselves."[45]

Viewer response to the McCarthy program was extraordinary. A CBS spokesman said it was "the largest spontaneous response" the network had ever experienced. More than twelve thousand telegrams and telephone calls had been received within forty-eight hours of the broadcast. Murrow's biographer notes that although the newscaster received "some hostile comment . . . the general reaction was not only favorable but highly approving." Within two weeks, reported a writer at the time, "some 22,000 letters had been received and sorted, of which all but approximately 2,500 were pro-Murrow." According to this count the radio was 9 to 1 in favor of Murrow, except for California where the response was 8 to 3. Friendly later estimated that between seventy-five and a hundred thousand wrote, telegraphed, or telephoned in response to the program: "We never really knew the exact count." He also reported that even after McCarthy, taking advantage of *See It Now*'s offer to respond on the air, presented a filmed half-hour rebuttal that strongly attacked Murrow, the mail "continued to run in Murrow's

favor . . . but the ratio did drop down to . . . two to one." An unfortunate side effect was that there were threats against Murrow's eight-
year-old son Casey, and that (as Friendly writes) "for years afterward
some one always met Casey at school and escorted him home."[46]

The critical response to the McCarthy program was, in the main,
quite flattering, except for McCarthy's media partisans, who responded
as might be expected: One suggested that *See It Now* should be retitled
"See It My Way," and a Hearst newspaper columnist referred to the
broadcast as a "hate McCarthy telecast" by a "pompous portsider."
Praise for the McCarthy program was widespread. A *New Yorker*
magazine writer dubbed the program "an extraordinary feat of journalism." A trade journal rhapsodized that "no greater feat of journalistic
enterprise has occurred in modern times." Jack Gould's enthusiasm for
the broadcast was so great that he began his comments by asserting,
"Last week may be remembered as the week that broadcasting recap-
tured its soul."[47]

Gould's enthusiasm for the broadcast, however, was tempered by a
fear of its implications, a fear that concerned a number of persons then
and still remains a worry for most observers of the electronic media
(especially given the growth of its impact and power since then). Gould
commented:

> It is difficult to see how Mr. Murrow could have done other than he did
> without abandoning his and television's journalistic integrity . . . but
> what was frightening about Mr. Murrow's broadcast . . . was . . . what
> if the camera and microphone should fall into the hands of a reckless and
> demagogic commentator.

Gilbert Seldes, an eminent, veteran commentator on the arts, also pon-
dered that point both then and later. He considered the program on
McCarthy "noteworthy," indeed "the most important single broadcast
in television" to that time, and yet he felt "in the long run it is more
important to use our communications system properly than to destroy
McCarthy." Moreover, the senator's reply, argued Seldes, demonstrated the "emptiness" of the equal time formula; Seldes said he had no
love for McCarthy, but the situation seemed akin to one in which "a
man clubbed another and then passed him the stick knowing full well
he could not use it effectively."[48]

It seems to me obvious that the *See It Now* program on Senator
McCarthy was neither fair nor objective. Nor could it be, given the

temper of the men who created it. Murrow's tone in constantly describing McCarthy as "the junior Senator from Wisconsin" was clearly meant to be pejorative and obviously reflected the broadcaster's distaste for the politician and what he stood for. A significant portion of the program consisted of McCarthy's statements (be they half-truths, distortions, or what have you) being corrected by an overserious Murrow. As one McCarthy biographer points out, "The editing portrayed Joe [McCarthy] . . . belching, picking his nose, contradicting himself, giggling at his own vulgar humor." A substantial portion of the program's footage depicting the senator stacked the deck against him visually. As one critic summed up the choice of footage: "It showed the Senator at his worst, or least coherent."[49]

The issues raised by this particular program remain crucial. There were and are those who feel, to use one historian's words, "that treatment of McCarthy was no crueler than McCarthy's treatment of numerous innocent witnesses before his committee." And there are those, like Gould and Seldes, who worry about the misuse of the media. Perhaps the questions raised are not answerable except from an individual point of view. What is clear—as one scholar pointed out a decade later—is that with this broadcast *See It Now* had turned "from making film *tell* something to making it *will* something."[50]

Just as there has been a divided response to the content of this particular program, so there has been a twofold response to the impact of *See It Now's* treatment of Senator McCarthy. A few year later Seldes argued that *See It Now* had carried the war aggressively into McCarthy's territory, and that "it was plain that the McCarthy who appeared a few weeks later" at the Senate hearings inquiring into his strange and strained relationships with the U.S. Army "had already suffered a tactical defeat and was aware of it." TV producer Fred Freed years later recalled the liberating effect of the program and how *See It Now's* action helped him and others at least to begin to combat McCarthyism, which had resulted in widespread blacklisting in the media industry: "Most of the time most of us just submitted to the pressure. We wouldn't admit it then, and it's painful to admit now. With *See It Now* that began to change. . . . Murrow stood up to him. Then others in the industry began to." A McCarthy biographer writing years later believes that the program damaged McCarthy, that it "had done what so many of the great news media had so long refrained from doing . . . laid bare the soul and techniques of a demagogue."[51]

See It Now had waited a long time to attack McCarthy. And there were and are those who felt it waited too long to join the small, stalwart band who had been willing to combat the senator (such as Eric Sevareid, a colleague of Murrow and Friendly at CBS, who had by 1952 already broadcast over radio several negative analyses of McCarthy, and in one commentary had unflatteringly likened him to an incompetent character in *Winnie-the-Pooh*). Typical is the recent study which maintains that Murrow's courage was "cautious," and that the "most remarkable thing about the program was that it was late" in attacking McCarthy. In the mid-1970s Jack Gould recalled that Murrow himself at the time said, "We're bringing up the rear." But I think the latter comment is more a matter of Murrow understatement than anything else. Given the low level of courage displayed in general by network broacasting executives, the fears that kept most controversy of *any* kind off the airwaves, and the hesitant history of the industry in dealing with such matters as blacklisting, one should not in retrospect slight the efforts of Murrow and Friendly. They may have been late in taking on the senator, but at the time they confronted the "ism" with the Radulovich program it was not yet clear which way the wind would finally blow. And even if there was a delay in confronting the senator, that delay did not diminish the impact the broadcast had at the time, an impact upon which almost all contemporary commentators agree. What was important was not that Senator McCarthy was being exposed as a "tricky operator," but that attention was being drawn to the situation by a man of "Murrow's stature" with a "vast television pulpit." Murrow probably summed up the situation best a few years later when he declared, "The time was right. . . . We did it fairly well. . . . There was a great conspiracy of silence at the time; when there is such a conspiracy and somebody makes a loud noise it attracts all the attention."[52]

It may be that Murrow is right when he avers that the program received "too much credit," but it is a sad footnote and a fascinating commentary on the recent writing of American history that while journalists and media types dealing with the period mention this *See It Now* program (whatever their approach to it), the works penned by professional historians do not. They usually touch on the televising of the Army-McCarthy hearings without taking into account the following: only the then relatively insignificant American Broadcasting Company network and the tiny Dumont network carried the hearings live during the day (reaching fewer than seventy-five stations). Moreover, ABC carried the hearings only as far as Denver. The National Broadcasting Company did carry the hearings to the West Coast for a few days but then, as an angry Seldes points out, "announcing that *there was not enough public interest to justify the expense*, contented itself with copious excerpts from the hearings shown late in the evening." Interestingly enough, CBS did not carry the hearings at all except for some clips shown on news programs late at night.[53]

While finishing up the McCarthy program Friendly had said to Murrow, "This is going to be a tough one to do." And Murrow replied, "They're all going to be tough after this." Some years later Friendly, commenting on this conversation and the subsequent history of *See It Now*, declared, "We have been swimming upstream ever since." The swim might have been easier if *See It Now* had pulled its punches and concentrated on innocuous subjects, but while the series did some lighthearted programs, it also continued to do programs that caused controversy. And as Friendly later wrote: "The attitude at CBS was 'Why does Murrow have to save the world every week?'"[54]

An unfortunate byproduct of the continuing controversy was the decision of the Aluminum Corporation of American (Alcoa), which had sponsored *See It Now* since its third program in 1951, to terminate that support at the end of the 1954-1955 season. The relationship between Alcoa and *See It Now* had been a good one; as Murrow said at the time, "I have a wonderful arrangement with my sponsor. They make aluminum and I make films." Alcoa's decision to sponsor *See It Now* had grown out of a desire to influence not a mass audience but specifically the kind that watched programs such as *See It Now*. TV was not a mass medium in the early 1950s—the cost of sets limited most viewers to what Friendly has described as "an up-scale elitist audience, one that a company would want to influence." And this audience Alcoa reached through *See It Now*. The company withstood heavy pressure over the years resulting from this sponsorship, but the company's priorities were changing: competition in the aluminum industry was steadily increasing, the company had decided to plunge into the consumer market and not just sell wholesale—institutional advertising no longer seemed pertinent. But the decisive factor was probably the question of controversy, which could affect its sales on every level. As Friendly recounts: "Alcoa salesmen had difficulty explaining why this company felt it necessary to sponsor programs against McCarthy . . . and 'for socialized medicine'—which is what some doctors thought our program on the Salk vaccine advocated."[55]

Alcoa never interfered with *See It Now*. As John Fleming, Alcoa's corporate liaison with the series, put it, "When you hire an editor you let him alone to work as he sees best." Nor did CBS interfere with *See It Now*, which operated with an autonomy akin to the "independence granted a columnist such as Walter Lippman or Arthur Krock" (to use Friendly's words). This freedom from corporate supervision owed much to Murrow's prestige, determination, and intimate relationship with William Paley, to whom Murrow had direct access.[56]

See It Now's continuing provocative stance seems to have undermined Murrow's status at CBS and to have led to the decisions to have the program irregularly scheduled and finally canceled. Indeed, how far that erosion had gone is indicated by the dramatic confrontation between Murrow and Paley over the end of *See It Now*. During the course of a long, heated argument Murrow angrily asked Paley, "Bill, are you going to destroy all this? Don't you want an instrument like the *See It Now* organization, which you have poured so much money into for so long, to continue?" And Paley replied, "Yes, but I don't want this constant stomach ache every time you do a controversial subject."[57]

The relationship between *See It Now*'s producers and their corporate superiors at CBS had never been an easy one. Paley had graciously called Murrow the morning of the McCarthy broadcast and said, "I'll be with you tonight, Ed, and I'll be with you tomorrow as well." Although it was clear at the time that Murrow and Friendly had Paley's approval, "with the advantage of hindsight it becomes apparent" (as one writer has noted) "that they did not have the official support of CBS as a corporation." Thus, for a number of their controversial broadcasts (including the Radulovich and McCarthy broadcasts), Murrow and Friendly found it necessary to pay out of their personal funds for *New York Times* advertisements announcing the programs, announcements that did not carry the CBS logo.[58]

See It Now's provocativeness upset and alienated Paley, but it was the changes in television broadcasting in the United States as much as the lack of corporate support within CBS that doomed the series. It was during the early and mid-1950s that television went national, with programs being aired coast to coast. Moreover, there was during these years, as one media study points out, "a fantastic growth pattern. . . . from 6 percent penetration of American homes by television in 1949 to 76 percent in 1956." And the year before, *The $64,000 Question* had debuted in June in the time slot just prior to *See It Now*, had achieved smash ratings almost instantaneously, and had started the quiz show boom.[59]

What Friendly and others in the industry called "opportunity costs" now came strongly into play. *See It Now*, according to Murrow's biographer, "had always been a sore spot with the company's accountants despite its prestige." It might often cost more than $100,000 to produce an individual program, and in the early days of *See It Now* Alcoa paid only $23,000 toward the cost of the program and an additinal $34,000 for the air time. By 1955 Alcoa was paying $55,000 for the air time, but Revlon—the sponsor of the much-cheaper-to-produce *$64,000 Question*—was paying $80,000 for its half hour. On seeing the first *$64,000 Question* show, a wary, concerned Murrow, already aware of the problems *See It Now* faced at CBS, turned to Friendly and asked, "Any bets on how long we'll keep this time period now?"[60]

The answer was not long in coming, and by the 1957-1958 season *See It Now* had returned to the intellectual ghetto of late Sunday afternoons. And then it was terminated. The economics of the situation as well as internal politics at CBS had resulted in what Friendly later called "The Strange Death of *See It Now*." What one critic has described as "consensus TV" now reigned. The axing of the series disturbed Murrow and Friendly. The latter later recalled, "When the end came Ed and I were very, *very* bitter."[61]

It has become fashionable in recent years to disparage the Murrow-Friendly collaboration, to downplay its impact, to downgrade Friendly, to deprecate Murrow for "working both sides of the street" (a reference to his efforts with *Person to Person*, the highly successful TV show which, in effect, made into an art nondemanding celebrity interviewing on television). It seems to me that these criticisms are at best quibbles. *See It Now*, in my opinion, is TV documentary at its best. The series admittedly had some clinkers; not everything it dealt with was vital; mistakes were made—but withal *See It Now* never compromised its integrity, and as with the Radulovich and McCarthy programs the series took an unpopular but necessary stand. In an extremely challenging and important speech to a 1958 convention of radio and television news directors, Murrow declared that he "did not advocate that we turn television into a 27-inch wailing wall," but he would "just like to see it reflect occasionally the hard, unyielding realities of the world in which we live." And that *See It Now* did, and did quite well.[62]

See It Now has spawned many imitations, but in my opinion none have lived up to the original. *60 Minutes* has lasted longer, has achieved greater commercial and ratings success, has managed to become an integral part of CBS. Certainly the *See It Now* presence is felt on that show; in 1981 its executive producer (Don Hewitt), managing editor (Palmer Williams), and one of its more distinguished producers (Joseph Wershba) were *See It Now* alumni, as were staffers such as cameraman Bill McClure. But peruse the recently published "complete text of 114 stories . . . of Season XII of *60 Minutes*," and you will be disappointed. The treatments lack depth and fire, the exposés are mostly of the obvious or of relatively powerless individuals, the subjects are a not-overdistinguished mishmash. *60 Minutes*, as one critic has pointed out, is "a feature magazine, designed for relaxed viewing."[63]

Relaxation was not the aim of the producers of *See It Now*, and the series did not relax viewers—it enraged them, it informed them, it convinced them. As TV documentary, *See It Now* does not seem to me ever to have been equaled. There are programs that have been slicker, but none more seminal for the form. Speaking to an English audience, Murrow once said, "There is . . . no substitute for the man who has at least a mild fire in his belly and is able to pierce that screen with his own conviction." That *See It Now* did, and did well—not always with every program, but certainly with great consistency and intelligence. The hardware has improved immeasurably since the 1950s, but *See It Now* still remains a superb model for anyone interested in the TV documentary.[64]

NOTES

1. Michael J. Arlen, *The View from Highway I* (New York: Farrar, Strauss & Giroux, 1976), pp. 3, 5; John Crosby, *Out of the Blue* (New York: Simon & Schuster, 1952), p. 284; Newton M. Minow, *Equal Time: The Private Broadcaster and the Public Interest*, edited by Laurence Laurent (New York: Atheneum, 1964), p. 52 (Minow's description of television programming unfortunately generally still holds true. He told his audience, the approxi-

mately 3000 delegates to the annual convention of the National Association of Broadcasters, "You will see a procession of game shows, violence, audience participation shows, formula comedies about totally unbelievable families, blood and thunder, mayhem, violence, sadism, murder, Western badmen, Western goodmen, private eyes, gangsters, more violence and cartoons. And, endlessly, commercials—many screaming, cajoling, and offending"); Michael Novak, "Television Shapes the Soul," in *Television: The Critical View*, edited by Horace Newcomb (New York: Oxford University Press, 1979), 2nd ed. p. 308.

2. Novak, "Television Shapes," p. 315; Arlen, *Highway I*, p. 51; Crosby, *Out of the Blue*, p. 237; Minow, *Equal Time*, p 308.

3. Tim Brooks and Earle Marsh, *The Complete Directory to Prime Time Network TV Shows: 1946–Present* (New York: Ballantine Books, 1979), p. 53; William Small, *To Kill a Messenger: Television News and the Real World* (New York: Hastings House, 1970), pp. 18–19; A. William Bluem, *Documentary in American Television* (New York: Hastings House, 1965), pp. 99–100; John Crosby, "The Demise of 'See It Now,'" *New York Herald Tribune*, 11 July 1958.

4. Helen Dudar, "A Post Portrait: Ed Murrow," *New York Post*, 1 March 1959; Sir Hugh Greene in "Good Night and Good Luck" (1975 BBC-TV Production), distributed by Instructional Media Services, Washington State University; Gary Paul Gates, *Air Time: The Inside Story of CBS News* (New York: Harper & Row, 1978), p. 13. How much Murrow still remains a touchstone in his profession is demonstrated by Dan Rather's reminiscenses. He recalls that the phrase "I think you have it in you to be another Ed Murrow" gets "vastly overworked" but still "it sings." And he found that in the mid-1970s, a decade and a half after Murrow left CBS, "it was astonishing how often" Murrow's name and work "came up" during program discussions at *CBS Reports*. Dan Rather with Mickey Hershkowitz, *The Camera Never Blinks: Adventures of a TV Journalist* (New York: William Morrow, 1977), pp. 160, 295. There is a splendid capsule profile of Murrow in William Manchester, *The Glory and the Dream: A Narrative History of America, 1932–1972* (Boston: Little, Brown, 1974), pp. 513–516. There is a somewhat more tough-minded but waspish assessment of Murrow in David Culbert's *News for Everyman: Radio and Foreign Affairs in Nineteen-Thirties America* (Westport, Conn: Greenwood Press, 1976, pp. 179–196.

5. Alexander Kendrick, *Prime Time: The Life of Edward R. Murrow* (Boston: Little, Brown, 1969), p. 139.

6. David Halberstam, *The Powers That Be* (New York: Knopf, 1979), p. 39.

7. Fred W. Friendly, *Due to Circumstances Beyond Our Control . . .* (New York: Random House, 1967), p. xvi; Edward R. Murrow, *This Is London* (New York: Simon & Schuster, 1941), from the introduction by Elmer Davis, p. viii; Lawrence S. Rudner, "Born to a New Craft: Edward R. Murrow, 1938–1940," *Journal of Popular Culture* 15 (1981): 101; Archibald MacLeish, "To Ed Murrow, Reporter," *Journal of Home Economics* 34 (1942): 361. There is a splendid two-record selection of Murrow's wartime broadcasts available: Fred W. Friendly et al., eds., *Edward R. Murrow: A Reporter Remembers*, vol. 1, "The War Years" (Columbia Records 02L 332).

8. Les Brown, *The New York Times Encyclopedia of Television* (New York: Times Books, 1977), p. 288; Janet Murrow quoted in Halberstam, *Powers That Be*, p. 44; William Paley, *As It Happened: A Memoir* (Garden City, N.Y.: Doubleday, 1979), p. 151; "TV

News Past and Present: A Conversation with Charles Collingwood" (broadcast over WNYC-TV, New York City, 27 September 1982).

9. Robert Lewis Shayon, "Murrow's Lost Fight," *Saturday Review of Literature*, 22 May 1965, p. 94; "Murrow at the Mike," *Newsweek*, 28 July 1947, p. 56.

10. *Current Biography, 1957*, pp. 196–197. Friendly insists that his middle name was Friendly and not Freundlich at the time he switched the names and that the family name had been changed much earlier (Friendly interview with the author, October 29, 1981). On the wall above his desk in his Columbia University office is a large picture from the turn of the century of a relative's store in Eugene, Oregon; on the plate glass window of the store is the word "Friendly."

11. Friendly, *Circumstances*, p. xvii; Murray Yaeger, "An Analysis of Edward R. Murrow's 'See It Now' Television Program" (Ph.D. diss., University of Iowa, 1956), p. 35; John Crosby quoted in *Current Biography*, p. 197.

12. Paley, *Memoir*, p. 299; Halberstam, *The Powers That Be*, p. 135; Robert Metz, *Reflections in a Bloodshot Eye* (Chicago: Playboy Press, 1975), p. 279; Gates, *Air Time*, pp. 106, 108; Arthur Barron quoted in Arthur Rosenthal, *The New Documentary in Action: A Casebook in Filmmaking* (Berkeley & Los Angeles: University of California Press, 1971), p. 145; Fred Freed quoted in David Yellin, *Special: Fred Freed and the Television Documentary* (New York: Macmillian), 1973, p. 20; Yaeger, "Analysis," pp. 36–37. Harvey Swados has penned a splendid profile of Friendly that attempts to assess and analyze the contradictory tendencies evident in the man: "Fred Friendly's Vision," in *Radical at Large: American Essays* (London: Rupert Hart-Davis, 1968), pp. 129–141.

13. Joseph Wershba, "Murrow vs. McCarthy: See it Now," *New York Times Magazine*, 4 March 1979, p. 22; Kendrick, *Prime Time*, p. 508. It is worth mentioning that Friendly's comments about Murrow in an oral history interview are quite respectful (Fred W. Friendly interview, Oral History Project, Columbia University, *passim*). Perhaps the best comments by Friendly about Murrow are to be found in "Good Night and Good Luck," when he tells the BBC interviewer, "Ed Murrow was no God. He was a great journalist and a great human being. . . . He made his mistakes like all the rest of us do."

14. Edward R. Murrow and Fred W. Friendly, *I Can Hear It Now* (Columbia m1495); Friendly, *Circumstances*, p. xviii. Despite the many imitations since then, the quality, style, and intelligence governing the making of this record and its successors have kept them from being cliché or old hat. To realize the superiority of *I Can Hear It Now* one need only compare it to one of its imitative competitors such as *Hark! The Years* (Capitol s282), which was narrated by Fredric March in a frenetic manner and punctuated by shrill music.

15. Quoted in Yaeger, "Analysis," p. 48; Kendrick, *Prime Time*, p. 317. There is an excellent, illuminating review of the first *I Can Hear It Now* album in Crosby, *Out of the Blue*, pp.237–239.

16. Kendrick, *Prime Time*, p. 329; Yaeger, "Analysis," p. 48.

17. Edward R. Murrow, "What's Wrong with TV?" *Reader's Digest*, February 1959, p. 55; Manchester, *Narrative History*, p. 516.

18. Crosby, *Out of the Blue*, p. 249.

19. Erik Barnouw, *A History of Broadcasting in the United States*, vol. 3, *The Image Empire* (New York: Oxford University Press, 1970), p. 45; Yaeger, "Analysis," p. 49; *New York Times*, 4 May 1952, p. 2:1; James L. Baughman, "*See It Now* and Television's Golden

Age," *Journal of Popular Culture* 15(1981):108. There is an interesting selection of *See It Now* transcripts in the Edward R. Murrow papers, Edwin Ginn Library, Fletcher School of Law and Diplomacy, Tufts University, Medford, Mass.; these papers have been microfilmed and are available from the Microfilming Corporation of America. There is also a limited selection of *See It Now* transcripts at the Billy Rose Theater Collection of the Performing Arts Research Center, New York Public Library at Lincoln Center, New York City (hereafter referred to as the Billy Rose Collection, NYPL). See also Edward R. Murrow and Fred W. Friendly, *See It Now: A Selection in Text and Pictures* (New York: Simon & Schuster, 1955).

20. Murrow quoted in Crosby, *Out of the Blue*, p. 247 (emphasis mine).

21. Murrow and Friendly, *Selection*, p. xi; Friendly, *Circumstances*, p. 3.

22. Barnouw. *Image Empire*, p. 54.

23. Murrow quoted in Yaeger, "Analysis," p. 57; Charles Montgomery Hammond, Jr., *The Image Decade: Television Documentary, 1965–1975* (New York: Hastings House, 1981), p. 40; Murrow and Friendly, *Selection*, p. xi.

24. Murrow and Friendly, *Selection*, pp. 31–32. *See It Now* (23 November 1952) had briefly touched on a similar issue when it dealt with the case of Harrison, N.Y., high-school officials who refused use of the school auditorium to persons who did not sign a loyalty oath.

25. David Caute, *The Great Fear: The Anti-Communist Purge under Truman and Eisenhower* (New York: Simon & Schuster, 1978), p. 22; Metz, *Reflections*, p. 282; Fred Cook, *The Nightmare Decade: The Life and Times of Senator Joe McCarthy* (New York: Random House, 1941), p. 3.

26. *McCarthyism*, edited by Thomas C. Reeves (Hinsdale, Ill.: Dryden Press, 1973), p. 2; *Webster's Third New International Dictionary*, 1961; Caute, *Great Fear*, p. 18.

27. Murrow and Friendly, *Selection*, pp. 31–32.

28. Ibid., pp. 32, 33. I was able to screen several *See It Now* programs, including this one, through the generosity of Fred Friendly.

29. Ibid., pp. 36, 38.

30. Yaeger, "Analysis," p. 133.

31. Friendly, *Circumstances*, p. 13; Murrow and Friendly, *Selection*, pp. 39–41.

32. Friendly in "Good Night and Good Luck"; Friendly, *Circumstances*, pp. 16–17: "Eyes of Conscience: See It Now," *Newsweek*, 7 December 1953, p. 65; Erik Barnouw, *Tube of Plenty: The Evolution of American Television* (New York: Oxford University Press, 1975), p. 177; *New York Times*, 25 October, 1953, p. 2:13; Paley, *Memoir*, p. 283; Murrow and Friendly, *Selection*, p. 43.

33. Yaeger, "Analysis," p. 95; Murrow quoted in Yaeger.

34. Leo Rossi quoted in Yaeger, "Analysis," pp. 157–158.

35. Barnouw, *Tube of Plenty*, p. 175; Friendly, *Circumstances*, p. 12.

36. Williams quoted in Yaeger, "Analysis," p. 65.

37. Friendly, *Circumstances*, p. 12; Friendly in "Good Night and Good Luck."

38. Friendly, *Circumstances*, p. 14.

39. Ibid., pp. 3–4; Barnouw, *Tube of Plenty*, p. 175; Murrow and Friendly, *Selection*, p. 53.

40. Laurence Bergren, *Look Now, Pay Later: The Rise of Network Broadcasting* (Garden City, N.Y.: Doubleday, 1980), p. 186; Kendrick, *Prime Time*, p. 97. An interesting side

note is pointed out by David Oshinsky in a recent biography of McCarthy (*A Conspiracy So Immense: The World of Joe McCarthy* [New York: The Free Press, 1983]). On the same day the *See It Now* show was broadcast, Senator Ralph Flanders (R-Vt.) made a speech critical of McCarthy and "this speech was only the beginning" (p. 397), culminating in his proposal in July of a resolution to censure McCarthy.

41. Friendly *Circumstances*, pp. 32–33; Friendly, Oral History Project, Columbia University, p. 18.

42. Yaeger, "Analysis," p. 29.

43. Transcript, Billy Rose Collection, NYPL, *passim*. It was also published in *Top TV Shows of the Year*, edited by Irving Settel (New York: Hastings House, 1955), pp. 61–71.

44. Transcript, Billy Rose Collection, NYPL, p. 10; Cook, *Nightmare Decade*, p. 446; Bergren, p. 187.

45. Wershba, "Murrow vs. McCarthy," p. 22; transcript, Billy Rose Collection, NYPL, p. 16.

46. *New York Times*, 11 March 1954; Kendrick, *Prime Time*, p. 54; Yaeger, "Analysis," p. 174; Friendly, *Circumstances*, pp. 43, 52, 58.

47. Quoted in Jack Gould, "TV and McCarthy," *New York Times*, 14 March 1954, p. 2:11; Jack O'Brian, quoted in Friendly, p. 13 (typical of the smear efforts directed against *See It Now* was Pan American Association, New York Inc., *What You Don't See in "See It Now"* [New York: Pan American Anti-Communist Association of New York, 1957], a pamphlet that among other things accused Murrow of having "favorably publicized Left . . . causes and . . . slandered anti-Communists" [p. 2], and of having repeatedly "shown his bias in favor of Left-wingers [p. 3]); Philip Hamburger, "Man from Wisconsin," *The New Yorker*, 20 March 1954, p. 71; "Radio, TV Takes the Stage in New McCarthy Tempest," *Broadcasting*, 15 March 1954, p. 31; Gould, "TV and McCarthy."

48. Gould, "TV and McCarthy"; Gilbert Seldes, *The Public Arts* (New York: Simon & Schuster, 1956), pp. 217, 226; Seldes, "Murrow, McCarthy and the Empty Formula," *Saturday Review of Literature*, 24 April 1954, p. 26. For a similar view even more forcefully expressed by someone who also opposed McCarthy see John Cogley, "The Murrow Show," *Commonweal*, 16 March 1954, pp. 163–164.

49. Thomas C. Reeves, *The Life and Times of Joe McCarthy* (New York: Stein and Day, 1982), p. 564; Baughman, "Golden Age," p. 108.

50. George Gordon, *The Communications Revolution: A History of the Mass Media in the United States* (New York: Hastings House, 1977), p. 271; Bluem, *Documentary*, p. 98.

51. Seldes, *Public Arts*, p. 20; Freed quoted in Yellin, p. 51; Cook, *Nightmare Decade*, p. 497.

52. Eric Sevareid, *In One Ear* (New York: Knopf, 1952), pp. 207–208; Edwin R. Bayley, *McCarthy and the Press* (Madison, University of Wisconsin Press, 1981), pp. 193, 195 (Gould reminiscence of Murrow statement); Harry Castleman and Walter J. Podrazik, *Watching TV: Four Decades of American Television* (New York: McGraw Hill, 1982), p. 88; Murrow quoted in Dudar, "Post Portrait," 27 February 1959. The most interesting account of the Army-McCarthy hearings is Michael Straight, *Trial by Television* (Boston: Beacon Press, 1954), who maintains that "those who watched learned for themselves what they would not have learned any other way" (p. 3).

53. Seldes, *Public Arts*, p. 235. A look through the following surveys of American

history, chosen at random—John M. Blum et al., *The National Experience* (New York: Harcourt Brace Jovanovich, 1981), vol. 2; David Burner et al., *The American PEOPLE* (St. James, N.Y.: Revisionary Press, 1980), vol. 2; Harry J. Carman et al., *A History of the American People—Since 1865* (New York: Knopf, 1967); Carl Degler, *Out of Our Past: The Forces That Shaped Modern America*, rev. ed. (New York: Harper & Row, 1970); Carl Degler et al., *The Democratic Experience: Civil War to the Present*, 5th ed. (Glenview, Ill.: Scott Foresman, 1981): Charles M. Dollar, ed., *America: Changing Times—Since 1865* (New York: John Wiley, 1979); John A. Garraty, *The American Nation*, 4th ed. (New York: Harper & Row, 1979), vol. 2; Ray Ginger, *People on the Move: A United States History* (Boston: Allyn & Bacon, 1975); Rebecca Brooks Gruver, *An American History: From 1865 to the Present* (Reading, Mass.: Addison-Wesley, 1981); Samuel Eliot Morison, *The Growth of the Republic*, 6th ed. (New York: Oxford University Press, 1969), vol. 2; Edwin Rosenzenc and Thomas Bender, *The Making of American Society—Since 1865*, 2nd ed. (New York: Knopf, 1978); Irwin Unger, *These United States: Questions of Our Past* (Boston: Little, Brown, 1978)—shows that none of these widely used books mention the McCarthy program, that four (Burner, Degler, Degler et al., and Ginger) don't mention the televising of the hearings. Three of these textbooks mention Murrow: Blum in passing, and Dollar and Ungar for his broadcasts from Europe. A survey of the following textbooks dealing with twentieth-century U.S. history as well as those dealing with more recent events reveals equally sparse coverage. See: Oscar Barck, Jr., and Nelson M. Blake, *Since 1900*, 5th ed. (New York: Macmillan, 1974); Frank Freidel, *America in the Twentieth Century*, 4th ed. (New York: Knopf, 1976); Walter LeFeber and Richard Polenberg, *The American Century: A History of the United States Since the 1890s*, 2nd ed. (New York: John Wiley, 1979); William Leuchtenburg et al., *The Unfinished Century: America Since 1890* (Boston: Little, Brown, 1973); Arthur Link and William B. Catton, *American Epoch: A History of the United States Since 1900*, 4th ed. (New York: Knopf, 1974); Forest Mac-Donald, *The Torch Is Passed: The United States in the 20th Century* (Reading, Mass.: Addison-Wesley, 1968); David Shannon, *Twentieth Century America*, 3rd ed. (Chicago: Rand McNally, 1974); Paul Conkin and David Burner, *A History of Recent America* (New York: Thomas Y. Crowell, 1974); Norman A. Graebner, *The Age of Global Power: The United States Since 1939* (New York: John Wiley, 1979); Eric F. Goldman, *The Crucial Decade—and After* (New York: Knopf, 1975); Robert D. Marcus, *A Brief History of the United States Since 1945* (New York: St. Martin's Press, 1975); William Leuchtenburg and the editors of *Life, The Great Age of Change* (New York: Time Inc., 1964); Lawrence S. Wittner, *Cold War America: From Hiroshima to Watergate* (New York: Praeger, 1974). All mention the televising of the Army-McCarthy hearings (albeit Marcus has them of the wrong McCarthy hearings), but only three (Conkin, Goldman, and Wittner) mention the McCarthy program of *See It Now*, and one of these unfortunately places it after the hearings.

54. Dudar, February 27, 1959; Friendly, *Circumstances*, p. 69.

55. Murrow quoted in Kathy Pedell, "This Is Murrow . . . ," *TV Guide: The First 25 Years*, compiled and edited by Jay S. Harris in association with the editors of *TV Guide* (New York: Simon & Schuster, 1978), p. 28 (the Pedell article originally ran in 1955); Friendly, *Circumstances*, p. 75; Friendly interview, 29 October 1981.

56. Fleming quoted in Yaeger, "Analysis," p. 56; Friendly, *Circumstances*, p. 9. Some questions have been raised about the extent of this autonomy. Helen Dudar, dealing with

the scheduling of the McCarthy program "without the knowledge of . . . CBS brass," asserted that "some observers" thought that was "as plausible as the idea of . . . a rocket team launching an Atlas Missile without notifying the Pentagon." (Dudar, February 27, 1959.)

57. Friendly, *Circumstances*, p. 92. This essay does not have the space to deal with the complex relationship between Paley and Murrow during the latter's last years. Murrow died of lung cancer in 1965. Suffice it to say that despite such acid-etched portraits as that penned by Halberstam ("And so on the occasion of the death of Edward R. Murrow, William S. Paley who had done so much to make him and almost as much to break him, and who wanted to be sure that the company got credit for Murrow, went on the air to say that he personally would miss Ed Murrow, as would everyone else at CBS," *The Powers That Be*, p. 154), there also seems to have been a less dark side. Murrow's biographer comments on Paley's interest in the ailing Murrow during the latter's last months and Paley's suggestion that "even if inactive Murrow could serve as a consultant to CBS, telling it 'what was wrong'" (Kendrick, *Prime Time*, p. 508). Paley, of course, has his own view: "Murrow would not have been Murrow nor I myself if we had not had differences of opinion during our long professional and personal relationship. These differences and their meaning have been distorted by careless writers who interpret disputes as estrangements" (Paley, *Memoir*, p. 297).

58. Paley quoted in Kendrick, *Prime Time*, p. 59; Bergreen, *Look Now*, p. 186.

59. William H. Read, *America's Mass Media Merchants* (Baltimore & London: Johns Hopkins University Press, 1976), p. 67.

60. Edward Jay Epstein, *News from Nowhere: Television and the News* (New York: Random House, 1973), p. 90; Kendrick, *Prime Time*, p. 339; Murrow quoted in Metz, *Reflections*, p. 204. There are some interesting comments on the economics of CBS News at the time in James L. Baughman's "The Strange Death of 'CBS Reports' Revisited," *Historical Journal of Film, Radio, and Television* 2(1982):29–30.

61. Friendly, *Circumstances*, p. 68; Richard Elman, "United States: Consensus TV," *Censorship* 2 (Autumn 1966):42–45; Robert Higgins, "Did You Know THIS Was Going On?" *TV Guide*, 19 February 1966, p. 11

62. *In Search of Light: The Broadcasts of Edward R. Murrow 1938–1961*, edited with an introduction by Edward Bliss, Jr. (New York: Knopf, 1967), p. 363.

63. *60 Minutes Verbatim* (New York: Arno Press/CBS News, 1980), p. ii; Andrew Hacker, "Exposing People for Fun and Profit," *Fortune*, 7 September 1981, p. 124.

64. *Variety*, 28 October 1959, p. 2.

2

Amos 'n' Andy and the Debate Over American Racial Integration

THOMAS CRIPPS

By 1948, the American popular press, the ruling Democratic Party, and even the most conservative of entertainment media, the movies, had signaled to their constituencies that the touchy issue of racial integration would move to the center of American attention. At the same time, Afro-Americans, especially the growing middle class, swelled the ranks of activist organizations dedicated not merely to older, ambiguous goals of "fair play" and "equality of opportunity," but to full participation in the main social and economic activities of American life.

The Columbia Broadcasting System, like most American broadcasters, had often behaved as though blacks did not exist. But as post-World War II racial activism grew into a genuine social movement, CBS acted with more than its usual indifference by announcing its plans to produce a television version of its twenty-year old radio program, *Amos 'n' Andy*. A comic anachronism that depended for its humor on stereotypical racial traits, the new television program provided the occasion for blacks to debate, both with CBS and among themselves, the precise nature of racial prejudice.

At stake was the right to a nationwide monopoly of broadcasting facilities through which the image of Afro-Americans was to be presented to an enormous American audience. On one side was a complex, increasingly political black bourgeoisie; on the other a highly visible weekly comedy that depicted blacks as feckless, verbally crippled, ineptly conniving parvenus with hearts of gold.

More than any other point of contention, the misrepresentation of the black middle class set black activists on edge. For decades, black intellectuals ranging from racial nationalists to assimilationists had looked to this class for leadership. Whether rooted in the antebellum free Negro community, in the sturdy Southerners who had graduated from Booker T. Washington's Tuskegee Institute, or in the urban Northerners who formed "the talented tenth" symbolized by the black philosopher, W. E. B. DuBois, this class had distinguished itself from the mass of blacks. Churched, stably employed, affiliated with an intricate network of clubs and fraternal orders, the middle class found in *Amos 'n' Andy* a polar opposite that demeaned aspiration, burlesqued the complex distinctions that marked black social classes, and presented to a national white audience an image of maddening oversimplicity.[1]

As early as 1931 black educator Nannie Burroughs spoke for the middle class when she complained of broadcasters who characterized blacks as a uniformly "ignorant, shouting, fighting, rowdy element," a contention summed up by John H. Law, a part-time actor: "The Negro intelligentsia dislikes the lump into one social group." By 1951, the year *Amos 'n' Andy* reached the television screen, these sentiments had been solidified into a movement led by the National Association for the Advancement of Colored People, which had already attained considerable success in changing the black image in Hollywood movies. Among the dissenters were Hollywood blacks who viewed the NAACP as a threat. As one of them, Ernestin Wade, put it, "Agitation from officials of Negro organizations in the past jeopardized the progress of Negro shows."[2]

Amos 'n' Andy, till then a blessedly invisible and therefore relatively innocuous comedy, had come to television in 1951 after more than twenty years on radio. On radio it had never aroused the single-minded wrath that seemed to mark the black response to the television version. For every critic who had complained, another could be found who saw merit in the show. As early as 1932, a survey of black students and "adult leaders" revealed a spectrum of opinion ranging from enjoyment to "marked resentment and emphatic disapproval," a finding later confirmed by a Chicago Urban League study reported in the black *Los Angeles Sentinel*. Another early critic, Bishop W. J. Walls, when he attacked the show emphasized not its substance but the uses to which it was put—"a commercialization of primitive weakness." Later, at the height of the NAACP campaign against the show, some of the nation's prestigious black newspapers expressed similar ambivalence toward the TV series.[3] To this day, despite persistent hostility toward the show, black collectors, scholars, and fans divide on the question of the racism in *Amos 'n' Andy*.[4]

Why did black activists devote so much time, energy, and expense to snuffing out *Amos 'n' Andy* if they knew as well as its makers and sponsors that the black community split in its opinion of the show and its impact? The answer is to be found in the rise of the black bourgeoisie to postwar political awareness and its recent success in influencing the racial content of motion pictures. Wartime propaganda had hinted at an enhancement of postwar black status; NAACP memberships had risen tenfold during the 1940s; CBS's announcement of the proposed series came in 1948, less than a year before the release of Harry S. Truman's Civil Rights Commission report, which had called for a "year of rededication" to American ideals of social justice; and, beginning in 1949, Hollywood dramatized these social changes in a cycle of "message movies."[5] In this social mood, CBS's decision to broadcast a television version of *Amos 'n' Andy* seemed a regressive flaunting of lily-white power in the faces of a formerly vulnerable minority. Moreover, CBS stood alone in its programming preferences, if we may credit a report written by the agent of Hugh Wiley, a writer of black Southern local-color stories. Wiley's agent explained a dry spell that began in 1947 as follows: "Stories dealing with the negro character are, unfortunately, impossible to sell," not merely because *Amos 'n' Andy* preempted the field but because of "extreme pressure" from blacks.[6]

Wiley's man had hit on the central difference between postwar and prewar black America—the national "pressure" that black middle-class Americans were capable of mounting against the networks. It was *their* taste, sensibility, and identity that CBS violated in its narrow depiction of blacks as urban riffraff, tricksters, Falstaffs, and snarling matriarchs marked by naive cunning, languid manners, and drawling malapropisms.

Before the war the NAACP had been a mere shadow of its postwar bulk, and black protest had been limited to empty protests over racial epithets and a few bids for ownership of low-wattage stations. Broadcasters, therefore, had done little to cultivate black listeners, and blacks had appeared on the air only in local broadcasts of religious music, prime-time guests shots by musicians, and a few servile roles in situation comedies and soap operas. As a social scientist put it, the black performer "introduces the humor, the clowning, and also enables the middle-class housewife to smile in a sort of superior, patronizing way."[7] At their best, radio programs occasionally included "on a 'sustaining' or unsponsored basis" the Hampton Institute Choir, Paul Robeson, Ethel Waters, and bits of jazz and vaudeville. Years passed between dramas such as CBS's *John Henry* (1932) and WMCA's made-for-New York show, *A Harlem Family* (1935).[8] The narrowest, most stereotyped black roles were reserved for the huge prime-time audiences who saw blacks only as obstreperous maids and valets in popular situation comedies. One of the best, *The Jack Benny Show*, played limitless variations on the relationship between a parsimonious employer and his irreverent, bumptious valet, Rochester (Eddie Anderson).[9]

Before World War II, blacks had felt powerless to act against this white monopoly of access to broadcasting, but the war helped shake the foundations of the social order, at the least in the form of necessitarian gestures toward enlisting blacks in a national effort, and at the most in the form of hints and promises of a better life after the war. Black journalists exploited the situation by demanding a "Double V"—a simultaneous victory over foreign fascism and domestic racism— thereby linking American war aims to black social goals.[10]

The broadcasters responded to the heat of the moment with dozens of shows, among them Roi Ottley's *New World a 'Comin'*; Wendell Willkie's *Open Letter on Race Hatred*, following the Detroit riot of 1943; Kate Smith's guest shot on *We the People* (1945), in which she urged an end to racism, not "at a conference table in Geneva" but in "your own home," a plea that drew twenty thousand requests for transcripts; a black doctor and a black soldier in the soap operas *Our Gal Sunday* and *The Romance of Helen Trent*; CBS's black situation comedy, *Blueberry Hill*; and scattered dramas written by leftists such as Norman Corwin. Together they eroded the monopoly held by the comic servants in *Fibber McGee and Molly*, *The Great Gildersleeve*, and their epigones.[11]

After the war, the liberal mood became, said Walter White of the

NAACP, a "rising wind" of social change. New shows that reflected the times included ABC's *Jackie Robinson Show*, which ranged from sports to social issues; WDAS's (Philadelphia) prize winning *Bon Bon Show*; and CBS's production of Katherine Dunham's *The Story of a Drum*.[12]

Typical of these programs was Richard Durham's self-proclaimed "rebellious, biting, scornful, angry, cocky" *Destination Freedom* (1948–1950), a series of 105 historical sketches produced at WMAQ (Chicago). Durham, a writer for *Ebony* and the *Chicago Defender*, introduced listeners to black history through such characters as abolitionist Harriet Tubman, rebels Denmark Vesey and Toussaint L'Ouverture, and a number of modern activists.[13]

Coincident with the trend of programming, black organizations took up fresh strategies: giving awards, prodding sponsors, enlisting the support of foundations, and joining in cooperative ventures. Sometimes they actually sponsored programs such as the Urban League's production of Erik Barnouw's *The Story They'll Never Print*, a drama about an unemployed black veteran that was chosen for Joseph Liss's book, *Radio's Best Plays*.[14]

Within the industry itself, researchers began to identify a heretofore untargeted audience of prosperous black listeners. WLIB, Harlem's station, for example, reported a "vast Negro market potential" of billions of dollars, a population then bursting into Greater New York, a college enrollment that had risen by 1000 percent, and an unemployment rate of only 4 percent. The trade magazine *Sponsor* confirmed the boom in black wealth in a story on "the forgotten 15,000,000" black consumers. *Ebony*, a glossy magazine that catered to this new class, ventured a linkage between black wealth, political power, and the coming medium of television. Pointing to evidence that blacks outpurchased whites in the pursuit of consumer goods, *Ebony* characterized sponsor-dominated television as "an amazing new weapon which can be all-powerful in blasting America's bigots."[15] With each new exposure of the prospective black audience, the broadcasters increased their repertoire of gestures from mere slanted programming to appointing Jackie Robinson a vice-president of WNBC. Among the performers, no less than nine groups campaigned for improved black opportunity in broadcasting.[16]

Coincident with this rising black presence, commercial television emerged as a visual medium that had only just become profitable after nearly two decades of technical development. As early as 1939, Julius Adams of the *Amsterdam News* had anticipated black attitudes toward the new medium and even toward *Amos 'n' Andy*. Because television seemed unconstrained by a racist tradition and not yet dominated by entrenched whites, Adams touted it as "Our New Hope." As to *Amos 'n' Andy*, Adams argued that although blacks had tolerated it during its invisible radio period, "it would be suicide to put a show like this on television."[17] By 1950, *Variety* agreed with Adams on the basis of a wave of black performers who had broken into TV: "Negro Talent Coming into Own on TV Without Using Stereotypes: A Sure Sign That Television Is Free of Racial Barriers."[18]

Indeed, in the three years between 1950 and 1952, the life span of the *Amos 'n' Andy* show, network executives embarked on "a new policy of cultivating the Negro audience"—at least according to the trade papers. When NBC hired a public relations firm to direct a series of seminars intended to lead toward "a more realistic treatment of the Negro on the air and the hiring of more Negro personnel," *Variety* characterized it as part of a "movement." In fact there was something to the story; all manner of memoranda passed among the topmost broadcasting executives, urging cooperation with the Urban League, "integration without identification" in casting radio shows, more black material, and "the creation of new program ideas designed to realize" these new goals.[19] But at lower levels executives complained of wooden, unresponsive black auditions, or claimed that "there are certain positions where you feel it might not be advisable to use Negroes," such as those who face the public.[20]

For a brief moment during the same period, a black production company broke the white monopoly on filmmaking for television. The All America company—a creature of William D. Alexander, a sometime funtionary in a black college and in the Office of War Information; Claude A. Barnett, president of the Associated Negro Press; and Emmanuel Glucksman, a white producer of B movies—made a deal with Chesterfield Cigarettes to combine stock shots from their own inventory and other sources with topical news film of black celebrities.[21] Unfortunately, ambition outstripped execution, and this idea—which had been pressed by black entrepreneurs for more than thirty years—ended up in syndication in small markets and profitless dates in Southern grind houses. Glucksman, who hated the rough-and-tumble of location shooting, settled for "talking heads" in claustrophobic office settings, stills, fabricated events, canned ceremonies such as sorority inductions, honorary degrees, Ralph Bunche laying a wreath on Gandhi's tomb, and a black family in Queens enmeshed in its symbols of, as the voice-over said, "gracious living," all of them punctuated by shots of Barnett plugging "our cigarette." *Variety* sniffed at the pioneering effort as "little more than a lot of name-dropping with pictures" fit only for the "southern markets" that eventually bought them at bargain prices.[22]

Into this world of newly felt, newly flexed, black middle-class consciousness, activism, and wealth descended *Amos 'n' Andy*, complete with baggy pants, plug hats, foul cigars, pushy wives, misfired schemes, and mangled grammar. Organized blacks were shocked, not so much at what they saw, but at the timing of its release in the year of liberal "rededication," at a cresting of black political consciousness. Indeed, at first it was not even altogether clear that Freeman Gosden and Charles Correll, the two white originators of the radio series, would decide to abandon blackface in favor of using black actors. In any case, organized blacks reckoned that no good could result from a genre of visual humor that made fun of the black bourgeoisie.[23]

From the moment the story broke in 1948, when the *Los Angeles Sentinel* reported that the *Amos 'n' Andy* radio show had begun integrating blacks into its cast, a confrontation between the NAACP and CBS seemed inevitable. And yet it should be seen that ambiguity clouded the issue. On one hand, organized middle-class blacks winced at the thought of their collective image resting in the charge of two white men whose adult life had been devoted to week after week of creating a nationwide running gag about blacks. On the other hand, blacks in show business pointed to increased opportunities for actors to be generated by the show. On the side of the NAACP, James Hicks of the *Amsterdam News* refused CBS advertising and complained that the show "stinks"; speaking for the actors, Billy Rowe of the *Pittsburgh Courier* labeled the NAACP group "pinks."[24]

With blacks unable to marshal a united front, CBS assembled a production team composed of two executives; Gosden and Correll; director Charles Barton; the veteran vaudevillian, Flournoy Miller, as consultant on racial matters; and a corps of black actors composed of new recruits as well as Johnny Lee and Ernestine Wade from the radio show. They began shooting at the Hal Roach Studio. The decision to record the show in film was a pioneering strategy founded upon hoped-for profits in syndication.[25] Their creature enjoyed a national premiere on June 28, 1951, impervious to the ineffectual black pressure against the show.

At this point CBS seemed to have won the day. Blatz Beer proved to be an eager sponsor. The Roach studio, working with an uncommonly high budget of $40,000, gave *Amos 'n' Andy* a showmanlike gloss: In Charles Barton, a veteran director of Abbott and Costello farces at Universal, they possessed an early master of television style with its cadenced sequences of medium close-ups and two-shots that quickly became conventions of situation comedies. Fortunately for CBS, Barton proved not a good journeyman director but an amiable, sentimental buffer between the originators of the show and the black staff, one of whom remembered Gosden as "an old Southern hardcore general" who tried to "make us mouth *their* words . . . to imitate *them*." For Barton the company was "the greatest family you ever saw," while one of the black actors agreed that "there was a lot of tension . . . because our director, Charlie Barton, was so human and considerate." CBS shrewdly played this angle in its press releases, which minimized the racial basis of the shows while emphasizing the "warm feelings" shared by the members of the company.[26]

The product of their labors played on similar sentiments. Putting aside the racial material that grated upon the sensibilities of organized blacks, from the premiere onward the shows presented happy people with small problems that were solved each evening by restoring equilibrium to some momentarily ruffled situation. The winsome characters were models for the next generation of television heroes— neutral, bland, goodhearted. Amos (Alvin Childress) was an island of sanity in a sea of manic connivance; Andy (Spencer Williams), a mixture of innocence and eye-winking worldliness; and Kingfish (Tim Moore), the potentate of a gimcrack lodge and a fabricator of rickety schemes. The women displayed a similar range of sense and eccentricity: even-tempered Amos had a wife to match; flirtatious Andy, a string of shallow disappointments; and Kingfish, a shrew who was the equal of his own comic pushiness. The supporting characters, all played by veterans such as Johnny Lee, Nick Stewart, Jester Hairston, and the Randolph sisters, represented various extremes of virtue and vice that provided a frame for the principals. As the show matured, the malleable characters grew away from some of the premises of the radio show in ways that allowed Kingfish to serve as a pejorative model beside which the others seemed saner, wiser, less avaricious, and therefore more humane, decent folk. In this way, the dignity of Afro-America seemed less at risk, and the race of the characters seemed to matter less than it had in radio.

Predictably, the first round of criticism of the show focused on the fringe characters and on Kingfish, whose malapropisms, feckless scheming, and anachronistic costumes and manners seemed a caricature of black middle-class aspiration. Even *Variety*, usually a defender of show business, complained of "the molasses-tempered janitor who is a throwback to the Stepin Fetchit era," and called for a toning down of exaggerated manners and stereotypes and a shifting of focus from burlesque to sympathy for the plight of the race. Led by the NAACP, the black middle class challenged what they took to be a parody of their historical struggle for social mobility in a hostile society.[27]

At first, the NAACP protest, which *Variety* played on page one, began with letters of complaint to the sponsor—Schenley Distilleries, the parent company of Blatz Beer—only hours after the premiere. In a few days the protest spread to various white liberal groups such as the American Jewish Committee, which proposed a team of consultants that included black psychologist Kenneth Clark of City College of New York and political scientist Robert MacIver of Columbia. The team was to draft an "unobjectionable" substitute program similar to the "loveable [and] admirable" *The Goldbergs* and other ethnic shows that had avoided alienating ethnic activists.

With many shows already "in the can," the network pointed out that the slightest changes would take weeks to reach television screens. Nevertheless, through the summer of 1951, the activists pressed on by means of outraged press releases, a rousing resolution at the NAACP convention in Atlanta, and nominal support from a small cluster of allies such as the United Auto Workers—and yet with scant results save for isolated gestures such as the decision of WTMJ-TV (Milwaukee) to drop the show.[28]

The snag in the NAACP campaign was not in its tactics but in the fact that the issue rested upon the ability of the organized black middle class to translate its own resentments into a collective black will to act.

Instead of this intended outcome, however, the campaign exposed an undercurrent of dissension in black circles. Newspaper columnists, actors with deeply felt loyalties to show business, and television viewers compromised the NAACP's claims to solidarity, thereby softening the drive for dignified portrayals of the black bourgeoisie. As Billy Rowe of the *Pittsburgh Courier* pointed out, if black audiences wished "to look at people of their own color, performing for people of every color," this desire was in itself an aspect of racial integration that doomed the NAACP to "fighting a losing battle."[29]

Indeed, Rowe had hit upon the vulnerable center of NAACP demands. Walter White of the NAACP, in attacking the white monopoly on American broadcasting, depicted this nettlesome fact *only* in terms of its slandering the middle class. By focusing on *Amos 'n' Andy's* caricature of the middle class as indecorous, prone to use "street slang," and no more than a nest of "quacks and thieves [and] slippery cowards, ignorant of their profession," White appeared to concede that the CBS show had been accurate in its depiction of the black lower classes.[30]

With few exceptions, the black newspapers took a position in the middle between the NAACP and CBS, either because they reflected their readers or because they hesitated to offend the broadcasters and advertisers from whom they derived revenue. Occasionally, a paper played both angles, blasting the show as "disgusting" while also running CBS press releases. On the extremes were the *Amsterdam News*, which refused advertising for *Amos 'n' Andy*, and Billy Rowe of the *Courier*, who touted the show as "the greatest television show on earth."[31]

Actors heatedly denied the NAACP's charge that *Amos 'n' Andy* smeared the middle class. Clarence Muse, for example, spoke for black Hollywood when he praised the show as an "artistic triumph" that played upon "real Negroes you and I know." In a swipe at the NAACP he announced, "I have switched to Blatz Beer." One of the most senior members of the cast and a former dirctor of feature films, Spencer Williams, also asserted the case for verisimilitude in opposition to the NAACP. Of one scene he asked rhetorically: "Now there's a situation that could happen in any home with any race of people, isn't that right?" Yet the actors' main concern was not so much art or social messages, but with their own version of striving for integration—job opportunities in Hollywood. One of their guilds, the Coordinating

Council of Negro Performers, threatened to picket the New York NAACP to make their point. Individual dissenters kept their counsel. "I knew it was wrong," said Nick Stewart years later, but "I went along with it."[32]

As the split in black opinion became evident, broadcasters, advertisers, and white journalists joined in a collective expression of astonishment at the inflexibility of the NAACP position. Indeed, one ad executive felt "nonplussed" because Blatz's advertising agency drew such vigorous fire while "making a frank bid for Negro trade . . . [through] a policy of integration in hiring . . . [and] taking pains to assure the show's complete acceptance." The advertising tradepapers agreed, *Printer's Ink* predicting that the show would "be with us for a long, long time," while *Advertising Age* reported that "most Negroes in this area do not go along with the NAACP." In general, the white press probably believed, with Harriet Van Horn of the *New York World Telegram and Sun*, that the NAACP was "a trifle touchy."[33]

The central issue in the debate never came into focus. Both sides assumed that they were in essential agreement on the future of blacks in American life—a benignly liberal drift toward an eventually painless, fully integrated place in the American social order. Indeed, in its primitive stages the genre of television situation comedy tended to promote, ratify, and reinforce this bland, center-left vision of the future by depicting American society as a self-correcting system that was responsive to demands for "fair play."

Television producers had quickly invented a formula that expressed their sentiments as they applied to various ethnic groups—the Jews in *The Goldbergs*, Nordics in *I Remember Mama* (a novel, a drama, and a movie before its TV debut), and the Italians in *Luigi* (a "thoroughly moral character . . . [and] not a one-sided stereotype," according to *Variety*), *Papa Cellini*, and *Bonino*, the latter starring Ezio Pinza of the Metropolitan Opera. All of them shared a pool of interchangeable parts: an extended family, crotchety but warmly sentimental old folks, happy problems happily resolved in twenty-eight minutes of air time, and a division of characters into an older generation encrusted with cultural survivals from the old country and a younger group of super-Americans who had assimilated the virtues of the new land.[34]

Unfortunately, *Amos 'n' Andy* was asked to perform similar service for an ethnic group whose history included slavery, discrimination, and exclusion from the opportunity for easy assimilation implied in the gently comic plots of the European ethnic shows. Thus their traits of eccentric manners, dialect, and other cultural baggage were perceived not as vestiges of a national culture but as the mocking of racial subculture that was an aberration of white American culture. Moreover, the black middle class that spoke against *Amos 'n' Andy* perceived itself as having successfully struggled to overcome the cultural bondage that the characters in the show seemed locked into. In fact, within the shows this point was given emphasis in that the central figures, Andy and Kingfish, spoke in rural dialects, wore slightly off-center-clothing such as derbies and flashy suits, and behaved with exaggerated, hat-in-hand diffidence and cunning obsequiousness, while only the minor figures—the clerks and functionaries—were allowed the crisp Yankee accents and officious surroundings that marked them as middle-class successes. Thus, the NAACP activists were correct in their resentments, especially in view of the fact that the American broadcasting system allowed them no adversarial voice on the air.

At the same time, the writers engaged to write the television version—Bob Ross, Bob Mosher, Joe Connelly, Jay Sommers, Paul West, Dave Schwartz, and others—took pains to depict most of the supporting characters with a neat, pristine middle-class politesse. The actors—Jeni LeGon, Napoleon Simpson, and others—reinforced the writers' intentions with self-confident, solid bits of business; well-spoken, modulated voices; and a firm sense of place as though they had been born in paneled offices. The set decorators followed the same line of thought. Exteriors—even an alley through which a white thief had escaped—were clean and devoid of trash. In the kitchens were full refrigerators, four-burner stoves, matching china; on the walls were the stock symbols of middle-brow culture—Barbizon landscapes, Van Gogh's *Bridge at Arles*, and Kingfish's favorite painting, Hals's *The Laughing Cavalier*; scattered about their parlors were the candy dishes and books of a typical middle-class room.

In the scripts, the writers left the blocking, shot selection, movement and business, and other fragments of characterization entirely to the director and the actors on the set. Thus the development of specific details of character were placed in the hands of the actors—an important factor to black viewers who might get derivative pleasure from seeing Sam McDaniel, or some other actor forced by Hollywood cir-

cumstance into a lifetime of demeaning roles, play a straight role, uncluttered by heavy-handed dialect. Finally, in the few shows in which a
heavy criminal appeared, he was sure to be played by Anthony Warde
or some other white denizen of B movies.[35]

The ambience of the sets was matched by the equally bourgeois
motivations of the characters. While it is true that neither of the two
principals succeeded at their erratic careers, their failure never resulted
from want of striving. The premise of the episode entitled "Jewel Store
Robbery," for example, is that Kingfish and Andy ruefully reminisce
about wasted opportunity. "Sapphire was right, Andy," says Kingfish.
"I done wasted my entire life. Me who had such a brilliant record in
school." Often at moments like these, the supporting characters appear
as contrasts against which to measure the principals. In this show, Roy
Glenn appears as a sleek, imposingly dressed, basso-voiced success.
The comic plot turns on the humiliating fact that Kingfish's circumstances have forced his wife, Sapphire, to hire out as Glenn's maid. At
the denouement Amos hammers home the point in a brief exchange
with Andy:

> I feel kinda sorry for the Kingfish. But you know, you can't much blame
> the Kingfish for wantin' the folks down in Marietta to think he's a
> bigshot up here. It's just human nature for everybody to want somebody
> to think they is important. I guess that's what keeps a lot of us going in
> life.

Moreover, the attention of the viewer is never allowed to stray from the
plot and the characters into current events along the racial front. White
characters, for instance, are never allowed to refer to race or even to
notice that the principals are black. In one show in which a gang of
white counterfeiters appear, they have a private opportunity to discuss
the blacks but identify them only as "those two birds upstairs."[36]

The plots reinforced the message put forth by the set decorations
and characterizations. In "Happy Stevens," for example, Kingfish and
Sapphire, cranky and backbiting from a marriage gone stale, seek help
from "the happy Harringtons," two white talk show hosts. But in the
end, they not only learn that they can live with themselves, unpropped
by the "cultured, charming chitchat" advocated by their radio coun-
selors, but also that the station prefers them to the white Harringtons.
In "Kingfish's Secretary" the situation is used not so much to depict
some small victory but rather to show how Kingfish has matured be-

yond his origins in Marietta. The dramatic contrast is provided by a Southern woman who has come north in answer to a matrimonial advertisement. The country woman suffers from comparision with the chic secretaries, primly dressed neighbors, well-stocked Harlem stores, and flippant dialogue of Harlem. Kingfish and Andy, with their slurred diction, outdated clothes, and perpetual suspension in midcareer between golden opportunities, suggest that although they are no longer bumpkins like the woman from the South, they are also still marching toward some form of bourgeois success. "That must be the scrubwoman," says Kingfish as he casually compares her with his own evolving parvenu style of life.[37]

Of all the shows, the most well known and affecting was a Christmas story that *Variety* described as "an almost classic bit." A simple story of a child's dream fulfilled at Christmastime, it provided a showcase for Andy to display his most deeply felt sentiments while seeking work that would allow him to buy a brown-skinned, talking doll for Arabella, Amos's precocious daughter. Andy's laying of the gift under the Christmas tree inspires Amos to compose a bedtime story in the form of a sentimental exegesis of the Lord's Prayer as it plays on the radio in the background, set to the music of Albert Hay Malotte.

As though challenging the NAACP, every incident, character, and set contributed to a touching domestic drama that was anything but an exploitation of black life. Indeed, the most persistently nettling quality of the program in the minds of black activists was not in the substance of plot or character but mainly in the survival of a stylized Negro dialect. Nevertheless, it often seemed balanced or disarmed by the middle-class accents that marked many of the shows. Thus, when Arabella asks crisply, "Wouldn't it be wonderful to have a white Christmas?" Andy replies with a favorite uncle's devotion, "Them's the best kind." Whatever Andy's small crimes against the language, he is treated with deferential respect by the janitor, who calls him *"Mistuh* Andy." And if Andy professes that poverty is "rebarrassin'," or uses some other comic neologism, the preponderance of supporting characters speak in Yankee accents appropriate to the setting. A coolly professional nurse; a department store executive played by Napoleon Simpson, a veteran of Hollywood jungle movies; a floorwalker played by Milton Woods, a star in "race movies"; and a string of winsome kids who sit on Andy's lap as he plays the store's Santa Claus all speak in radio-announcer American.

In the end, Andy has played out a perfect bourgeois scenario: he has focused on a goal, worked for wages to accomplish it, deferred his own gratification, and ceremonially presented the fruits of his labors in a socially correct call on Arabella's parents. And he has accomplished all this at considerable psychic cost to himself in that he chose not to present Kingfish with a gift and had been insulted for it.

Every setting, prop, and gesture reaffirmed the form and substance of middle-class life. When Andy calls, Amos and his wife are enjoying a Christmas Eve pause in front of their tree. At the sound of the doorbell, Amos puts on a dark jacket, straightens his tie, and receives his old friend with a formal handshake. The rooms are jammed with the same icons of conventionality that have dressed the sets of all the programs in the series.

As though to confirm the theological sources of Andy's selfless behavior, the last scene is devoted entirely to Amos's interpretation of the Lord's Prayer. Up to this moment, every two-shot close-up of the characters has been in conventional television style—a succession of fixed, eye-level shots of "talking heads," intercut with reaction shots edited for easy continuity. Here, however Barton lowers the camera angle, tilting up on Arabella's bed, a setup broken by cutaways that tilt down on the recumbent and reverent girl. The sequence asserts Amos's fatherly authority and gives him an imposing presence through which to give a line-by-line exegesis of the prayer—which plays, *sotto voce*, on the radio. Amos's resonant expression of humanity's need for a deity, and his evoking of a natural order in which mankind may live with a hope for community, harmony, and brotherhood ends with a shot of falling snow, seen through the window from Arabella's point of view.[38]

Over the seventy-odd weeks of production, these softly decent characters and homilies balanced the shambling presence of Kingfish, thereby blunting the case of the NAACP. *Variety*, which frequently spoke for show business and for liberalism, used the Christmas show as a swipe at what it considered off-target militance. "Despite the hassle over civil rights currently engulfing the nation in this Presidential election year, *Amos 'n' Andy* isn't going to influence any viewer one way or the other," declared the trade paper. "If anything, the series shrewdly brings out some of the best characteristics of the Negro." Indeed, even though the cast was solidly black in almost every show, *Variety* inferred a subtle integrationist message that logically followed from "the great value of showing a Negro family living normal lives in normal surroundings sharing the emotional and religious experience of all people."[39]

Gradually the NAACP saw its image as defender of the oppressed take on an unaccustomed ambiguity as a pressure group whose "touchiness" in attacking the "most liberal" of the networks ruined the careers of black actors and polarized black opinion. Apart from the younger generation of black Hollywood, which shared the dismay of the NAACP at "the harm" done by *Amos 'n' Andy*, countless black actors and loyal listeners felt put upon by "outsiders" and, according to actress Lillian Randolph, "various white groups" who used the NAACP as a weapon to "eliminate the Negro actors [and] put [me] out of business."[40] Musician Lionel Hampton, the most conservative of black performers, set forth this economic line in its broadest social terms: "I look upon the new 'Amos 'n' Andy' television show as an opening wedge toward greater opportunities and bigger things for scores of our capable artists who haven't been able to get a break in video until this new Blatz-CBS show started." Blatz released the results of a poll that supported the performers against the NAACP, claiming that 77 percent of black New Yorkers liked the show. In 1952, Estelle Edmerson, a young graduate student, surveyed the actors and confirmed a deep vein of resentment at the NAACP pressure on their livelihoods, a strong sense of accomplishment, and gratitude toward the sponsor and network. They felt grateful for "a toe in the door" (Willie Best) and to be able "to eat three times a day" (Roy Glenn); they refused to "see anything objectionable" on the air (Eddie Anderson); they complained of organized blacks that "we, as a race, are too sensitive" (Johnny Lee); and they praised "the baby entertainment medium, television, [that] has accepted the Negro entertainer" (Cab Calloway). Ruby Dandridge extended Calloway's opinion by pointing to CBS's hiring of Flournoy Miller, whom "they ask for opinions when in doubt as to the insults to the Negro people." Whites such as Ed Sullivan also testified "that TV as a medium was made to order for Negro performers." Dissenters—most of them trained actors such as James Edwards, Juano Hernandez, and Frank Silvera—insisted on "the harm" done to liberalism by the show.[41]

In the end, the ambiguities both in the content of *Amos 'n' Andy* and in the splintered black response to it undercut the NAACP campaign to remove the show from the air. This is not to cast the organization as a lone figure in hopeless cause. By August 1951, the National Urban League had opened its own letter-writing campaign, which also attracted several white liberal groups. But intellectuals such as George Norford, drama critic of the *Amsterdam News*, and G. James Fleming, a political scientist from the Virgin Islands and an *Amsterdam News* reporter, began to hope to divert the attention of blacks toward a demand for "an open communications system" rather than the divisive question of whether or not *Amos 'n' Andy* excluded or burlesqued black bourgeois behavior. Indeed, the NAACP itself by 1954 turned its attention to studying the black broadcasting marketplace, ways to develop a "National Negro Broadcasting Council," and eventually a means of producing "network-calibre, quality programming" for independent Negro-appeal stations. One enthusiastic advocate told Walter White of the NAACP that radio—if not television—was "potentially the greatest instrument of progress that has ever been available to a minority race," a source of "cultural self-expression on a mass scale," and a source of jobs and income.[42]

Nevertheless, in the short run the NAACP had failed to cast *Amos 'n' Andy* as an enemy of the entire black world. Instead, the show had been characterized as a slander against only the black middle class. Thus, instead of fulfilling a *Chicago Defender* prediction that the "disgusting" revival of "stereotyping" would "be crushed . . . by the frontal assault of an enlightened and protesting people," the campaign merely sputtered out. Blatz's decision to withdraw from sponsorship at the end of the 1953 season was depicted in the trades not as a defeat at the hands of the NAACP, but as a quest for a higher-class image accomplished by picking up the prestigious *Four Star Playhouse*.[43] The show survived in syndication, often earning solid ratings and audience shares. Far into the 1960s *Amos 'n' Andy* played as a "strip," or daily program, usually in fringe time but occasionally in prime.[44] In the large markets such as New York, heavyweight sponsors like Trans-World Airways bought the time slots. And when it finally expired in major markets it played on in small-time Southern metropolitan areas, remembered not as a vanquished enemy, but almost as a martyr—"one of the alltime major casualties of the radio-to-video transition," according to *Variety*.[45]

Why had the NAACP engaged in what seemed like a fruitless enterprise that split blacks and alienated white liberals? What had been gained by the playing out of the episode? The answers are not entirely clear, but they lie in the shifting goals and rising hopes of the postwar black leadership. World War II had enlarged black goals to include the possibility of eventual full integration into American life at the precise moment of a boom in memberships in black activist organizations. Simultaneously, *Amos 'n' Andy* arrived in full view of the television audience, complete with symbolic baggage from an older time in black history and broadcasting history. Solidly rooted in a segregated world, by its existence, even on television, it seemed to cast doubt over black social goals and to mock the newly powerful, organized black middle class. The virtues of black aspiration and success were simply too deeply imbedded in the fabric of the programs to invite appreciation by organized black activists—even though evidence suggests a faithful audience of black viewers.

NOTES

1. Black middle-class values are taken up in David G. Nielson, *Black Ethos* (Westport, Conn., 1980), and August Meier, *Negro Thought in the Age of Booker T. Washington, 1885-1915* (Ann Arbor, Mich., 1965).

2. The quotations are from Estelle Edmerson, "A Descriptive Study of the American Negro in United States Professional Radio, 1922-1953" (Master's thesis, University of California-Los Angeles, 1954), pp. 115, 87, 94. NAACP activities are recorded in that organization's files in the Library of Congress.

3. H. B. Alexander, "Negro Opinion Regarding *Amos 'n' Andy*," *Sociology and Social Research* 16 (March 1932): 345-354; Bishop J. Walls, "What About Amos 'n' Andy?" *Abbott's Monthly*, December 1930, pp. 38-40, 72, the latter in James Weldon Johnson Memorial Collection, Beineke Library, Yale; *Los Angeles Sentinel*, 18 March 1948.

4. The Enoch Pratt Free Library of Baltimore reported that especially among "older" patrons demand was so heavy "you could hardly get hold of" some tapes. (telephone interviews with Florence Connor and Carolyn Houck, Pratt Library). Also available in Afro-American Studies Program, University of Maryland, College Park, Md., the director of which, Al-Tony Gilmore, is writing a book on *Amos 'n' Andy*. See also James Wolcott, "Holy Mack'el!: Amos 'n' Andy Videotapes Are Hot Items on the Nostalgia Market," *Esquire*, January 1981, pp. 11-12.

5. President's Committee on Civil Rights, *To Secure These Rights* (Washington, D.C., 1947). A good essay and bibliography on the period is Richard Polenberg, *One Nation Divisible: Class, Race and Ethnicity in the United States Since 1938* (New York, 1980), chap. 3, p. 330.

6. David Freeman, Jaffe Agency, to Hugh Wiley, 26 March 1952; 21 April 1952, Wiley Papers, Bancroft Library, Berkely, Calif.

7. L. S. Cottrell quoted in Paul F. Lazarsfeld, *Radio and the Printed Page* (New York, 1940), pp. 56-57, and in Edmerson, "Negro in Radio," p. 195.

8. J. Fred MacDonald, "Stride Toward Freedom—Blacks in Radio Programming," paper loaned by author, pp. 7–14, later a chapter in his *Don't Touch That Dial!* (Chicago, 1980).

9. Sample of Benny-Anderson dialogue in MacDonald, "Stride Toward Freedom," p. 11a. Black ambivalence toward Rochester can be seen in Edmerson, "Negro in Radio," pp. 185-187 (newspapers and *The Negro Yearbook* cited), and in Anderson himself, telephone interview between Anderson and Cripps, June 1970, in which he claimed never to have crossed boundaries of bad taste nor depicted unreal characters.

10. See *Pittsburgh Courier*, 4 March 1942, for an example. A rich literature includes John B. Kirby, *Black Amercans in the Roosevelt Era: Liberalism and Race* (Knoxville, Tenn., 1980).

11. For a sample of reviews of local and prime time network programs see *Variety*, 7 October 1942, p. 26; 11 March 1942, pp. 18, 35; 13 May 1942, pp. 32–33; 20 May 1942, p. 36; 10 Febraury 1943, p. 30; 17 February 1943, p. 28; 3 March 1943, p. 33; 8 April 1942, p. 30; 15 March 1944, p. 53; 3 May 1944, p. 1; 22 March 1944, p. 3; 16 February 1944, p. 43; see also MacDonald, "Stride Toward Freedom," pp. 25–33.

12. *Sponsor*, December, 1949, p. 44, on Robinson, cited in Edmerson, "Negro in Radio," pp. 12, 45; synopsis of *Story of a Drum*, CBS 15 February 1946, in Katherine Dunham Collection, Box 7, Morris Library, Southern Illinois University, Carbondale, Ill.

13. Docments from *Destination Freedom* Collection, Institute for Popular Culture Studies, Northeastern Illinois University, cited in J. Fred MacDonald, "Radio's Black Heritage: *Destination Freedom*, 1948–1950," *Phylon* 39 (March 1978): 66–73.

14. Edmerson, "Negro in Radio," p. 165, and conversations between Barnouw and Cripps, 1975–1976. Edmerson's informants, pp. 350–359, cited sponsors who feared pejorative associations with blacks ("nigger flour") and "a mixed reception from Negroes themselves." Thus civil rights groups inquired into broadcasting as a weapon. Ann Tanneyhill of the National Urban League, for example, argued: "I do hope we will be able to move into the fields of motion pictures and radio in 1948. We 'scooped' other race relations agencies on the comic book but I fear they will beat us to the draw on motion pictures and radio." *Morning for Jimmy* file, NUL Records, Library of Congress.

15. "The Forgoten 15,000,000," *Sponsor*, October 1949, pp. 24–25, 54–55; Edmerson, "Negro in Radio," pp. 350–354; "Selling the Negro Market," cover story in *Tide*, 20 July 1951, in NAACP Records; "Can TV Crack America's Color Line? *Ebony*, May 1951, p. 58. *Ebony* from 1948 through 1952 gave heavy coverage to television as though believing its own assertion that "television has supplied ten-league boots to the Negro in his fight to win what the Constitution of this country guarantees."

16. *Variety*, 9 January 1952, p. 32; 3 September 1952, p. 26; 6 February 1951, p. 31; 11 January 1950, p. 28 (in which George S. Schuyler's talk show is seen as "in line with a new policy of cultivating the Negro audience").

17. *Amsterdam News* (New York City), 12 August 1939.

18. *Variety*, 3 May 1950, pp. 30, 40.

19. On programming, see *Variety*, 8 February 1950, p. 58; 19 April 1950, p. 24; "Television," *Ebony*, June 1950, pp. 22–25; *Variety*, 11 January 1951, p. 28; 10 September 1952, p. 30; 22 October 1952, p. 27; 26 November 1952, p. 30. On policies of executives, *Variety*, 8 November 1950, p. 26; 17 January 1951, p. 26; 18 July 1951, p. 1.

20. Edith Tedesca, CBS personnel, quoted in Edmerson, "Negro in Radio," p. 103.

21. Glucksman-Barnett correspondence in Barnett Papers, Chicago Historical Society, NUL interceded for blacks seeking entry into broadcasting, as in placing lyricist Joe Lutcher as a prospective writer of Camel cigarette commercials, thereby providing another crack in the white monopoly. Wesley R. Brazier to Guichard Parris, 5 December 1952, Series 5, Los Angeles 1944–61 file, box 42, NUL Records.

22. Reels are scattered among Clark College, Atlanta; Library of Congress; and Kit Parket, Carmel, Calif.; Glucksman to Barnett, 25 August 1954; *Variety*, 11 August 1954, p. 41.

23. *Amos 'n' Andy* began in 1929 on Chicago radio, moving eventually to network broadcasting, recordings, two RKO films in 1930, and animated cartoons (cartoon in Library of Congress, films on KDKA-TV, (Pittsburgh); *Variety*, 9 October 1930, p. 31; 20 August 1930, p. 4; 8 October 1930, p. 22. See also Norman Kagan, "Amos 'n' Andy: Twenty Years Late, or Two Decades Early?" *Journal of Popular Culture* 6 (Summer 1972):71–75.

24. Quoted in Kagan, "Amos 'n' Andy," pp. 71–75.

25. *Los Angeles Sentinel*, 18 March 1948; *Variety*, 1 February 1950; 28 April 1948, p. 1; 4 October 1950, p. 30; 5 November 1950, p. 1, the latter for a report of the national post-prime time sneak preview.

26. Interviews, June 1970 and the summers of 1976 and 1977, between the author and Nick Stewart, Bill Walker, Ernest Anderson, Jester Hairston, Alvin Childress, Sig Mickelson, and Charles Barton.

27. *Variety* 4 October 1950, p. 30; C. L. Dellums to Walter White, 6 December 1950, NAACP Records.

28. *Ebony*, May 1951, p. 21; *Variety*, 4 October 1950, p. 30; *Color*, clipping; Dellums to White, 6 December 1950; Lindsay II. White et al. to Lewis S. Rosenstiel, Schenley Distillers, copy, 27 June 1951 (all but *Ebony* and *Variety* in "*Amos 'n' Andy*" file, NAACP Records).

29. *Pittsburgh Courier*, 7 July 1951; *Variety*, 4 July 1951, p. 1; Walter White to Committee, copy, 10 July 1951; White, memorandum for file, 11 July 1951, and on 10 July 1951 marked "not to be given out," in NAACP Records. The committee included the topmost rank of the national NAACP, along with Ralph Bunche, journalists Norman Cousins and Lewis Gannett, Louis T. Wright, Channing Tobias of the YMCA, and Algernon Black of the National Council of Churches.

30. *New York Times*, 22 September 1951; Walter White to "subscribing newspapers," copy, 12 July 1951; Gloster B. Current to "NAACP branches and state conferences," copy, 16 July 1951; NAACP press release, "Why the Amos 'n' Andy TV Show Should Be Taken Off the Air," 15 August 1951; press release, "New Protests Mark 4th Week . . . 26 July 1951"; Ardie A. Halyard, Milwaukee Branch, to Current, 27 July 1951, NAACP Records.

31. Walter White to newspapers, 2 August 1951; White to Billy Rowe, 27 July 1951, NAACP Records, in which White argued that the shows affected society to the point of causing a riot, and demanded proof of Rowe's linkage of the NAACP with the Communist Party.

32. For the mixed black response see *Chicago Defender*, 23 June 1951 (Fred O'Neal); 7, 14, 28 July 1951; 18 August 1951 (CCNP); *Variety* 28 January 1953, p. 1 (NBC defense), 24 June 1953, p. 1 (sponsors); *Defender*, 29 September 1951 (UAW); 25 August, 18 August

1951 (anti-NAACP actors); 8 September 1951 (Negro Masons' split); 29 September 1951 (clerical protest); *Variety*, 8 August 1951, p. 1 (statements by Lester Walton and Noble Sissle); *Negro Achievement* 9 (November 1952), p. 40, latter in Johnson Collection, Beineke Library, Yale.

33. W. Richard Bruner, "Amos 'n' Andy Hassle Won't Stop TV Show," *Printer's Ink; Advertising Age*, 13 August 1951; Arnold M. Rose, "TV Bumps into the Negro Problem," *Printers' Ink*, 2 July 1951, p. 36; Walter White, "Negro Leader Looks at TV Race Problem," *Printer's Ink*, 24 August 1951, p. 31; *New York World Telegram and Sun*, 27 July 1951; *Interracial Review*, September 1951; *New Leader* 15 October 1951; Gosden and Correll quoted in *Advertising Age*, 13 August 1951; Harold Doman and Thelma Eastman, draft petition on "integration," 31 July 1951; Lindsay H. White and James E. Allen, NAACP, copy, to Lewis S. Rosenstiel, Schenley, 27 June 1951; Walter White to newspapers, copy, 2 August 1951, all in NAACP Records.

34. *Variety*, 23 August 1950, p. 28, 24 September 1952, p. 30 (*Luigi*); 1 October 1952, p. 101 (*Cellini*); 16 September 1953, p. 31 (*Bonino*); Walter White memorandum, 10 July 1951, recounting the role of Edward J. Lukas, American Jewish Committee, in influencing the content of the *The Goldbergs*, NAACP Records.

35. "Happy Stevens," "The Kingfish's Secretary," and "The Rare Coin" in Enoch Pratt Free Library; scripts in Library of Congress and in Special Collections, UCLA.

36. "The Jewel Store Robbery," in Pratt Library, script in Library of Congress.

37. Source as in note 35.

38. "The Christmas Show," viewed through the courtesy of Professor Al-Tony Gilmore, chairman, Afro-American Studies, University of Maryland, College Park, Md.

39. *Variety*, 31 December 1952, p. 18.

40. Edmerson, "Negro in Radio," pp. 89, 117, 126–129, 192, 391–393, 396, 403.

41. Hampton quoted, *Pittsburgh Courier*, 4 August 1951, in Edmerson, "Negro in Radio," p. 391; Blatz sample in *California Eagle*, 23 August 1951, also in Edmerson, p. 393. Her other interviews derived from pages cited in note 40.

42. Interview between George Norford and the author, 29 October 1970, in which Norford recalled a tension between feeling that the shows were "funny as hell" and his opposition to network exclusivity that denied blacks access to the air; conversations with Professor Emeritus G. James Fleming of Morgan State University, especially one on 31 October 1975. On the NUL campaign, see Ann Tanneyhill, NUL, to Frank Stanton, CBS, 10 August 1951; Tanneyhill to Bill Chase, 10 August 1951; Tanneyhill to Lewis S. Rosenstiel, 10 August 1951, Series 7, Box 1, NUL Records. On the NAACP's inquiry into a "National Negro Broadcasting Council" and some form of "network-calibre" programming for blacks, see Harry Novik, WLIB, to Walter White, 10 January 1951; 7 July 1954; and David D. Osborn et al. to White, [July 1954], 19 pp., in NAACP Records.

43. *Chicago Defender*, 7, 14, 28 July 1951; *Variety*, 18, June 1952, p. 28 (Blatz's withdrawal); 11 March 1953, p. 25 (*Four Star* and also the outsized "nut" of *Amos 'n' Andy*); *Variety*, 8 August 1951, (a page-one story on the threats of Lester Walton, a veteran black drama critic, and Noble Sissle, a famous bandleader, to picket NAACP offices as a means of dramatizing black opposition).

44. In the decade following the suspension of production, *Amos 'n' Andy* remained a staple of the syndication market, generally in a pattern of good solid ratings in southern states and through the West to Bakersfield, and in smaller markets. Thus in the same

summer week in 1955, it finished first among syndicated shows in Little Rock but ninth in Washington. Where it was possible to measure, it seemed to play equally well in northern towns such as Evansville and southern towns like Shreveport, but also in large markets where heavy black populations resided such as Detroit. One week in 1956, it was number one in New Orleans with a rating of more than 50 and an audience share of more than 80, while one month later in New York, in keeping with its pattern of flopping in large markets, it finished tenth with a rating of 7.5, against *Looney Tunes*. This trend also included less clearly measurable traits, among them the possibility that when *Amos 'n' Andy* was opposed by programs that were slanted toward children, the adults in the family overrode the tastes of the young. In Shreveport in the summer of 1961, for example, *Huckleberry Hound* finished fourth with a rating of 16 as against the 22 posted by *Amos 'n' Andy*. Gradually, through the early 1960s, even though the same viewing patterns persisted, the size of the figures tailed off. Ratings consistently fell below 20, even in southern and small-town markets, and even in towns such as Dayton, Bakersfield, Atlanta, Charlotte, and New Orleans the show regularly finished ninth or tenth in the local race for hegemony in syndication. Sample made by Alma Taliaferro Cripps and Paul Hagan Cripps for the years 1954–1963.

45. *Variety* continued to cover the story even as the combative elements of it diminished. See 2 July 1952, p. 24; 31 December 1952, p. 18; 13 May 1953, pp. 38–39; 16 September 1953, p. 21; 3 June 1953, p. 25; 13 January 1954, p. 25. For postmortems in addition to the *Esquire* article cited in note 4, see "The Case of the Missing Roast Beef," *Ebony*, April 1958, p. 143; "Requiem for the Kingfish," Ebony, July 1959, pp. 57–64; Edward T. Clayton, "The Tragedy of Amos 'n' Andy," *Ebony*, October 1961, pp. 66–73 (which reported that "no other Negro show has been able to find a national sponsor"); and Thomas Cripps, "The Films of Spencer Williams," *Black American Literature Forum* 12 (Winter 1978):128–134.

3

The Rise and Fall of Milton Berle

ARTHUR FRANK WERTHEIM

"When the history of the early days of commercial television is eventually written, several chapters will no doubt be devoted to the strange art of Milton Berle," wrote Philip Hamburger in *The New Yorker* in 1949. Hamburger was impressed by the comedian's extraordinary popularity on NBC's *Texaco Star Theatre* and how millions of Americans ritually watched Mr. Television, the name Berle acquired because he was the medium's first star. His following was "a phenomenon of massive proportions," the writer declared.[1]

On Tuesday evening, known as Milton Berle Night, fans habitually turned on their sets at 8:00 P.M. to laugh at the comic's vaudeville slapstick routines. Viewers preferred to be entertained at home by seeing a "snowy" black-and-white picture on their new receivers rather than listening to their favorite radio program. Radio had kept Americans amused at home for over twenty years. Now it was being challenged by a more powerful and seductive medium that depended more on the eye than the ear. Since only 9 percent of homes had televisions in 1950, most Americans watched the Berle show at friends' houses or stood in smoky, crowded neighborhood taverns.[2] Throngs also gathered on sidewalks in front of appliance store windows displaying television sets for dealers knew this was a way to attract buyers.

Broadway and movie theaters supposedly lost customers on Tuesday night, and some nightclubs and restaurants closed. During the week viewers talked about the skits they had seen and eagerly awaited the next program. Berle's fame was widely publicized when his picture appeared on the cover of both *Time* and *Newsweek* for May 16, 1949.

Stories about the show's popularity circulated in newspapers and magazines. One laundromat advertised, "Watch Berle while your clothes whirl." One of Berle's writers, Jay Burton, remembered that a New York store usually open at night posted a sign on the window that read "Closed. Went home Tuesday night to see Uncle Miltie." Avid fans apparently sat through the one-hour program without going to the bathroom, because the commercials could also be amusing. Detroit reported a large increase in water usage due to flushing toilets immediately following the show's conclusion. Although certainly some stories were exaggerated for publicity purposes, they nevertheless suggest the program's enormous appeal.[3]

The Berle craze, which ran from 1948 to 1951, resembled the *Amos 'n' Andy* mania on radio during the early 1930s. Both series had phenomenal ratings in the early years of their mediums. The two programs were also responsible for increasing NBC's revenues and making the broadcasting industry financially profitable by attracting advertising to other network shows. Like Freeman Gosden and Charles Correll, the stars of *Amos 'n' Andy*, Berle became an overnight sensation and media celebrity.

Why were so many television viewers captivated by Berle? A major factor was the comedian's style of comedy, which derived from urban vaudeville humor. Berle's routine appealed to early television's main audience, which was located primarily in cities. Between 1948 and 1952 most TV stations were situated in major metropolitan areas. From 1952 to 1954 television began expanding into small-town and rural regions due to coast-to-coast network broadcasting via coaxial cable and the licensing of new stations. During those years the Berle show began to drop in the ratings, and before long the comedian became television's first prominent victim. Although Berle has been the subject of many popular magazine articles and has coauthored an unusually frank and revealing autobiography, he has been neglected by television historians.[4] A discussion of *Texaco Star Theatre's* content, production, and reception and an analysis of the comedian's style and career is crucially important for understanding the cultural power of television in its early years.

Born on July 12, 1908, on West 113th Street in Manhattan, Berle started in show business at an early age. His father, Moses Berlinger, a paint salesman and shopkeeper, was frequently ill and had difficulties earning enough money to support his wife and five children. Berle's mother, a department store detective, was the backbone of the family, and she recognized and nurtured her son's talent. As a youngster Berle showed signs of being a natural comic. He diplayed the characteristics of a "*schlemiel* child," the name psychologists Seymour and Rhoda Lee Fisher have given to children with clownish behavior patterns. In their study they found parallels in the childhood of other professional comedians and "certain troubled children" who used "the ridiculous to cope with life—much like the *schlemiel* of Yiddish folklore." As one of five children and the youngest of four sons, Berle constantly demanded and received attention. He was reputed to be a "fresh kid" and a cutup who liked to show off, do imitations, and mug in front of a mirror. At home he put on shows for the neighborhood children using a clothesline for a curtain and wooden grocery crates for a stage on which he sang, danced, and cracked jokes. One Halloween the five-year-old Berle dressed as Charlie Chaplin wearing his father's baggy suit, derby, and cane and a false mustache made from a piece of his mother's fur muff. A theater manager spotted him on the street and liked his costume so much he convinced his mother to enter him in a Chaplin imitation contest. Berle won the competition, and his mother decided that her son should become a child performer.[5]

In his autobiography Berle remembered how he first appeared in local amateur shows as a vocalist and impersonator and then joined touring children's vaudeville shows. Accompanied by his mother—who was his agent—and his younger sister, he travelled from one town to another and lived in cheap hotels and boarding houses, where his mother often cooked meals on a portable stove. He soon obtained child roles in silent movies filmed at the Biograph studios and worked for other motion picture companies. The youngster appeared in films with Mary Pickford, Marion Davies, and Pearl White. In 1920 Berle made his Broadway stage debut in a revival of *Floradora*, receiving $45 a week. At age twelve he teamed with Elizabeth Kennedy in a successful boy-girl act on the Keith-Albee vaudeville circuit performing a sketch in which he sang, danced, and impersonated. The team toured big-time theaters for four years, including New York City's Palace in May 1921.

As a child star Berle did not really have a normal boyhood. He had little formal schooling, and early in life had the responsibility of earning money for the family. His experience matches that of other comedians interviewed by the Fishers, who were

> called upon to be adult beyond their years. . . . To an unusual degree, they were expected to care for themselves and to act as caretakers for their brothers and sisters. . . . The comics' images and thoughts about their parents suggest the possibility that their dedication to absurdity as adults is a response to having been treated absurdly as children. . . . In childhood, the comics felt they did not have the right to be dependent or childlike. They were supposed to be super self-sufficient.

Berle admitted that the constant pressure to obtain the best child roles was responsible for his brash character and ambition to succeed.

> I had learned that you had to fight for everything you wanted or chances were somebody else would get it. . . . I had learned to fight for attention on a stage and fight with my fists off stage. I had all the confidence of poverty—nothing to lose and everything to gain by fighting.

For Berle and other children like him, show business could be a glamorous way of earning a living and moving up in society. The attention and flattery Berle received also boosted his ego. "You take a kid at the age of five," he wrote, "and make him the star of the family, and then take that same kid out into the world and make him a star with everybody catering to him as if he were something more than another perishable human being, and it's a miracle if that kid doesn't grow up to be a man who believes he's Casanova and Einstein and Jesus Christ all rolled into one." Thus Berle's life as a child entertainer had a marked influence on his personality on and off stage.[6]

At age sixteen Berle had grown too tall for a boy-girl act, and he began instead to appear alone as a vaudeville comic single. He studied other comedians, particularly Ted Healey, and gradually developed a fast-paced monologue and flippant wise-guy stage personality. He had an exceptional talent for mimicry and received an ovation for impersonating Eddie Cantor in blackface. To get laughs he sometimes surprised the audience by his zany antics, such as falling into the orchestra pit. He added variety to his repertoire by doing a soft-shoe dance and singing popular songs. Sometimes he dressed in drag, an idea he got from watching female impersonators and the annual drag balls in New York City. For several years the comedian played the minor vaudeville circuits, but he gradually moved up and in the late 1920s became a headliner. At the Palace (1929) and other major theaters he was a well-known comic master of ceremonies. He did a clever monologue, introduced the acts, and often obtruded in their performances to get laughs. His rapid-fire delivery of successive one-liners and compressed jokes that aimed to keep the audience continually laughing typified the urban vaudeville stand-up comic. This style would also dominate Berle's routines on television.

When vaudeville declined in the early 1930s Berle became a successful nightclub performer and also took roles in several Broadway shows. Between 1934 and 1949 the comedian starred in six radio programs, but they were never popular hits and rarely lasted more than a season. He disliked working with a prepared script, preferred to ad-lib, and enjoyed the give and take of a live audience. A body and face comedian, he projected a raucous type of comedy that was not suited to radio and needed to be seen rather than heard.[7]

When Berle entered television in 1948 programming was still very limited. Prime-time evening hours in 1947 were dominated by sports programs such as boxing on the *Gillette Cavalcade of Sports* and live telecasts of wrestling and the roller derby. Some quiz, news, and children's programs were also scheduled. A few pioneer series did begin in 1947, particularly the *Kraft Television Theatre*, *Howdy Doody*, and the puppet show *Kukla, Fran & Ollie*, but big-name stars from radio, stage, and films had not yet tried television. The networks, however, aimed to upgrade and expand their programming for the 1948-1949 season.[8]

In spring 1948 Berle was starring in the *Texaco Star Theatre* radio broadcast when Myron Kirk of the Kudner Agency, Texaco's advertising representative, told the comedian that the oil company was seeking a host for television's first large-scale variety show. Texaco executives knew that popular comics had helped sell their products on radio because the company had sponsored Ed Wynn as the Fire Chief in the early 1930s and Fred Allen in the 1940s. Berle was anxious to enter the visual medium because he thought it suited his talents. His autobiography recounts how he made his television debut in Chicago as early as 1929, when he and the actress Trixie Friganza appeared on a closed-circuit experimental braodcast by the United States Television Corporation, owned by F. A. Sanabria. "My instructions were to do eight minutes and keep it clean, and don't move around too much," Berle recalled.

> Of the actual broadcast, all I can remember is a small room and fierce heat from the lights and the heavy make-up we had to wear. We were part of history, but I don't think either of us made history. The broadcast was sent out to maybe twelve people in Sanabria's company who had sets.[9]

Texaco tried out different masters of ceremony during the summer of 1948. Berle hosted the premiere on June 8 with guests Pearl Bailey, Harry Richman, Bill "Bojangles" Robinson, and Señor Wences. He chose to stay with the comedic style he had perfected in vaudeville and nightclubs.

> I thought about it, and decided to take the advice I had given to so many others when their big break came. Don't go looking for something new. Do what you have done best, what got you to your big break. So I suggested to the powers at Texaco a show in which I would serve as host, do some of my routines and introduce guest stars, who would do their specialties, and then I would mix it up with them for some comedy.

He hired the writer Hal Collins to help him remember routines he had done in the past. Berle's show was a hit with the audience and Texaco signed him to host the telecasts during the 1948-1949 season.[10]

The production of the *Texaco Star Theatre* reflected the newness of television. The show originated live from New York City, where it was broadcast from Studio 6B in the RCA building at Rockefeller Center. The four cameras, which were mounted on platforms in front of a small stage about thirty-six feet wide, blocked the views of some of the studio audience. The picture was often out of focus, and sometimes the cameras missed the comic action. "There were shrieks of laughter from the studio audience," compalined one critic, "but the all-electronic audience was treated only to glimpses of the principal parties—a flying wig here, a broken baton there, a mad figure zooming across the screen." Berle occasionally had his back to the camera. The hot lights caused him to perspire and wipe his forehead with a handkerchief while on stage. The microphones were extended from booms and visible on the screen. The performers could not wear white shirts or jewelry because these articles reflected the television lights. Painted backdrops were rolled up and down for scene changes. Once Berle, dressed in drag, got his skirt caught in a rollerdrop and was lifted off the stage in a screaming rage. Another time some bears in an animal act got diarrhea and the dancers that followed had to perform on a slippery stage. Even the show's weekly budget—$15,000 in 1949 and $40,000 in 1950—was low considering that the average cost of a one-hour program during the 1979–1980 season was over $400,000.[11]

It took an entire week for the staff to prepare each telecast. By 1950 Berle had a staff of about one hundred people including writers, production assistants, musicians, scene and costume designers, prop and cameramen, technicians, and regular cast members. On Wednesday morning, the day after the program, Berle met with his writers and assistants at his office to discuss ideas for the next show. The writers suggested jokes for the comedian's opening monologue, including topical gags from the week's news. Musical numbers and a finale were also tentatively selected. The writers met again on Thursday at Hal Collins's apartment to further develop Berle's material. The writer Jay Burton recalled that Berle "demanded a lot of material but he was never hard on writers and had respect for them." Berle chose the best jokes and skits on Saturday, "picking maybe three from every twenty that each writer came up with." A script was typed and copies given to the performers and staff for rehearsals on Sunday and Monday. The singing and dancing acts and Allen Roth's orchestra rehearsed in the ballroom of the Henry Hudson Hotel while the comedy sketches were tried out at the Nola Studios on Broadway.[12]

Berle avidly worked on many details of the production. He edited the writers' lines, selected the musical arrangements, directed the dancers and musicians, chose the scenery and costumes, and checked the camera angles. The comedian kept a whistle around his neck and blew it each time he gave a direction in order to save his voice for the telecast. The staff created a gambling pool based on how many times Berle blew the whistle during the dress rehearsal. The comedian constantly called on the cast to perform better. He "pushed and shoved and bullied during those hysterical years," he admitted. Once Berle criticized the singing of Metropolitan Opera star Robert Merrill. "You've got to build up to the last note, take it an octave higher, and hit it hard!" admonished the comedian. "If I tried that at the Met the critics would murder me," replied Merrill. "They might murder you at the Met but they'll love you in vaudeville!" said Berle.[13]

The dress rehearsal in Studio 6B began on Tuesday morning and lasted until evening. Berle did not rehearse his monologue because his timing depended on the musicians and crew laughing at the jokes for the first time on the telecast. There were always frantic last-minute changes and problems with timing the show. Often there were not enough hours to rehearse every part. Berle worked under enormous pressure, for the problems he faced in television were horrendous. In vaudeville the comedian had years to perfect his act, and he could repeat the same routine before different audiences in various cities. In radio the comic had worked from a prepared script. Now Berle was faced with staging a live weekly program for thirty-nine consecutive weeks and creating new jokes and skits for every show.

The Berle hour was produced by the Kudner Advertising Agency, whose executives aimed to have the series strongly identified with the Texas Oil Company. The show's title—the *Texaco Star Theatre*—was borrowed from the company's radio program. Naming the series after the sponsor was a practice common in radio and early television (e.g., the *Colgate Comedy Hour* and the *Kraft Television Theatre*). When advertising time became more expensive in the early 1950s, the networks began packaging their own programs and selling commercial spots to several sponsors on a one-hour program. Compared to the large amount of advertising on current prime-time television, there were only three commercials on the *Texaco Star Theatre*, and they were entertaining.

Texaco advertisements featured humorous song and comedy. Opening and closing singing commercials were performed by the four Texaco Men dressed in gasoline station uniforms. This was carried over from radio, where singing commercials had been successful sales gimmics. At the program's beginning a bell and siren sounded, the curtain opened, and the Texaco Men ran out on stage singing a catchy tune:

TEXACO MEN

Oh, we're the men of Texaco
We work from Maine to Mexico
There's nothing like this Texaco of ours
Our show tonight is powerful
We'll wow you with an hourful

Of howls from a showerful of stars
We're the merry Texaco Men
Tonight we may be showmen
Tomorrow we'll be servicing your cars.

FIRST MAN

I wipe the pipe, I pump the gas
I rub the hub, I scrub the glass

SECOND MAN

I touch the clutch, I mop the top
I poke the choke, I sell the pop

THIRD MAN

I clear the gear, I block the knock
I jack the back, I set the clock

FOURTH MAN

So join the ranks of those who know
And fill your tanks with Texaco

TEXACO MEN

Sky Chief—fill up with Sky Chief
And you will smile at the pile of new miles you will add
Fire Chief—fill up with Fire Chief
You'll find that Texaco's the finest friend your car has ever had.[14]

Ex-vaudevillian Sid Stone performed the middle commercial doing a spoof of a sidewalk pitchman. Wearing a checkered sports jacket and derby, the fast-talking con-man street salesman set up his sample case of wares before the camera and exclaimed: "Awright, I'll tell ya what I'm gonna do!" Rolling up his sleeves, he began selling some funny invention:

Now friends, just a minute. Through the courtesy and kind permission of the Texas Company, Texaco, Pennsyltucky, I'm gonna offer for the first time, a brand new gimmick (*holds up casserole*)—my magical electrobiological incubator. For you people who haven't been eating chicken lately, due to the high cost of living, I'm gonna show you how to get one any time you want it. With the aid of my magical incubator, I'm gonna produce a real, live chicken right before your very eyes. You simply take a pinch of dehydrated chicken powder, drop it in the incubator—(*demonstrates*)—place the incubator over the hand thusly, say the magical words—avva jibabba, jibabba . . . and here we have a real live chicken . . . (*lifts incubator, finds egg in hand*). Well, what do you know! She got away again!

Then suddenly Stone would sneak in a commercial for Texaco:

And with every incubator, I'm gonna throw in, free of charge, my forget-your-worries writing pad . . . All you do is write down what you want to forget—(*demonstrates pad, has acetate paper, when you lift, writing disappears*)—like your wedding anniversary, or your mother-in-law's birthday—lift the paper and it disappears . . . It can help you forget anything . . . even automobile worries . . . For instance, you take your car in for a fall checkup, and your Texaco dealer inspects it thoroughly. Check! Worry number one disappears . . .

Stone's sales pitch "Awright, I'll tell ya what I'm gonna do!" became a popular expression across America.[15]

The *Texaco Star Theatre* format closely resembled an old-fashioned vaudeville bill. Several variety acts and guest-star appearances were performed between comedy routines, and the commercials became acts in themselves. A curtain opened and closed before each act to give the impression of a theater. The director rarely experimented with video techniques and instead conceived the program as a vaudeville show before cameras with standard long shots and close-ups. Acrobats, jugglers, dancers, and unicyclists were the types of performers seen on the screen. Each program was highlighted by guest stars, including Frank Sinatra, Sid Caesar, Phil Silvers, Dean Martin and Jerry Lewis, and Tallulah Bankhead. The guests performed their specialties, but they also did unexpected comedy bits. Comedian Gracie Fields once sang in a bathing suit and opera singer Lauritz Melchior appeared in blackface. Accustomed to having to pay at a theater or nightclub to see the same stars, the television audience enjoyed the novelty of the free entertainment.

As comic master of ceremonies Berle performed many routines he had done in vaudeville. He did an opening monologue, introduced the acts, and often broke into their repertoire just as he had at the Palace and elsewhere twenty years before. He clowned with the dancers, took pratfalls with the acrobats, and sang funny duets with singers such as Elvis Presley (Elvis & Pelvis). Berle impersonated a child with missing teeth and a large lollipop in a spoof of *Howdy Doody* with "Buffalo Bob" Smith. Another time he acted in a takeoff on the opera *The Barber of Seville* with Lauritz Melchior, who dumped a pail of lather on the comic's head.

Berle did anything to get a laugh, and often his slapstick depended on being the fall guy. At any mention of the word "makeup" a character would run from the wings and whack Berle with a huge powder puff. He was repeatedly hit in the face with cream pies and squirted with soda water from a seltzer bottle. His hair was pulled and his clothes torn apart. Other old-time vaudeville stunts included Berle cutting off the tie of a spectator and sticking his fingers in a performer's mouth. He mugged frequently throughout the program and could make many types of comic facial expressions. One writer said his face resembled "a pound of silly putty with store teeth stuck to it."[16]

Viewers especially enjoyed Berle's ludicrous costumes. After the singing commercial the Texaco Men introduced the star, who made a grand entrance clothed in some outlandish outfit. When they introduced Berle as the man who discovered America he arrived standing on a boat, dressed as Christopher Columbus. On other occasions he entered on a rocket ship, wearing a Buck Rogers outfit; in a bathtub, dressed as George Washington crossing the Delaware; and on a chariot, draped in a Roman toga. Introduced on one program as "America's number one television star whose jokes go back to the Stone Age," Berle appeared as a caveman. In his hand he carried a large club and with the other dragged a dummy by the hair. He tossed the dummy into the audience, ran over to the orchestra, threw music sheets on the floor, snatched a violin, and smashed it on a stand. Then he ran back to the audience, grabbed a mink coat and returned to the stage. The frenzied Berle hour was always marked by preposterous pranks.[17]

Berle did as many as five costume changes in a program. He had a dressing room near the stage where a valet and an assistant helped him change clothes and apply makeup. He appeared as Superman, Santa Claus, Father Time, Sherlock Holmes, Charlie Chaplin, the Easter Bunny, and in many other roles. Berle did several female impersonations which, as mentioned earlier, he had performed in vaudeville. He imitated Cleopatra, a ballerina, and a French can-can dancer. His impersonation of the Brazilian singer Carmen Miranda drew huge laughs. He wore several layers of beaded necklaces around his neck, large round earrings, and a hat topped with artificial fruit. Berle appeared on the cover of *Newsweek* in this disguise. Most celebrities accepted his mimicking in good fun. One exception was the Metropolitan Opera star Dorothy Kirsten, who called Berle's imitation of her "horrible" and threatened to sue the comedian.[18]

Berle's opening monologue was usually related to his costume. On a Thanksgiving broadcast he arrived on stage dressed as a pilgrim:

> Get a load of me . . . You've heard of Pilgrim's 1620—I look like Milgrims twelve-ninety-five!
>
> I insured my jokes with Lloyd's of London—and that's the kind of joke that can make Lloyd's leave London!
>
> But I love Thanksgiving . . . My brother Frank and I have Thanksgiving all year round. He's always saying "thanks" and I'm always giving!
>
> Come on folks, laugh—you're slowing down the show—I feel like a pilgrim that's not making any progress!
>
> I love Thanksgiving, because that's the time of the year you have turkey stuffed with chestnuts—Of course with the high taxes this year—you'll be lucky to have chestnuts stuffed with turkey!
>
> Last year I had a wonderful Thanksgiving dinner. Jack Benny invited me to his house—the prices were very reasonable!
>
> What a dinner that was. Everybody was there. Vishinsky wanted to come—He heard we were cutting up turkey!
>
> Believe me—if all the turkeys in the world were laid end to end— that's the part I would get![19]

The comedian's rapid monologue was a combination of vaudeville-type insult jokes, topical gags, and wordplay. He told running gags about his brother Frank and his mother, who often sat in the audience and laughed out loud at his jokes. Berle especially liked to tease spectators in the audience:

> Don't laugh, lady . . . Look at the old bird you came in with! And you're no chicken yourself! Boy, what an audience tonight . . . As I look into your faces it reminds me of a garden of roses. Here and there I see a weed! That cute blond over there. You look like Judy Holliday . . . and the guy next to you looks like "Death Takes a Holiday."

Another technique Berle employed was to make himself the butt of a joke:

That little boy over here. It's late why don't you go home and let your mother put you to sleep. Oh, she sent you here for me to put you to sleep!

Pun jokes and malapropisms were used frequently:

While I was in the park, I saw the statue of Nathan Hale all covered with ice and snow . . . It made me very happy because Tallulah Bankhead said she'd be on my show when *Hale* freezes over!

If a joke "died" Berle was ready with the inevitable "saver":

That man down there—will you please take your foot out of the aisle. After the next joke, I may want to make a quick getaway![20]

In his monologue he made fun of his reputation as "The Thief of Bad Gags"—a name given to him by the columnist Walter Winchell. Berle's renown as a joke stealer actually began as a promotional stunt in vaudeville with a rival comedian. Berle believed that all jokes were public property, and as a stand-up comic in vaudeville and nightclubs he had freely borrowed gags and routines from other comedians. The accusation, however, was exaggerated and Berle made it a running gag on his TV show. On one program he came out dressed as a policeman and said, "I've got a lot of cop jokes tonight; every one of them was copped from somebody else."[21]

Topical gags from the day's headlines also appeared in his monologue. Once he joked about the current cold weather and the federal government price freeze initiated to stabilize prices during the inflation resulting from the Korean War.

How do you like the snowstorm we just had? Looks like Mother Nature and the government were partners. They froze everything. Boy it was so cold last week I hadda move in with Gabriel Heatter!

Berle's fans especially enjoyed his quick ad-libs and snappy one-liners about everyday life. "I've got twenty-five thousand jokes in my head," he said. "I have a library of humor which could furnish about eight hundred and fifty thousand jokes or joke ideas. And I follow the news so closely that I always have a stack of topical gags." Berle's rapid delivery, frenetic activity on stage, and even the swift progress of the show matched the fast pace of city life.[22]

The brisk manner of his routines led *Newsweek* to call him "television's whirling dervish." "Shouldn't he be investigated by the Atomic

Energy Commission?" was the caption under his photograph on *Time* magazine's cover. Berle was a performer with inexhaustible energy. He entertained the studio audience with a two-hour "warmover" after his program went off the air. During the 1948–1949 season Berle also did a radio show for Texaco on Wednesday night and continued to do night-club engagements. He performed at many charitable benefits and hosted TV's first telethon for the Damon Runyon Cancer Fund on April 4, 1949.[23]

Berle's humor was never above the audience's heads, because the comedian aimed to make his gags obvious or "lappy." They should be "laid right into the audience's lap," he said. Berle was not a wit or satirist like Fred Allen or W. C. Fields, but a "common man's common comedian," as *Newsweek* called him. "He wanted everyone to get it," said Jay Burton. "He was not interested in eight people at Harvard getting the joke." [24]

The program's popularity also had to do with its family orientation. Promotional hype for the show claimed that parents complained of the comedian keeping their children up past bedtime. But Berle seemed to take seriously the responsibility that came with being the nation's first TV idol. At the end of a typical show he would speak sincerely to the children in the audience. One night Berle ad-libbed:

> Since this is the beginning of a new season, I want to say something to any of you kiddies who should be in bed, getting a good night's rest before school tomorrow. Listen to your *Uncle Miltie* [italics mine] and kiss Mommy and Daddy good night and go straight upstairs like good little boys and girls.

The name Uncle Miltie soon caught on with his fans, and even Berle began using the nickname when he said good night to the children at the program's end and told them to be careful crossing the street.[25]

Berle's television personality was another important reason for his success. "Personality is what people tune in to watch or turn out to see," said the comedian. He personified a flippant city slicker—a character most viewers could understand, since in 1950 nearly twice as many Americans lived in urban areas as in rural regions. After World War II the cities were being populated by organization men and clerical workers taking white-collar jobs in expanding corporations. Audiences in cities were more "hip," Berle noted in 1951.

> The comic intelligence of audiences across the country has changed. It
> has improved vastly. You don't have to tell an audience you're going to
> ad-lib and then explain that it means you're going to add lines that aren't
> in the script—and then explain what a script is.

Berle's slapstick comedy routines had tremendous appeal with these
earliest network television viewers. His visual comedy inherited from
vaudeville and silent movies adapted well to the new medium, and his
TV career illuminates the taste of early television audiences.[26]

The most significant element in understanding Berle's popularity is
that during its height (1948-1951) the comedian's audience was almost
exclusively urban. Approximately 75 percent of the television audience—around 5 million viewers—watched Berle each week in 1949.
The *Texaco Star Theater* was mainly shown live and on kinescope in only
twenty-four cities, because television developed slowly in rural areas
and coast-to-coast television via coaxial cable did not begin until late
1951. During Berle's peak years the size and scope of the television
audience was very limited. Because of problems of channel assignments
and interference the Federal Communications Commission ordered a
freeze on new television station licenses between September 1948 and
July 1952. Consequently, by 1952 there were only 108 operating stations located in 63 major metropolitan areas; of these stations, 64 were
NBC affiliates. As of February 1, 1949, *Variety* reported that there
were just 1,082,100 television receivers in the nation, of which 450,000
(41.6 percent) were in New York City. Most of the remaining sets (40.9
percent) were in Philadelphia, Washington, D.C., Boston, Chicago,
Detroit, and Los Angeles. About 35 percent of Berle's 5 million viewers
were in New York City, and a majority resided in cities on the East
Coast. Thus Berle was not entertaining a wide geographical cross section of Americans but primarily viewers in cities, particularly in places
such as New York.[27]

The *Texaco Star Theatre* certainly had a New York look. This was
partly because the show was televised from Manhattan and resembled a
type of vaudeville show one might have seen at New York's Palace
Theatre in the 1920s. Most of the publicity stories about the show
concerned the city, where undoubtedly Berle was extremely popular.
By his style of delivery and stage mannerisms Berle represented a type
of New York Jewish stand-up comic from the urban vaudeville and
nightclub circuits. In his monologue the comedian often told many

New York City jokes that referred to places in Manhattan. One, for example, dealt with hotels in the city:

> Boy what a New Year's Eve I had. I made the rounds. Went to the Essex House—The Town House—The Hampshire House—and wound up in the station house!

Other wisecracks mentioned such Manhattan landmarks as Gimbels department store and the Bronx Zoo.

> Don't laugh lady . . . This is Columbus 1492—what's yours . . . Gimbels $10.75!
>
> Come on folks . . . hurry up and laugh . . . I'm due back in the Bronx Zoo in an hour!

Such "inside" jokes illustrate Berle's technique of often playing to his large New York audience.[28]

The *Texaco Star Theatre* was the number-one-rated show in 1949 and 1950. Between October and April 1951 the program obtained an average Nielsen rating of 61.6, meaning that a little over 60 percent of TV-equipped homes were tuned to the Berle show. This was the second highest seasonal rating in television's history (*I Love Lucy* received a 67.3 rating in 1952–1953). It must be remembered, however, that these ratings were then taken in so-called television cities—urban areas where Berle's vaudeville-style humor had proven appeal. The high ratings really signify the perfect match between Berle's citified comedy style, the limited size and scope of the urban audience, the lack of competitive programming, and the novelty of television.[29]

Tradition has it that millions of Americans bought television sets especially to see Berle, and there was a large increase in sales during the height of his popularity. There were only about a half-million receivers in the country when Berle began the *Texaco Star Theatre*. Over 6.1 million television sets were sold in 1950—almost twice the number purchased during the entire decade of the 1940s—and by the end of 1951 Americans had bought more than 15.6 million sets. The percentage of TV households increased from 9 percent in 1950 to 23.5 percent in 1951. By the time Berle discontinued his program in 1956 a substantial majority of American households (71.8 percent) had television, and this figure included a growing percentage of rural viewers. Berle joked about the buying fad: "Since I've been on television they've sold a lot of sets. My uncle sold his, my father sold his . . . " Although the number of buyers who bought sets just to watch Berle is impossible to tabulate, one can assume that the comedian's popularity was an important factor at least during the early stage of the sales boom.[30]

The extraordinary success of the *Texaco Star Theatre* caused the networks to schedule more comedy and variety programs. "It was something like the Alaskan gold rush of 1898," recalled television writer Max Wilk, "as every comic—male or female, high or low, stand-up or fall-down, monologuist, quick-change artist, top or second banana, talking woman or straight man, dialect specialist or pantomimist— who'd ever induced the vaguest snicker from an audience was rushed by his eager agent to attend a top-level meeting with equally eager advertising men, sponsors, and network executives." NBC had become the leading network because of Berle's show. Rival CBS consequently created a major variety program in 1948, *Toast of the Town*, starring Ed Sullivan. According to network president William Paley, the newspaper columnist was hired to host the Sunday night show "because the CBS programming department could not find anyone like Milton Berle." Comedians Sid Caesar and Imogene Coca were featured on the *Admiral Broadway Revue* (1949), a forerunner of *Your Show of Shows* (1950). Comedy began to dominate nighttime scheduling by 1950. That year Jackie Gleason starred on Du Pont's *Cavalcade of Stars*, Groucho Marx began *You Bet Your Life*, and Jerry Lester hosted television's first late-night comedy-talk show, *Broadway Open House*. Realizing that TV was becoming America's favorite home entertainment, the radio comedians began turning to television. Both Bob Hope and Jack Benny had their first specials in 1950. Comedy revues with rotating hosts also became popular that year, including the *Four Star Revue* with Ed Wynn, Danny Thomas, Jack Carson, and Jimmy Durante, and the *Colgate Comedy Hour* starring Martin and Lewis, Eddie Cantor, Fred Allen, Abbot and Costello, Jerry Lester, and Phil Silvers. If it "wasn't for Berle," said Jackie Gleason, "a lot of us wouldn't have gotten a break either. When he became Mister Television, those network guys began saying: "We gotta get comics. They want funny stuff. Let's get funny-men."[31]

Comedy programs like *Texaco Star Theatre* helped increase network revenues as advertisers were attracted by television's mass appeal. "Obviously, the great problem is to attract audiences that will buy enough of the products of the advertiser to pay for the show," commented a

Newsweek columnist. "Milton Berle is the best audience getter the medium has yet turned up." NBC initially lost money in television, but beginning in 1949 it started to reduce its losses. Total broadcast revenue and network time sales tripled in 1950. This was the last year the industry was in the red, and in 1951 it made a $41.6-million profit.[32]

Television also proved profitable for Berle. He was the highest-paid comedian in 1949, earning $5,000 a week on TV, a small sum compared to today's high salaries but an impressive amount for the time. The successful comedian formed Milton Berle Enterprises, Inc., a holding company consisting of several corporations organized around his earnings in TV, nightclubs, radio, the theater, and other financial investments. Afraid of losing him to another network in 1951, NBC signed a $200,000-a-year contract giving it exclusive use of his services as actor, director, writer, and producer for thirty years.

If the urban masses loved Berle's humor the critics often disapproved of his style. Writing in *The New Yorker*, Philip Hamburger found the comedian's clowning and mugging tasteless. "He crooks his elbow and simultaneously bends his fingers in a clawlike gesture that gives him the air of a singularly distressed primate," he wrote. "He twists his mouth and reveals his teeth in an exertion that, at least to me, signifies nothing." Jack Gould, *New York Times* television critic, called the season premiere in September 1949 "not a particularly enchanting evening."

> The idol of Channel 4 was in there working as hard as ever with a gag, costume change and spectacular sitdown, but the result at best was only so-so vaudeville and not very bountiful Berle. . . . The sketches, which have been assuming an increasing importance on his show, were what shortchanged Mr. Berle. The routine in which he played a Kentucky colonel started of well, with engaging by-play from a couple of stooges, but it dragged on past the point where it had much life. The other turn built around the *Howdy Doody* show and Bob Smith died on its feet, the idea of Berle and the guests being members of the Peanut Gallery never being fully realized. Berle's writers are going to have to settle down for the winter.

In his 1950 and 1951 reviews Gould frequently found Berle's routines dull and repetitious. He criticized the comedian for intruding on his guest stars' acts and suggested he acquire more "humility" on stage. "Time," he wrote, "has caught up with Milton Berle."[33]

Under pressure to keep his number-one rating during the 1951-1952 season, Berle often did show signs of strain in his performance. This was his fourth season on the air. His slapstick routines were no longer novel, and the skits were often predictable. The *Texaco Star Theatre* was rated the top program in September 1951, but between January and June 1952 it dropped as low as number twenty. Berle blamed his problems on the fact that he was only on three out of every four weeks. "When I came back after a week off," he wrote, "I had to work twice as hard to pull the show back up." He complained that the press was too critical of the show's planned applause (the program was the first to have a blinking electric applause sign). He justified sharing the spotlight with his guests by saying that this allowed the stars more time on camera. Berle, however, often did overdo his competitive banter with guest stars and occasionally upstaged them. Another problem was that he was beginning to face competition in the ratings from other programs, especially the domestic situation comedy *I Love Lucy*, which began in October 1951. This show and other comedy programs were not offering their viewers old-style vaudeville, but a style of humor more geared to the dimensions of television and appealing to urban, suburban, and rural audiences.[34]

These difficulties led Texaco and its representative, the Kudner Agency, to change the format for the 1952-1953 season. Goodman Ace and a new team of writers were hired to create the programs for this fifth season on the air. Ace did away with much of the slapstick and concentrated on creating a "new" and less boisterous Berle who would attract a wider variety of viewers. He organized each program around a comic situation in which Berle was seen behind the scenes having some difficulty while preparing for his TV broadcast. Fewer guests were used and instead new regulars were hired, including Fred Clark, Arnold Stang, Ruth Gilbert, and the ventriloquist Jimmy Nelson. Jack Gould felt the season opener lacked "purpose, direction, style, and wit," but he admired Berle's attempt to change his style. "It is not every player who will try to mend his ways in Macy's window," he wrote. Although the 1952-1953 *Texaco Star Theatre* was rated fifth in the seasonal ratings, Texaco decided to drop the program because of its declining popularity. The bland comedy situation format did not really fit the comedian who for years had depended on a certain amount of riotous slapstick to get laughs. Nor was Berle happy with his new role: "I was not the Milton Berle of the crazy costumes and all the zany schticks my audiences had come to expect."[35]

Berle continued on television for three more seasons, but his popularity continued to decline. Between 1952 and 1954 coast-to-coast coaxial cable and newly licensed TV stations brought the Berle program to more potential viewers. While the number of operating stations inreased from 108 in 1952 to 354 in 1954, Berle's ratings did not increase. His citified comic style was not really suited to the new small-town and rural audiences.[36]

Berle's problem as a "city" comedian reflected a long-standing urban versus rural conflict in American culture. In the past this tension had often influenced politics and social history, as for example in the "dry" 1920s when rural sections generally supported the prohibition of alcoholic beverages while urban areas opposed the law. Well before television, the comic stereotypes of the old-fashioned and intolerant "hayseed" and the dishonest and overly sophisticated "city slicker" had frequently appeared in stage plays, vaudeville, radio, movies, and newspaper and magazine illustrations. Later popular "rural" television shows like *The Beverly Hillbillies*, *Green Acres*, and *Hee Haw*, or programs starring Andy Griffith and Jim Nabors, poked fun at country life but at the same time exuded rural values not common to city-slicker types like Berle. Nielsen testings of local markets have revealed that preferences for comedy shows can vary regionally and that a "city" comedian popular in the urban Northeast might not be popular in the South. An American Research Bureau survey published in *Variety* in May 1954 reported that in Charlotte, North Carolina, Berle's rating was only 1.9, compared to a figure of 56.3 for his competition, *Death Valley Days*. Given the choice between a popular "Western" program and Berle, rural viewers seemingly preferred the former.[37]

The comedian's rating continued to decline as the TV audience expanded. The *Buick-Berle Show* was rated sixth in 1953-1954, but dropped to thirteenth the following season. Lucille Ball, Jackie Gleason, Groucho Marx, Bob Hope, Jack Benny, Martha Raye, and George Gobel captured more viewers than Berle in 1954-1955. Then Buick switched to rival Jackie Gleason—a blow to Berle's pride. During the 1955-1956 season he did a color telecast from Hollywood every three weeks, but this program failed to make the top fifteen and was rated as low as eighty-fourth on the charts.[38]

In fall 1955, CBS hired Phil Silvers to play Sergeant Bilko in a situation comedy scheduled opposite Berle. Silvers, who had recently impersonated Berle in the Broadway comedy *Top Banana*, did not at first like the competiton. "Why did you let CBS do this to you?" asked Berle over the telephone. "It was a big secret," said Silvers, speaking of the broadcast schedule. "They never told me. I hate playing opposite you." When Silver's sitcom was moved to 8:00 P.M. instead of 8:30 P.M. it began to pass Berle's show in the ratings. "You rat," said Berle to Silvers. "You had to go on Tuesday?" Despondent about his low ratings and unhappy about his role as a "passive straight man" for the last four seasons, Berle did not want to do a show for the coming year. Fearing the loss of a mass audience and advertising revenue, NBC agreed to the comedian's wishes. "Whatever instinct there was in me that made me want television when other entertainers avoided it now gave me the feeling of the end of something," he wrote.[39]

Berle never did make a comeback in television. He was the host of the *Kraft Music Hall* (1958–1959) and of *Jackpot Bowling* (1960–1961), in which he performed comedy routines between bowling frames. During the 1960s he made several television guest appearances, but he worked more frequently in nightclubs. Because of their contract, NBC was forced to pay Berle when he was not performing. "We don't like to pay people for not working any more than they like to take the money for nothing," said Mort Werner, NBC's vice-president for programming in 1964.

> We listened carefully to every one of Milton's ideas; they just didn't seem to work out for one reason or another. And a year ago he told us he wasn't interested in doing a weekly variety show. We let him do a *Defenders* for another network, and he subbed for Ed Sullivan on his show one time that I know of. But we can't let him do too much of that—we're not in this business to help out the competition.

In 1965 Berle renegotiated his contract and agreed to accept $120,000 annually if he could appear on other networks. In 1966 the comedian hosted a variety program on ABC, but it was canceled during the season.[40]

Ironically, Berle's particular type of urban vaudeville comedy was responsible for both his rise and demise. Berle arrived at the precise time TV needed a star. Excited by the novelty of television, viewers in American cities, particularly New York, first found Berle hilarious and were responsible for his popularity. Yet even these fans began to tire of his vaudeville slapstick routines and switched to other programs when the prime-time schedule expanded. Berle's main failing, however, was his inability to attract a large audience outside the cities. The comedian's decline reflected television's ruthless competitive rating system. When Texaco attempted to save the program by changing the format in 1952, Berle was given a new role that really did not fit his type of comedy. Then when he was floundering in the ratings both Texaco and later Buick dropped his program. Thus Berle quickly became one of television's first victims, and, perhaps, one of its most poignant ones.

Because his style was so influenced by urban vaudeville humor, Berle failed to sustain a truly national following. Despite his occasional charm he did not have an amiable stage personality like Red Skelton, who remained on TV for twenty seasons. Nor did he excel in character comedy like Jack Benny, who was a television favorite for sixteen seasons. Berle also never became a perennial comic institution like Bob Hope, who could appeal to a wide variety of viewers. Nor was Berle able to expand his repertoire as television grew. He was unable to take a sketch, as Jackie Gleason did on *The Honeymooners*, and turn it into a permanent situation comedy. Berle's comedy flowered during a special time and place. The comedian was best as a comic master of ceremonies in slapstick skits that seemed funny when television was new and the audience limited primarily to major metropolitan areas. Berle, however, was undoubtedly a significant force in the shaping of early television programming, and his popularity made clear to others that this new medium could have vast influence on the American public.

NOTES

The author would like to thank Thomas Cripps, Peter Rollins, Bert Spector, and John E. O'Connor for their perceptive and instructive comments on this article.

1. Philip Hamburger, "Television: The World of Milton Berle," *The New Yorker*, 29 October 1949, p. 91.

2. Cobbett S. Steinberg, *TV Facts* (New York: Facts on File, 1980), p. 142.

3. Milton Berle and Haskel Frankel, *Milton Berle: An Autobiography* (New York: Dell, 1974), p. 297; author's interview with Jay Burton, 2 August 1981.

4. Berle and Frankel, *Milton Berle*.

5. Seymour Fisher and Rhoda Lee Fisher, "Schlemiel Children," *Psychology Today*, September 1980, p. 64. Berle was not one of the comics interviewed by the Fishers. For biographical details pertaining to Berle see Berle and Frankel, *Milton Berle*; "Milton

Berle," *Current Biography* (New York: H. W. Wilson, 1949), pp. 44–45; "Milton Berle: Television's Whirling Dervish," *Newsweek*, 16 May 1949, pp. 56–58; "The Child Wonder," *Time*, 16 May 1949, pp. 70–72, 75–76.

6. Fisher and Fisher, "Schlemiel Children," pp. 66–67; Berle and Frankel, *Milton Berle*, pp. 121, 301.

7. Arthur Frank Wertheim, *Radio Comedy* (New York: Oxford University Press, 1979), pp. 388–389; John Dunning. *Tune in Yesterday: The Ultimate Encyclopedia of Old Time Radio, 1925–1976* (Englewood Cliffs, N.J.: Prentice-Hall, 1976), pp. 415–416.

8. Tim Brooks and Earle Marsh, *The Complete Directory to Prime Time Network TV Shows, 1946–Present* (New York: Ballantine, 1979); Alex McNeil, *Total Television: A Comprehensive Guide to Programming from 1948 to 1980* (New York: Penguin, 1980).

9. Berle and Frankel, *Milton Berle*, p. 136.

10. Berle and Frankel, *Milton Berle*, p. 294.

11. Hamburger, "World of Milton Berle," p. 92; Steinberg, *TV Facts*, p. 135; Joel Edwards, "Behind the Scenes with Milton Berle," *Coronet*, April 1951, pp. 83–87.

12. Interview with Jay Burton; Berle and Frankel, *Milton Berle*, p. 299.

13. Berle and Frankel, *Milton Berle*, p. 301; Edwards, "Behind the Scenes," p. 85.

14. *Texaco Star Theatre* script, 11 October 1949, Jay Burton Collection, Doheny Library, University of Southern California, Los Angeles.

15. *Texaco Star Theatre* script, November 2, 1948, Jay Burton Collection; Brooks and Marsh, *Prime Time TV Shows*, p. 403.

16. Gilbert Millstein, "Bringing Things to a Berle," *New York Times*, 8 August 1951, p. 6:70.

17. *Texaco Star Theatre* script, 4 March 1952, Jay Burton Collection.

18. "Radio and Television," *New York Times*, 7 June 1949, p. 54.

19. *Texaco Star Theatre* script, 21 November 1950, Jay Burton Collection.

20. *Texaco Star Theatre* script, 6 February 1951, Jay Burton Collection.

21. Edwards, "Behind the Scenes," p. 87.

22. *Texaco Star Theatre* script, 6 February 1951, Jay Burton Collection; Robert Sylvester, "The Strange Career of Milton Berle," *Saturday Evening Post*, 19 March 1949, p. 150.

23. "Television's Whirling Dervish"; "The Child Wonder," *Time*, 16 May 1949.

24. Goodman Ace, "Berle's Still Berling," *Look*, 7 April 1953, p. 54; "Television's Whirling Dervish," p. 57; interview with Jay Burton.

25. Berle and Frankel, *Milton Berle*, p. 312.

26. *Bicentennial Statistics* (Washington, D.C.: United States Bureau of the Census), p. 373; Millstein, "Bringing Things to a Berle," p. 70.

27. Erik Barnouw, *The Golden Web* (New York: Oxford University Press, 1968), p. 258; Leo Bogart, *The Age of Television* (New York: Frederick Ungar, 1972), p. 9; *Variety*, 2 March 1949, p. 30; Steinberg, *TV Facts*, p. 142.

28. *Texaco Star Theatre* scripts, 1 January 1952, 11 October 1949, 16 January 1951, Jay Burton Collection.

29. Brooks and Marsh, *Prime Time TV Shows*, p. 802; McNeil, *Total Television*, p. 965; Charles Champlin, "Reunion of Uncle Miltie's Million-Member Family," *Los Angeles Times Calendar Magazine*, 26 March 1978, p. 47; "The Child Wonder," p. 70; "Television's Whirling Dervish," p. 56.

30. Steinberg, *TV Facts*, p. 142; Max Wilk, *The Golden Age of Television: Notes from the Survivors* (New York: Delta, 1977), p. 54.

31. Wilk, *Golden Age*, pp. 52–53; William S. Paley, *As It Happened: From Radio to Television* (Garden City, N.Y.: Doubleday, 1979), p. 238; Berle and Frankel, *Milton Berle*, p. 347.

32. "Television's Whirling Dervish," p. 58; Steinberg, *TV Facts*, pp. 196–200.

33. Jack Gould, "Programs in Review," *New York Times*, 25 September 1949, p. 2:11; Jack Gould, "Radio and TV in Review," *New York Times*, 20 September 1950, p. 62.

34. Berle and Frankel, *Milton Berle*, p. 332.

35. Jack Gould, "New Milton Berle," *New York Times*, 21 September 1952, p. 2:13; Berle and Frankel, *Milton Berle*, p. 334; Brooks and Marsh, *Prime Time TV Shows*, p. 802; Steinberg, *TV Facts*, p. 475.

36. Brooks and Marsh, *Prime Time TV Shows*, p. 803; Champlin, "Reunion," p. 47.

37. For example, a 1967 Nielsen survey revealed how viewing preferences differed by geographical regions. The less-populated South included the "countrified" Red Skelton and Andy Griffith among the top ten programs, but these two comedians were not among the top ten in the Northeast, where the "citified" Jackie Gleason and the Smothers Brothers were rated the top two shows. (see Steinberg, *TV Facts*, p. 162); *Variety*, 5 May 1954, p. 36.

38. Brooks and Marsh, *Prime Time TV Shows*, p. 803.

39. Phil Silvers, *The Laugh Is on Me* (Englewood Cliffs, N.J.: Prentice-Hall, 1973), pp. 207-208; Berle and Frankel, *Milton Berle*, p. 348.

40. Dwight Whitney, "How to Make Millions Without Really Working," in *TV Guide: The First 25 Years* (New York: Simon & Schuster, 1978), p. 102.

4

History Comes to Life and
You Are There

ROBERT F. HOROWITZ

The introductory credits come on to the television picture. A title appears. As the credits roll on, an announcer says, "April 9, 1865, Grant and Lee at Appomattox." There is a slight pause, and then, as if the voice were entombed in the bowels of the earth, comes the statement: "YOU ARE THERE." The picture instantly shifts to the CBS newsroom, where Walter Cronkite is seated at the anchor spot. Cronkite proceeds to give the viewer background information on the news event and then announces, "All things are as they were then, except 'You Are There.'" The next scene is the start of the historical reenactment of the climax of the Civil War.

This was a typical beginning for approximately 140 presentations (there were about two hundred broadcasts between 1953 and 1957, counting reruns) of one of television's most successful efforts at dealing with historical material, the CBS network program, *You Are There*. Based on authentic material with scripts structured around actual quotations, *You Are There* attempted to reconstruct history faithfully as it had been made, with the added feature of television reporters and cameras.[1] During its four-year run, the award-winning show maintained a high standard of programming and was consistently entertaining, informative, and instructive.

The study of a docudrama (a dramatic recreation of a historical event) involves consideration of a number of factors and questions. The quality of the research that went into the production, the historical accuracy of the presentation, the amount of fictional material that was utilized, the effectiveness of the method of integrating factual information into a dramatic framework, the way action scenes were handled, and the sophistication of the ideas discussed in the broadcast all have to be analyzed. An evaluation must also determine how the intellectual climate of opinion influenced the interpretations presented. Was there, for example, a tendency to avoid controversial topics and strong ideological statements? Did the programs tend to view major historical figures in terms of hagiography? Was patriotism used as a conceptual framework? Determining the answers to these and related questions will be an effective way of analyzing one of television's first attempts at dealing with historical topics.

The concept of recreating historical events as if they were breaking news stories, the brainchild of the writer-performer Goodman Ace, was first attempted on radio. Ace originally met with difficulty in getting the program on the air, since the vice-president for programming at CBS, Davidson Taylor, was against the concept. Taylor was firmly convinced that the CBS chairman, William S. Paley, would dislike the idea. Thus, in an effort to get the proposal off the ground, Ace enlisted the support of writer-director-producer Robert Lewis Shayon, journalist Edward R. Murrow, and the distinguished radio critic John Crosby. The last wrote two laudatory articles about the show, after listening to a pilot demonstration record. But Taylor still objected. Finally, Ace was scheduled to confer with Paley about a summer replacement show, and the writer decided to go over his superior's head. In Taylor's presence, Ace discussed the summer shows with Paley, but when the conference was drawing to a close he launched into a description of his idea for a program called *CBS Is There*. Paley was impressed, and he asked Taylor, "Why aren't we doing that?" Taylor responded, "Oh, we're going to . . ."[2]

CBS Is There went on radio on July 7, 1947. The program covered the gamut of historical recreations from ancient to modern times, and utilized the services of such prominent correspondents as John Daly, Don Hollenbeck, Harry Marble, and Richard C. Hottelet. In 1948 the name of the program was changed to *You Are There*, and it continued as such until its demise in 1950. The original television version went on the air February 1, 1953, and continued through October 13, 1957.[3] The program was well received by viewers, but when the audience began to demand more action, the show was replaced first by *Air Power* and then by *Twentieth Century*, which were both more documentary in form, and which appealed to a male-dominated audience.[4]

In remembering the *You Are There* series, many—including some professional television people—seem to think of it as a children's program, but this is erroneous. The audience for the show was predominantly adult, and the broadcasts were directed at these viewers; the target age range was from high-school students on up. The original executive producer, William Dozier, indicated that several episodes were to be concerned with historical topics "within the memory of adults," because he wanted strong audience identification.[5] Hence, approximately 25 percent of the shows were on subjects within the living memory of the audience.

Those who may have doubts concerning the sophisticated nature of the material intended for an adult audience should consider the complexity of theme and characterization in several episodes. In *Cortez Conquers Mexico*, for example, there is a scene between Cortez's Indian woman interpreter and the conquistador. Before the scene, mention had been made of charges leveled against Cortez by Spanish authorities, including the accusation that he had had an un-Christian relationship with his interpreter. The Aztec woman (played by Eartha Kitt) says to Cortez (and here I am paraphrasing), "I have been your interpreter. I have cared for you, and cooked for you. I have been your wife." Cortez averts her eyes and answers, "I have a wife across the sea." The Indian woman retorts, "All soldiers have wives across the seas." Such a sophisticated conversation, which hints at interracial sex, would clearly not appear on a television program directed at children. That this dialogue was spoken on an adult show broadcast in 1953 was remarkable in itself.

The program entitled *The Fate of Nathan Hale* was not simply the story of a young patriot who died for his principles, but of the complex interplay between Hale and his captor, Captain John Montressor. The viewer sees the soul-searching of the two protagonists as they seek to understand each other's views and principles. This is accomplished in a crisply written script that avoids the childish and maudlin sentimentality which all too often accompanies interpretations of the Nathan Hale story.[6] Rather than play upon schoolbook patriotism, the episode on the Boston Tea Party went on to suggest that both John Hancock and Samuel Adams may have had ulterior motives for opposing the unloading of the East India Company's tea. Adams was charged with trying to gain political power by creating an incident, and Hancock (a merchant widely known at the time as a violator of British regulations) was berated for desiring economic gain, since he had not been picked as one of the consignees for the tea. Although these accusations were strongly denied by the characters in the drama, the script introduced them in such a way that the viewer was left with the impression that the drive for power and wealth may indeed have been a motive for the actions of some of the patriots. This is an interpretation much more subtle and complex then the "good guy versus bad guy" tradition that appears in television shows specifically directed at an audience of 7- to 12-year-old children, and which usually simplifies history.

In order to deal effectively with history in any form, the research behind a project must be accurate and thorough. Although the producers did not enlist the services of professional historians as advisors, *You Are There* was well researched. The program had a full-time staff that read many of the pertinent primary and secondary sources available on a particular topic. This material was then assembled by the in-house researchers into a coherent package and presented to the producer, director, and writers, who converted the data into a show. According to the first producer, Charles Russell, 60 percent of the dialogue came from letters, speeches, newspapers, or other published sources, while the rest of the script consisted of "accurate historical sentiments put into appropriate words by our writers."[7]

The thoroughness of the research was made abundantly clear after *The Crisis at Valley Forge* was criticized for inaccuracy. Dozier wrote a letter to the *New York Times* indicating the primary and secondary source materials—*The Writings of Washington*, Schachner's biography of Burr, the letters of Col. John Laurens, etc.—that had been utilized; he proved that on the specific items in question, *You Are There*, and not its critic, was correct.[8]

The writers took very little dramatic license with historical facts. One obvious exception was the encapsulation of time, by which events that happened over two or three days, or even a week, were presented as if occurring in one day. This was required for dramatic unity and to present necessary information to the viewer in a coherent fashion. All good historical dramas use this time-altering technique.

One example of the reduction in time is the opening scene of *Grant and Lee at Appomattox*. We see generals Lee, Longstreet, and Alexander and two aides discussing the military situation, receiving reports on the fighting, and ultimately coming to the conclusion that the only course open to the Army of Northern Virginia is to surrender. In actuality, these discussions and reports took place over a two-day period, from April 7 to 9, and not on the early morning of April 9. Everything that they talked about *did* occur, but not all on the morning of April 9. The statements were historically accurate; the time-frame was not.

The overall presentation was consistently historically correct, but some of the particulars were inaccurate. The sequence of events shown may have been slightly out of chronological order, a speech may have been slightly altered for better dramatic effect, or to improve the transition from one scene to another, and on rare occasions the director presented a scene that was clearly fictional in form, if not in content. (The scene with Emerson and Thoreau on Concord Bridge in *Webster's Sacrifice to Save the Union* is an example of such fictionalization and will be discussed later.) Thus, Cronkite's statement, "All things are as they were then, except 'You Are There,'" is vaguely misleading (time encapsulization, for example, was never made explicit to the audience), for it creates a false sense of exact re-creation, which is clearly impossible in any dramatic presentation.

Dozier's choice of Cronkite as the anchorman was a brilliant piece of casting that greatly increased the audience's willingness to accept the verisimilitude of the program. Cronkite had become a household name following his superb in-depth coverage of the 1952 political conventions. In his correspondent's role, Cronkite has always managed to come across as hard working, knowledgeable, controlled, and unassuming, a man with real enthusiasm for the people and events he is covering. He has always had that special quality that television demands, of being able to project both trust and authority at the same time.[9] When Cronkite says, "All things are as they were then, except 'You Are There,'" the audience tends to sit back with the belief that this is true: all things are the way they were then. In point of fact, *You Are There* was a fairly successful effort at accurate historical re-creation. It was not absolutely faithful, for a certain amount of poetic license necessary for dramatization was taken, but the finished product was quite close to the historical record. It was Cronkite, however, the voice of authority, who communicated a strong sense of authenticity for the show.

By the early 1950s, the cold war, the bomb, Korea, the desire to maintain the status quo, and the anti-Communist crusade had created an atmosphere where, in large segments of the society, "fear became a way of life."[10] It was, above all, the era of the blacklist. In June 1950, the little pamphlet *Red Channels* was published, which supposedly described Communist influence in radio and television, and the blacklist in the broadcasting industry began in earnest. Around this time, J. Edgar Hoover attacked CBS as the "Communist Broadcasting System," greatly upsetting Paley. Frightened by this hostile climate, CBS executive vice-president Joseph Ream instituted in late 1950 a system of loyalty oaths for the network. Those who refused to sign the oath or who had "questionable" pasts were dismissed or allowed to resign quietly. CBS then established a security office, and it soon became the practice for producers to obtain clearance from the network before any actor, director, or writer would be allowed to take part in a program scheduled to appear on the air. Often a name would come back with the single statement, "Unacceptable," and no further explanation. In short, as John Henry Faulk has written, CBS openly engaged in the practice of blacklisting.[11]

In 1953, AWARE, Inc., a vigilante group, was set up to fight the so-called Communist conspiracy in the entertainment industry, and CBS quickly established a good working relationship with the new organization. The historian of the blacklist, Stefan Kanfer, has said that "by 1955 an appearance on a CBS program constituted a visa to the white list."[12] CBS, which at various times both before and after 1953 has been considered the most liberal of the major networks, became the most sensitive to organized pressure from the right, and acquiesced more willingly than its rivals.[13] It was under these conditions that *You Are There* was produced. Charles Russell claimed that he was "walking a tightrope" in producing the show and stated that certain ultracontroversial events would never be done.[14]

The drive to maintain the status quo, and the fear and timidity that dominated the political life of the country in the early and mid-1950s, also influenced the intellectual mood. As the 1950s became the decade of the "end of ideology," the intellectual life of the nation took on a decidedly conservative tone. Nowhere was this more evident than in the writing of American history. The old Progressive school of historiography, which stressed economic, class, political, and sectional conflict as its interpretive structure for explaining American history, had gone as far as it could go. Historians no longer wrote of class conflicts between "the haves and the have nots," of ideological disputes between conservatives and liberals, and of sectional differences between East and West. Instead of cyclical discontinuity, scholars turned to discussing the persistence of particular unifying and enduring traditions and themes in American history. This new school of thought, which took hold of American historiography, became known as the Consensus interpretation, and presented a view of American history emphasizing continuity and lack of conflict. According to this interpretation, all Americans of whatever ethnic background or station shared an underlying common outlook, common goals, and a common ideology. Whatever disagreements arose among Americans were really just disputes within an ongoing "liberal tradition." Consensus historians believed that the United States never experienced the great class conflicts that had torn Europe apart in the eighteenth and nineteenth centuries. Accordingly, the American people were in agreement on the basic fundamentals and principles of a liberal society.[15]

This intellectual climate of opinion stressing historical continuity influenced the emerging television industry and affected *You Are There* in several ways. The individual shows did not avoid interpretation; a point of view was expressed, but strong ideological statements were scrupulously avoided. While there was criticism of individuals, overt criticism of American institutions and traditions was carefully avoided. There was very little substantial analysis in the episodes, and any ideological bent that came across was created more by mood than by explicit statement. Perhaps the best way to describe how *You Are There* interpreted American history is to examine a few specific shows: *The Boston Tea Party*, *Webster's Sacrifice to Save the Union*, and *Grant and Lee at Appomattox*.

The Boston Tea Party offers a historical interpretation that is a combination of patrician nationalism in the tradition of George Bancroft and the Progressive school of thought. Patrician nationalism is apparent in the sense that the dispute between the Colonies and Great Britain was

presented in the script, at times, as a clearcut issue of American liberty
versus British tyranny. The good, sober people of Boston were determined to keep their rights as freemen, and they were united in their
opposition to Parliamentary tyranny: it was "no taxation without representation." Like Bancroft, *You Are There* saw only the selfish side of
British actions.[16]

Three aspects of the Progressive interpretation emerged, each
suggesting that the American Revolution was also based on economic
and personal interests. From the speeches of Hancock, Adams, and the
other patriots, the viewer learned that many colonists believed that the
tea plan was a conspiracy of the British government and the East India
Company to force America to recognize English dominance. At the
heart of the Progressive interpretation was Hancock's statement that the
real issue was monopoly. If the tea were allowed to land, the East India
Company would be given a lock on the colonial tea trade, and, if this
occurred, Britain would soon control all of the Colonies' overseas trade.
This, in turn, would lead to the destruction of the American economy
and create a state of vassalage for the colonists. Finally, the show qualifies as Progressive history for the sophisticated explanation it gives
regarding the motives of men such as Hancock and Samuel Adams.
Like the leading Progressive historians, Charles Beard and Vernon L.
Parrington, *You Are There* did not view the founding fathers as men who
existed just below gods, and who acted only out of pure love of principle, but as individuals who may have allowed self-interest to influence
their actions. What is not found in the episode, however, is the Progressive idea that there was a complex class conflict in America over the
question of who should rule at home once independence was
achieved.[17] Instead, we are told that the colonists were united not only
in their opposition to the landing of the tea, but also in their understanding of how to move against the British. This, of course, fit in with
the intellectual climate of opinion in 1953: all America united against its
enemies. The most complete modern historical book on the Boston Tea
Party was published by Benjamin Woods Labarre a decade later.
Labarre's study was based on exhaustive archival research, and presented an interpretation quite similar to that of *You Are There*.[18] This, of
course, only confirms the high quality of the research done for the
show.

The Daniel Webster presentation was really history as mythology and hagiography. The basic historical facts of the show were correct: Webster's famous March 7, 1850, speech was presented accurately, and so were the positions and attitudes of John C. Calhoun, Henry Clay, and the abolitionists. The premise of the broadcast was that in giving his March 7 oration in favor of Clay's compromise proposals on slavery, Webster helped preserve the Union, but in the process he sacrificed his political career. In his speech Webster was shown coming out against the positions of the northern abolitionists and supporting a new tougher fugitive slave law. He also talked much more about the grievances of the South than of the North, blasted the idea of peaceful secession, and gave a powerful and moving plea for the Union and nationalism. Because of Webster's great effort the Compromise of 1850 passed, and the nation was saved from civil war for a decade. According to the program, his assumption of a basically pro-Southern stance in his speech ended Webster's political career. Unfortunately, a good deal of this interpretation is myth and symbolism, and a few major points need to be discussed.

First, according to the best scholarship now available, Webster really did not sacrifice his political career. It is true that he was savagely attacked for his betrayal by the antislavery forces led by Theodore Parker, Horace Mann, John Greenleaf Whittier, and Ralph Waldo Emerson, and that for well over a year he was persona non grata in certain circles in Boston. But that is only one side of the story. It was also true that the Cotton Whigs (northern businessmen with economic ties to the South) and other commercial men of Boston approved of what the Massachusetts senator had done, and Webster received supportive petitions with thousands of his constituents' signatures. A few months after his oration, President Zachary Taylor died and the new president, Millard Fillmore, appointed Webster secretary of state, hardly the position of a man whose political career was over. And, in 1852, when he was a serious candidate for the Whig nomination for president, his defeat had more to do with a poor campaign organization and the political baggage of a forty-year career than with his March 7 speech.

Although suggesting otherwise may have resulted in a more dramatic program, Webster's address really did not turn the tide in favor of the compromise. The senator swung very few northern Whig votes over to the side of Clay's omnibus bill. In fact, Clay's plan actually failed in the Senate. The Compromise of 1850 eventually passed the Congress because of three factors: President Taylor, who opposed the idea of a compromise, died, and his successor, Fillmore, favored it; Clay, disheartened by his failure and worn out by his effort, took a leave of absence from the Senate; and, finally, the compromise was now directed by the pragmatic Stephen A. Douglas, who broke up the omnibus bill into individual pieces of legislation. Only in this way did the Compromise of 1850 become reality, but by that time Webster was no longer in the Senate. Thus, although he did make a contribution, Webster was not the decisive factor in its passage, and he did not sacrifice his career by supporting it.[19]

The script was an outright glorification of the senator. He was portrayed as a great, noble man of vision, intellect, and irreproachable patriotism. We see Webster the defender and protector of the Union, but nothing is said about Webster's self-interest. In point of fact, the senator was a fiercely political animal, and his career had been at a standstill since the mid-1840s. Webster's course of action was directed at saving the nation he loved, but it was also an effort to revive his political fortunes. The latter concept is not addressed at all in the broadcast. *You Are There* presented a hagiographic picture of Webster, which served to confirm his history-book image.

Although this interpretation of Webster is open to question, it was a view that was prevalent in American historiography at that time, and it is deeply embedded in American historical mythology. The leading historian of the Civil War and Reconstruction Era in the 1950s, Allan Nevins, presented an explanation of Webster and the Compromise of 1850 that in many respects was in line with much of the material broadcast on *You Are There*.[20] In 1964, a program was done on Daniel Webster for the *Profiles in Courage* series, and the Massachusetts senator was still portrayed as having destroyed his political future because of his principled stand on the Compromise of 1850. The question of whether or not the compromise was effective is a value judgment that historians have been arguing about for a century. The position that it was effective was dominant in 1955, and even as late as 1976 David Potter, while not glorifying Webster or condemning the antislavery views, looked favorably on the compromise.[21] The *You Are There* interpretation fit in perfectly with the American people's need to believe that, in a crisis, great men can find rational ways to solve problems with sober compromises, and that only in extraordinary circumstances, as in 1861, is this not the case. Such an interpretation is part of the myth that perceives American history as a unified national experience, and *You Are There*, in this respect, came close to a Consensus view of history. Still, "Webster's Sacrifice to Save the Union" filled a symbolic need of the American people (in the 1950s) to feel a sense of unity. And, as we all know, in certain circumstances myths and symbols may be more important than historical reality.[22]

Grant and Lee at Appomattox (produced in 1955) offered the viewer a clearly Consensus version of American history, even though the subject matter concerned the final phases of a great conflict. The effect of this program was to create the impression that the Civil War was a war free of ideology, and that with the conflict ending, the nation would soon be unified again. One scene with Northern soldiers sitting around a campfire effectively captures this notion. It was a brothers' war; and as one soldier said, after having visited the rebel lines, "You would have thought that we were fighting in the same army." The bitterness that was felt on both sides was downplayed to the degree that the viewer is left with the impression that there were no enduring philosophical or political differences between the North and the South.

You Are There did effectively create the mood of many of the fighting men in 1865. The script was well written and the background information and facts of the story were accurate. One comes away from the broadcast with an understanding of the emotions and feelings of the participants. The sorrow, pity, and empathy of the Northern soldiers for the defeated Southerners are unmistakable. Grant's hope for the future, his gratification at the thought that the fighting will soon be over, his desire to show respect for Robert E. Lee and to make sure that the general did not feel humiliated were all factually correct.[23] Lee's pain at the act of surrender, his dream that it could have been different, and the genuine respect, love, and admiration that he felt for his officers and men come through to the audience. Grant did firmly believe, as did Lincoln, that the war should end "with malice toward none and charity for all." If this is what one wants to highlight, then it is easy to present a Consensus interpretation. But that was only part of the story.

Two elements were lacking in the presentation. First, we never learn why the war was fought. The Civil War was, after all, not only about preserving the Union; it was also a struggle to kill slavery. There were clear ideological and political differences between the North and the South; without them the war would not have been fought. Cronkite's overview should have mentioned these crucial facts at some point. Secondly, not all of the participants were happy with the outcome. Lee's nephew, Fitzhugh Lee, refused to surrender, and he led his men through the Union lines to fight on. General Philip Sheridan was upset at the leniency of the terms, and would have been only too happy to annihilate the remainder of the Army of Northern Virginia.[24] The radical Republicans in Congress were, of course, planning to enforce a much harsher peace.

In 1972, David Wolper Productions did a television documentary entitled *Surrender at Appomattox*. Filmed as if a newsreel camera had actually recorded the final days of the Civil War, the show had a "you are there" quality about it. Narrated by Hal Holbrook, with Bruce Catton as the historical consultant, the show was much more factually detailed than *You Are There* (at fifty-two minutes it was double the length of the original show). Although there were re-created interviews in *Surrender at Appomattox*, there was no effort at real dramatization; Holbrook's narration is constant throughout the film. The program was historically accurate, visually exciting, and a quality production in all ways.

The Consensus interpretation was completely absent from the Wolper production. In contrast to the less critical view of *You Are There*, a decidedly antiwar attitude comes across in Holbrook's narration. Of course, the intellectual climate of opinion was different in 1972 from what it had been in 1955. As a purveyor of historical information, and as television entertainment, *Surrender at Appomattox* was superior to the *You Are There* version. Yet the later show was not as moving as "Grant and Lee at Appomattox." Although it passed over other important issues, the *You Are There* production managed to capture an idea that is deeply embedded in the American people's conception of their history, and that was absent in the more sterile 1972 effort. As William McFeely has recently stated: "The surrender at Appomattox is enshrined in American history as the great sacrament of reconciliation. Differences were overcome and disparities made one in the meeting of two brilliantly different men. . . . In their disparity, Lee and Grant were the perfect celebration of the mass of reunification."[25] *You Are There* captured this feeling of a "mass of reunification" and a "sacrament of reconciliation," and thus recreated the essence of the meaning of the meeting at Appomattox for generations of Americans.

Given the intellectual climate of opinion at the time and the political necessity to create a view of a united America, it would have been remarkable if *You Are There* had not presented a Consensus view of Appomattox. Harmony, stability, and continuity were the requirements of the day, and the story of the events at Appomattox Courthouse lent themselves perfectly to a Consensus interpretation of American history, which the historian John Higham once called "a massive grading operation to smooth over America's social convulsions."[26]

During the course of its four-year run, no one school of historical thought dominated *You Are There*'s approach to interpreting American history. While *The Boston Tea Party* and other earlier shows evoked elements of the old Progressive view, by 1955 the emerging Consensus interpretation was influencing more of the broadcasts. The only aspect of American historiography that was carefully avoided was the idea that American history has at times been driven by class conflict and ethnic and racial tension. *You Are There* tried to be as noncontroversial as possible and to be in the mainstream of American mythology. But none of this should be surprising, given the era when the program was produced. What is surprising is the high level and sophistication of the ideas that were presented on a show that was intended for a mass audience.

As a television program, *You Are There* was a well-crafted piece of work. The show was done live for approximately the first year and a half, and then the producers switched to a filmed format. But whether it was filmed or live, the program came across the same way: as a filmed stage play. There was little real action; everything was conveyed by the spoken word and by gestures. Scenes of action were left to the imagination. In *The Boston Tea Party* the viewer sees a picture of a ship at a wharf, and Cronkite gives a narration of what occurred. But you do not see any of the "Mohawks" climbing aboard the ship and throwing the tea into Boston Harbor. Battle scenes were represented by sounds of guns going off in the distance, while actors carried on a discussion. A clear example of this method was the opening segment of *Grant and Lee at Appomattox.* The cannons roar, an actor describes a battle, but you do not *see* any fighting. You hear the hoofbeats of Grant's horse, as a soldier yells "There goes Grant," but you do not *see* the general.

In the early years of television production, many techniques such as these were carryovers from radio, where so much was inevitably left to the imagination. Of course, when the show was broadcast live from a sound stage, it could not be done in any other way. The nonactive format became established as a mode of operation, and when the show went to a filmed version, for reasons of continuity the method was maintained. It was also too expensive to have action-packed scenes filled with actors riding across the countryside and running up and down hills.[27]

There were three aspects of *You Are There* that were not effective. The first was that the production staff not only tried to re-create a historical event as a drama, but they attempted to do it in the form of a news broadcast. Reporters were interpreting the events for the audience, and they were breaking into the story to do interviews with the participants. This had a jarring effect on the narrative, and it often broke the dramatic continuity of the production. It was a needless distraction. Cronkite's opening and closing narrations were usually well done and were necessary to the drama, but the central story would have been more realistically handled without the breaking news story gimmick.

On occasion, *You Are There* ran into difficulty getting certain pertinent points of view across within a dramatic context. One example was in the broadcast on Webster, where the writer and director wanted to present the abolitionist position on the Compromise of 1850. This had already been partially accomplished by interviewing Joshua Giddings outside the Senate chamber. But now they wanted to give the New England abolitionists' attitudes, and so the scene shifted to Concord Bridge, where Henry David Thoreau and Ralph Waldo Emerson were waiting to be interviewed. This contrivance did not work at all. Such a meeting never took place, and this takes something away from the claim of historical accuracy. Moreover, it was highly artificial. Emerson and Thoreau did hold the opinions that were expressed, but a more realistic way of presenting them might have been created. Such incidents were the exception, not the rule, on *You Are There*.

Finally, the show ran into difficulty when the creators tried to integrate actual newsreel film with recreated dramatizations. The effort was a mistake, and the shows that attempted such integration—*The Evacuation of Corregidor, December 7, 1941, VJ Day,* and *The Rise of Adolf Hitler*—had a false quality to them. The difference between the dramatization and the newsreel film was too evident to the viewer, and in this context the historical recreations came across as less than authentic. Fortunately, the use of real news footage was a rare occurrence during the program's four years on the air.

All in all, *You Are There* was an effective attempt at presenting history on television.[28] After each show was over, if one had listened and watched carefully, one could explain how a particular event happened, why it happened, and what effects it had in the immediate future. It was an impressive and creative method of handling historical material. The *You Are There* programs were dramatically sound, informative, and accurate portrayals of historical events, and although the production techniques of television have now moved way beyond the sedentary stage-piece version of action that was presented, for their time they were extremely fine television broadcasts. As an interpreter of American history, *You Are There* was an accurate mirror of the intellectual climate of opinion in the 1950s, and the degree of intelligence and sophistication that came through was a definite achievement for mass-audience television.

NOTES

1. *New York Times*, 2 September 1953; John Dunning, *Tune In Yesterday: The Ultimate Encyclopedia of Old-Time Radio* (Englewood Cliffs, N.J., 1976), p. 655; "Almost Nothing but the Truth: How 'You Are There' Gets There with the Facts," *TV Guide*, 28 May 1954, p. 11.

2. Robert Metz, *CBS: Reflections in a Bloodshot Eye* (Chicago, 1975), pp. 131–134; "CBS Is There Again," *Newsweek*, 9 February 1953, p. 55.

3. Dunning, *Tune In Yesterday*, pp. 655–656; *New York Times*, 8 February 1953; Vincent Terrance, *The Complete Encyclopedia of Television Programs, 1947–1976*, 2 vols. (South Brunswick, N.J., 1976), p. 450; Martin Mayer, *About Television* (New York, 1972), p. 162.

4. Gary Paul Gates, *Air Time: The Inside Story of CBS News* (New York, 1978), pp. 89–90.

5. Cleveland Amory, review of *You Are There*, *TV Guide*, 9 October 1971, p. 28; "CBS Is There Again," p. 55; *New York Times*, 22 March 1971.

6. *New York Times*, 2 September 1953.

7. "Nothing but the Truth," p. 11.

8. Edward Pinkowski to Radio-Television Editor, *New York Times*, 24 January 1954; William Dozier to Radio-Television Editor, *New York Times*, 28 February 1954.

9. Gates, *Air Time*, pp. 199–200, 207; David Halberstam, *The Powers That Be* (New York, 1979), pp. 240–243.

10. Stefan Kanfer, *A Journal of the Plague Years* (New York, 1973), p. 150.

11. Kanfer, *Plague Years*, pp. 8, 107–108, 122, 154; Metz, *CBS*, pp. 266, 281–284; John Henry Faulk, *Fear on Trial* (New York, 1964), pp. 235–236, 263, 356.

12. Faulk, *Fear on Trial*, pp. 10–11; Kanfer, *Plague Years*, pp. 211, 232.

13. Halberstam, *Powers That Be*, p. 137.

14. "Nothing but the Truth," p. 11.

15. Richard Hofstadter, *The Progressive Historians: Turner, Beard, Parrington* (New York, 1968), pp. 437–466; Robert A. Skotheim, ed., *The Historian and the Climate of Opinion* (Reading, Mass., 1969), pp. 41–45, 61, 72–74; Gerald N. Grob and George Athan Billias, eds., *From Puritanism to the First Party System* (New York, 1972), pp. 9–18.

16. Grob and Billias, *From Puritanism*, pp. 86–88, 128.

17. Skotheim, *Climate of Opinion*, pp. 20–22; Grob and Billias, *From Puritanism*, pp. 130–133.

18. Benjamin Woods Labarre, *The Boston Tea Party* (New York, 1964).

19. For views more in line with my own, see Irving Bartlett, *Daniel Webster* (New York, 1978) pp. 240–292; Holman Hamilton, *Prologue to Conflict: The Crisis and Compromise of 1950* (New York, 1966), pp. 76–83, 149–150.

20. Allan Nevins, *Ordeal for the Union: Fruits of Manifest Destiny, 1847–1852* (New York, 1947), pp. 286–314, 336.

21. David M. Potter, *The Impending Crisis, 1848–1861*, completed and edited by Don E. Fehrenbacher (New York, 1976), pp. 90–120.

22. For a fascinating look at the use of myths in American history see James Oliver Robertson, *American Myth, American Reality* (New York, 1980), especially the first three chapters.

23. Bruce Catton, *Grant Takes Command* (Boston, 1969), pp. 463, 465–466; Douglas Southall Freeman, *R.E. Lee: A Biography*, vol. 5 (New York, 1935), pp. 121–123, 139–143; Bruce Davis, *To Appomattox: Nine April Days 1865* (New York, 1959), pp. 346, 350–351, 379–387.

24. Catton, *Grant Takes Command*, pp. 462-463; Freeman, *Lee*, p. 130; Davis, *To Appomattox*, p. 390.

25. William S. McFeely, *Grant: A Biography* (New York, 1981), p. 216.

26. John Higham, "The Cult of 'The American Consensus': Homogenizing of Our History," *Commentary* 27 (February 1959):94; Skotheim, *Climate of Opinion*, p. 202.

27. "CBS Is There Again," p. 55.

28. During the 1971–1972 television season, CBS presented a children's version of *You Are There*. Like the program of the 1950s, the research for the shows was of high quality, and the presentations were for the most part factually correct. But the effort to simplify historical material for a younger audience gave the program a pedantic air, which limited the dramatic effect. Additionally, in the 1970s version, the news correspondents were actually seen, creating a sense that the journalists were more important than the event they were covering. The finished programs were choppy and distracting, and as drama they did not reach the high level of the earlier productions.

5

Marty: Aesthetics vs. Medium in Early Television Drama

KENNETH HEY

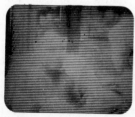

Live drama fitted neatly into the demands of early television broadcasting. Each play had a complete script, called for a minimum of set constructions, could be aired live with professionals accustomed to continuous acting, could draw upon vast literature already in existence, and needed a most elementary variety of camera shots to generate adequate emotional impact. In short, television drama as part of broadcasting represented the primitive and yet innovative conditions of prevideotape, pretelefilm programming. Its demise in the mid-1950s demonstrated how technological advancement could fail to produce a better program. Telefilm productions asserted thrill and excitement and forgot the ideas that at least appeared in some form on live television drama.

The financial system behind television drama devolved from the economics of radio and television broadcasting in general. In the 1950s, as television took hold nationwide, that financial system received considerable attention. The House Committee on Interstate and Foreign Commerce (85th Congress), charged with studying ways to regulate the television industry, considered television shows from the viewpoint of their sponsors. Since advertisers supported various programs "to attract audiences for the commercial message," the House committee characterized television stations and networks as "advertising media." T. E. Nelson, a 1950s industry booster, carried the governmental designation further. "Television?" he told a group of Boston executives. "He's the high-powered salesman who comes to see you; he demonstrates his merchandise in actual use, right in your living room. That's television—sellovision—the only complete sales call in all advertising."[1] From 1949 to 1956, the era of live television drama, broadcast sponsors expanded their advertising expenditures elevenfold, from just over $57 million to around $1.2 billion.

In this context, television drama served as a crucial link in the message-medium-receiver cycle of broadcast advertising and assumed a position as part of the sponsor's image and message. Thus, live drama appeared on shows named the *United States Steel Hour, Hallmark Hall of Fame, Philco-Goodyear Television Playhouse, Lucky Strike Theater, Revlon Theater, Kraft Television Theater, Ford Theater,* and others. These programs belied qualitative as well as societal attitudes of their sponsors and incidentally blurred the distinction between dramatic impact and commercial appeal.

Broadcast sponsors connected commercial image with dramatic message because support for television theater involved financial risk. In 1948, *Life with Mother* required only $23,000 to stage on Broadway, but it ran continuously for several months. Just a few years later, one single hour of live television drama cost anywhere from $25,000 to $50,000 and could not be repeated without another infusion of capital. But if the costs remained substantial, potential returns kept rising. In 1946, about ten thousand television sets sat in living rooms primarily in large cities; three years later that figure had jumped to 1 million, and by 1955 32.5 million sets delivered sponsors' messages to home audiences.[2] That type of market possibility made broadcasting even at its higher prices worth the risks.

Eric Bentley explained the economic realities of Broadway productions. "No play shall be performed," he admitted. "unless a small group of wealthy men will bet on its having a long run."[3] For television, Bentley's statement could be altered slightly: "No play shall be broadcast on television unless a small group of wizened producers convince another group of wizened advertisers that the production would attract potential customers for a sponsor's product." The actual television show wedged itself in between sponsors and viewers and linked the two together. Television author Rod Serling complained that writing plays for such a commercial scheme created aesthetic difficulties because every ten minutes the writer lost the audience to "twelve dancing rabbits selling toilet paper." More accurately, the national image of United States Steel, Ford Motor Company, and other industrial giants exuded concepts like progress, leadership, strength, and growth, and those social values insistently limited the dramatist's range but also enhanced a mediocre play's appeal. A play to be produced needed to reflect (or at least not contradict) the image of the main advertisers. The combination sought a middle level of quality that paralleled industrial production—very few great products and very few complete failures.

"The whole objective in the [Hallmark] Hall of Fame Series," explained producer-director George Schaefer, "was to present the very best in entertainment that had a positive side to it, an affirmative value. . . . Underneath, there must be a positive hook, a positive result that is to come out of it." For Schaefer, the series' tendency toward blatant optimism matched his own personality. "This is definitely part of my own nature," he admitted. "It's all that middle-class morality ingrained in me."[4] In the completed cycle of communication, middle-class audiences watched programs sponsored by companies whose marketing strategy depended upon the middle class and which preferred plays that pandered to middle-class values. The audience, while it could sometimes be challenged, was never to be offended, lest it vent unexpressed rage against the sponsor's products.

To shield sponsor investment and to placate marketing's hypothetical middle-class audience, live television drama adhered to two basic assumptions, which directed all programming policy: that the audience coast-to-coast revealed a stark uniformity of taste and that a good program exhibited "dead centerism." Robert E. Kintner, president of NBC in the 1950s, illustrated the first assumption when he commented: "I think the taste of America is almost identical from Maine across to California."[5] In corporate terms, regional, ethnic, and other variations in taste, attitudes, morality, and life-styles sifted through a commercial sieve and mixed into a national culture that television shaped and served. The second assumption—dead centerism—arose to cover the yawning gaps in the first assumption. This policy insisted that programs not offend particular beliefs held in particular sections of the country and that content remain complimentary to the sponsor's image when describing details of an identifiable group or character. Thus, Reginald Rose's *Thunder on Sycamore Street* (1954), a story about neighborhood bigotry, underwent revision to fit broadcast assumptions. The good neighbors of Sycamore Street directed their anger at a convict rather than a Negro because studio producers worried that the author's intended attack on racial bigotry and segregation would alienate white southern audiences. In a similar vein, the American Gas Association, sponsor of the much-heralded *Judgment at Nuremberg* (1959), forced the deletion of all references to lethal or dangerous gases.[6]

The dualistic assumptions guiding program policy ameliorated some financial liabilities for live television drama, but they could not protect a series from weak plays and uninteresting stories. At community theaters or movie houses, each member of the audience had paid the price of admission, and even if dissatisfaction led members of the audience to leave at intermission, they had already deposited money at the ticket booth. But the television viewer had other options and other activities beckoning at all times, and a theater-ticket sale translated in television to a delayed purchase of a sponsor's product. This reality of television financing made live drama differ considerably from its stage predecessors. The influence of the commercial medium upon traditional drama resulted in a new form of drama—the teleplay—and a new mode of presentation—the teletheater. This article examines the structure and meaning of both the teleplay and the teletheater and traces their origins to stage and radio drama. For detail, the *NBC Television Playhouse* (Philco and Goodyear sponsored) and one of its programs, *Marty* (1954), serve as specific examples. *Marty*, written by Paddy Chayefsky, managed to create an effective emotional response from the viewer despite structural difficulties. It also bridged the closing gap between television and film, helping create a single entertainment industry. To appreciate how *Marty* represented both the past and the future of television's cultural significance, background studies of both postwar drama and media businesses must precede specific analysis.

Television drama did not spring to life full grown when television first beamed to a national audience. The people who produced, directed, acted, and staged television plays switched to the newer medium from legitimate-stage work. Their efforts on behalf of the national, living-room theater evolved from the patterns of postwar drama, which itself responded to a perceived sense of alienation, loneliness, isolation, and declining human potential. But while the theater emphasized the limitations on human development and understanding, middle-class society in general enjoyed a surprisingly affluent postwar life-style, which spawned a broad-based optimism dependent upon real growth in the economic sector. Whereas television adopted stage tactics in matters of presentation, design, and acting, it altered the overall messages to fit the audience that watched television. To understand fully how this transformation took place and the extent to which it happened, a look at postwar drama in the United States might be advantageous.

The postwar American stage split into two distinct factions, one pursuing adventurous innovation and the other continuing standard, popular drama, both old and new. According to Martin Gottfried in *A Theater Divided*, the factions represented a "right wing" and a "left wing" view of stagecraft. The left wing, an appellation given because of the theater term for the off-stage area as a "wing," founded its theory in "art" and individual expression. "Left wing morality," Gottfried explained, "is based in the ideal. It demands truth, honesty, purity, and at the same time will overlook any human failings except hypocrisy. . . . While demanding charity and responsibility in social areas, it insists upon selfishness and egoism in the pesonal, managing to be anarchistic and communistic simultaneously."[7] Major "left-wing" playwrights such as Jean Genet, Eugene Ionesco, Samuel Beckett, Harold Pinter, and Edward Albee did not consider their works as messages to be communicated but as theater works which happened. In short, the event and the conception took precedence over the message and the word.

The "right wing," on the other hand, grounded its theory on professionalism and methods related to quality of production. Scenery, lighting, and costume framed a realistic world, while acting, especially with the Method, focused on actors as emotional extensions of characters portrayed. All of these united under a directing style that emphasized a tight, clean, and ordered presentation of the script as written. Right-wing drama remained "naturalistic in style and literary in form," and depended upon "plot and realism. . . . All [the right-wing plays] were melodramas, all were stories, all were realistic, all were mechanically geared to get the message across."[8] That "message," according to Gottfried, fitted the working mentality of the producer, who was primarily a person with business interests. "His theatre is fundamentally his taste and his taste is middle-class and middle-aged."[9] For emphasis Gottfried detailed the world view infused through right-wing drama:

> It means a belief in God, a respect for law, a love of country, a need for order, a sense of family, a concern with appearance, a willingness to be organized, a recognition of the good in social responsibility. It means an interest in melodic music, representational art, story fiction, rhymed poetry. . . . It means a belief in cornerstones—of marriage, social systems, maturity. It means an acceptance of the various interdenominational non-sectarian, middle-class values, ranging from the Ten Commandments to the Boy Scout oath. And, in general, the ethical foundation upon which Western society is built.

Several right-wing writers like Arthur Miller, Tennessee Williams, William Inge, and others accepted progressive "reform ideas" and honed a sharp moral edge on subjects like alcoholism, mental illness, illegitimate children, juvenile delinquency, and even political terror. "Despite their apparent worthiness," Gottfried warned, "these are nearly all platitudes, many of them ill conceived. They represent the comfortable ideals for a comfortable society that has lost the interest, and consequently the power, to think for itself."[10] At its best, right-wing drama left the audience with an impression that the play had confronted something significant and that the derived effects satisfactorily replaced missing substance.

Summer stock tended to perform the traditional works of writers from Gottfried's right-wing school. With a repertory schedule and a transient audience, summer groups needed to latch onto works already known to the general public and easily mounted with available professionals. Extensive innovation required extra time, energy, and money, while conventional script properties offered latitude in style and subject. Many professionals involved in summer-stock direction and production had learned their trade from university theater programs like the Drama School at Yale University, and institutional programs tended to rely upon the same right-wing tradition. Thus, the authors included in basic drama textbooks, from Shakespeare to Chekov to O'Neill, received the greatest attention in summer stock. Of the authors contemporary to the rise of television drama, Miller and Williams won the largest following in summer theater.

Postwar authors like Miller and Williams projected a fatalistic if not cynical attitude toward human frailties. Unforgiving, unyielding, broken, violent, forceful, rude, illiterate, greedy, and unfair characters peopled the highly emotional plays these authors produced. Most of their characters faced personal shortcomings and fell victim to their own flaws. Miller's *Death of a Salesman* (1949) and *All My Sons* (1947) as well as Williams's *A Streetcar Named Desire* (1949) and *Garden District* (1954; filmed as *Suddenly Last Summer*, 1957) contained characters who lived lives of illusion or escape and who in the course of dramatic denouement confronted an unfair reality. "The intensity of the confrontation," John Howard Lawson explained in *Theory and Technique of Playwrighting* (1960), "will determine the tragic element in the drama."[11] In general, the tragedy seemed extreme and the human toil considerable, often surpassing any balanced perspective on the sins committed. Postwar dramatists of national reputation limned an ominous message of failure and mendacity that presaged calamitous consequences ahead. For a nation recovering from a world war and enjoying the benefits of a cranked-up economy, the yelling in the wind could only be taken as good drama. Thus, the right-wing dramatist utilized a realistic setting to hammer home a fantastic message of social importance. Even though much of the real nightmarish agony seemed linked to sexual frustration or excess, these dramas left the audience with a sense of important social comment in the midst of highly charged emotional rhetoric; it was good theater.

Television dramatists tended to accept right-wing interests in stage-as-reality and drama-as-character-study. While producers and directors shifted easily from summer stock to live television, TV writers like Paddy Chayefsky, Rod Serling, Reginald Rose, and others, all of whom were influenced by Miller and Williams, felt compelled to alter the despairing fatalism of the more prominent playwrights. The major conflict in these television dramatists' works revolved less around illusion versus reality and more around tradition versus modernity, an issue influenced by the medium for which they wrote. If Miller and Williams mixed personal feelings with social comment, the television playwright mixed personal perspective with changing social conditions as viewed through a new electronic medium. Unlike their theater counterparts, television characters confronted their situations with a greater sense of inevitability and acknowledged more readily the movement of time and the influence of progress. Furthermore, whereas the former dramatists emphasized despair at the insensitivity of humans toward other humans and anguish at the degradation of modern life, the television dramatists focused on doubt and potential shortcomings, most of which dissolved after troubled consideration. Williams's inarticulate and violent hero underwent reworking in Chayefsky's plays, reappearing as an articulate (albeit in slang) and vulnerable commoner. Miller's corrupted and condemned villains resurfaced in Serling's teleplays as powerful and sometimes successful men who probed and exploited human weaknesses but somehow remained faithful to the rules of the games they played. The psychological malaise of other writers like William Inge, whose midwestern towns became haunts for sexually stunted or mentally overwrought adolescents, played differently in Reginald Rose's social and political diorama of community emotions and interpersonal conflicts.

Guilt, a socially imposed questioning of self-worth, pervaded the plays of Miller, Williams, and Inge, but surfaced only ocassionally in Serling and others, and then only in the meager shape of regret. In Serling's *Patterns* (1956), a young executive never confronted his moral sliminess the way Williams's Chance Wayne in *Sweet Bird of Youth* (1959) did. John Proctor in Miller's *The Crucible* (1953) paraded Salem's communal guilt through the courtroom and exposed the selfishness involved in corrupting true faith with wicked vendetta. But the Cantor in Chayefsky's *Holiday Song* (1953) questioned only his own faith, received guidance, stumbled upon a "miracle," and then rediscovered his faith. While both Proctor and the Cantor challenged accepted viewpoints, the individual's relationship to society missed critical examination in Chayefsky's work. Society shouldered the blame in Miller's study of overzealous conformity, while self-doubt and normal questioning merely bothered Chayefsky's protagonist. The individual received primary attention in all these plays and others like them, but their central messages differed with the medium of presentation. Theater drama tended to criticize society (social comment) while original teleplays examined individual conflicts (moral comment) created within a larger society.

The "message," which postwar right-wing theater drove home repeatedly, revolved around some variation on what Michael Wood labeled "the problem." The "problem" story nearly reached generic form early in the 1950s because specific problems—alcoholism, racism, impotence, violence, divorce, etc.—became interchangeable within the plot outline. "Now all [the writer] has to devise," Ring Lardner, Jr., wrote of the TV writer's interest in "realism," "is the particular distortion which will enable him to present a segment of life without facing up to its consequences."[12] Theater, film, and television captured each problem from the same point of view: weak individuals wrestled and defeated or lost to their problems. *The Lost Weekend* (1953), *Thunder on Sycamore Street, The Crucible, A View from the Bridge* (1955), *Gentleman's Agreement* (1947), and so on all depicted characters with problems; the protagonist wavered, tilted, and swayed with forces beyond his control, and then finally succumbed to their treachery alone or overcame the problem through some interpersonal relationship. The stories never explained any problem completely, and with some false premise about its origins, the answer could only seem facile, especially given the limitations of time (television) and space (the stage). As a result of poorly described problems, solutions likewise became interchangeable. William H. Whyte, Jr., in *The Organization Man* explained how corporate structures defined problems as breakdowns in communication and as a result believed that renewed communication solved all problems.[13] That corporate attitude became an aesthetic when applied to television's problem stories. Explanations varied slightly: failure to talk to all participants, failure to listen to complaints, to explain self-doubts or suspicions, to hear others' questions, etc. Thus, solutions forged within a generally complacent soceity involved reopening channels of communication, a structured response to personal problems that suited the broadcast industry quite well.

Overall, stage drama tended to describe a guilty society, corrupted by its own self-interest, declining into slothful failure and peopled with morally brittle and psychologically damaged characters. The stage outlined a pessimistic, if not cynical world, where seeds of corruption blossomed in violent dehumanization. Compared to comfortable middle-class standards, postwar drama seemed like a window into a house of horrors peopled by oddballs transported from some alien culture. Teleplays, on the other hand, satisfied the postwar social, economic, and even psychological makeup of their middle-class audience. They tended to depict a wholesome society, occasionally misguided by commonly felt desires, peopled with morally delicate but psychologically normal characters. At its norm, the living-room screen enfigured an optimistic, although often troubled, world in which doubters recovered and slackers found their way. More importantly, most were forgiven their transgressions.

Stage plays featured a visceral reaction to general human conditions, while the teleplay demanded an empathetic response to specific human problems. While the stage worked toward a general point about human intention through a specific, if contrived, situation, the teleplay demonstrated a normal point about routine life through an average, if inauthentic, situation. Both could be called "realistic," but stage realism resulted from the play's applicability to human emotions and conditions as well as its style of portraying the play's central idea. Screen realism resulted from the play's believability and acceptance of the characters and situations. If a connection could be made between the two, it would be that the stage portrayed a metarealism around its counterpart in television.

Despite these obvious and yet significant differences between stage and television plays, one curious theme runs through nearly all their works. From the stage's castrated heroes, suicidal salesmen, and raped females to the screen's doubting religious figures, corporate executives, and impassioned jurists, characters in these plays hoped to salvage some dignity and decency from a difficult world. Miller's Willy Loman (*Death of a Salesman*), Williams's Blanche DuBois (*A Streetcar Named Desire*), Inge's Madge (*Picnic*), Serling's executive (*Patterns*), Chayefsky's Marty (*Marty*), and countless others sought some respect from a society that hounded them with their shortcomings. Women too old to marry, men failing in their work, men too old to marry, women failing in their duties, all received constant reminders of their weaknesses, and all slavishly sought to regain respect and dignity either through self-awareness or through some special relationship. Even though television characters always discovered their self-worth while stage characters often collapsed under external criticism, the search and the questioning placed importance on personal honor, a peculiarly strong postwar preoccupation.

Live drama and teleplays shared this preoccupation with respect and dignity, not only because of the postwar era's neurotic search for identity, but simply because of the people who created as well as watched the two media. For some, Gottfried's right-wing theater presented the upper-middle-class ideals of the Broadway producer, but did television realize similar ideals? Norman Felton, producer for the *Lucky Strike Theater*, acknowledged the program's orientation: "It is my opinion that television began when few people had sets and those few were usually the well-off, conservative, higher educated element—as with any new gadget. The people we were producing for were generally people like ourselves. So we produced programs . . . that pleased us."[14] Television producers and studio personnel as well as the sponsors' marketing specialists, all well-paid technicians, savored the benefits of an affluent economy. Not surprisingly, they wanted teleplays to express optimistic and progressive ideas and to elevate respect and dignity to positive, social objectives.

On the whole, the teleplay, because of its live stagings and commercial backing, borrowed extensively from its theater cousin. The "realism" and conservatism of the right-wing theater tradition affected the teleplay most directly, although the demands of television production forced the theater world view to undergo modification in order to appeal to a wider, middle-class audience. But teleplays involved more than themes and stories, because they blended theater effects with the expansive features of an electronic medium. The unique combination of traditional drama and modern technology created the teletheater, the commercial-based mode of presenting the author-based teleplay.

According to Carol Serling, wife of the playwright, live television drama enjoyed the benefits of several media. "There was the immediacy of the theatre," she told a television audience, "the coverage of radio and the flexibility of film. It was all there. And yet for the writer it had the narrowest scope of any art form, if you could call it an art form."[15] Theater immediacy involved a sense of live on-stage acting, which depended upon a studio, staged look. Eric Bentley commented that Broadway set designs at that time followed two paths: the old-fashioned stereotyped set and the new-fashioned stereotyped set. The older version included a living-room set—armchair, fireplace, doorway, stairway—all usually placed around a piano. The newer style featured the same interior space but matched it with an exterior set so characters could move freely from their living room to the sidewalk, as in *Death of a Salesman* and *A Streetcar Named Desire*. A single variant on the latter style pictured a front porch with neighborhood surroundings, as in *All My Sons* and *Picnic*. For live drama, television extended the new-fashioned stereotyped set. But not only did the characters move through various rooms, out the door, and into other buildings, but the audience—via the camera—followed them.

The mobile audience, what Carol Serling called "the flexibility of film," allowed the teletheater director to expand the stage to include a realistic sense of movement and changing environment. In the most innovative dramatic series, especially those of producer-director Franklin Schaefer of *Ford Theater* or Albert McCleery of *Hallmark Hall of Fame*, stage settings and camera movement intertwined in such a way as to fandangle the viewer.[16] The enclosed theater became a continuous arena that included movement inside and outside of different sets. McCleery's "hot camera" followed actors in "cameo close-up" around the studio in a turning, spiraling movement, sometimes exceeding 360 degrees and always countermanding the distinction between stage space and audience space. Schaefer worked with stage designers to create moving walls, furniture, and fixtures to permit the dollying camera to follow the characters and action at an engaging distance. The effect of such kinetic eavesdropping left the audience with a sense of having overheard part of another person's life. McCleery created a mystifying experience in pursuit of theatrical reality, while Schaefer generated an intensified experience in imitation of an invaded privacy. Their use of "the flexibility of film" represented the widest range of interpretation for television's entrenched realism.

George Schaefer worked for *Hallmark Hall of Fame* but also directed theater and film, and his comments concerning the media and their differences offer exemplary insights into the dialectic between creators and audience. For all three media, Schaefer maintained one goal: "I attempt to tell a story, build a mood and develop characters for an audience in all three media. However, once I've gotten an understanding of the basic material and a belief that what I see in the script can be communicated, I approach each medium quite differently." Live theater focused on the ticket-buyers assembled in front of the action: "In the theatre I think in terms of performance, of casting actors who can fill the house." To satisfy this dimension, Schaefer sought a unified response from the audience through coordinated set designs, costumes, actor movement, and timing to allow similar ideas to grow on the audience. "The smart director [for the stage] looks for the laugh or gasp which shows that everybody is ahead of the production. He recognizes that the audience makes the play happen." To that extent, the stage did not exude the director's presence. In film, the continuity got lost. "In any film work, you're dealing with hundreds of fragments. . . . Each [scene] has its own life, its own truth. Each one will be lit, rehearsed and shot separately—a huge, tedious undertaking compared to the other two ways of working." The whole concept of editing raw footage forced the film director into a different working style. For television, Schaefer explained, "you try to secure actors with some stage training who can sustain and modulate a performance; however, the audience is sitting at home. . . . You don't have to unite the audience. . . . Part of the audience can hate the scene, part can like it, some can even scorn it or laugh at it; as long as the scene's exciting and involving the audience, it's successful in television terms." But above these craft differences, the director on television assumes greater control over what the audience concentrates on and what perspective the viewer takes of the character. Rather than stage left or right with variations based on location of seats, the screen director selects "the size and content of the image, and the sound that's heard behind it. The results can be wonderful."[17] Because television combined certain film capabilities with important stage appeal, television pleased Schaefer most: "I enjoy working in electronic television more than in the other two media."[18]

Despite the advantages, television writers and directors also inherited one medium's vice: radio's advertising message. Even though legitimate theater contributed writers, producers, directors, and actors to stage new teleplays, the structure and concept of actual teletheaters—television dramatic series—evolved from radio. Radio theater approximated in electronic systems the audience-active medium of the novel. Unlike the theater or screen re-presentation of literary works, the radio and novel demanded that the receiver create his or her own visual field. Beyond this fundamental point, audience identification of character types depended upon different attributes for each medium. For radio, voice differentiation affected audience reactions, while on television facial expressions and gestures gained primary attention. But despite these differences, overriding connections brought the two media together. Radio theater, like teletheater, played to audiences that remained in their homes surrounded by the distractions and comforts of domestic life. Moreover, television was heir to the same corporate structure, advertising system, and technological power struggle that dominated radio. The same national broadcasting companies, the same announcers, the same programs, and the same production perspective dominated both media, and ineluctably brought their live theater productions into close approximation in aesthetic and theme. For programming, Eric Barnouw, writing on radio drama in 1945, commented:

> While a skillfully informative program, challenging the listener to attention and thought, never fails to reach a large segment of available listeners, it is also true that a larger audience can generally be found for the program that invites mental ease instead of thought—that appeals to emotions more directly than to intelligence, and that provides escape into imaginary wish fulfillment rather than the more demanding attention to actual problems. . . . When drama is involved, this means drama with old artificial formulas, the pat plots that reinfore childish ways of thinking, and the stock characters that often strengthen stereotyped concepts of whole groups of people.[19]

In Barnouw's opinion, radio operated on the same dual assumptions that would mark television broadcasting and developed insulting programs that categorized and formulaically limited all human endeavor.

Unlike the theater, both radio and television dramas remained subservient to the media tyrant: time. Problems appeared and disappeared within a preselected period of air time, and no extra consideration, no matter how important, could be forced upon that time slot. Although both radio drama and television drama could outdistance live theater by continuing a story over several broadcasts, standard programming of original plays rarely chose the serial structure. Both media enjoyed the benefits of special effects like electronically induced fades of sound or image and the ability to move locations quickly by applying a conventionally accepted transition device. These and other tricks like them granted media theaters a breadth and streamlined pace that the seat-bound theaters could never equal.

The most fundamental element radio theater bequeathed television involved the formal presentation of the play itself. Unlike live theater, the teletheater borrowed from radio a scoping technique of program presentation. The scoping technique inserted a series of incidents between the beginning of the program and the beginning of the play. The ritualized opening gave familiarity and theater "dim light" time to the program and helped settle the family around the living-room receiver. But more important to the programmer, it offered an appeal to the home-bound audience to stay tuned. The general scope technique required three parts: the series introduction, the commercial message, and the dramatic "frame." Frank Nagler in *Writing for Radio* (1939), a how-to book for potential authors, explained the importance of a solid series introduction:

> The introductory announcements must be made extremely attractive (through sound effects, novel descriptions, unusual methods of presentation) because they are the first thing the audience hears of your program.[20]

The type of opening depended upon the program's strengths. For example, *Favorite Story*, a weekly theater of classic adaptations, opened with a statement from its movie-star host:

> "This is Ronald Coleman inviting you to radio's most dramatic half-hour . . . [*timpani roll*] 'Favorite Story.'" [*Music, with a decidedly classical motif, rises to a pitch and then decrescendoes into silence.*]

Another form started the music first:

> [*Plodding mystery music reaches a dramatic pitch, both in volume and timbre and cuts off.*] Announcer: "And now it's time for 'Big Town.'" [*Music starts again; this time with melodious soothing sound.*] "The makers of Rinso present Edward G. Robinson in 'Big Town.'"

This would be followed by a commercial message, which was short, direct, and to the point. In general, it mentioned the product's name, suggested its benefits, and then closed with the understanding that further information would be forthcoming later in the hour. The *Hallmark Card Theater* included a lengthy statement that began:

> [*Violin music in background throughout*] "For more than a third of a century, quality has been a habit with the makers of Hallmark Cards. They are the kind of cards you can be proud to receive . . . [*much more*] And now as usual here's Richard Kalmar, well-known Broadway actor and producer to preside over tonight's Hallmark program. Mr. Kalmer."

The tone of the opening depended upon the joint influences of the product's image and the dramatic selection for the evening. For *Big Town* Rinso soap acted like the series' newspaper reporter confronting a dirty urban problem. For Hallmark cards, the warmth and glow of a greeting card reflected the *Reader's Digest* genre, which tugged at the heart and toyed with the tear ducts.

After the opening hook and the commerical message, a narrator's "frame" introduced the evening's story, highlighting missing details like set location and inciting incident. Standard radio programming required the series narrator to give a background for incidents to be heard and to state the results of an incident that might have been omitted.[21] For example, one episode of *Big Town* started with the following:

> "Mr. Robinson is heard as Steve Wilson, managing editor of the Illustrated Press. Ona Munson plays the part of Lorelie Kilbourne, Steve's charming assistant. On this particular morning they met for breakfast at their favorite cafe, lingered long over an extra cup of coffee and arrived late at the office of the Illustrated Press."

During the final phrase, office sound effects rose in the background, giving the impression that doors had opened and people had scurried past. In this manner the radio series scoped through a series "hook" to a short commerical message, and finally into the opening story "frame." After that, the actual play started.

When television programmed live drama, the same scoping technique appeared. The series hooks varied considerably, and in fact varied from season to season within each series When *Lucky Strike Theater* first opened on television, the establishing camera shot pictured a paper puppet stage that contained a cut-out Lucky Strike insignia and the words *Lucky Strike Theater*. Within three years, *Lucky Strike Theater* had added the title *Robert Montgomery Presents* and opened with a conspicuously professional shot overlooking the stage set, including cameras, lights, crew, and actors. "From New York City," injected a voice-over narrator. An orchestral fanfare accompanied the audience's brief glimpse of preshow excitement, and as the camera panned slowly left, the same voice-over technician called "On the air, Mr. Montgomery." Thus, when Robert Montgomery, standing to overlook the upcoming drama from his raised vantage point, finally appeared, he had been established as the program's trusted leader. "Good evening ladies and gentlemen. Welcome to Lucky Strike Theater." The transition from amateurish puppet theater to professional preparations reflected the gradual escalation of commercial appeal that marked the first few years of television drama. *Ford Theater* opened its program with a sound-and-light spectacle that eventually took recognizable shape as a steel plant forging metal for a new car. The brilliant fanfare music accompanied a visual transition from smelter to open road, where a new Ford zoomed across the countryside. The camera work—like the editing and music—functioned smoothly, adding an air of technological quality to the advertisement. The voice-over narrator stated a no-nonsense line: *"This* is the Ford Theater." The media techniques, like the message they transmitted, sounded highly professional, and the play that followed the opening maintained that product image.

As in its radio ancestry's example, television's series hook and brief commercial message led to the narrator who delivered the "frame" for the ensuing drama. In "The Closed Door" (1952), Robert Montgomery introduced a medical drug, sodium amytal, during his first appearance standing above the studio set. After the commercial message, however, which featured Dorothy Collins singing a brief message about the cigarette, he appeared inside the set. The camera opened right on a newspaper headline that set the mood; the camera withdrew to include the yelling newsboy, and dollied farther back to include Montgomery buying a paper, looking at the headline, and then telling of the murderous adventure to follow. The omniscient narrator situated inside the set became a standard feature of the Montgomery style and continued to appear in series like Rod Serling's *Twilight Zone*. The trusted voice and face placed inside the theatrical world indicated a protective attitude toward the public. But more important, the narrator bridged the problematic commercial gaps between acts. After each commercial break, the narrator standing inside the set would refresh the viewer's memory, tease the interest with a question, and then let the camera enter the scene. Thus the scoping technique, which introduced the series, the product, and the story, also introduced a narrator-persona who lent continuity to the show and who reconnected story-line patterns broken with commercial messages.

In radio, the commercial message separated dramatic acts and was introduced by music and a brief silence; in television, the same advertisement breaks appeared after the series theme song, a slow camera dissolve, and appropriate "dead" air time had prepared the viewer. Both instances offered a few moments repose before the commercial onslaught. At their best, these messages extended the image and quality of the show broadcast. In general, however, the commercial messages exceeded in quality the accompanying drama because advertisers took fuller advantage of the potentialities of film. Editing, sound, lighting, dialogue, and camera techniques on film looked and sounded more dynamic than live television studio work. Whereas the drama piqued interest and increased tension, the commercial released that build-up with a display of technology and skill to take the breath away. Cars on the highway, tires rolling down the road, beautiful models demonstrating makeup, lived-in sets with fireplaces and holiday greeting cards, recipes on paper converting quickly to beautiful dishes of luscious food, and the dynamic thrust of industrial development—what chance did live theater have next to such bravado statements? Nonetheless, the trusted narrator reappeared after a slow dissolve from the commercial and reintroduced the story line.

What effected a structured conservatism in the weekly dramatic series was simply the ritualized form that the scoping technique foisted on the teletheater. The opening hook delivered familiarity across the airways and piqued the interest of a complacent audience. The commercial message paid respect to the patrons and offered thanksgiving to economic forces behind the divertissement. The narrator's frame introduced the details of that evening's story and thus moderated the viewer's entrance into the electronic theater. The story line ended at various points throughout the program to remind the listener of how the entertainment reached them and to suggest that they support the program by purchasing the advertised product. The connection between drama and commercial message intimated that the viewer could become a patron for the price of an essential commodity, a product they needed anyway. If they enjoyed the teletheater, the juxtaposition suggested, then they would enjoy the product as well and would also insure the theater's future appearance. The narrator then reframed the story and escorted the viewer back into the events. At the end, commercial messages, the end-summary frame, thanks to the cast, and a short concluding "hook" for the next week's story ended the ceremony. Like a benediction, the end frame summarized the service and promised more next week.

The teletheater ritual reached the public under the double scrutiny of station executives who enforced the "similar taste" and "dead centerism" assumptions of broadcasting and of advertising agents who amended the image and content of each play to suit the sponsor's general policy. The integrity and quality of the on-screen works depended upon the writers, directors, producers, camera operators, crews, and actors who worked under such conditions. Unlike the stock theater from which most crews had learned the trade, television "stock" did not seek intimacy from the local community stage. While they both operated under the domineering influences of money and audience appeal, television, by its national spread, realized greater risks for greater gains and thus imposed greater tension. Rather than intimacy of locale, the teletheater sought intimacy of character and familiarity of situation, an aesthetic perspective that paralleled in feeling and interest the teletheater's commercials. But while these situations sometimes spawned innovative and interesting teleplays, the general quality seemed mediocre. The "golden age" of television theater could better be renamed the "cradle years of a baby whose birth," according to Rod Serling, "may not have been accidental but whose process of maturing was far from being planned." To enhance screen quality, practitioners had to overcome structural limitations. Live TV drama director Fielder Cook characterized the situation in a more positive tone. The era remained golden in his mind because live performance eliminated post-production meddling by overinterested sponsors. "That those plays got on the air at all," he wrote in the *New York Times*, "was generally regarded by the advertisers and network executives as a miracle—and not a wholly technological one—and the freedom enjoyed by the creative participants approached the near absolute the closer we got to airtime and jumping off 'live.'"[22]

Teletheater production was a child born of the union between radio drama and live theater. With a programmatic structure developed from radio and a thematic and formal construction derived from the theater, live television drama added to its initial high popular culture crossbreeding the considerable range and advantage of photography. The product survived a rough childhood but grew to assume a few years of rich adult life before passing out of existence due to developments within the photographic medium. As part of the evolution of television entertainment, live drama fell victim to videotape and ratings. Based on viewing a sizeable but hardly exhaustive portion of the several thousand dramas created during the best years, several tentative conclusions can be drawn.

First, in terms of programming and audience experience, the entire ritual from opening "hook" to closing "frame" created the teletheater series. The act of television viewing in general and dramatic experience in particular formulated the response and affected perceptions as much as the play's content. The mood and tone established with the opening hook directed the viewer's mind toward the drama; the commercial breaks suggested distancing; the narrator lent continuity, familiarity, and trustworthiness; and the sponsors' associations outside the theater initiated dramatic impact. The opening series of shots worked like an usher to seat the ticket buyers, the commercial break worked like the dimming lights, and the narrator-host made personal what the theater-goer's program made impersonal. As the camera dissolved away from the narrator and into the setting, the curtain had been drawn. As the same camera faded after the first act's last line, the curtain slowly closed, and the same was true of the play's final line. The commercials worked like radio commercials to remind the audience that the play was being seen thanks to the graciousness of some large corporate entity and that gratitude could be shown with an appropriate store purchase. The whole ritual was honest and forthright; the corporate society presented entertainment for its customers, much as the paternalists at the turn of the century "took care" of their employees. It was a ritual of paternity and affirmation of authority and acceptance.

Such a ritual affected dramatic form, and the teleplay differed considerably from its theater parent. The teletheater's overall form could be drawn in a pattern:

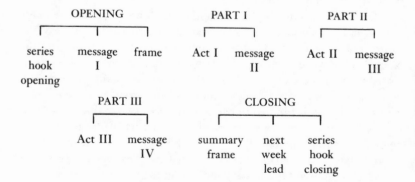

The teleritual superseded in power the teleplay, and thus the drama had to fit into the larger ritual; the teleplay pattern looked like this:

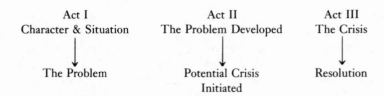

Act I	Act II	Act III
Character & Situation	The Problem Developed	The Crisis
↓	↓	↓
The Problem	Potential Crisis Initiated	Resolution

The ritualistic tension that resulted from the commercially induced dynamic between programming hour and dramatic presentation surfaced most obviously in the emotional arc that the plays followed. Each act had its own "curtain" suspense, and each curtain suspense needed to be greater than the previous one. The result was an escalation of emotions through the final act. That arc could be drawn in the following manner:

The most important element of the structural-emotional whole is that each teleplay act delivered emotionally sensitive viewers straight into a commercial message. Thus, the range of dramatic impact remained confined within the limited potentialities of short periods of time and the commercial message benefited from the peaks that each act created. Despite television producers' comments to the contrary, this format limited intimacy. The camera, the narrator, the commercial break, the contrived emotional range, and the controlled dramatic arc all served to put distance between viewers and the play, and yet made them susceptible to the message the advertisement presented. The few truly impressive teletheater presentations—and *Marty* was one—overrode the programmatic limitations, attracted audience attention, and studied important issues.

Using the programmatic design to distance the viewer from the action insulated the audience from tragic or emotionally intense situations. While it may have been alarmed, moved, or irritated, a television audience could rarely be put through a cathartic or thoroughgoing personal reaction. The effect of this structure related closely to the programmatic ritual that showed a paternalism of sponsor toward audience. The limited emotional range effected a condescension that permeated regular teletheater presentation. In the standard narrator-host program, the narrator informed the audience of important details and after each commercial retold the events from just two minutes prior. He also lectured the audience on what was important and what to see in the next segment. The acting generally tended toward the melodramatic, probably because the plays themselves lacked depth. Yet acting artificially controlled or relentlessly overdrawn became the dramatic tool necessary to reach the precommercial "curtain" peaks. Reaction shots, slow dissolves, and facial expressions became the bread and butter of teletheater productions. Overly melodramatic at some points and blandly editorial at others, the teleplay lacked polish because it lacked the time necessary to prepare quality work. The difference was made up through actor histrionics and camera operation, as the director concentrated more and more on camera-based theater rather than idea-based drama. Like right-wing theater, the television audience was to be impressed with the program rather than charged with an idea. Another condescending feature of most teleplays involved heavy moralizing. Miracles, simple vindication, easy resolutions, and positive reinforcement for commonly held values made the teleplay less challenging than other dramatic presentations and gave the audience little new material to assimilate. If the drama were social, the teleplay pointed out how bad things were: "Look at all that bigotry/prejudice/hatred/evil." If the drama were historical, the teleplay pointed out the curiosities: "Look at all those costumes/sets/evils." If the drama were personal, the teleplay pointed out all the problems of living: "Look at all those problems/ obstacles/evils." For whatever the situation, "evils" served as the foil, and perseverance/honesty/morality and so on worked as a solution. Thus, the ritualized format controlled the dramatic form and affected the content, and the ritual of affirmation condescended to an audience that registered support in terms of mass viewer numbers.

Because of the condescension permeating the teleplay as well as the demands of television production and the interests of those who created the works, teleplays tended toward a practical storytelling aesthetic. Every culture has had its storytelling entity—from ancestor to shaaman—and postwar America had television theater. Since the producers did not want to "lose" their audience and because of the general attitude about what that audience was, the teletheater utilized a minimum number of attention-getting media techniques. Besides the few special examples cited earlier, blurred screen for story transition (either to a dream sequence or a flashback) and camera movement (dolly shots, tilting and panning camera) captured the range of dynamic television. Most setups included two and at the most three cameras, and most conversations transpired over a two-shot, two-camera setting. The "art of television" never entered into the producer's mind because the story within the play remained the center of attention. The realistic, direct-expression aesthetic worked in support of the ritualized theater and limited emotional range to instill a soothing, if not calming, response to the depicted "problem"; that, in turn, furthered emotional distancing, an essential element for ensuring adequate ratings.

The final general conclusion that can be drawn based on the teletheater viewing completed to date involved the era in which the live television drama occurred. The teletheater was a product of the McCarthyism then haunting the industry's executive suites and impinging upon the lives of several creators. Thus, teleplays frequently made references to saying prayers, thanking God, avoiding communism, rejecting authoritarianism, loving America, trusting neighbors, distrusting strangers, admitting guilt, surviving difficulties, overcoming evils, and the like. While such comments were rarely heavy-handed, and while anticommunism never appeared as acceptable subject matter, their presence kept the sponsors clear of any negative responses from potential or existing customers. The "dead centerism" and uniformity-of-taste theories of television broadcasting clearly affected content and methodology of teletheater production, almost eliminating investigation of actual social conditions such as racial injustice, demagoguery, urban blight, suburban flight, and other depressing realities. The teletheater's structure implied an industry assumption that Americans, at least those with television, did not want to think about let alone look at those actual problems.

For the writers and directors trained in the more socially conscientious legitimate theater, the newer medium must have generated some moral doubts. With its commercial appeal and mass audience, television drama seemed to butt up against the basic tenets of artists and their works. In the romantic's image, an artist remained a rebel and supported efforts to undo conservative, stable institutions. A true craftsperson resisted the temptation of mechanized or industrialized production. As a loner the artist needed to point the opposite direction from modern, production-oriented societies and offer alternatives in the form of rich, challenging, and innovative ideas. How could a modern artist reconcile these attributes with the demands of a corporate, commercial, electronic, and seemingly ill-conceived teletheater production?

The difficulties of converting to the newer form of theater can be read through Paddy Chayefsky's play *Printer's Measure* (1954, *Philco-Goodyear Playhouse*).[23] The story tells of an old craft-oriented printer, Mr. Realy (Pat O'Malley), and his resistance and then acquiescence to a linotype machine in the printers shop. The agony of the surrender to the modern era is heightened through the disaffection of the old man's young apprentice (Martin Newman), who due to family financial demands goes to school to qualify for lucrative work as a linotype operator. Money and machinery win over work satisfaction and craftsmanship. In a line that seemed to point the stage playwright to the new medium, the mother informs the young apprentice that old values may always be amended: "If you cannot hold on to old things," she moralizes, "we must make peace with the new." The television playwright, at the most basic and constant level, learned to produce results and to communicate directly. The media dramatist did not master the word and dramatic form as the stage writer did because time and program ritual did not encourage subtlety and because professional criticism no longer affected the product. The television writer investigated the "how" of events, while the stage writer appraised the "why." Not only had they abandoned Gottfried's concept of left-wing theater, they had abandoned the risks of right-wing drama for the convenience of quick, direct communication. It seemed they had forgone the short story for the business letter.

One subconscious response to this new condition of drama work can be gleaned from the number of teleplays that dealt with a rebellious individual caught in the mainstream of an indifferent world. From Joan of Arc to the fading printer, the theme of oppressive surroundings affecting sensitive or creative characters reappeared frequently. While this situation may have reflected the general historical themes of the

ity and range of productions throughout television programming. Broadway plays, like *A Trip to Bountiful* starring Lillian Gish and introducing Eva Marie Saint, came directly to the *NBC Television Playhouse* and appeared on the screen as near to the original performance as possible. Literary classics, like *Cyrano de Bergerac*, underwent major revisions and often cutting before reaching the living-room screen, but they appeared with great frequency. Short stories by noted authors like F. Scott Fitzgerald frequently reached the weekly playhouse, as did adaptations of well-known novels like Dickens's *Great Expectations* (1954) and *David Copperfield* (1954). Television documentaries like *Vincent Van Gogh* (1953) developed and grew during this period and assumed a qualitative position next to regular theater adaptations. As the NBC theater became more popular, however, and reached weekly ratings on a par with game shows, variety shows, and other traditional big-market programs, more original teleplays reached production. Several playwrights, like Horton Foote (*Young Lady of Property; A Trip to Bountiful*), Robert Alan Aurthur (*The Basket Weaver; Man on a Mountaintop*), Tad Mosel (*My Lost Saints*), N. Richard Nash (*The Happy Rest*), David Shaw (*Rescue*), and Paddy Chayefsky worked constantly for NBC creating new plays for the weekly show. Three staff directors—Vincent J. Donahue, Delbert Mann, and Arthur Penn—coordinated with the associate producer, Gordon Duff, on production and with the general operations director, William Nichols, on play selection and casting. Actors and actresses varied throughout the playhouse's years on television, but the screen brought to national living rooms name performers like Grace Kelly, Betty Miller, Kim Stanley, Rod Steiger, Gene Lyons, and others. For its years on television, the staff of NBC's weekly playhouse, like teletheaters on other stations, struggled to produce quality drama within the preordained structure.[29]

The person behind *NBC Television Playhouse* was Fred Coe, an innovator and traditionalist keen on the potential of television. Born in Alligator, Mississippi, in 1914, Coe attended Peabody College for Teachers in Nashville, and from 1938 to 1940 Yale University's Drama School. After completing his studies, he returned to Nashville, where for five years he directed community theater and drama for radio station WSM. In 1945, he moved to NBC in New York City as production manager, which meant writing, directing, and producing various shows on early television. "When the Playhouse did its first show in

October, 1948," he wrote five years later, "all of us were convinced it was our mission to bring Broadway to America via the television set."[30] The camera operated like a frontal audience, actors worked through entire live productions, and the dramatist's works remained sacrosanct, even though whole scenes were ripped from Broadway originals to meet program time requirements. To further the effect of realism and to outdo live theater, Coe sent camera crews around New York City to gather location file footage that could be intercut throughout the drama to lend authenticity to transitions and believability to chosen sets. In 1954, when Coe picked his all-time favorite *Playhouse* productions, he selected two literary adaptations, one original documentary, and seven original teleplays, one of them Paddy Chayefsky's *Marty*, perhaps the most popular production of the entire era.[31]

Paddy Chayefsky was born in New York City in 1923 and attended The City College of New York. During World War II, he served in the Army and wrote *The True Glory* (1945), a government film about purple-heart bravery. After the military hitch, Garson Kanin, who had seen Chayefsky's government work, sent the young writer $500 to study at the Actor's Lab of Hollywood. Several short works led to a junior writer's contract with Universal-International. While writing piecemeal dialogue for B movies, Chayefsky's first major writing success reached print in *Cosmopolitan*. "The Great American Hoax" told the story of an aged man who, to regain lost employment, impersonated General Motors' Charles "Engine Charlie" Wilson. Publicity and chance brought the impersonation to Wilson's attention, and the motor magnate personally reinstated the displaced employee. The old man's granddaughter pointed to the story's central theme when she exclaimed, "All of a sudden it came to me, like a burst of lightning, that nothing is more important than your dignity. It's more important than a high standard of living or being assistant to the head." Chayefsky's biographer, John M. Clum, explained that this theme remained with the scriptwriter through most of his career: "The basic theme of the novella is one that Chayefsky would use over and over—that of the man who will stage a seemingly quixotic battle to maintain his position in an impersonal world."[32]

In 1952, Chayefsky wrote several radio dramas for the *Theater Guild of the Air* and *Cavalcade of America* and sketched several scripts for television series like *Danger* and *Manhunt*. By the end of 1952, the young media writer had signed with NBC to work on the *Playhouse* series, and two of his works—*Holiday Song* and *The Reluctant Citizen*— were aired before the year ended. His "commonplace realism" saturated his early teleplays. In each of them, the Old and New Worlds collided, leaving the older generation with glowing memories of an honest past and with problems from an unpleasant present. The following year, six Chayefsky teleplays appeared on the *NBC Television Playhouse* series, and one of them, *Marty*, won the greatest acclaim for the author. He had adjusted himself to the new medium, and his teleplays blended admirably with the medium's structural demands.

"Realism, in the theatre," Chayefsky once wrote, "is a synthesized business; what one achieves is really the effect of realism. In television, you can be literally and freely real. The scene can be played as if the actors were unaware of their audience. The dialogue can sound as if it had been wire-tapped."[33] Because the author had limited experience with the stage, he can be forgiven his misinterpretation of dramatists and stagings in the live theater. But the comments on television suggest the direction his personal aesthetic took. The common person with common problems deserved to speak a dialogue of common language. The idiomatic, the class-ridden, the ethnic, and the unassimilated language of Chayefsky's best characters marked his work as realistic in effect and appearance, even if slightly fallacious in underlying theme. In the single-viewing series approach, Chayefsky's characters came across as well-molded entities speaking from the heart. Biographer Clum explained that television and Chayefsky consummated a marital combination made in media heaven.[34] The author never wrote large-scale drama and discouraged large-scale productions, the two things the medium could not manage. The author's focused stories attached themselves to a single character and followed him or her through a simple life "probed sympathetically." His narrative remained contrived and controlled, forcing the audience to ignore every irrelevant detail and to concentrate on the streamlined features of a well-trimmed story line. "Dramatic construction, as far as I am concerned," explained Chayefsky, "is essentially a search for reasons. That is to say, given the second act curtain incident, construction consists of finding reasons why the characters involved in the incident act as they do."[25] Contemplation, theorizing, argumentation, debate, and similar traits of intellectual activities disturbed the flow of well-written narratives. Action and

reaction, the basic visual dialogue between opposites, motivated a Chayefsky drama.

Marty represented the epitome of Chayefsky's aesthetic development. The author described *Marty* and *The Mother*, his next teleplay, in
the same way:

> They both deal with the world of the mundane, the ordinary, and the
> untheatrical. The main characters are typical, rather than exceptional;
> the situations are easily identifiable by the audience; and the relation-
> ships are as common as the people. . . . I set out in *Marty* to write a love
> story, the most ordinary love story in the world. I didn't want my hero to
> be handsome, and I didn't want the girl to be pretty. I wanted to write a
> love story the way it would literally have happened to the kind of people
> I know.[36]

Marty tells the story of a young butcher (Rod Steiger) and his attempts to take control of his life. Marty's mother (Esther Minicotti)
harasses her son about marriage and family obligations while organizing
his life for him. His best friend, Angie (Joseph Mantrell), badgers the
young worrier into seeking companionship at the local singles dance
hall. Inhibited by male prerogatives and stereotypes, Marty reluctantly
meets Clara (Nancy Marchand), a plain-looking young woman with a
decent and kind personality. Guided by the independence gained from
his new relationship, Marty overcomes the stifling effects of his posses-
sive mother and aimless chum, and he responds positively to the challenge of love and shared responsibility that Clara offers. With stability from an adult heterosexual relationship, Marty sees his various
roles—as butcher, friend, son, and lover—in proper perspective, and
this gives his life meaning.

Chayefsky thought *Marty* fitted into its times by examining the
details of personal trials. "These are strange and fretful times," he
wrote in his *Television Plays*, "and the huge inevitable currents of history
are too broad now to provide individual people with any meaning to
their lives. People are beginning to turn into themselves, looking for
personal happiness. The offices of psychoanalysts are flooded with
disturbed human beings; the psychiatric clinics of hospitals are too
terribly understaffed to handle the demands of the public. Hardly a
newspaper, at least in New York, does not carry a syndicated psychia-
trist or similar columnist. The jargon of introspection has become
everyday conversation." *Marty* intentionally highlighted this introspec-

tive period and allowed the author to examine "the Oedipal relationship, the reversion to adolescence by many 'normal' Americans, and the latent homosexuality of the middle class."[37] In short, Chayefsky thought he had a simple and sympathetic story that contributed simple answers to the complex and immense problems of the postwar era of fretful confusion.

Despite the author's overblown interpretation, the work has maintained a certain charm over time. Phrase repetition, ironic conversation, smooth scene transition, efficient camera manipulation, and interpretive settings manufacture a feeling of intimacy mixed with objectivity. The language is that of second-generation immigrants, and the situation converts into socialization and assimilation when Marty meets a woman outside the Italian community of his upbringing. Marital independence in a modern, urban life overtakes the extended family of the traditional, ethnic community. The dynamism of the first attracts and wins Marty away from the aimlessness and misguided features of the second. Like television itself, Chayefsky's play captures the appeal of an emerging national culture over and against the uniqueness of a fading parochial (read "pluralistic") culture. If, as Chayefsky suggested, the "currents of history" were too large to "provide individual people with any meaning to their lives," then the response to that situation—an independence that rejected tradition and embraced an unknown future—resonated with the national, corporate culture that created those same large and amorphous "currents of history." By rejecting tradition, Marty surrendered to the forces behind the initiating malaise.

Even though Chayefsky misunderstood the main currents of American thought and misinterpreted the ideas that motivated writers in the contemporary theater, he did understand practical, common personalities. What he missed in the grander scheme of social and literary operations, he recouped in wisdom and experience in matters relating to daily routine. Based on his experiences as a junior writer in the movie business, he understood Hollywood, and when an independent studio approached him about filming *Marty*, Chayefsky's learned skepticism served him well. His humbling experiences in Hollywood's film factory taught him that writers rarely received any satisfaction from an industry intent on praising every collaborator except the original story's writer. He learned that the words, the phrases, and even the story could fall before the director's "imagination" and the actors' "interpretation." He knew production details depended upon a "what-had-worked" mentality rather than a "try-something-new" adventurism. He understood how open-ended screen presentations frequently lost a simple story in a mélange of special effects, elaborate sets, and numerous scene shifts. Movement replaced content and effect overwhelmed meaning. These memories loomed large in Chayefsky's mind when representatives from Hecht-Hill-Lancaster productions offered to buy the film rights to *Marty*.

As independent producers freed from the constraints of studio narrowmindedness, Harold Hecht, Harold Hill, and Burt Lancaster soothed Chayefsky's doubts with a contract that left the author with nearly total control over the filming process. The author accepted only $13,000 for his work, but parlayed his foresworn bonus into immense production authority: he could attend every rehearsal and do all rewriting, the entire script would be rehearsed in sequence prior to shooting, and, most important, the television director, Delbert Mann, would direct the film version as well.[38]

Delbert Mann emerged from the same theatrical roots as producer Fred Coe. Born in Lawrence, Kansas, in 1920, Mann studied drama at Vanderbilt University and whetted his professional appetite on community-theater work in Nashville. After his 1941 graduation and a short stint in the Air Force, he entered Yale Drama School. When his graduate studies ended, he acted and directed for the Twin Theater Company in Columbia, South Carolina, for several theater seasons. During the off season, he worked as stage manager for summer stock groups in Wellesley, Massachusetts. In 1949, Fred Coe lured the young director to the National Broadcasting Company in New York City to serve as assistant director to the *NBC Television Playhouse*. From 1949 to 1955, Mann directed more than 100 hour-long teleplays, including Chayefsky's *Marty* and *The Bachelor Party* (1953), both of which Mann converted to the big screen.[39] "Delbert Mann's finest gift as a director," Chayefsky wrote, "lies in his ability to see the whole show in its proper shape. This is a rare quality in a director. . . . Delbert also has a keen understanding of normal bourgeois life. He is an amiable middle-class fellow himself, who looks rather like a young associate professor of sociology."[40]

John Clum has noted that the film's success resulted from the story's "effective blend of a romance with a happy ending that was presented

within the framework of a naturalistically conceived setting and characters."[41] Clum based his interpretation on the story's strength and the
obliteration of normal barriers between television and film. That obliteration, however, resulted from the original contract and the ignorance
of director and screenwriter on matters related to film production. By
maintaining allegiance to *both* the story and the medium of origin, the
film played like a large-screen, commerical-free television show. Rather
than expand the television story, the collaborators diminished the
adapted medium's range. Instead of elaborating on the lives of different
characters, the creators worked visual detail into the lives presented in
the teleplay. Chayefsky's healthy skepticism matched with Mann's
cinematic innocence guided the two toward a product that sustained the
drama's integrity, extended realistic presentation over and against the
normally fantastic medium, and focused the film medium's unlimited
range on the mundane. Ironically, in an era of big screen decadence,
musical fantasies, and rewarmed Westerns, *Marty* had unmistakable
charm, not only in its story, but in its direct, uncluttered method of
presentation.

The strengths of *Marty's* television appeal resulted from its appro-
priateness to the teletheater ritual and its adjustment to the structure's
possibilities. As Fred Coe explained, the standard teleplay fell naturally
into three acts, the form Chayefsky used for *Marty*. The structure and
emotional curve of those three acts, however, also satisfied the tripartite
teleplay structure created by the teletheater's commercial demands. Act
I begins in a butcher shop, moves to the local bar, and ends at Marty's
house. In that sequence, the audience meets Marty, Angie, and Mrs.
Pilletti, the three interacting characters in the Bronx Italian world as it
has been experienced for years. The act ends with Mrs. Pilletti
badgering Marty to frequent the Waverly Ballroom, where he might
meet a nice young woman to marry. Customers bother Marty, friends
bother Marty, and now his own mother bothers him. Pestered to extremes, he finally explodes as the act ends:

Ma, waddaya want from me?! Waddaya want from me?! I'm miserable
enough as it is! Leave me alone! I'll go to the Waverly Ballroom! I'll put
onna blue suit and I'll go! And you know what I'm gonna get for my
troubles? Heartache! A big night of heartache!

After pacing the floor and expressing his frustration, Marty returns to the dinner table, calms down, attacks his food, and finally gets control of himself enough to comment humorously on his mother's mistaken reference to women as "tomatoes." Just as he finishes his last line, the camera dollies out, signaling the audience to retreat from Marty's problems; slowly, the screen fades into darkness and into the first commercial break.

The final speech of Act I, much like a missing narrator, summarizes the action already seen, and it reminds the viewer of Marty's problems. His low self-esteem, his mother's overburdensome influence on his life, and his struggle to avoid inevitable pain in personal relationships all are concentrated into the words of his final oration. His speech focuses attention on emotional vulnerability and not ideational interplay and on a specific situation rather than general conditions. Audience empathy and vulnerability have reached a peak. When the camera dissolves into the advertisement, the structural shift encourages the transfer of the audience's emotions from the drama to the commercial message.

Act II starts at the ballroom and ends back at Marty's house. Through a siginficant part of the act, effective intercutting between action at the ballroom and at home develop tension between the mother's latest problems with her sister Catherine (Augusta Ciolli) and Marty's newest acquaintance. Aunt Catherine's interruption of her son and daughter-in-law's marriage results in complaints and a final agreement that she live with her sister, Marty's mother. That family crisis intimates possible tension between Mrs. Pilletti and the love affair simultaneously blossoming at the Waverly. The act concludes with Clara and Marty leaving his home, having pricked Mrs. Pilletti's curiosity and paranoia. As the young couple leaves, the camera examines the mother's fear-ridden face and suggests that she has connected her future with that of her abandoned sister. The crisis between Marty's surrounding influences—his mother and Angie, whom he left at the ballroom—and his personal feelings has been etched into the viewer's mind; or said another way, the individual versus society—the whole romantic dichotomy—has taken shape in this ethnic Italian community. As with the first act, empathy reaches a peak as consequences of Marty's good fortune turn against the mother. Whereas the first act concluded with Marty's sense of despair, the second act ends with Mrs.

Pilletti's worry over her impending loneliness. Once again, the audience experiences an emotional "curtain" scene that foreshadows a further collision of personalities and even life-styles in the following act.

Act III commits Marty to action over the protestations of his friend, Angie, and the mildly stated worries of his mother. After listening to his companions belittle women and his mother belittle Clara, Marty charges to the phone and calls his overnight flame. The act finishes on a feverishly high emotional pitch as Marty finally unwrinkles his brow and breaks into a full smile. He ridicules Angie about getting married and dials Clara's number with unaccustomed vigor. He has direction, and the world, willy-nilly, moves along with positive purpose. The first act ended with emotional browbeating, the second with worry and misguided fear, and the third finishes with an emotional high that gracefully skirts answers to the problems raised at each of the two previous "curtain" events. The mother, who badgers Marty as the first act ends and who worries over her future as the second act ends, never figures in the final act's "curtain" scene. Family structures, ethnic traditions, and lower middle-class life-styles get pushed to the side as Marty falls in love with a teacher and will presumably move up and out of his station on the wings of two incomes, a liberated identity, and a clear conscience. As before, the audience, having been plied with the middle-class idea of progress and identity, moves right into a commercial message offering another commodity to support that same life-style.

Criticism never played a role in determining content or even reactions to teletheater productions because it could not affect viewers. Unlike film audiences whose choices might be affected by critical comments, teletheater audiences made their choices without critical input. Thus, written records of contemporary responses are difficult to locate. But since *Marty* in film form approximated its teleplay origins, responses to the film could still be instructive. The teletheater ritual—crucial to the television experience—did disappear and thereby permitted more direct contact with the characters. The strength of Chayefsky's story overstretched the normally required pauses and carried through the entire ninety minutes. Extra dialogue gave greater depth to the young family bothered with Aunt Catherine's presence, and pacing gave the bar scenes a greater sense of despair. But only a few extra location shots added anything to the stagelike sets. In looks and development, the film and the teleplay worked in similar ways. The emotional curve of the two changed radically, however, because of the differences in media presentation. With the teletheater screening, each "curtain" event needed to build sufficient suspense to maintain interest into and through the commerical. But in the movie house, such artificial pitches would only seem what they in fact were: weak attempts to create identification with characters and to generate intrigue where little existed. In the film version, the emotional arc moved through a slow incline to a peak in the final scene, and then dropped quickly into the closing credits. The mother's worried expressions seemed less significant, and certainly Marty's Act I speech worked as an extension of his daily routine rather than as a momentous explanation of his wounded world view. In short, while the two versions of Chayefsky's play resembled each other in many ways, the transfer from teletheater to movie house altered substantially the dramatic arc because of the demands placed upon the play by its respective commercial backers. Nonetheless, film criticism may be worth investigating as a means of understanding contemporary responses to the characters depicted.

Catholic magazines understandably supported the film unanimously. *America* printed a review that explained why *Marty* was different from most films available in the public domain: a small budget led to a direct, simple story; a basic honesty of story created a sympathetic look at life's common problems; authentic details conveyed "a vibrant and immistakable [sic] ring of truth." The magazine praised Chayefsky because his "respect and affection for his characters was [sic] a blessed relief from the current tendency to portray the so-called average man in the inane and patronizing caricature of *The Life of Riley* and *Ma and Pa Kettle*." *Catholic World* similarly praised the film because it was "such a canny observation of real life with a sound development of character." Not only were the characters consistent with the magazine's view of "real" life, but the entire setting and action revealed an essential understanding of life as lived in the Bronx. "The authentic background," the reviewer continued, "the unadorned glimpse of the American middle-class milieu, the sensible integration of both the Catholic and the Italian elements in Marty's background, and the overall air of simplicity and honesty make *Marty* a wonderful experience."[42]

John McCarten of *The New Yorker* contrasted *Marty* with other films of the time. "It is neither high, wide, nor handsome," he conceded, "and it has been photographed with a camera designed to present films of the type we used to know and love before Cinemascope opened new and lunatic vistas for our enjoyment." Arthur Knight agreed. In his *Saturday Review* commentary, he praised the author's originality, and concluded: "*Marty* is a small work, a chamber work if you like. But in this day of elephantiasis of the screen, it proves more refreshing than the first breath of spring." Knight carried his compliments into the realm of criticism for the film industry. "For what this lovely, touching, wonderfully human picture reveals is that a fine T.V. script provides a better basis for a film than possibly any other source of movie material outside of the *bona fide* original."[43] He explained that the camera united films and television and that this central instrument of creation caused problems and possibilities only those two media faced. From television drama, which enjoyed immediate connections with the live theater, teleplays had by the mid-1950s moved into the center arena of film production.

"There must be millions of Martys," Knight conjectured, but, in fact, many connections between television and films moved the two industries into overlapping production. Whereas radio broadcasters extended authority over early television and maintained its management throughout, television theater gave way to telefilm productions and the live teletheater disappeared, a victim of the industry's "progress." Movie studios produced telefilms for broadcasting, actors and directors moved freely between the two media, movie studios released pre-1948 films for television viewing, and the Academy Awards program moved onto television. What had been competitive enterprise became in practice one big entertainment industry. As a result, small "chamber works" like *Marty* gave way to "spectacular adaptations" from popular novels.[44]

For a story like *Marty*, with its depictions of common problems and common life, to facilitate the cohabitation of two giant entertainment industries was an irony lost on most critics of the time. "Hardly a moment on the screen since Chaplin made the last scene in *City Lights*," intoned the *Time* reviewer, "does more deep and tender credit to the human race than this [ballroom scene]. Like a penny in the gutter a heart catches the light. It isn't much, and there are millions like it, but it's coin of the realm, and only a proud child, no matter what his age, will pass it by."[45] In a society concerned with organization men, corporate buildup, domestic turmoil in civil rights, and governmental tyranny, perhaps the simple story needed telling less for the specifics and more for the release. Like its style and even its message, *Marty* was a final glimpse over the shoulder for a society working more and more into a national, popular culture. Curiously enough, the story told of the demise of traditional culture, and the medium reemphasized the rise of national communications.

NOTES

1. Quoted in Irving Bernstein, *The Economics of Television Film Production & Distribution: A Report to TV Screen Actors Guild* (Los Angeles : Screen Actors Guild, 1960), p.4.

2. Ibid, p. 3.

3. Eric Bentley, *The Dramatic Event: An American Chronicle* (New York: Horizon Press, 1954), p. 245.

4. Quoted in Edith Efron, "He Confesses He's a Square," *TV Guide*, April 18, 1970, pp. 10–11.

5. Quoted in Bernstein, *Economics of Television*, pp. 6–7. Bernstein discusses these programming assumptions in greater detail.

6. Reginald Rose, *Six Television Plays* (New York: Simon & Schuster, 1956), p. 107; Michael Kerbel, "The Golden Age of TV Drama," *Film Comment* 15 (July–August 1979):19.

7. Martin Gottfried, *A Theater Divided: The Postwar American Stage* (Boston: Little, Brown, 1967), p. 83.

8. Ibid, p. 241.

9. Ibid, p. 40. The indented quote is from pp. 48–49.

10. Ibid, p. 49.

11. John Howard Lawson, *Theory and Technique of Playwrighting* (New York: Hill & Wang, 1960), p. xxvii.

12. Michael Wood, *America in the Movies, or "Santa Maria, It Had Slipped My Mind"* (NewYork: Basic Books, 1975), pp. 131–135; Ring Lardner, Jr., "T.V.'s New 'Realism,' Truth Sans Consequences," *The Nation*, August 13, 1955, p. 132.

13. William H. Whyte, Jr., *The Organization Man* (Garden City, N.Y.: Doubleday/Anchor, 1957), pp. 39–40.

14. Quoted in Cecil Smith, "Four-In-One Marks Return of Felton," *Los Angeles Times*, 14 May 1970, p. 4:21.

15. Carol Serling, typescript of interview by Sonny Fox Productions, Hollywood, Calif., p. 1.

16. Rudolph Roderick, "Albert McCleery," *Entertainment World*, 21 November 1969, pp. 15–16. See also "Albert McCleery," *Current Biography* (February 1955), pp. 25–27. General conclusions about directorial style expressed in this section derived from program viewing at the University of California at Los Angeles Television and Film Archives. The author wishes to thank Dan Epstein for guidance through the vast collection.

17. "George Schaefer," *Dramatics*, March/April, 1979, pp. 21–25, interview transcription from Indiana University Oral History Project.

18. Ibid.

19. Eric Barnouw, *Radio Drama in Action* (New York: Farrar & Rinehart, 1945), p. viii.

20. Frank Nagler, *Writing for Radio* (New York: Ronald Press, 1939), pp. 80-81.

21. Sherman P. Lawton, *Radio Drama* (Boston: Expression Publishers, 1938), p. 132.

22. Rod Serling, *Patterns: Four Television Plays with the Author's Personal Commentaries* (New York: Simon & Schuster, 1957), p. 8: Fielder Cook, "Why Early TV Was a Golden Era for Drama," *New York Times*, 14 February 1982, p. D:31.

23. *Printer's Measure, Holiday Song, The Big Deal, Marty, The Mother,* and *The Bachelor Party* are in Paddy Chayefsky, *Telvision Plays* (New York: Simon & Schuster, 1955).

24. Quoted in Jack Hellman, "Light and Airy," *Variety*, 7 March 1968, unpaginated clipping in Delbert Mann Biography file, Margaret Herrick Library, American Film Institute, Beverly Hills, Calif.

25. Chayefsky, *Television Plays*, p. 132.

26. Robert Whitehead, "From Stage to T. V. Screen," *Theater Arts*, October 1956, p. 69.

27. Gore Vidal, "Television Drama, Circa 1956," *Theatre Arts*, December 1956, p. 85.

28. Fred Coe, "TV-Drama's Declaration of Independence," *Theatre Arts*, June 1954, pp. 29-32. The quotes below are from p. 87.

29. "Coe, Fred(erick)," *Current Biography Yearbook* (New York: H. W. Wilson, 1959), p. 74.

30. Coe, "Declaration," p. 29. For other information see Coe entry in *Current Biography Yearbook*, 1959.

31. Coe, "Declaration," p. 87.

32. John M. Clum, *Paddy Chayefsky* (Boston: Twayne Publishers, 1976), p. 26. Most of the biographical information in this section comes from pp. 15–40.

33. Quoted in Clum, *Chayefsky*, p. 36.

34. Clum, *Chayefsky*, p. 31.

35. Ibid, p. 32.

36. Chayefsky, *Television Plays*, pp. 173–174.

37. Ibid, pp. 132, 174.

38. Clum, *Chayefsky*, p. 91–93.

39. Hazel Flynn, "Mann Likes Plenty of Pre-Rehearsal," *Citizen News*, 29 January 1964, unpaginated clipping in Delbert Mann Biography File, Margaret Herrick Library, American Film Institute, Beverly Hills, Calif. See also "Biography of Delbert Mann," Paramount Studios (May 1957).

40. Chayefsky, *Television Plays*, p. 264.

41. Clum, *Chayefsky*, p. 96.

42. "Films," *America*, 30 April 1955, p. 139; "Film and T. V.," *The Catholic World*, April 1955, p. 63.

43. John McCarten, "The Current Cinema: Up from TV," *The New Yorker*, 23 April 1955, pp. 133–134; Arthur Knight, "If You Can't Lick 'Em, Join 'Em," *Saturday Review*, 26 March 1955, pp. 25–26.

44. Kerbel, "Golden Age," p. 19.

45. "The New Pictures," *Time*, 18 April 1955, p. 110.

6

Nightmare in Red: A Cold War View of the Communist Revolution

PETER C. ROLLINS

As a public service in the fall of 1952, the National Broadcasting Company began to air a half-hour series entitled *Victory at Sea*. The twenty-six episode documentary drew a large audience including highbrows like Bernard DeVoto as well as people in the street. Reviewers lauded the artistry of these compilation films* dealing with U.S. naval operations in World War II, but, as one member of the production team has recalled, *Victory at Sea* was one of the rare public-affairs programs that "could consider itself a barroom success." Thorough research in the world's film archives, masterful editing, rich musical orchestration, and an eloquent script convinced network executives that documentaries for television could be both artistic and popular, could both inform and make a profit—perhaps even in prime time.

In 1953, the *Victory at Sea* production team became NBC's *Project 20* group, hoping to continue the momentum of *Victory at Sea*'s success. Henry Salomon was the group's senior producer, but significant creative contributions were made by Donald Hyatt (assistant producer),

---

*Compilation films consist of footage "compiled" from existing film archives. The pioneer compilation film series was Frank Capra's *Why We Fight*, eight powerful orientation films produced during World War II. *Victory at Sea* brought *Why We Fight* compilation methods to television.

Richard Hanser (writer), Daniel Jones (film researcher), and Robert Russell Bennett (orchestrator). Until his death in 1958, Henry Salomon's historical vision dominated *Project 20*'s studies on contemporary issues; after 1958, Donald Hyatt's interest in Americana and historical paintings pointed *Project 20* in a nostalgic direction. *Nightmare in Red* is a classic early Salomon production; paradoxically, the Salomon vision and showmanship—which made *Nightmare in Red* a success scheduled against *The $64,000 Question* in 1955—seriously compromised the program's historical value. In its confusion between the attractions of drama and information, nonfiction television remains a genre in search of an aesthetic. The promises and problems of nonfiction programming can be traced back to the pioneer in network documentary, *Project 20*.[1]

Victory at Sea was based on Admiral Samuel Eliot Morrison's history of U.S. naval operations during World War II, an enormous project that Salomon, a former student of Morrison's at Harvard, helped to research and to write. With the enthusiastic support of Harvard classmate Robert W. Sarnoff—who would remain a constant protector of *Project 20* within the NBC bureaucracy—Salomon brought the epic story to television.[2]

Victory at Sea was an instant hit. Like many thousands of loyal *Victory at Sea* viewers, Bernard DeVoto, editor of *Harper's*, dropped everything to watch each new episode: "For twenty-six Sundays last year, neither the telephone nor the doorbell was answered at my house between 3:00 and 3:30 P.M." *The New Yorker* hailed the series as "certainly one of the most ambitious and successful ventures in the history of television."[3] The series won practically every major award for which it was eligible, including the Freedom Foundation's George Washington Medal, an Emmy from the Academy of Television Arts and Sciences, and the best documentary award from five major trade magazines, along with a host of outstanding achievement awards.

Henry Salomon's vision of history appealed to a cold-war television audience. The program lauded America's role as an international warrior in a global crusade for freedom; it taught that the United States was a nation which, innocent of geopolitical designs, could be brought into world struggles only when its cause was moral. Bernard DeVoto warmed to the Salomon vision: "The word 'liberation' has lost the face it had ten years ago, but gets it back when you look at *Victory at Sea* . . . repeatedly, you see tears of ecstasy of people greeting their deliverance . . . they are ravished by the fulfillment of hope." DeVoto suggested that postwar Americans were in need of the message *Victory at Sea* offered: "We forget too easily; everyone should see the whole series every year. It will be all right with me if Congress sees it twice a year."[4]

Indeed, most *Project 20* films of the Salomon era are parables of freedom. In *Victory at Sea* (1952), the allies are "free men [who] have given free men a chance to be free." During the Pacific campaign, "the children of free peoples move the forces of tyranny from the face of the earth—it is, it *will* be so, until the forces of tyranny are no more."[5] Throughout *Nightmare in Red* (1955), the words of the poet-prophet Alexander Pushkin remind the Russian people (and American television viewers) that, despite eras of oppression, "the heavy hanging chains will fall, the walls will crumble at a word, and Freedom greet you in the light, and brothers give you back the sword." *The Twisted Cross* (1956) traced the eventual triumph of freedom over Hitler's totalitarian regime. *Call to Freedom* (1957), an ambitious program about Austria's postwar liberation, intercut excerpts from Beethoven's *Fidelio*—a paean to freedom—with its documentary report. Shortly before his death in 1958, Salomon announced that he would explore the theme in depth through "a new series of television programs dealing with the conflict between democracy and Communism in the middle of the present century."[6]

The theme of freedom was personally important to *Project 20* staffers. Richard Hanser remembers the outlook as "an American viewpoint, the freedom and unfettering of humanity." As a photojournalist in 1948, Hanser, a veteran of World War II, returned to Europe to cover the Berlin Airlift. On one memorable occasion he was allowed to steer an airlift plane en route to the embattled German capital. In a newsreel entitled "Berlin Powderkeg," scriptwriter Hanser depicted the courage and ingenuity of free peoples locked in conflict with totalitarianism. Freedom was no mere abstraction.

Donald Hyatt has a similar memory about the *Project 20* team's interest in freedom as a theme: "We had just come through the war. We were sensitive people seeking out of that war themes that we wanted to do over again, themes of freedom, themes of brotherhood." While Hyatt readily admits that some will find such feelings "simplistic" and "corny," he is still proud of the common sense of "dedication, a patriotic spirit" among the *Project 20* members: "Even our Assistant Editor had been in the Battle of the Bulge." In the thirteen hours of images, narration, and music that was *Victory at Sea*, Salomon, Hanser, and Hyatt eloquently celebrated their chosen theme.[7]

Victory at Sea's success convinced NBC that there was an audience for historical compilation films. The staff was asked to remain together under the designation *Project 20*, a name emblematic of the ambitions that Salomon had for the series: "This title derives from the 20th century and our aim to dramatize its major themes with a blending of film, music, and spoken narration."[8] Privately, Salomon stressed to his team that "we are not documentarians, we are dramatists, we are playwrights." The next challenge was to find a worthy encore for *Victory at Sea*.[9]

The study of modern totalitarianism seemed promising, and research began on a general approach to both fascism and communism. As Donald Hyatt remembers, "There was a change in the subject from *Victory at Sea*, but not a change in theme."[10] Once film research began, the discovery of numerous caches of hitherto unseen footage suggested a division of the study into two separate programs. The rise of Soviet communism would be studied in an hour-long program, which Salomon initially wished to call *Red Tide*, but finally renamed *Nightmare in Red*. A second program, eventually entitled *The Twisted Cross*, would exploit the rich film resources captured from the Germans and conveniently located in the Washington, D.C., area.[11] Common to both programs would be two general themes, the nobility of the human spirit—despite political oppression—and the eventual liberation of humankind from its oppressors.[12]

Both films would aim at the timeless core of each experience, with each ending on a philosophical note, "a reflection on knowing ourselves better as a result of the particular experience explored by the film."[13] While the rise and fall of Nazism might be effectively explored in such general terms, would such a moralistic vision be supple enough to explain Soviet history and the appeal of world communism to Third World peoples? Could an American drama about liberation provide sophisticated international insights?

Borrowing extensively from the Russian fiction film, *Potemkin* (1925), the opening moments of *Nightmare in Red* explode visually and musically.[14] Shots of a shipboard mutiny are followed by scenes of street riots, culminating with the famous tour de force of dynamic montage, the Odessa Steps massacre. Juxtaposed with this uproar is a quiet aftermath: static shots of empty streets and men in chains are supported by discordant musical pulses that are barely audible. This alternation between unstable revolution and autocratic counterrevolution succinctly summarizes *Nightmare in Red*'s interpretation of Russian history: repressive regimes (first Czarist, then Communist) may enjoy years of success, but the Russian peasants periodically arise to throw off their chains. Unfortunately, the average Russian is so politically inept that schemers inevitably return to power. The pendulum of Soviet history swings regularly from one extreme to the other without resting at a liberal center.

Two Russian writers provide insight into the tragedy of Russian history. In a quote read by narrator Alexander Scourby, Leo Tolstoy explains to his people the fruitlessness of their unconstructive rages: "Change must come to Russia . . . but every revolution by force only puts more violent means of enslavement in the hands of those in power." Scourby then reads the previously given quote from Alexander Pushkin, who offers solace for those yearning to breathe free. There is always hope that the next liberation will succeed in bringing to birth a viable, liberal society. Such was the dream in 1917 and, according to *Nightmare in Red*, such was still the hope of the ordinary Soviet citizen in 1955. The remaining forty-four minutes of *Nightmare in Red* explore the details of this thesis.

Segment one examines the Romanoff dynasty, using recently discovered court footage to exploit the pathos of a doomed kingdom. Czar Nicholas II is described as an ineffectual ruler who would rather fiddle with his cameras or vacation in the Crimea than fulfill the responsibilities of office. The czarina is no happier with the family's lack of privacy, but is more autocratic. Neither the royal family nor the aristocracy will admit the existence of "a spectre of revolution . . . behind the marble pillars and splendid villas." The closing minutes of this portrait of Russia's *ancien régime* are a masterpiece of showmanship. Hollywood filmmakers have often employed dress balls to dramatize the twilight of aristocracy. As early as 1914, D. W. Griffith's *Birth of a Nation* evoked the poignant demise of the Confederacy through such a scene. Twenty-five years later, David O. Selznick's *Gone With the Wind* followed suit. Using fiction footage from *The Anna Cross* (1954), *Nightmare in Red* attempts to evoke a similar mood of dramatic irony. The narrator explains that "in the Crimea, in the capital of St. Petersburg, at the country seats of the great landowners, the privileged few dance away the ominous years of fancy dress . . . in heart-breaking ignorance." Dancers in *The Anna Cross* are shown in close-up, including shots of faces, feet, and swirling dresses. After a waltz, a serpentine line of dancers tries to keep up with an intoxicating musical tempo. At dawn, tipsy aristocrats depart, crowded into open carriages. They ride past a municipal employee extinquishing street lamps. Using a visual pun, the narrator cites Lord Raglan: "'The dancing years are ending, the party is over. The lamps are going out all over Europe. We shall not see them lit again in our lifetime.'" Maximum pathos of the final days is evoked by the skillful weaving together of music and fiction footage.[15]

Section two traces Lenin's rise to power. While the Czarist regime crumbles during World War I, Lenin enters the picture, a tool of the German high command: "We send Lenin into Russia just as we send shells and poison gas against an enemy." Visual and aural elements support this interpretation. Shots of Lenin are intercut with dynamic shots of railroad cars, engine stokers, tracks, all images dramatizing the sponsored arrival of the "brilliant, bitter, dedicated man." Certainly German assistance cannot be denied, but the implied conclusion offered by *Nightmare in Red* is obviously incorrect. As a leading textbook on modern history aptly notes: "Lenin and the Bolsheviks did not bring about the Russian revolution. They captured it after it had begun. They boarded the ship in midstream." A long battle scene from the Russian fiction film *Ten Days That Shook the World* (1928) is used to communicate a sense of the puissance of Lenin's revolutionary leadership.

Once in power, Lenin reveals the realpolitik behind his promises. In signing a treaty with the Germans, Lenin is accused of forsaking allies "who are still fighting to the death in France." No mention is made of Lenin's assumption that the world war was a product of the inner contradictions of capitalism. Domestic events are shown in an equally nightmarish light. Lenin declares that his government "seeks the frank liquidation of the idea of democracy by the idea of dictatorship." As a supporter of "rabid terrorism," he murders the royal family, an event presented with pathetic music and tender phrasing by narrator Alexander Scourby, along with a tearlike dissolve. Lenin's portrait could hardly be more negative.

Lenin's regime, although it promised to uplift society, was little more than a new chapter in Russia's tradition of repression. Section three of *Nightmare in Red* provides disturbing details to drive this message home. Images of starving children, some of them eating the lice that infect their ragged clothing, are shown while the narrator makes the film's first reference to nightmares: "'Equality!' cried the Communists, and there comes the equality of the slaughterhouse and the democracy of the cemetery. The dream of a brave new world, of a new heaven and a new earth, develops into a *nightmare* of starvation and economic collapse" [emphasis supplied]. An Allied blockade of Russia during this period goes without notice, but not the privations it caused—those are Lenin's fault. When Lenin resorts to the New Economic Policy (1921–1927), which allowed private enterprise to function as a stopgap measure, playful street pictures and jolly music join narrator Scourby in ridiculing the failure of Communist dogma.

Segment four tracks Stalin's bloody footsteps. When Stalin attempts to foster bootstrap industrial growth, he is condemned for personal cruelty. The first five-year plan "makes enormous strides at enormous human costs. But the workers who survive cannot eat heavy industry, cannot wear it, cannot live in it." *Nightmare in Red* does not mention that the Soviet Union was forced to industrialize without the help of outside capital, yet—despite the obstacles—industrial production increased by 236 percent during the first five-year plan. By 1938, the Soviet Union had become the world's foremost producer of tractors and locomotives. *Nightmare in Red* neglects to evoke the excitement with which these heroic efforts at economic development were greeted by the Russian people. As millions of college freshmen have since learned:

> . . . the feeling that everybody was busily toiling and struggling to create a socialist fatherland was perhaps the most distinctive achievement of the new system. Workers had a real belief that the new industrial wonders were their own. The sense of participation, of belonging, which democracy had given to the average man in the West in political matters, was widely felt in the USSR in economic matters also. People rejoiced at every new advance as a personal triumph. It became a national pastime to watch the mounting statistics, the fulfilling of quotas or hitting of "targets."[16]

Quoting the Grand Inquisitor from Fyodor Dostoevski's novel *The Brothers Karamazov* (1880), *Nightmare in Red* discounts the popularity of Stalin's programs: "the mass surrender of personal will and freedom—

once Nicholas, now Stalin." Stalin signs of every description—Stalin rugs, Stalin commemorative bowls, and, as a climax of film rhetoric, a balloon-hoisted Stalin pennant—are briskly edited in a montage designed to prove that the Russian people are being brainwashed. Much screen time for section four is expended on the purge trials of 1936-1938. No historian would want to defend the trials, but the emphasis devoted to them by *Nightmare in Red* is excessive.

When World War II arrives in segment five, *Nightmare in Red* shows that Russians fight for "Mother Russia." Just as Lenin did in 1918, Stalin in 1939 signed a disastrous treaty with the Germans. *Nightmare in Red* blames Stalin for the horrible war to follow:

> "It is time for fear when tyrants seem to kiss." Stalin's comrade Molotov, and Hitler's, von Ribentropp, sign their so-called "friendship pact" in the Kremlin. Hitler has his green light for World War II. Stalin has switched it on.

Later, the two dictatorships share their common interest in booty, "this time over the corpse of Poland, the corpse of peace." They are birds of a feather.

Eventually, Germany violates the pact. Handsome, bareheaded German soldiers are welcomed by civilians somewhere in the Soviet Union, proving the spiritual bankruptcy of the Communist regime: "The myth of the people's devotion to Communism in the land of workers and peasants explodes as the workers and peasants greet the Germans as liberators." Staged scenes from German propaganda films are introduced to support this argument. Civilians greet German troops with flowers and hand salutes and tear down pictures and statues of Stalin, replacing these graven images with portraits of "Uncle Adolf." A montage of Georgians, Armenians, and Mongols in German uniforms stresses how many nationalities fought Stalin's regime under the German flag. For musical support of this counterrevolution, a tune in a minor mode is introduced in counterpoint with the revolutionary leitmotif. The world war is finally won by the "Russian soldier who fights not for Marx or Lenin or Stalin, but for one another—for Mother Russia." Stalin promised, as the film explains, that the effort was "part of a struggle of the peoples of Europe and America for their independence and democratic freedoms." The postwar period brings no such freedoms to Russia.

Segment six of *Nightmare in Red* treats the cold war. Mounted guards outside the Kremlin remind the viewer of previous agents of repression who quelled the 1905 revolution. Moscow is described as a "symbol and magnetic core of an empire more powerful, more vast than any dream of any czar." The new empire is ruled by the Party, which has "unbridled sway" over the people who constitute 97 percent of the nation's population. The new aristocracy rules from the Kremlin "as master and warden casting a lengthening shadow." Section one of *Nightmare in Red* concluded with a dress ball. By introducing a cocktail party for Russia's technocrats at this point, *Nightmare in Red* asserts that there are historical parallels. Tables are crowded with liquor, fancy hors d'oeuvres, and bowls of fruit; a rhumba accentuates the sybaritic tone of the visuals. The rhumba is allowed to overlap shots of urban slums, accenting an ironic contrast between the life-style of workers and the luxuries enjoyed by Soviet officials. Stalin is quoted to justify the inequities.

Despite the tyranny of the czars, despite the repression of Lenin and Stalin, "the people and their faith endure." Surely the average Russian has been severely tested: "The state, knowing no creed but blind obedience, demands a captive mind, a captive spirit, a captive body. It must forever barricade its borders against the infection of freedom from without, against the escape to freedom from within." The final minutes of section six provide the title material for *Nightmare in Red*. The film takes us to dungeons below ground. Using fiction footage illuminated by high-contrast lighting, the camera pans victims in overcrowded cells, men and women herded together. The camera follows a simulated flashlight, which blinds the prisoners. A montage designed to evoke the idea of oppression follows: after a number of shots of individual faces, a tracking shot moves through a crowded cell holding nearly one hundred prisoners. As the nightmare continues, prisoners are herded onto flatbed trucks where they are netted down like cargo. Trains then take them in crowded freight cars to Siberia where they dismount in snow at gunpoint. The final shots of *Nightmare in Red* concentrate on the corner of a barbed-wire stockade, shot from a low angle. The NBC logo is imposed over this last image.

Commentary for these concluding moments plays on verbal connotations, sounds, and allusions. While we look at suffering innocents in underground cells, the narrator intones:

First the Cheka, with its motto: "The Cheka does not judge, it strikes." Then came the NKVD, and the MVD, then came the KGB, ever-changing ominous initials which all mean secret police, which mean terror conscious and subconscious, which mean the power of reality, a *Nightmare in Red*: "My father chastised you with whips, but I will chastise you with scorpions." An ancient prophecy comes true.

The verbal rhetoric reinforces the sense of confinement and oppression provided by the visuals.

The only hope for the Russian people is an ancient one, revolution. Continued repression will eventually lead to a new outburst, recalling the dream of liberation announced by Pushkin in the early moments of the program: "Deep in Siberian mine, keep your faces proud; the bitter toil shall not be lost, the rebel thought unbowed. The heavy-hanging chains will fall, the walls will crumble at a word, and Freedom greet you in the light, and brothers give you back the sword." The Manichean conflict between liberty and tyranny could not be more dramatically rendered as barbed-wire images close the film.

Nightmare in Red surprised the *Project 20* team by creating sponsor problems. Initially scheduled for broadcast on November 13, 1955, the program was delayed when Pontiac withdrew its support. Donald Hyatt remembers: "Salomon was livid over it and said it was typical of sponsor thinking." Since *Nightmare in Red* was the series premiere, the entire *Project 20* effort seemed to be in jeopardy.

Only fragments of the story exist, and few of those fragments are on paper. Donald Hyatt has reflected: "No one in this part of the world works on paper; they use the telephone."[17] There were many who could have made such telephone calls; prescreenings of the program to at least twenty-three advertising agencies and corporations were only part of an aggressive NBC promotional campaign. A host of corporate executives, political figures, and reviewers had screened *Nightmare in Red* by the end of July 1955. Although a number of alternate sponsors were enthusiastic, Pontiac began to ease up on the accelerator.[18]

Some time during the summer prescreenings, Pontiac's advertising staff began to worry about *Nightmare in Red*'s bleak anti-Communist closing. In addition, members of the Soviet delegation in Washington who attended a prescreening launched a protest. Both negative responses eventually reached the desk of Charles E. Wilson, secretary of defense and former chairman of the board of General Motors. All sources agree that Wilson was responsible for withdrawing Pontiac support. Pontiac's reasons for not sponsoring an anti-Communist film throw light on the complex relationship between American history and American television.[19]

Some members of the Eisenhower administration (1952-1960) were sincere in their efforts to chip away at the cold war glacier. In mid-July 1955, President Eisenhower traveled to Geneva to attend a summit conference with the Soviet Union's new heads of state, Nikita Krushchev and Nikolai Bulganin, the first such meeting in ten years. After a subsequent foreign ministers' conference in October 1955, many world citizens began to have some hopes that a "spirit of Geneva" would improve East-West relations. Although mistrust continued after the meetings, gestures were made by both sides to improve mutual understanding and trade. American businessmen were especially interested in "alleviating difficulties in performing usual business and maintenance services within the USSR," but the Russians were deaf to most American suggestions.[20] Secretary Wilson was particularly interested in demonstrating that American corporations could do business without becoming bogged down in political rhetoric. Sponsoring a program like *Nightmare in Red* in the face of Soviet complaints was simply impolitic, a gesture that would stir up trouble; hence the phone call.

In a front-page story in mid-October, *Variety* validated the commercial motivation: "General Motors is adopting discretion as the better part of democratic valor and future trade. . . . General Motors is a world-trading outfit and has been in the forefront for over 30 years of efforts to reduce barriers to business among nations. In coming face to face with the political embarrassment of *Nightmare in Red*, General Motors was completely consistent."[21] By mid-November, *Variety* reported that Armstrong Cork had picked up the program and would be scheduling it for late December, preempting its *Circle Theater* program, but with *Circle Theater* host John Cameron Swayze introducing and closing the program. If Pontiac had been concerned about Soviet feelings, reviewer reactions clearly indicate that the automobile manufacturer had shifted into reverse at just the right time.

Reviewers accepted *Nightmare in Red* as a factual, objective study of the Russian revolution and its contemporary implications. In his introduction, host John Cameron Swayze encouraged such responses by explaining, "The film is real, and through the knowledge it imparts, perhaps people can prevent getting caught in a *Nightmare in Red*." Since Swayze's *Camel News Caravan* was one of the leading evening network news programs, such a statement firmly stamped the program to follow with an imprimatur of fact. A closing by Swayze completed the nonfiction frame.[22]

Sid Shalit of the *New York Daily News* was representative in his responses to *Nightmare in Red*. The film was factual: "There's no fiction or editorializing. . . . None was needed. The story it told by authentic, sometimes blood-curdling newsreel shots, some of them never shown publicly." The film was a patriotic lesson: "America's Red Quislings wouldn't enjoy *Nightmare in Red*. . . . Even the dumbest Commie stooge might begin to suspect that documentary films like these— ninety percent of them Russian made—can't be faked." For Mr. Shalit, *Nightmare in Red* was not an interpretation at all, but an object lesson, "a chunk of history-in-the-raw which every free citizen in the world should try to see, and remember."[23]

One reviewer boiled the lesson down to a homily: "Over here, when there's a knock on the door at night, it is simply a neighbor borrowing a cup of sugar or collecting for a worthwhile charity . . . not the secret police inviting you to your own funeral."[24] Although not usually known for critical insights about film and television, the Honorable John W. McCormack of Massachusetts took time to speak for the program two days after its second broadcast. Congressman McCormack was especially pleased by what he considered to be the program's objectivity, its use of "thousands of feet of factual, unembellished motion picture film," its cool appeal to the intellect: "In presenting the world menace that is Communism, this film is a true public service."[25] The conservative *National Review* felt that the program's insights would be especially instructive during a dangerous post-Geneva thaw in the cold war: "It should be shown throughout the world, often, and particularly in those countries recently and noisily visited by Bulganin and Krushchev."[26] All such reviewers reminded their readers of the contrasting blessings of the American way.

At the opposite extreme of the political spectrum, *The Daily Worker* launched a diatribe against "NBC-TV's orgy of hatred." The Communist newspaper resented the use of Nazi propaganda films and decried the cynical treatment of Communist objectives: "If an ignorant cop or a stoolie were to write the history of the Soviet Union, it would be something like NBC's nightmare." The reviewer noted than an Irving R. Levine-narrated program for NBC, *Look at Russia*, had been more balanced, stressing "what Americans and Russians have in common." The Levine presentation, according to *The Daily Worker*, provided insight, revealing that the Soviet Union was "hardly the gigantic prison the USSR is made out to be in the nightmare."[27]

Somewhere between the saber rattlings of Congressman McCormack and the righteous indignation of *The Daily Worker* were some thoughtful responses about *Nightmare in Red* as an interpretation—rather than a mere presentation—of history. Marya Mannes came away from a preview impressed with the power of documentary for television: people in the industry were beginning to recognize the power of "facts, used as the instrument of art." She hoped that "this growing and infinitely useful form of art—the documentary in depth—becomes part of the American diet, so deficient in the vitamins of thought." Ms. Mannes was somewhat troubled, however, by potential misuses of such programs. Given the combined power of images, words, and music, the genre could be dangerous in the wrong hands: "Another team could have made a different picture from frames on the cutting room floor."[28]

In a review for *Senior Scholastic*, Patrick Hazard recommended the program to teachers because of its point of view: students could develop critical viewing skills by dissecting the program. Hazard recommended that teachers assign student teams to critique such elements of cinematic rhetoric as editing ("Ask them if a single execution would have given the intended effect"), music ("Ask your students to feel how music reinforces mood"), and point of view ("The problem of editorializing in a documentary must be stressed"). Hazard undercut claims to objectivity by suggesting that Soviet filmmakers could turn the tables on *Project 20* with an anti-American film entitled "*Nightmare in Red, White, and Blue*, in which racial discrimination, waterfront racketeering, juvenile delinquency and comic books are shown as the essence of American life." Hazard's observations about the plasticity of the compilation medium—as well as his classroom suggestions—are still valid.[29]

The passage of almost thirty years provides some perspective on *Nightmare in Red* as a documentary that may—or may not—have performed a service for its cold-war audience. Two fundamental questions need to be asked, questions readers are urged to ask of any documentary broadcast over the commercial medium of television: first, did *Nightmare in Red* provide new insights, or did it cater to existing prejudices? Second, were the resources of visual language employed for the purposes of drama at the expense of information?

1. Did *Nightmare in Red* Provide New Insights?—Americans were intensely disturbed by the aftermath of their second world war to end all wars, and the threat of world communism—sometimes called "Godless communism"—was at the heart of their anxiety. For a short time Senator Joseph McCarthy convinced a troubled public that its new problems were somehow linked to betrayal of public trust by officials and intellectuals. The Berlin crisis, the Korean War, and the fear of subversion were all part of America's cold-war nightmare.

A number of prominent historians in the 1950's warned that Americans needed to understand how their "revolutionary" heritage differed from the revolutionary developments in Russia, Asia, and South America. Daniel Boorstin exhorted Americans to appreciate their unique political experience: "We must refuse to become crusaders for liberalism, in order to remain liberals." Harvard professor Louis Hartz suggested that *the* question for Americans in the 1950s was a rephrasing of a conundrum articulated in the nineteenth century by Alexis de Tocqueville: "Can a people 'born free' ever understand peoples elsewhere that have become so?" Especially in the case of Russia, George Kennan's *American Diplomacy: 1900–1950* argued for a detached approach that ruled out both the option of intervention and the hope for internal revolution. The Soviets needed time to evolve toward Western institutions and values: "Let them be Russians; let them work at their internal problems in their own manner."[30]

Nightmare in Red, rather than tapping these new perspectives, succeeded as drama—but failed as history—in its unremitting attack on every Soviet motive, goal, and achievement. In the cause of drama, the czar's fall is treated with great pathos, stressing the victimization of a trapped family rather than providing any insight into the cruel necessity behind the execution. Lenin and Stalin make domestic and foreign policy decisions strictly to retain power, and neither allies nor Russia's peasants are spared in such selfish designs. As a result, according to *Nightmare in Red*, the basically religious and apolitical Russian masses yearn for liberation. When the expected revolution occurs, the Russian people will espouse liberal democracy, their "true" political heritage.

Using the phrasing of Tocqueville's questions, *Nightmare in Red* had the responsibility to help those born free (Americans) understand peoples elsewhere who were supposedly struggling to become so (Russians). Revolutionary violence and bloodshed, extensively shown and discussed by the documentary, have always been an unavoidable, tragic experience when entrenched interests have resisted change, but typically present, too, have been noble ideals and dreams of a better life—the very fuel of revolutions. Instead of balancing its portrait, *Nightmare in Red* imputed the worst motives, introduced the most lurid anecdotes, and discounted Communist ideology as a verbal smokescreen concocted to sway public opinion. The revolution itself is reduced to a bloody and cynical game of musical chairs in which one self-interested elite replaces another. Rendering dramatically the theme of oppression invited the filmmakers to paint too many shadows; conversely, efforts to predict a liberating rebellion unrealistically prevented the historian-filmmakers from exercising even a modicum of empathy. In short, the complexity of history was sacrificed to fit a narrow, preestablished theme. One historian who uses *Nightmare in Red* in classes dealing with American perceptions of Russia has observed: "Sometimes I think it's merely that everything Russian is evil . . . the film does not inform nearly so much as it preaches. This is what I find so objectionable."[31]

At a time when such theatrical films as *My Son John* (1952) and television fiction programming such as *I Led Three Lives* were manipulating viewer fears and prejudices about communism, the mass-media list of nightmares was long enough. In not fighting against the tide of xenophobia, *Nightmare in Red* failed to fulfill its responsibilities as a documentary. Marya Mannes, an otherwise friendly critic of Salomon's efforts, found *Nightmare in Red* lacking in this regard, failing to show "what went on in Russian minds and hearts during those convulsive years and what it is that has kept Communism alive and strong."[32] Although Third World films such as *The Battle of Algiers* (1966) have made impressive attempts to show the appeal of revolutionary ideology, it is safe to say that Americans still need documentaries to illuminate this insight.[33]

2. Which Was More Important, Drama or Information?—Henry Salomon, Richard Hanser, and others frequently referred to a quotation from Walt Whitman to explain their combined aesthetic and historical objectives: "I seek less to display any theme or thought and more to

bring you into the atmosphere of the theme or thought—there to pursue your own flight." Most scholars who have studied *Project 20* concur that the series dealt "more with feelings than with facts."[34]

Newsreels present pictures of events, but only documentaries that strive toward art take the care to match and weave compositional textures.[35] *Nightmare in Red*, like other *Project 20* programs, was skillfully edited to yield the maximum feeling from compositional elements of archival footage. For example, it is no accident that *Nightmare in Red* finds Leo Tolstoy in a garden where he warns about the excesses of revolution; nor it is fortuitous that the film associates Lenin with an impact montage involving a train racing across the countryside. In both cases, compositional elements help to interpret the historical figures: Tolstoy shows the repose of reason while Lenin is a man of violence. Inclusion of Lenin's wife—who was afflicted by exopthalamosis ("pop-eyes")—adds a scurrilous piece of negative imagery to further undercut Lenin's image as a leader. In practically every scene, *Nightmare in Red* reflects a similar careful crafting of form to content; as a result, viewer feelings are masterfully orchestrated.

If a compilation film is a study of history, then its credibility is jeopardized every time dramatic considerations tempt the filmmaker to include visually exciting—but historically anachronistic—pictures. Despite their technical excellence, *Project 20* films during the Salomon period must be criticized for their cavalier attitude toward the historical authenticity of cinematic materials. Jay Leyda has warned compilation filmmakers, "As little as five fictional feet in an otherwise scrupulous compilation can shake the spectator's belief in the whole film, *including its ideas*. Even though he does not identify a shot as false, merely to sense that something is wrong, to get a whiff of arrangement can poison for him the whole setting of the tiny falsehood."[36] No one on the *Nightmare in Red* project seemed to be concerned with such niceties, for a combination of faked nonfiction footage plus fiction materials crowd some twenty minutes of the fifty-four-minute program.

In section five, *Nightmare in Red* dramatizes the disaffection of nationalities who greeted invading German troops as liberators. While no one would deny that Mongols, Armenians, and other groups did indeed fight briefly against the Red army, the documentary's method of telling the story is extremely problematic. Without indicating its source, *Nightmare in Red* employs extensive footage from Nazi propaganda films. The section includes scenes staged for Nazi cameras, and many anti-Communist moments in this section use whole, unaltered sequences from such Nazi propaganda. In 1942, these scenes must have been effective proof to native Germans that their expansive war was just, but incorporating such materials whole-cloth into a historical film some thirteen years later is clearly a showman's choice, presenting history that was crafted into drama rather than illuminating the drama in history. The materials here—and elsewhere—were chosen for their emotional impact, not for their veracity. The ploy is comparable to quoting without citation from a John Birch Society pamphlet in a serious essay opposed to fluoridation. Distortions in the quoted material would discredit the essay for discerning readers.

Fiction materials are generously included in *Nightmare in Red* to achieve maximum emotional effect. The chaotic nature of periodic outbursts of revolution in Russian history is supported visually by little else: the 1905 revolution is seen through Eisentein's *Potemkin*, with segments selected to underscore *Nightmare in Red*'s theme of senseless violence rather than Eisenstein's theme of revolution for a good cause; the last flickering moments for aristocracy are played upon extensively through the use of a lavish studio production, *The Anna Cross*, a Russian film that had nothing whatsoever to do with the revolution; the dynamic 1917 Communist takeover is excitingly communicated by long sections from the film *Ten Days That Shook the World* (1928) and other fiction sources. Last but not least, the final scenes—which caused so much consternation at the Russian Embassy, the Department of Defense, and Pontiac's ad agency—were totally fictional. They were used because they were, from an editor's perspective, enormously compelling pictures.[37]

It is silly to criticize a compilation film for being an interpretation of reality. As CBS documentary producer Burton Benjamin has observed, "If the compilation film is 'just a collection of newsreel clips,' then a history book is 'just a collection of library clips' and no history makes sense."[38] The basic problem with *Nightmare in Red*'s use of fiction materials had two components, perhaps only one of which would still exist in the 1980s. First, from a production standpoint, it seems clear that fiction materials were selected because they dramatically conveyed a predetermined slant, not because of the novel pictorial or documentary insight they supplied. The polite name for such filmmaking is "persuasion"; an unfriendly label is "propaganda."

A second aspect relates to the television audience: were 1955 viewers capable of joining *Project 20* filmmakers in the search for inner truths through fiction? Turning back to the often cited remark of Walt Whitman, once brought into the "atmosphere of the theme or thought," would audiences know in what direction to "pursue [their] own flight?" When asked this question by a Macon, Georgia, history teacher, film researcher Daniel Jones responded, "The huge American television audience, besides being intelligent, is sophisticated enough to realize these passages are re-enactments and introduced because of their effectiveness, to tell the story better."[39] An extensive survey of reviews indicates that only one newspaper columnist, Ethel Daccardo of the *Chicago Daily News*, even noticed the fictional materials.[40] Staged scenes, fiction footage, and *Nightmare in Red*'s thesis were accepted without much critical reflection, presumably on the premise that pictures don't lie, especially pictures introduced by John Cameron Swayze. Then and now, the temptation to use whatever "works" visually is always present in the editing room, leading network documentarians in the direction of drama for drama's sake rather than toward Salomon's stated objective—drama as a device to discover the inner meaning of history.

Project 20 and television Documentary after *Nightmare in Red*—For *Project 20*, the Pontiac incident was a small bump in the road, not a serious collision. Within NBC, patrons like Robert W. Sarnoff and Sylvester "Pat" Weaver assured that nervous programmers could not interfere: "The network could never have applied pressure; that would have got their neck in a noose." (At that same time, however, sponsor pressures were placing such controversial CBS programs as Edward R. Murrow's *See It Now* [Alcoa Aluminum] in jeopardy.) The Salomon team was ensconced on a very privileged corporate perch: "Had we been outsiders, we would have been decimated . . . the Sarnoff power gave us freedom."[41]

Viewer interest helped to vindicate *Nightmare in Red* and the series of programs to follow. When broadcast two days after Christmas 1955, *Nightmare in Red* received a Nielsen rating of 23.9 (or approximately 9,420,000 homes), the best rating ever achieved in a difficult spot opposite CBS's *$64,000 Question*; the second broadcast on January 24 resulted in an equally impressive audience draw.[42] The advertising manager for Armstrong Cork, Pontiac's replacement, was elated: "In the history of this company, no effort of ours has ever provoked so much favorable response from so many people."[43] Subsequent *Project 20* programs would receive even higher ratings. As *Playboy* later marveled, *Project 20* served to "enable the Sarnoffs, the sponsors, and the FCC—and even the public—to have its cultural cake and eat it, too."[44]

Avoidance of controversy also helped the series after 1955: *The Twisted Cross* (March 24, 1955; 32.4 Nielsen rating) assailed a long-since-toppled totalitarian regime; *The Great War* (October 16, 1956; 20.8 Nielsen rating) exploited the drama of a "singing war"; *The Jazz Age* (December 6, 1957; 35.2 Nielsen rating) played on nostalgic emotions; the turbulent era before 1900 was brought to the screen in a deceptively blithe program entitled *The Innocent Years* (November 21, 1957; 27.0 Nielsen rating). The only Salomon program after *Nightmare in Red* to address contemporary issues was *Call to Freedom* (January 1, 1957; 27.2 Nielsen rating). Reviews were not enthusiastic about *Call to Freedom*'s mixture of the oil of opera with the water of documentary. Donald Hyatt remembers that the program lacked the compelling force of *Nightmare in Red*: "Yes, Austria has its freedom and its opera open, but there is nothing deep to reflect on. . . . In the sense of drama, it doesn't work."[45] It may also be true that the theme of liberation, dramatic to a 1955 audience, was no longer so gripping in 1957. The one potentially controversial project, *That War in Korea*, was left on the shelf until the Kennedy years (November 20, 1963). In 1965, even a friendly observer of *Project 20*'s work had to admit that few programs "have taken a position contrary to the collective viewpoint."[46]

When Henry Salomon suddenly died in January 1958, at the age of 40, Donald Hyatt's tastes and interest led *Project 20* still further from controversy. Hyatt's debut as producer was *Meet Mr. Lincoln* (February 11, 1959; 26.6 Nielsen rating), a program that both justified continued support of *Project 20* and established a new style. Hyatt employed "stills-in-motion" techniques over Matthew Brady photographs to bring the Civil War years to life. The dignity of human beings was still an important theme, but it was focused more toward cultural expressions than politics and power. Enduring programs such as *The Real West* (March 29, 1961) and moving religious evocations such as *The Coming of Christ* (December 21, 1961) or *He Is Risen* (April 15, 1962) further explored spiritual themes while refining a stills-in-motion style.[47] By 1967, *Project 20* had produced over twenty-five major documentaries for television.

It is difficult to overestimate the importance of *Project 20* to the history of television documentary. As *Variety* noted in its obituary for Henry Salomon: "The Project 20 series was given prime evening time and not restricted to the Sunday afternoon 'intellectual ghetto' of public affairs programming."[48] With sponsorship from Prudential Insurance, CBS used *Victory at Sea* techniques to assemble *Air Power* (1956), narrated by Walter Cronkite and organized into the same twenty-six-episode format as its seaborne predecessor. Between 1957 and 1961, another CBS series entitled *The Twentieth Century* churned out 104 compilations. Under the direction of Burton Benjamin, *The Twentieth Century* hoped to evoke in film "the smaller story which did not dominate history's headlines."[49] Controversy was successfully avoided in such programs as *Paris in the Twenties*, *The Movies Learn to Talk*, and other evocative historical compilations. Not to be outdone, ABC—the little fellow—came out in 1960 with a twenty-six-episode series on World War II entitled *Winston Churchill: The Valiant Years*. Eyewitnesses to history, on-camera narrators, and new footage at historic sites enriched both the CBS and ABC descendants of *Project 20*. Not only the techniques of *Project 20*, but its personnel circulated among the networks: editor Isaac Kleinerman moved to CBS, where he became an award-winning producer on *The Twentieth Century*; after working as a researcher for *Victory at Sea* and *Nightmare in Red*, Mel Stuart took his archival lessons to CBS and then on to David Wolper Productions.

The major networks began to lose interest in the compilation genre some time in the early 1960s. Many producers—quite incorrectly—assumed that the world's archives had been fully exploited, forgetting that what made compilations interesting were the historical visions guiding them, not simply old pictures strung together with narration. Of greater significance was the appearance of new technologies, to include light cameras, "fast" film, and excellent portable tape recorders. Investigative reporting—once the monopoly of print journalism—was now possible for television. Compilations left the television screen, although they continued to be a classroom staple.[50]

The birth of cable television seemed to have renewed an interest in compilation as a genre. In 1981, Home Box Office (HBO) aired a compilation series entitled *Remember When*. Not even the presence of Dick Cavett—entering and exiting the actuality footage by means of a special effect called "ultramat"—could hide the flaws of productions marred by dated historical interpretations, anachronistic film materials, and redundant narration. Rather then picking up where *Project 20* left off, *Remember When* seemed to be produced in total ignorance of the NBC legacy.

The compilation film has great potential for the exploration of history, only some of which was tapped by *Project 20*. As audiences become more visually literate, we must ask compilation filmmakers to tell us who we were on the condition that they relate that information— vividly, but honestly—to who we are and who we need to become. Henry Salomon's promise for *Project 20*—to use archival films to explore the past for the benefit of the present—still awaits fulfillment.[51]

Notes

1. A number of public documents have been useful to this study of *Project 20*. An early analysis which, while friendly, was not devoid of criticism is Albert J. Abady, "Project Twenty: An NBC Television Network Series" (Master's thesis, Pennsylvania State University, 1965). Very useful for those interested in *Project 20* after Henry Salomon's death is Philip J. Lane, Jr., "NBC-TV's Project 20: An Analysis of the Art of the Still-in-Motion Film in Television" (Ph.D. diss., Northwestern University, 1969). The only book to devote attention to *Project 20* is A. William Bluem, *Documentary in American Television: Form, Function, Method* (New York: Hastings House, 1965). I concur with Bluem's perception that there was a Salomon era (1951–1958) and then a Hyatt era (1958ff.) for *Project 20*. This paper is restricted to the political and aesthetic visions of *Project 20* during the Salomon years, for which *Nightmare in Red* stands as a representative program. Those interested in a still narrower and earlier focus are invited to consult Peter C. Rollins, "*Victory at Sea*: Cold War Epic," *Journal of Popular Culture* (1972): 463–482. The delightful quotation about *Project 20's* "barroom success" is from Richard F. Shephard, "Fact plus Flourish: Project 20 Combines Two Elements on TV," *New York Times*, 25 December 1966, p. 2:15.

2. The importance of Robert Sarnoff's concern for Salomon's projects cannot be overemphasized. Artistic liberties allowed stemmed from the Sarnoff connection, one Harvard man helping another against the Lilliputians at Rockefeller Center. As Richard Hanser told me, "It was one case in which nepotism worked out well." Richard Hanser and Donald Hyatt graciously shared their opinions, clippings, and precious time with me during interviews conducted in fall, 1981. I wish to thank them for all their courtesies. Travel support by the W. K. Kellogg Foundation made the interview opportunity possible, as did support from the Columbia University Seminar on American History/ American Television. Quotations from interviews will be cited as Hanser interview or Hyatt interview.

3. The DeVoto comment is from "The Easy Chair," *Harper's*, January 1954, p. 8; Phillip Hamburger's "Far-off Places: TV's *Victory at Sea*" provides the encomium from *The New Yorker*, 1 April 1953, p. 79. These are representative responses to a program still being broadcast on late-night television in 1982.

4. DeVoto, "Easy Chair," p. 8.

5. All further quotations from *Project 20* programs are drawn from viewing notes. This statement is from an episode of *Victory at Sea* entitled "The Fate of Europe."

6. "Henry Salomon, TV Official, Dead," *New York Times*, 2 February 1958, p. 86.

7. Hyatt interview.

8. As quoted in Marya Mannes, "Channels: The Hot Documentary," *The Reporter*, 17 November 1955, p. 38. This article is also part of Lewis Jacob's massive anthology, *The Documentary Tradition: From Nanook to Woodstock*, 2nd ed. (New York: W. W. Norton, 1979), pp. 296–300.

9. Hyatt interview.

10. Hyatt interview.

11. Hanser interview.

12. Hyatt interview.

13. Hyatt interview.

14. Viewing notes were taken from two prints of *Nightmare in Red* owned by the Audiovisual Center, Oklahoma State University, Stillwater, Okla. 74078, prints renting for less than $20. Many other university audiovisual centers also rent the film. McGraw-Hill sells prints of *Nightmare in Red* for about $600. Viewing prints for scholars are available at the Library of Congress in Washington, D.C., and the Museum of Modern Art in New York City.

15. Information about purchased film materials has been drawn from a file entitled "Nightmare in Red—legal," the Donald Hyatt personal papers, hereafter cited as *NIR*—Legal File.

16. R. R. Palmer and Joel Colton. This and the previous textbook quotation are from *A History of the Modern World* (New York: A. A. Knopf, 1965), pp. 723, 721.

17. All Hyatt's remarks are from the Hyatt interview.

18. Details about promotional efforts have been gleaned from memoranda in the *Project 20* papers, Wisconsin Center for Film and Theatre Research, Madison, Wis. This collection contains a number of manuscript materials, some of which were scanned for me by John E. O'Connor during a research visit to the center.

19. This narrative description has been pieced together from the Hyatt interview plus two articles from *Variety*, "Television's *Nightmare in Red*: Pontiac Exits 'Hot' Programs," 19 October 1955, p. 1 (hereafter referred to as "Pontiac Exits,") and "Armstrong to Take On Anti-Commie *Nightmare* That 'Pard' Pontiac Axed," 23 November 1955, pp. 1, 16.

20. This representative quotation is from "East-West Contacts Stalled," *Facts on File*, November 1955 (New York: Facts on File, 1956), p. 375.

21. "Pontiac Exits," p. 1.

22. The Swayze remarks have been taken from program summary cards, Program Analysis Division, NBC. I wish to thank Ms. Betty Reed and Ms. Julie Radin for their cheerful and intelligent assistance, and I urge television scholars to tap this little-known resource for research dealing with both fiction and nonfiction programs.

23. Sid Shalit in *New York Daily News*, 27 December 1955. This review was found among the private clippings and papers of Richard Hanser.

24. From a colorful review among Hanser clippings, *sans* bibliographical data.

25. From a speech delivered 26 January 1956, reproduced as an offprint found among Hanser clippings.

26. "*Nightmare in Red*," *The National Review*, 18 April 1956, p. 6.

27. *Daily Worker*, 30 December 1955, p. 6. The Levine documentary had aired in October 1955. According to *The Daily Worker* diatribe against *Nightmare in Red*, the program "was a friendly attempt to show the things that Russians and Americans have in common such as traffic problems, housing shortages, television, sports, etc." Russians were presented as human beings; the country's atmosphere was portrayed as liveable.

28. Mannes, "Hot Documentary," p. 38.

29. Patrick Hazard, "*Nightmare in Red*," *Senior Scholastic*, 6 October 1955, pp. 34, 53.

30. Although ideas of the "consensus historians" here cited are now considered passé by many, their challenges to existing formulations represented, at least for the 1950s, new strategies for understanding the American liberal tradition in an international context. The Boorstin warning is from *The Genius of American Politics* (Chicago: University of Chicago Press, 1953), p. 188. Louis Hartz discusses the relevance of Tocqueville's observations in *The Liberal Tradition in America: An Interpretation of American Political Thought Since the Revolution* (New York: Harcourt, Brace, 1955), p. 25. George Kennan's extremely influential ideas were collected in *American Diplomacy: 1900–1950* (Chicago: University of Chicago Press, 1951), where an evolutionary approach toward Russia was urged, pp. 136–137. As interpretative historians, the *Project 20* team should have been aware of the writings of Boorstin, Hartz, and Kennan; a new documentary should always consult the most recent studies available.

31. Letter received from Professor John Walz, department of history, California State University, Hayward, Calif., 20 February 1982. I wish to thank Professor Walz for his interest in this project. Other historians who sent letters of advice and criticism were Bert Spector (Harvard Business School), David Culbert (Louisiana State University), Taylor Stults (Muskingum College), Leslie Fishbein (Rutgers University), Thomas Cripps (Morgan State University), and Paul Vanderwood (San Diego State University). Each suggestion prodded thought, as did the suggestions of my Oklahoma State University colleagues, Leonard Leff and Gordon Weaver.

32. Mannes, "Hot Documentary," p. 38.

33. This excellent fiction film was directed by Gillo Pontecorvo and is available for rental from Audio Brandon Films.

34. *Project 20* press kits and promotional materials repeat this notion in a variety of ways. Both Abady and Lane cite such statements with approval, a notion with which—in principle—this article does not quarrel.

35. The best study of compilation film history and aesthetics is Jay Leyda, *Film Begets Film: A Study of the Compilation Film* (New York: Hill & Wang, 1964). Leyda spends considerable time examining the successes and failures of the genre, 1898–1963. *Project 20* productions are briefly discussed in a chapter entitled "Smaller Screen—Larger Audience," pp. 97–100.

36. Leyda, *Film Begets Film*, p. 130.

37. *Nightmare in Red*, Legal File, Hyatt papers.

38. "The Documentary Heritage," *Television Quarterly: Journal of the National Academy of Television Arts and Sciences* 1 (1962):32. This article is included in Jacobs, *Documentary Tradition*, pp. 301–306.

39. The exchange between Daniel Jones and Florence Blair, a social studies teacher in Macon, Georgia, is discussed in Abady, "Project Twenty," pp. 62–64. Abady was

skeptical about the defense: "The sophistication and ability of the 'huge American audience' to distinguish between actuality and theatrical footage raises doubt in this writer's mind" (p. 63).

40. Daccardo reviewed *Nightmare in Red* in the *Chicago Daily News* ("Russ TV Gives Grim Picture," 29 December 1955, p. 39) and just prior to the second broadcast ("Red Film Is 95 Pct. Newsreels," 24 January 1956, p. 35). Daccardo's misuse of the word "newsreel" is characteristic of the primitive state of television criticism and indicative of the vulnerability of audiences. There are very few "newsreel" materials in *Nightmare in Red*, although footage from documentaries, propaganda films, and actualities are abundant. No one seemed to know what to call the new programs. At various points in research for this article, the following terms were employed by producers and critics: telementaries, think films, films of life, nonfiction programming, docudramas, fact dramas, actuality dramas with a hard spine. In 1981, the search continues for a language to describe the proper role for the nonfiction film.

41. Hyatt interview.

42. All statistics in this section have been culled from NBC materials in the files of Richard Hanser.

43. As quoted in Henry Salomon, "Timidity Will Get You Nowhere," *Variety*, 25 July 1956, p. 32.

44. "On the Scene: Donald Hyatt, a way out of the Vast Wasteland," *Playboy*, April 1962, p. 103.

45. Hyatt interview.

46. Abady, "Project Twenty." The entire paragraph from which this quotation is taken is of interest. "Perhaps the time has come to return to battle with popular misconceptions rather than popular conceptions. This era has blundered through eras corroded by mistakes—Prohibition, McCarthyism, and others. Although most Project 20 themes have been enlightening, few have taken a position contrary to the collective viewpoint—a viewpoint with which most of the country agrees: Mark Twain was one of America's finest men of letters, the Jazz Age was exuberant, patriotism is good for America. There are other histories to be told" (p. 88).

47. *The Real West* is still used constantly for history classes in the Southwest; Richard Hanser's theological training meshed effectively with Donald Hyatt's eye for painting on the religious projects.

48. "Death of Salomon at 40 Cuts Short One of TV's Most Promising Careers," 2 February 1958, p. 32. Thanks are due J. Fred MacDonald of Northeastern Illinois University for this and other useful sources. Professor MacDonald's "The Cold War as Entertainment in 'Fifties Television," *Journal of Popular Film and Television* 7 (1978):3–31, highlights the ways in which cold-war concerns became part of television's fiction and nonfiction programming.

49. Quoted in Bluem, *Documentary in American Television*, p. 169.

50. History teachers have begun to make their own compilations for the classroom, a development made difficult by the high cost of film and television production. British aspirations and achievements are discussed in Paul Smith, ed., *The Historian and Film* (Cambridge: Cambridge University Press, 1976), pp. 121–85. American developments are evaluated in Peter C. Rollins, "*Storm of Fire* and the Historian as Filmmaker," *The History Teacher* 12 (1979), 539–48. David Cuthbert and Peter Rollins have recently com-

pleted an historical compilation designed to train the student eye along lines suggested in the review of *NIR* by Patrick Hazard (above, p. 17). Entitled *Television's Vietnam: The Impact of Visual Images*, the video production comes in 150 min. and 60 min. formats and is accompanied by a workbook. (OSU Audiovisual Center).

51. Leyda, *Film Begets Film* is an indispensable starting point. Ultimately, the ideal compilation filmmaker will have the cinematic eyes of a Hyatt, the historical vision of a Salomon, the verbal gifts of a Hanser, and the musical ear of a Bennett. Perhaps this is too much to expect of an individual; unfortunately, it is also doubtful that such a talented group will ever be assembled again. As a result our classrooms will suffer from inferior productions unable to balance the demands of history and art.

7

A Clash of Cultures: The Smothers Brothers vs. CBS Television

BERT SPECTOR

Videotaped earlier that same week, this night's *Smothers Brothers Comedy Hour* is being aired by CBS on Sunday, February 25, 1968. After the half-hour station break, Dick Smothers stands alone on stage to introduce the next guest.

Dick opens with a curious comment: "We are very fortunate to have back on our show a man who was on our first show of the season."[1] In the world of prime-time television variety shows, special guests rarely make more than one appearance on any given show per season. Dick then winds his way through a typically effusive show-business introduction, and whatever curiosity has been piqued by his opening statement is quickly forgotten in the glow of Dick's recital of his next guest's unmatched contributions to the world of entertainment.

But curiosity ebbs only momentarily as Dick hints—too vaguely and generally for the uninformed viewer to make much of those hints—of a not-so-typical show-business career, and perhaps even an intricate tangle of circumstances that surrounds this appearance:

> We're very proud to have this man on the show, not only because he's a great man, a fine man, but also beause he performs rarely on television. In fact, he's only made one major television appearance in the last 17 years. Well, ladies and gentlemen, I'm happy to present on our show for the second time, Mr. Pete Seeger.

Appears rarely on television? Only once before in the last seventeen years? Now, for the second time on the Smothers Brothers show? Dick Smothers's message is there, to be dug out. Pete Seeger was blacklisted from commercial network television for seventeen years. The Smothers Brothers broke that blacklist earlier this season. Now, they have brought him back. But why?

Seeger is first seen on a rocking chair, his long legs shot out stiffly in front of him, his head back slightly, holding a five-string banjo. The television audience can see that some sort of an inscription is etched onto his banjo head, but the camera never allows the viewer to make out the words: "This machine surrounds hate and forces it to surrender."[2] He opens with a playful ditty about growing old, then stands and walks to center stage. The camera's close-ups are not kind to Seeger's craggy, deeply lined, frankly homely face. His pilling sweater adds to a rather unkempt appearance certainly not typical of television performers. But Seeger seems absolutely unselfconscious, and as he begins to sing again, the camera settles rather comfortably on his lanky frame.

His next number is more serious than the first, as he works his way through short verses of songs documenting the painful history of the country's past wars: the American Revolution ("Yankee Doodle"), the Civil War ("John Brown's Body"), the Spanish-American War ("Damn, Damn, Damn the Filipinoes"), and World War I ("I Don't Want No More of Army Life"). Subtly highlighted by the songs, and not so subtly by the introductions that accompany them, is the fact that past as well as present American wars have generated heated, often respected opposition. Both Abe Lincoln and Mark Twain were war protesters, the audience is told.

Seeger has now set the proper stage. Literally without fanfare, he simply reaches for a twelve-string guitar that has been placed beside him on stage, and begins to sing:

It was back in 1942, I was a member of a good platoon.
We were on maneuvers in Louisiana one night by the light of the moon;
The captain told us to ford a river, that's how it all begun.
We were knee deep in the Big Muddy,
The big fool said to push on.

This song, Seeger's own "Waist Deep in the Big Muddy," is the reason Seeger has been invited for a second appearance on the Smothers

Brothers' show. In fact, he sang this very song on the first show, in September 1967, but the song never made it to the air. In only one of his many battles with CBS, Tommy Smothers had fought for this second appearance, and fought for Seeger's right to sing "Big Muddy." That battle he won; others he did not. But the confrontations themselves became one of the central facts of the Smothers Brothers' career with CBS. The confrontations, that is, plus one other not unimportant fact: the Smothers Brothers show became one of the most popular programs on television, and remained popular until CBS abruptly canceled it near the end of the 1968–1969 season.

In the winter of 1966, Sunday-night prime-time television was dominated by one show, NBC-TV's venerable family Western, *Bonanza*. In an attempt to unseat the Cartwrights from their weekly throne, CBS had called forth some of its high-powered stars. Both Garry Moore and Judy Garland tried and failed to woo viewers away from the Ponderosa. *Bonanza* seemed invincible.

Then came the Smothers Brothers.

Most television critics quickly dismissed Tom and Dick Smothers. Where a bankable television star like Garry Moore and an internationally known celebrity like Judy Garland had failed miserably, how could this young, offbeat, comedy/folk duo possibly succeed? Only one writer, Jack Gould of the *New York Times*, saw a more important aspect to the confrontation. Tom, aged thirty, and Dick, then twenty-nine, could "be the forerunners of the next generation of artists," predicted Gould, "who must be brought along if the medium is to protect itself against the inevitable obsolescence of the oldtimers who currently dominate so much of television comedy."[3]

But in 1966, at the height of the Vietnam War, antiwar protests, urban riots, and the "greening of America," young performers like the Smothers Brothers would not simply be "brought along." Instead, Tom and Dick infused their prime-time show with the kind of overt political satire and social commentary that network executives had managed to avoid and ignore since the medium's inception.

And what started as a prime-time confrontation between CBS and NBC over rating points quickly escalated into a more significant battle between the Smothers Brothers and their own timid, basically conservative network hierarchy.

Tom and Dick Smothers began performing folk songs in San Francisco in 1958. Like their good friends Dave Guard and Nick Reynolds, of a newly organized San Francisco group calling itself the Kingston Trio, the Smothers Brothers learned about folk music from listening to the records of Josh White, Bob Gibson, then Pete Seeger and the Weavers. However, unlike Seeger and the other folk musicians who clustered around *Sing Out!* magazine in New York City, the Smothers Brothers steered clear of any and all political involvement. Not only were they unsympathetic to the radicalism of Seeger and Woody Guthrie, but they seem to have been totally unaware of the long-standing and intimate relationship between folk music and the American Communist Party.[4] Much closer in spirit to the Kingston Trio than to Pete Seeger's group, the Weavers. Tom and Dick Smothers were, in those early days, politically naïve.[5]

The only political organization with which Tom had any contact at all in the late 1950s was the liberal Committee for a Sane Nuclear Policy. He remembers seeing SANE demonstrators on campus, and also admits that like many other students of his generation he felt little kinship with such political activism. "I was just as shortsighted and nonpolitical as anybody else," he confesses.[6]

So, instead of relying on political and topical music, the Smothers Brothers based their act on parodies of folk songs. The Weavers' "Tzena, Tzena, Tzena," for instance, became a rousing song about a camel race. Tom slyly ended his rendition of "I Never Will Marry" by snickering, "But I'll fool around a lot." Let the "ethnic" musicians— that's what Tom and Dick called people like Pete Seeger back then— take folk music seriously. The Smothers Brothers played their music strictly for laughs.

Ironically, the Smothers Brothers' career was enhanced by folk music's sudden burst of popularity in the late 1950s and early 1960s. In July 1960, under the heading "Folk Frenzy," *Time* magazine took note of the "sudden" upsurge of folk music on American campuses.[7] That upsurge was not nearly as sudden as *Time* would have its readers believe, however. Pete Seeger himself, blacklisted from television and nightclubs, found all through the 1950s that college students were "the one sector of American society that didn't give a shit for the blacklist."[8] He had been performing folk music on small liberal-arts campuses since 1953. But the real "frenzy" began in 1957 when Dave Guard and Nick Reynolds teamed up with Bob Shane to form the Kingston Trio. The young trio performed folk tunes and new ballads in a folk style similar to that of the old Weavers. Instead of the electrified guitar and percussion backing that typified so much of the popular music at the time, the trio accompanied themselves on the acoustic guitar and banjo. In the fall of 1958 Capital Records released the Kingston Trio's version of an old mountain ballad first recorded by Frank Proffitt, "Tom Dooley." The record shot to the top of the charts. By the early 1960s, the airways were flooded with the sound of folk and pseudo-folk music. Groups like the Terriers, the Highway Men, the New Christy Minstrels, and Peter, Paul and Mary, and individuals like Joan Baez and Bob Dylan enjoyed popularity and commercial success of their own.

Within several years, the Smothers Brothers themselves were appearing in folk clubs across the country: New York City, Denver, Chicago, Los Angeles. Jack Paar introduced them to national television audiences on his *Tonight Show*, while their "live" recordings sold remarkably well. Their act became familiar to millions of Americans: Tommy on guitar, Dick playing bass fiddle; Tommy playing "the dumb one," flubbing his lines, losing his temper, shouting at his calm, seemingly sane and well-adjusted younger brother, "Mom always liked you best," and offering as his favorite snappy comeback to insults, both real and imagined, "Oh, yeah!" After nearly a decade of building a reputation in the entertainment industry, the Smothers Brothers received an invitation from CBS to star in a prime-time television variety series.

The Smothers Brothers Comedy Hour was born as a mid-season replacement in the winter of 1966. At the time, *McHale's Navy, My Three Sons,* and *Gilligan's Island* dominated television comedy. Lucille Ball still played at some variation of her Lucy Ricardo role. Only a few critics like Jack Gould sensed the possibility that the Smothers Brothers might rock the foundations of television comedy. Unexpectedly, the Smothers Brothers turned their show into a kind of prime-time showcase for the generally antiestablishment trends of the counterculture. They presented their audience of 30 million viewers with folksingers, little-known rock groups, and social satire of a kind not then seen on television.

At first, the Smothers Brothers faced the expected squabbles over what the network deemed to be "blue" material. A reference to "breasts" in an Elaine May sketch had to be cut from the very first show. Sam

Taylor, editor of CBS-TV's West Coast Department of Program Practices, regularly reviewed show scripts and carefully weeded out material deemed inappropriate. Jokes using the word "conception," Taylor wrote in one memo, "are not acceptable." Likewise, the verse in the song "The First Time Ever I Saw Your Face" that begins "The first time ever I lay with you" could not be put on the air. CBS vice-president Perry Lafferty chafed at a line from a *Romeo and Juliet* satire in which Nanette Fabray asks Tom (as Romeo), "Did you get that girl in trouble?" That line never made it to the air.[9]

Apparently, by February 1968 those standards had relaxed a little. Jokes about female nudity and sex became somewhat acceptable, certainly more common with the popularity of Johnny Carson on *The Tonight Show* and the phenomenal success of *Laugh-In*, both on NBC-TV. Knowing now that such traditional bawdy humor could help attract an audience, CBS allowed lines in 1968 that they almost certainly would have cut in 1966. A mock poll conducted on the February 25, 1968, show has Dick Smothers asking Pat Paulsen, as an advertising executive, about the quality of programs on television:

Dick: What do you think is the most important concern for an advertising agency?

Pat: The most important thing is to find the right program for the right advertiser. For instance, one of our clients was the Dearform Brassiere Company, and we linked them up with the perfect show.

Dick: And what was that show?

Pat: "The Big Valley."

Whether the cause of humor had been advanced any, the flexibility to use such "blue" material had clearly grown in two years.

But problems of this kind had plagued television comedians since the earliest years of the medium and were to be expected. What troubled network executives much more was the fact that Tom was beginning to direct his humor down decidedly political avenues. "A lot of sacred cows were being knocked down then," says Tom to explain his slowly emerging political awareness. Additionally, the Smothers Brothers were keenly sensitive to the changing attitudes of the young audience that had lifted them to popularity in the first place. "All across the country, people became aware," points out Tom. "We just happened to be two kids," he says with studied understatement, "who had a television show."[10]

Antiwar messages and references to drugs began creeping into the material. On the same show as the *Romeo and Juliet* skit, a mild, indirect drug reference considerably perturbed Perry Lafferty. Actress Leigh French appeared as a "hippie" in what was to become a regular feature on the show, "Tea with Goldie." The announcer invited the audience to "share a little tea with Goldie," and Leigh French explains, "I'm *drinking* it today."[11] Lafferty ordered that line cut. Again, the change over a two-year span is obvious when the hostess of "Tea with Goldie" ends a "helpful hint" segment on the February 25, 1968, show by noting, "Remember, ladies, if you have a groovy hint, you just roll it up and send it in. And if it's really groovy, we'll share it."

The resistance to Tom and Dick came not just from Lafferty, but also from Michael Dann, CBS director of programming. Dann and Lafferty fought the brothers at every turn. "The whole series was a weekly clash over something," recalls Tom. "It was always something."[12]

Dann did not wish to muzzle the singers entirely and thereby jeopardize the show's popularity. He did, however, insist on prohibiting the use of comedy built around two themes: religion, and opposition to the Vietnam War. Dann, for example, purged a statement made by folksinger Joan Baez in support of the antiwar movement. At the taping, Baez introduced a song by dedicating it to her husband, who, she told the audience, was then in jail for resisting the draft. After the censor went to work, however, Baez's pronouncement emerged considerably altered. "I want to dedicate this song to my husband," Baez was heard to say, "who is in jail."[13] For what, viewers might have wondered? Holding up a bank?

Such political censorship occurred with regularity. A seven-and-a-half-minute segment involving Harry Belafonte singing "Lord, Lord, Don't Stop the Carnival" against a backdrop of film clips from the riot-marred 1968 Democratic convention in Chicago never made it to the air. Tom was even more infuriated that CBS sold five minutes out of that same show to the Republican National Committee to plug the candidacy of Richard Nixon. Neither did pointed religious satires by comedian David Steinberg get on the air, at least not in their entirety. The show was not to be used, insisted CBS-TV President Robert Wood in an angry memorandum to his young stars, "as a device to push for new standards."[14]

What was taking place from week to week was a clash of cultures between CBS and the Smothers Brothers. The performers and writers of the show were all relatively young and sensitive to the emerging countercultural values of America's youth. And that sensitivity explains in large measure the popularity of the show. But the uniqueness of social commentary on prime-time television perplexed and upset CBS executives.

Before the Smothers Brothers, television censorship mainly meant dealing with four-letter words, sexual references, toilet jokes, and plunging necklines. Now, Tom and Dick introduced political humor. To make matters worse, the social commentary of the Smothers Brothers came not from the political right, but from the left. Observed Tom at the time, "Nobody bothers hawks like Bob Hope."[15] The identification of the show with countercultural values may seem politically harmless, certainly not revolutionary, from a vantage point of later years. But television executives, like many other traditionally oriented Americans tended to exaggerate the threat such countercultural values represented.

In attempting to fashion a manifesto of the counterculture, Charles Reich argued in *Greening of America* (1970) that the coming revolution "will originate with the individual and with culture and will change the political structure only as its final act." Abbie Hoffman placed a similar stress on the presumed forces of the counterculture. In 1967 he attempted to end the war in Vietnam by performing an exorcism of the Pentagon building, apparently intending to levitate it and thus disintegrate the entire military-industrial complex. "When I appear in the courtroom," Hoffman declared on the eve of the 1969 Chicago conspiracy trial in which he was a defendant, "I want to be tried not because I support the National Liberation Front—which I do—but because I have long hair . . . because I smoke dope."[16]

Abbie Hoffman never appeared on the Smothers Brothers show, of course, but there was plenty of long hair (none of it sported by the squeaky-clean-cut Smothers Brothers themselves) and joking, easy references to drugs. If Abbie Hoffman and Charles Reich felt that long hair and drugs were the vanguard of the coming revolution, then Robert Woods, Perry Lafferty, and Michael Dann might have felt that there was good reason to keep the air clean of such subversive elements.

It was just this intense desire to maintain some semblance of control over the show's content that led Michael Dann to institute a policy unique in all of television for this one show, whereby the network allowed its affiliate stations to preview each individual tape of *The Smothers Brothers Comedy Hour* two days prior to the Sunday-night airing of the show. In that way, each affiliate director could decide for himself or herself whether to air that particular show.[17] In fact, it was pressure from local affiliates that CBS executives most often cited as the reason for their queasiness over the Smothers Brothers' show.[18]

Still, it is amazing how much satire did make it to the air each Sunday night. As the show zoomed into the top ten and, remarkably, knocked *Bonanza* out of its number-one slot, Lafferty and Dann became increasingly tolerant of the political and social comedy of the Smothers Brothers.

Take the February 25 exchange between Dick Smothers and black actor Scooey Mitchell. While race riots wracked urban America for several years (particularly the months following the assassination of Martin Luther King, Jr., in April 1968), black actors appeared only occasionally on television, and in roles little differentiated from their white counterparts (Bill Cosby in *I Spy*, and Diahann Carroll in *Julia*). Frank discussion on television about the lack of black representation on the airways was rare, comedy built on such a premise rarer still. It is in that context that the Smothers-Mitchell dialogue seems like something of a breakthrough. Anger and an awareness of hostility, hypocrisy, and bad intentions crackle just beneath the surface on a remarkably gentle exchange between Dick and a black television viewer (Mitchell) improbably named "George Wallace":

Dick: Tell me, Mr. Wallace, are you still having trouble with that name of yours?

George: Yeah, it's a drag. People keep calling me and asking if I'm running for President.

Dick: Well, are you running?

George: . . . No, I'm not running anywhere. Not unless he wins. *Then* I'll run.

After dismissing the incipient presidential campaign of Alabama governor and staunch segregationist George Wallace, the skit pokes some fun at one of the well-known side benefits of the unfortunate race riots:

George: (*Pointing to his television set*). I just got this set yesterday. My cousin got it for me. Walnut cabinet, full color, 27-inch picture tube. I got one of these remote controls . . . My cousin got it for me. Eight dollars.

Dick: Wow. Where'd he get such a bargain?

George: I don't know where he got it. But he told me when I watch it to sort of (*casts a furtive glance over his shoulder*) watch it like this.

Finally, the "interview" get to the heart of the matter:

Dick: Being a television viewer, what is your reaction to the current programs?

George: I'm glad you asked me that. I don't believe television programs give a true picture of life in this country. It's unfair.

Dick: How can you explain that?

George: Well, look. The Flying Nun is white. Gomer Pyle is white. Tarzan, with all the running he does around in the jungle, *he's* white . . . And ten percent of the country is Negro. And the only colored star we got is Smokey the Bear.

Dick: But, Mr. Wallace. I seem to see more and more Negroes on television every day.

George: Yeah, but you get tired of watching basketball games.

Dick: What about commercials?

George: Well, the commercials aren't any better than the programs are. A friend of mine was in a commercial where he shaved under water.

Dick: Well, what's so unfair about that?

George: With an electric razor?

Dick: Well, there must be some way to get more Negroes on television.

George: Well, look. I told you before, ten percent of the population is Negro. Right?

Dick: Right.

George: So therefore, one out of every ten programs should have a Negro star. Simple.

Dick: One out of ten. That sounds fair.

George: Sure.

Dick: But if it were true, you know, some very big stars would have to be replaced by negroes. Even one of the Smothers Brothers might have to be colored.

George: Naw. You can forget about that, baby.

Dick: Why?
George: We'd probably get the dumb one.

A slightly more traditional, but nonetheless pointed jab at television over the empty-headedness of programming and advertising executives came later in the same skit. Dick is now "interviewing" Pat Paulsen playing the head of a large advertising agency. It is a head, the jokes make clear, endowed with little more than hot air:

Dick: What do you look for when you decide to sponsor a show?
Pat: Truth and quality, but most of all integrity.
Dick: But what if the show is not a hit?
Pat: Then we dump integrity and go for junk . . .
Dick: Don't you think this will drive people away from watching shows on television?
Pat: On the contrary. A recent survey shows that, today, more people watch shows on television than on any other appliance. Toasters are second.

To drive home the final point, Dick ends the poll bit by reminding viewers that "movies are better than ever."

Pointed political satire was prominent on that February show. The Smothers Brothers show clearly and openly aligned itself with the antiwar movement (Goldie draws the peace sign with foam, and the emblem of the antiwar movement also appears on the breast pocket of guest Dan Rowan's blazer), and by early 1968 the antiwar movement was also, decidedly, an anti-President Johnson movement. Up to several months before this show, political experts assumed the president would be a shoo-in for his own party's nomination, and a likely victor over whoever the Republicans might put up in the fall. Eugene McCarthy, a senator from Minnesota, was challenging the president in the New Hampshire primary, to be held the following month. But his challenge, based almost entirely on opposition to the war, was given little serious chance. The junior senator from New York, Robert Kennedy, offered his own objections to the president's conduct of the war while he waited, Hamletlike, on the sidelines.

But already, by the time the show was taped, Johnson had cause for unease. The Tet offensive of late January–early February had held up for all to see the extreme vulnerability of the American position and the hollowness of Johnson's assurances of ultimate victory. Polls were beginning to pick up slippage of his popularity and an increase in public support for the antiwar position.[19] Pat Paulsen, a Smothers Brothers regular, conducted a mock campaign for the presidency that proclaimed the show's message in only slightly veiled humor:

Question: Mr. Paulsen, why are you running for the highest office in the nation?

Pat: A lot of people think we're doing this for laughs, but we're really serious about it. We feel that when the election comes, there'll be no choice for anybody. Therefore, we want to put somebody in the White House to add a little charm and brightness.

The contrast between Paulsen's last line and his dour appearance adds the only touch of humor to this otherwise dead serious declaration of alienation.

Paulsen gets the biggest laugh of the night's show with another line aimed directly at the president. It is when he is playing the advertising agency executive who is explaining the necessity of finding the right program for the right advertiser:

Pat: But the best match we ever made was when we got a call from the White House, and President Johnson hired us to promote his popularity.

Dick: Well, what show did you get for him?

Pat: "Mission Impossible."

Paulsen was right. Almost precisely a month later, Johnson withdrew his name from consideration for the nomination.

And then, of course, there was the appearance by Pete Seeger.

Pete Seeger began his performing career in March 1940 when he appeared, along with Woody Guthrie, at a New York City benefit organized by actor Will Geer (later to costar in CBS-TV's hit series *The Waltons*) on behalf of California migrant workers. After World War II, Seeger brought together a group, called People's Songs, with the idea of promoting both folk music and radical politics. In fact, Seeger's involvement with left-wing political groups dated back to his undergraduate days at Harvard, where he was a member first of the socialist American Student Union and then of the Young Communist League. After leaving Harvard he eventually joined the American Communist Party and remained a member, active to the extent that his schedule and temperament allowed, through the early 1950s.[20]

It was in 1948 that Seeger, together with Lee Hays, Ronnie Gilbert, and Fred Hellerman, formed a singing group called the Weavers, with the expressed purpose of downplaying the political content of the folk music in an attempt to reach a broader, popular audience. The Weavers succeeded beyond Seeger's wildest imagination. In November 1949 they were performing at Max Gordon's small New York City club, the Village Vanguard. Seven months later, Decca Records released the Weavers' first single, "Tzena, Tzena, Tzena" backed by "Goodnight, Irene" (somewhat cleaned up from Leadbelly's original version for popular consumption). The public response to the Weaver's music must have stunned all concerned. *Billboard* heralded "Irene" as a record "likely to achieve popularity," and by mid-July listed both "Tzena" and "Irene" among the nation's best-selling pop singles. In August, when "Irene" soared to number one, *Billboard* proclaimed it as possibly "the biggest hit of the era."[21]

The Weavers' popularity demonstrated remarkable staying power. Their second release, "Roving Kind," reached *Billboard's* top twenty. *Cashbox*, the trade journal of the jukebox industry, recognized the Weavers' phenomenal impact by featuring them on an August 1950 cover. The *New York Daily Mirror* put on a charity benefit and invited the Weavers to share the spotlight with Milton Berle. The quartet quickly became, in *Billboard*'s words, a "hot class spot," appearing at the best clubs in New York, Las Vegas, and Hollywood. For the 122 weeks after the release of "Irene," a Weavers record appeared on *Billboard*'s best-seller list seventy-four times. For twenty-five of those weeks, in fact, two Weavers' songs appeared simultaneously.[22] The irony of all this popularity is that, during its entire span, the Weavers were being blacklisted.

Pete Seeger was no stranger to political attacks from the right. The Almanac Singers, one of Seeger's early folk groups, had been denounced as "Fifth Column propagandists" in the *Atlantic Monthly*, and as "the American Communist's favorite ballad singers" on the front page of the *Chicago Tribune*. In 1947 a group of three ex-FBI agents began publishing the weekly newsletter *Counterattack* "to obtain, file, and index factual information on Communists, Communist fronts, and other subversive organizations." Pete Seeger's name, along with that of the other Weavers, appeared often on its pages. When the editors of *Counterattack* issued *Red Channels* in June of 1950 as a special report on communism in the entertainment industry, Seeger was one of the entertainers featured.[23]

The television industry responded immediately to the appearance of *Red Channels*. General Foods, the sponsor of a new television version of the popular radio series *The Aldrich Family*, slated for a September 1950 premiere on NBC, abruptly fired actress Jean Muir from a leading role. Muir had been listed in *Red Channels* and, as a General Foods' spokesperson explained, "Using her would have been akin to sending out a poor salesman in an area where the salesman was disliked." While General Foods had no concern with the particulars of the charges against the actress, the spokesperson admitted, and while in fact the company regarded *Red Channels* as a "terrible menace," the company felt it had no choice but to fire Muir. "She had apparently become a controversial figure," concluded the spokesperson, and would only "alienate the goodwill of a great many customers." Apparently thinking along the same lines, Stokely-Van Camp withdrew its sponsorship of an NBC show scheduled to use the Weavers in June 1950.[24] Pete Seeger did not appear on commercial television for the remainder of the decade, and in fact did not break through the anti-Communist blacklist until September 1967.

While the entertainment industry blacklist had no officially designated beginning and end, two watershed years can be identified: 1950 for the beginning, and 1960 for an end. *Red Channels*, whose appearance coincided almost precisely with the opening of the Korean War, heralded the coming of the blacklist for that portion of the industry centered in New York City. The blacklist settled on Hollywood that same year, marked by the final Supreme Court decision to send the Hollywood Ten (a group of left-wing screenwriters whose fiery appearance before the House Un-American Activities Committee (HUAC) in 1947 led to contempt-of-Congress convictions) to prison. Confident in the legal righteousness of its position now, HUAC reopened its Hollywood hearings and began amassing names of "subversive" entertainers. Prior to 1950 only the Hollywood Ten lost jobs because of their refusal to cooperate with HUAC; starting that year, the lists grew and grew.

The end of the blacklist is somewhat harder to pinpoint. Cracks began to appear as early as 1957 when the Motion Picture Academy awarded its Oscar for best screenwriting to Robert Rich. The academy soon learned, much to its embarrassment, that no such person existed: "Robert Rich" was a pseudonym for Dalton Trumbo, one of the notorious Hollywood Ten. That incident exposed a well-known industry "secret" that scores of blacklisted writers had continued to work throughout the decade under assumed names. The sham of the industry's self-righteous anticommunism had been revealed, though the blacklist itself had not yet been openly defied.[25]

Then, on January 20, 1960, *Daily Variety* reported that producer Otto Preminger had hired Dalton Trumbo to write the screenplay for *Exodus*. That a major Hollywood producer working on an expensive motion picture was willing to risk hiring an identified, unrepentant Communist represented the first open defiance of the blacklist. Suddenly, the floodgates flew open. One major studio after another discovered the "courage" to defy the blacklist. In May 1960 MGM disclosed plans to distribute a foreign-made film by blacklisted writer Jules Dassin (*Never on Sunday*); and Twentieth Century-Fox openly hired Sidney Buchman, another blacklisted writer. The next month, the Screen Writers' Guild reached an agreement wherein no producer could deny screen credit to a writer just because he or she had been identified before HUAC as a Communist (a practice accepted throughout the 1950s). Almost simultaneously, Sam Spiegel announced the hiring of another blacklisted writer, Michael Wilson, to work on one of the industry's most expensive projects, *Lawrence of Arabia*. *Exodus* opened in New York in December and, despite condemnation by the American Legion, became an immediate box office success. The following January, newly inagurated President John Kennedy joined his brother, Attorney General Robert Kennedy, in attending a public showing of *Spartacus*, another movie written by Trumbo and subjected to an American Legion boycott. The president made no comment about the politics behind *Spartacus*. In fact, he made no comment at all about his attendance. Like millions of other Americans, he was apparently interested only in seeing a good movie, and was unconcerned with the political background of the screenwriter. The Hollywood blacklist had indeed ended.[26]

Blacklisted actors began making their way back onto television as well, but much more slowly. The fact that Seeger could not break through the blacklist until 1967 was due, in part, to the man himself. While many other blacklisted writers and performers were being condemned for political activism that had taken place in the past, most often in the Depression years, Seeger remained defiantly and openly radical. Not only did he refuse to cooperate with HUAC when called to testify in 1955, but he declined to seek the Constitutional protection of the Fifth Amendment. Instead, he told the committee that questions about his political beliefs were none of their business. He escaped imprisonment only when his one-year sentence was overturned on a technicality. Seeger sang at his first anti-Vietnam War demonstration in 1954 and, throughout the 1950s and 1960s, was an active voice in the peace and civil rights movements.

Even so, the television industry displayed a special sensitivity to political radicalism. All through the early and mid-1960s, Columbia Broadcasting System's record division released and promoted Pete Seeger records while Columbia's television division avoided him entirely. The decision to use or not use Seeger, then, was based not so much on the political preferences of CBS corporate executives, but rather on the structure of the particular industry.

Several special characteristics seem to increase the vulnerability of television to political pressure groups. First, unlike the other mass media, television came of age during the height of America's anti-Communist crusade. In 1948, just as HUAC shifted its attention from Communist infiltration of the motion picture industry to the accusations against Alger Hiss, television developed a national audience. The number of cities served by television stations jumped in that year to twenty-three as compared to only eight in 1947. At the same time, sales of television sets climbed 500 percent and, with 172,000 homes owning sets, the potential audience for television programs soared an astronomical 4,000 percent. Network profits grew accordingly. In 1950, when *Red Channels* appeared on the desks of television executives, CBS-TV earned $4.1 million. Within four years, that figure had grown to almost $11 million. The television industry formed its consciousness at the very peak of the anti-Communist crusade, and timidity became a deeply embedded feature of the industry's executives.

Then too, the potential size of the audience makes television unique in comparison to other media. In 1953 television reached into 21 million homes. By the mid-1960s, 55 million homes, or 94 percent of the total, were equipped with at least one set. With a potentially immense audience, television executives aimed their product at a much broader range of the public than did other media. A successful nightclub act, for example, need attract only several thousand patrons in each city. A "gold" album, the pinnacle of commercial achievement in the record industry, comes with the sale of only five hundred thousand records in a nation with over 61 million phonographs. Even movies play to audiences significantly smaller than television's. In 1950, 36 million Americans attended movies each week, and that figure rose to just over 40 million by the 1960s.

What all these figures mean is that a single popular television show can, and usually does, outdraw a week' s total nationwide movie attendance. Nightclubs, records, and to a lesser extent movies can appeal to a limited, specific subgroup within the general population and still remain commercially successful. Television executives, however, constantly aim at a television audience of tens of millions. Jokes about drugs and long-haired rock musicians might appeal to some groups, but would they attract and keep an audience of 40 million? That each single rating point can be worth millions of dollars in revenue leads executives to ponder long and hard this question of mass taste.

Television's direct relationship with commercial sponsors makes it especially responsible to certain pressures. With nightclubs, records, and motion pictures, an entertainment "package" is sold directly to the public. In television, however, networks must first sell their product to sponsors. While pressures can and have been applied by individual radio stations against certain record companies,[27] that control is entirely indirect and comes only after a record has been produced and distributed. Television arranges for sponsorship before airing a show, thus allowing censors the unparalleled opportunity for prior censorship over programming.

Particularly in the early years, television allowed advertisers almost total control over program decisions, continuing a practice that originated with radio. The television industry offered for purchase entire periods of broadcasting time. The sponsor, then, could completely "own" a television program and make all decisions concerning its content. Sponsors were directly associated with specific programs in the minds of an audience ranging into the millions, and those sponsors felt strongly that their corporate image was linked to the program. Thus the commercial structure of the television industry made it especially susceptible to the pressures of the blacklist.

The practice of total program sponsorship ended in the early 1960s when steeply rising production costs forced sponsors to share commercial time and thus give up the complete ownership of a show. By mid-decade, independent "package companies" produced nearly 90 percent of all evening entertainment programs. Sponsors still maintained a critical position within the industry, but their loss of absolute control contributed to the general demise of the blacklist in the early 1960s.

From the industry's beginning, sponsors sought to avoid alienating any segment of the potential market. *Sponsor*, a journal designed specifically for the broadcast industry, advised in its premiere issue of 1946 against mixing merchandising with controversy of any sort. "Censorship," it editorialized, "is integral to the purpose of creating good will." The businessman must always "echo public taste" while avoiding "the opposite values." Since broadcast sponsors function as businessmen, *Sponsor* urged them to have "no association with political, artistic, or literary avant-garde." For a sponsor to intrude political or social "preferences" into programming "is to invite counter-attack."[28]

With or without sponsor pressure, network executives found anticommunism to be an expedient posture. The unique structure of the television industry played an important role in reinforcing corporate conservatism. Networks depend on sponsors to provide program revenue, but they also depend on local station affiliates to provide them with a national market. But government regulations have created a fragile relationship between the networks and their local affiliates. Congress created the Federal Communications Commission (FCC) in 1934 to regulate the broadcast industry, and in 1940 the FCC promulgated rules governing the relationship between the local licensee and the networks. Those rules, particularly the ones concerning program "clearance," allowed local station owners an expected degree of power over industry operations.

One critical FCC directive allowed networks to own and operate no more than five television stations around the country. To develop a truly national market and thus attract large sponsors, networks turned to local television stations as necessary outlets. Local stations contracted to carry national programming. But the 1940 FCC rules allow local stations to reject *any* network offering they might find unsuitable, even if that station has signed a contract to carry the program. Thus, local affiliates have the final word on whether to "clear" a network offering. Each additional outlet is, of course, critical in determining how much a network can charge for advertising time. Network executives are understandably reluctant to alienate station owners. It is true that if a local station declines to carry an inordinate number of network shows, the network can retaliate by withdrawing its affiliation. But the network would first want to be sure to have another outlet available in the same market, and the number of available outlets in any one market is strictly limited both by the economics of station ownership and by FCC regulations over licensing. Making matters more difficult during the opening years of the blacklist, the FCC had, due to the chaotic growth of the industry after World War II, decreed a freeze on license granting that lasted from 1948 to 1952.

Those rules and regulations had the effect of accentuating the cautious attitude of network executives, who realized they had to be extremely sensitive to the expectations, whims, and prejudices of local affiliate owners. CBS learned that lesson from the problems it encountered throughout the 1950s in arranging clearance for news shows featuring the controversial Edward R. Murrow. For most of the decade, over half of its affiliates refused to carry Murrow's regular news documentaries. So network executives, those of CBS in particular, well knew the potential difficulties of using allegedly subversive or even controversial performers and offering them to local affiliates.

Pete Seeger ran headlong into the conservatism of network television several times through the 1960s. The most dramatic example was ABC-TV's failure to use him for their *Hootenanny* show, the one show on television devoted to the folk-music boom for which Seeger, more than any other single performer, was responsible. (Even the word *hootenanny* was introduced to folk circles by Seeger and Woody Guthrie.) Richard Lewine, the head of the independent packaging company producing *Hootenanny*, explained that neither Seeger nor his former singing group, the Weavers, would be considered for the show since they were not "punchy enough . . . We wanted better singers . . . groups that would carry a national audience." After pressure from other folk singers (Joan Baez, Bob Dylan, and Peter, Paul, and Mary were among those who refused to appear after learning of the Seeger ban), Lewine dropped all pretense and announced that Seeger and the Weavers would be "considered" after all, but only if they signed a loyalty oath.[29] No loyalty oath was signed, and neither Seeger nor the Weavers appeared.

The anti-Communist crusade had lost much of its steam by 1963, but it had not died completely. Crises in Berlin and Cuba reminded the American public that Soviet communism still exerted strong influence over world affairs. Public opinion polls taken as late as mid-decade indicated that a good many Americans considered internal communism to be a threat. Almost half the respondents thought Communists had been involved in civil rights demonstrations, while 59 percent disapproved of moves to legalize the Communist Party.[30] The best Seeger could do by 1966 was to appear on CBS-TV's Sunday morning noncommercial program, *Camera Three*. But Seeger was determined to end all that, and he told an interviewer that year that one of his major personal goals for 1967 was to "try to break through the television blacklist."[31] Indeed, in 1967, seventeen years after the appearance of *Red Channels* and seven years after the collapse of the Hollywood blacklist, Seeger received an invitation to appear on the Smothers Brothers' show.

"We want America to sit back and think while they're watching our show," explained Smothers Brothers' coproducer Saul Ilson. "Not that we're doing these things to be controversial," he added, "but to let our audience know that we know what's going on." For that reason, Tom Smothers decided to invite Seeger. Ilson explained that decision by saying, "Nobody seems to be breaking new ground on TV, so we look upon Pete's appearance as an important event." Tom added, "I wanted Seeger in because he's a famous folk singer. Like the Weavers and all those people, he's a legend to me."[32]

Predictably, neither Perry Lafferty nor Michael Dann shared that enthusiasm for Seeger. Lafferty spoke up first. "We're getting nasty letters *now*," he told Tom. "Now you're going to put this Pete Seeger on? I don't want him!"[33]

But Tom was more determined than ever. At the beginning of his show's run on CBS, he had been given complete artistic control, which meant that he had the right to select his own guests. So there really was not much Lafferty could do about Seeger. "Okay, but," Lafferty added ominously, if somewhat vaguely, "you're going to have to pay the consequences."[34]

From his New York City office, Michael Dann informed the press that the Smothers Brothers had submitted Seeger's name on a list of planned guests and the network had routinely approved. No, he said, he had not bothered to seek the consent of the show's sponsors, or for that matter even to contact them.[35]

Amid a great deal of publicity and self-congratulations on its corporate bravery, CBS permitted Seeger to sing on the Smothers Brothers' show. And for a while at least, the network basked in the warm glow of liberal approval. "Mr. Seeger's long banishment from the networks did not prevent him from being heard by large and enthusiastic audiences in concerts and on records," came a typical response, this from the *St. Louis Post-Dispatch*. "It will be good to see and hear him again on TV."[36]

But, as it turned out, CBS was not quite as ready for Seeger as it first appeared. In 1967 nobody but a few right-wing extremists raised the issue of Communist infiltration of the entertainment industry. But the nation was sharply divided at the time on the conduct and propriety both of the Vietnam War and the domestic opposition to that war. And Seeger insisted on using his prime-time access to convey his own resistance to the war in Vietnam. When Tom asked Seeger what he wanted to sing on the program, Seeger listed several songs and then added, "I'd also like to sing 'Waist Deep in the Big Muddy.'"[37]

That song was a new composition by Seeger that attacked President Johnson and the war indirectly, through the use of parable.

It told of a World War II incident in which a commanding officer ordered his platoon to forge the Big Muddy River while on a routine training march. Having no idea that the river was both deep and dangerous, the commander nearly drowned the entire platoon before being swept away himself. In the critical sixth stanza, Seeger related the incident to current events: all you have to do is read the newspapers to realize that we are once again "Waist Deep in the Big Muddy," while "the Big Fool says to push on."

Columbia Records had just released a Seeger album with "Waist Deep" as the title song. But what CBS would accept on its records, it refused to tolerate on its television network. Michael Dann complained to Tom that some listeners might interpret the sixth stanza as an attack on the president and his handling of the war, to which Tom replied, "Oh, don't be ridiculous."[38]

At that point, some CBS executive suggested a "compromise." Maybe Seeger could sing "Waist Deep" but without the sixth stanza. Pluck out the offending words. Seeger, naturally, would have no part of that suggestion and Tom stood by his guest. "That stanza is the whole point of the song," he argued. "He's got to sing the whole song."[39]

At the taping session, Segger sang "Waist Deep" in its entirety. The audience exploded into applause, and Tom thought, "It was wonderful." Michael Dann thought otherwise. "We felt that other music would make a better contribution to the show," Dan explained as he ordered the "Waist Deep" segment removed from the tape shown over the air.[40]

The issue might have died at that point if not for Seeger's insistence on making the dispute public. Immediately phoning a reporter for the *New York Times*, he explained what had happened. "It's important for people to realize that what they see on television is screened," he emphasized, "not just for good taste, but for ideas."[41] Tom joined the battle by inviting Seeger to return for the February 25, 1968, show.

When Tom and Seeger met to tape the new show, Tom inquired, "Want to try 'Waist Deep' again?"

"Yup," replied Seeger, "I sure do."

"Let's go for it," answered Tom.[42]

This time around, Michael Dann and the rest of CBS relented. Their change of heart may have been due to the avalanche of bad publicity following their first show. Additionally, the fact that the popularity of the Smothers Brothers had continued to climb did not lessen Tom's clout with the network. So this time, "Waist Deep" made it to the air.

The day following the February 25th show, the *Times* reported only one noticeable ripple. In Detroit the local CBS affiliate director had previewed the tape and erased the section containing "Waist Deep."[43]

Ironically, the Seeger victory came in the next-to-the-last season of the Smothers Brothers' show. Despite its continued increase in popularity, the show fell victim to the network axe in April 1969. CBS spokespeople claimed that Tom had reneged on his agreement to make program tapes available for prescreening. The tape of the April 14 show, which contained an appearance by antiwar activist Dr. Benjamin Spock, had allegedly arrived at corporate headquarters several days late. CBS leaped at that excuse to rid itself of the troublesome Smothers Brothers.[44]

Even then, the controversy did not die. Tom publicly chastised the network in general and William Paley, chairman of the board, in particular. Pointing to Paley's friendship with Richard Nixon and his expressed desire to be appointed ambassador to the Court of St. James, Tom wondered aloud whether a deal might have been struck between the two. Just three months after Nixon's inauguration, Paley removed from the air the one show that contained any criticism of the president.[45] (In any event, Paley never received his appointment.)

The final act of the dispute commenced when Tom and Dick hauled their former employers into court. CBS, the brothers alleged, had violated their contractual agreement by canceling the show before the end of the 1968–1969 season. The U.S. District Court in California agreed, awarding Tom and Dick Smothers $776,300.[46]

In his 1970 survey of popular arts in America, Russel Nye quickly dismisses the Smothers Brothers. "The only extensive attempt at satirically edged social commentary, that of the Smothers Brothers in 1968," writes Nye in *The Unembarrassed Muse*, "proved inept and immature."[47] But the significance of the show was that political commentary was there at all. This is not to say that the Smothers Brothers were radicals or that their show represented the coming to prime-time commercial television of political radicalism or the values of the counterculture. They were hardly in the vanguard of public opinion when it came to the war, civil rights, or even drug use. Instead of leading opinion, they seemed to reflect the views already extant in large segments of the public.

What can be said, however, is that the absolute dread and total rejection of political content, a last vestige of the McCarthy era, had at last been broken. Within a year of the departure of *The Smothers Brothers Comedy Hour* from CBS, shows like *Laugh-In* and *All In the Family* delighted audiences and soared to the top of the ratings charts with their own brands of social and political humor.

In a real way, Tom and Dick Smothers had paved the way.

NOTES

1. This and all subsequent quotations from the 25 February 1968 show are taken from the program tape provided to the author by Smothers, Inc. The author would like to thank Smothers, Inc., for its cooperation.

2. Seeger's inscription was in response to the more fiery, radical words scrawled by Seeger's long-time friend and mentor, Woody Guthrie, on his own guitar: "This machine kills fascists."

3. *New York Times*, 16 October 1967, p. 91.

4. For a discussion of that connection see R. Serge Denisoff, *Great Day Coming: Folk Music and the American Left* (Urbana, Ill., 1971); Richard A. Reuss, "American Folklore and Left-Wing Politics" (Ph.D. diss. Indiana University, 1971); Bert A. Spector, "'Wasn't That a Time?': Pete Seeger and the Anti-Communist Crusade, 1940–1968" (Ph.D. diss. University of Missouri, 1977).

182   AMERICAN HISTORY/AMERICAN TELEVISION

5. Tom Smothers, interview with author, New York City, 20 April 1979.

6. Ibid.

7. *Time*, 11 July 1960, p. 81.

8. Pete Seeger, interview with author, Beacon, New York, 1–2 October 1975.

9. *New York Times*, 16 April 1967, p. 2:21; CBS memorandum, 16 October 1967, *The Smothers Brothers Comedy Hour* Collection, Theater Arts Library, University of California-Los Angeles; *New York Times*, 27 January 1968, p. 58.

10. Tom Smothers interview.

11. *New York Times*, 27 January 1968, p. 58.

12. Tom Smothers interview.

13. Robert Metz, *CBS: Reflections in a Bloodshot Eye* (New York, 1975), p. 301.

14. Mertz, *Reflections*, p. 303; Tom Smothers interview.

15. *Look*, 24 June 1969, p. 29.

16. Charles Reich, *The Greening of America* (New York, 1970) p. 4; Norman Mailer, *Armies of the Night* (New York, 1968), pp. 138–139; Abbie Hoffman, *Woodstock Nation: A Talk-Rock Album* (New York, 1969), p. 8.

17. Metz, *Reflections*, pp. 294–301.

18. Tom Smothers interview.

19. In 1966 Gallup polls showed that 16 percent of the public thought U.S. military involvement in Vietnam had been a mistake. That figure rose to 41 percent in July 1967 and 45 percent in January 1968. At the same time, those who disapproved of the manner in which President Johnson was handling the war rose from 22 percent in 1965 to 52 percent in July 1967 and 50 percent in February 1968. For results of Gallup polls, see George Gallup, *The Gallup Poll: Public Opinion, 1935–1971* (New York, 1972), pp. 1967, 2074, 2099, 2105.

20. Pete Seeger, letter to author, 15 August 1977.

21. *Billboard*, 24 June 1950, p. 35; *Billboard*, 15 July 1950, pp. 36, 40, 44; *Billboard*, 22 July 1950, pp. 20, 24, 26, 28; *Billboard*, 19 August 1950, p. 13.

22. *Cashbox*, 12 August 1950, cover; *Billboard*, 13 January 1950, p. 14; *New York Post*, 8 September 1950, p. 17; *Los Angeles Mirror*, 2 February 1951, p. 6; *New York Times*, 1 April 1951, p. 11,x; *Variety*, 23 May 1951, p. 56; *Chicago Herald-American*, 6 June 1951, p. 21; *New York Daily News*, 18 September 1950, p. 5.; *New York Daily Mirror*, 18 September 1950, p. 5.

23. *Atlantic Monthly*, June 1941, pp. 661–672; *Chicago Tribune*, 5 January 1943, p. 1; on the founding and early history of *Counterattack* see Merle Miller, *The Judges and the Judged* (New York, 1952), pp. 36, 63–66; *Red Channels: Report on Communist Influence in Radio and Television* (New York, 1950), p. 90.

24. The General Foods and Stokely-Van Camp stories comes from a lengthy article on *Red Channels* in *Sponsor*, 8 October 1951, pp. 28–29, 75–80.

25. Bruce Cook, *Dalton Trumbo* (New York, 1977), pp. 256–262.

26. Ibid., p. 276; Howard Suber, "The Anti-Communist Blacklist in the Motion Picture Industry" (Ph.D. diss. University of California-Los Angeles, 1968), pp. 138, 150–153, 158–159; *New York Times*, 5 February 1961, p. 39.

27. In the 1950s, for instance, some AM stations barred records by Chuck Berry and Jerry Lee Lewis because of the "immoral behavior" of those two singers. George Denisoff, *Solid Gold: The Popular Record Industry* (New Brunswick, N.J.), p. 377.

28. *Sponsor*, November 1946, p. 40; *Sponsor*, 10 September 1951, p. 30.

29. *Variety*, 20 March 1963, p. 66; *New York Post*, 21 March 1963, p. 95; *New York Post*, 22 March 1963, p. 94; *San Francisco Chronicle*, 5 April 1963, p. 43; *Billboard*, 13 April 1963, p. 1; *Broadside*, April 1963, pp. 8–11; *Variety*, 27 May 1963, p. 35; *Broadside*, August 1963, p. 12; *New York Times*, 6 September 1963, p. 71; *Hootenanny*, March 1964, p. 29.

30. Gallup, *Opinion*, pp. 1971, 1976.

31. *Melody Maker*, 3 December 1966, p. 18.

32. Ilson quoted in *New York Times*, 25 August 1967, p. 72; Tom Smothers interview.

33. Tom Smothers interview.

34. Ibid.

35. *New York Times*, 25 August 1967, p. 72.

36. *St. Louis Post-Dispatch*, 2 September 1967, p. 94.

37. Tom Smothers interview.

38. Pete Seeger, *Pete Seeger Sings and Answers Questions at the Ford Hall Forum*, Broadside Records, Album No. 502.

39. Tom Smothers interview.

40. *New York Times*, 13 September 1967, p. 95.

41. *New York Times*, 13 September 1967, p. 95; *Newsweek*, 25 September 1967, p. 118.

42. Tom Smothers interview.

43. *New York Times*, 15 February 1968, p. 87; *New York Times*, 27 February 1968, p. 87.

44. *Look*, 24 June 1969, p. 27.

45. Tom Smothers interview.

46. *New York Times*, 25 September 1969, p. 95; *New York Times*, 7 April 1973, p. 16.

47. Russel B. Nye, *The Unembarrassed Muse: The Popular Arts in America* (New York, 1970), p. 412.

8

Television's Nixon: The Politician and His Image

DAVID CULBERT

The appearance of now Vice-President Nixon on the TV National hook-up was the greatest event that ever happened for T-V. It is simply the very greatest help that any new industry ever had to get started.
—Speaker, Los Angeles Chamber
of Commerce, January 1953[1]

Television came of age during the 1952 campaign. In 1948 there were but sixteen commercial television stations and 170,000 sets, mostly in the northeast. Four years later there were 108 stations and more than 15 million sets. The origins of political television are closely related to the early career of Richard M. Nixon. Were it not for television, he probably would have been dropped from the Republican ticket in September 1952. Were it not for television, he might very well have been president in 1960. This essay will discuss three notorious television appearances by Nixon in 1952, 1960, and 1974, paying attention to details of production and visual content, and attempting to relate each to American society during those years. We will be concerned with effects, not causes; the general question of the precise impact of television on political decision making in American society still awaits a definitive answer. Nixon understood a great deal about manipulation, and how it relates to visual communication. His personal experience showed the way to countless other politicians, in the process helping establish television's central position in selling images to the prospective voter.

Enthusiasts of communications technology have often imagined a new mass medium that would make possible greater individual participation in political decision making. 1952 saw many of these heartening promises made—and believed. Both political parties agreed to meet in Chicago in the same amphitheater to make possible, for the first time, complete nationwide television coverage of the party conventions.[2] There was another first—the convention hall was air conditioned, and advertisers took note. Sponsors sold viewers two expensive "new" necessities: room air conditioners and television sets. In magazine advertisements Jane Russell, admittedly clad in very little, said she kept cool with a handsome "desert sand" room unit; a boiling-hot couple, in a full-page ad, tried to recall the previous winter when they begged for heat. Television manufacturers sold sets against a backdrop of the 1858 Lincoln-Douglas debates. History would be made before your eyes. *Time*'s July 14, 1952, cover showed a map of the United States with a giant eyeball inside. Three television cameras suggested that for the first time, the professional politicians would be routed: the all-seeing eye of television would make it impossible for deals behind closed doors.[3]

If such statements smack of boosterism to a later generation, it is worth noting that party professionals took them seriously indeed. The networks distributed press releases in which they proudly explained their new technology for bringing the entire convention to the home viewer.[4] For example, the "newly-perfected wedge-wipe amplifier device" (split screen) meant that viewers could see two pictures at once. Two mobile units (the size of the van suggests *barely* mobile) permitted such innovations as covering an event outside the convention amphitheater. Walkie-talkies and "peepie-creepies" (mobile camera units on the convention floor) meant that delegates could be interviewed on the spot. Of course the mobile camera required a muscular operator—it weighed ten pounds, plus a fifty-pound transmitter strapped on one's back.

Zoom lenses seemed especially dangerous. During the Republican convention some viewers noticed with displeasure that during invocations delegates "milled around . . . without any show of respect or reverence for the Almighty." Rows of empty seats, or sleeping delegates, made the convention appear less dignified than civics textbooks might have lead one to believe. At least one viewer complained to the Democratic National Committee that delegates paced back and forth near the speakers' platform in hopes of having their pictures seen on TV back home.[5]

The Democratic National Committee's official program warned delegates that "at any moment long distance lenses of television cameras may center upon you personally, subjecting your every expression and casual gesture to the appraising scrutiny of a million eyes!" Every convention hotel-room door had a card hung on it: "YOU'RE BEING WATCHED. Be in your seat tonight at 8!"

Such viewer aids as a "magnetic totalizer" helped keep the balloting clear. According to a CBS press release, a "novel 'elephant race'" showed the "Taft vs. Eisenhower race for the 604 votes needed for nomination" by "the horizontal progress of two white elephants across the viewing screen."[6] Millions of Americans bought or rented television sets to see both conventions gavel to gavel. Dull or not, seeing a convention was new. Viewers were forming visual images of candidates, and television let them see things the candidates did not wish seen.

Politicians agonized about how to use the new medium. Some feared it would make them look ridiculous, or expose their undesirable qualities. How, they wondered, could they hide from a camera that threatened? Instant "experts" offered conflicting advice, some not terribly helpful. The Democratic National Committee issued a booklet with some basic tips: "Men *must* shave before facing the television camera." The leader of a "campaign clinic" held in Washington at the House of Representatives told his audience: "I recommend staying away from programs below the dignity of a Congressman, and wouldn't participate in 'girdle races' or any audience participation shows."[7]

CBS-TV operated a coaching school for candidates, also in Washington, where Speaker of the House Sam Rayburn was told that his bald head offered a target of opportunity for the floodlights television broadcasting required. Rayburn worried about letting someone apply pancake makeup to the top of his head. He said some experts told him white suits were best for television, but the CBS instructors insisted otherwise. Rayburn watched himself on camera to see why wide, sweeping gestures were inappropriate. The use of telephoto lenses clearly bothered him. "Can't a man ever have a moment to relax?" he was quoted as asking. "Well, when I want a smoke, I guess I'll just step down behind the platform." Actor Robert Montgomery, installed as television expert in the White House soon after the Eisenhower victory in November 1952, had his own curious tips. He informed would-be political performers that the use of makeup was *not* advisable. One memorandum from Montgomery's White House office told politicians about the effectiveness on television of chalk talks with a blackboard, a flannel board, even "an Army overcoat or helmet when you discuss defense expenditures." No wonder surviving news kinescopes sometimes have the flavor of the amateur hour.[8]

Speaker Rayburn's worries about television suggest a fundamental fact of life about the 1952 campaign overlooked by partisans, who have described the campaign in terms of Stevenson the witty egghead and Nixon the mud-slinging master of dirty tricks. Both parties eagerly bought a substantial amount of television time; both hoped the new medium, in combination with still-important radio, would do the trick. Both parties used extensive advertising agency assistance. If neither quite understood what might work, it was not for lack of trying. The important role of advertising agencies in the campaign led someone to rewrite a popular Pepsi Cola singing commercial of the day:

> Eisenhower hits the spot
> One full general, that's a lot
> Feeling sluggish, feeling sick?
> Take a dose of Ike and Dick.[9]

A.C. Nielsen ratings help us understand how much attention was given to television in the closing days of the campaign, beginning in early September. Eisenhower bought time for nine nationwide telecasts; Stevenson, fifteen. The best television rating Stevenson got was on September 23, 1952, when he followed Nixon's "Checkers" speech with a speech of his own. Most of the network political broadcasts reached between 3 and 5 million homes. Only Nixon's Checkers speech did better, with nearly 9 million viewers and over 7 million radio listeners.[10] No wonder the Los Angeles Chamber of Commerce speaker considered Nixon's speech the greatest thing ever done for television.

By September 1952, Eisenhower appeared a sure victor in November. Then came a headline story in the *New York Post* on September 18, charging that Nixon had a slush fund which made a mockery of promises to clean up political corruption in Washington. Eisenhower's campaign strategists, who had never liked Nixon, eagerly seized the partisan story. The influential *New York Herald Tribune*, unofficial organ of the Republican party, in an editorial the next day called for Nixon's resignation. As Garry Wills explains so brilliantly in *Nixon Agonistes*, it was the Republican party hierarchy, not the media attacks, that made the *Post* story so serious. Nixon learned that Stevenson had a slush fund of his own, and argued that one is guilty of no crime in making use of a personal campaign fund. The story of the Checkers speech thus has little to do with whether Nixon was guilty, or whether he cleared himself by what he said. The biggest media event of the 1952 campaign concerns Nixon's decision to use the medium of television to take his case directly to the American people.[11]

It was improvisation all the way, starting with Nixon's television adviser. Edward A. (Ted) Rogers was thirty in 1950 when he volunteered to help Nixon in his California senatorial race. A graduate of Cornell University, Rogers that same year had joined the Los Angeles office of Dancer-Fitzgerald-Sample, an advertising agency, where he gained some experience in television. In 1961, at Nixon's request, Rogers prepared a memorandum on what his duties had been in producing the nationwide Checkers speech on September 23.[12] The story of what happened can be reconstructed from Rogers's detailed description.

When the slush fund story broke on Thursday, September 18, Nixon was scheduled to speak in Portland, Oregon, the next day. Campaign adviser Murray Chotiner "began to talk" with Rogers in Portland on the nineteenth about a telecast. Chotiner wanted enough time for a national press buildup, and Rogers said he could not get on the air before Tuesday night, the twenty-third. In 1952 programs could originate only from New York, Chicago, or Los Angeles.

Saturday the *Herald Tribune* called for Nixon's resignation. Late Sunday night, the twenty-first, Chotiner told Rogers that Nixon was ready to cancel his campaign train, fly to Los Angeles, and prepare for the sudden television event. Chotiner gave Rogers a piece of paper that night with the name "Carroll Newton" on it and his home phone in New York City. Newton worked for the advertising agency Batten,

Barton, Durstine & Osborn (BBD&O), and handled all Republican requests for network television time. Newton agreed to get time cleared on all three networks for the broadcast, which meant preempting sponsored time by paying the sponsor not to air its program. Rogers said he wanted the Nixon broadcast as close as possible to the highly popular hour-long *Milton Berle Show*. The Nixon broadcast was set for 9:30 to 10:00 P.M., Eastern Daylight Time, over NBC. To get *Suspense*, the regular program at that hour, preempted, Newton made a personal call to the president of the Auto-Lite Corporation in Toledo.

About 2:00 A.M. Monday morning, still in Portland, Rogers called a close personal friend in Hollywood, John Claar, camera director for the *Eve Arden Show*. Claar galvanized NBC personnel into action. Claar and NBC representatives met Rogers at the Ambassador Hotel on Monday the twenty-second, upon his arrival by plane from Portland. After selecting the El Capitan theater in downtown Los Angeles as the studio, Rogers and Claar went to NBC's scene docks, selected the library set (Nixon told Rogers on the plane that a library would be more "natural" than an office set), and had it shipped to the El Capitan. "From that point forward," Rogers writes, "we worked straight thru Monday night into Tuesday. I wrote the open and close somewhere in there, and got it sent to NBC for mimeo."[13]

Nixon told Rogers he would see him briefly on the afternoon of the twenty-third, to go over what he would say. In the meantime, on Monday afternoon Rogers frantically looked for a Nixon lookalike to come to the studio for lighting and camera placement. In the primitive television world of 1952, it was unheard of to try to light a telecast without the talent being on hand for a number of careful adjustments. A local television-time salesman, Dan Lincoln, was pressed into service and ordered to show up at the El Capitan first thing Tuesday morning.[14] Rogers wrote that with the exception of himself,

> from that point forward until RN walked into the studio minutes before air, no one connected with the telecast, in any capacity, had any contact with RN. We constructed the telecast, item by item, with what I call 'Preventive TV.' This means that no matter what RN would do, because we didn't know what he would do, we placed cameras so that we could get a picture. I had a large shallow oval of a white line painted on the floor downstage of the library set (between RN and the TV cameras and hardware), and when RN came in, for instance, we told him that as

long as he didn't cross that white line, we would get a picture and a good one.[15]

Tuesday afternoon Rogers spent about thirty minutes with Nixon at the Ambassador Hotel, while Nixon "talked through" what he might say. Rogers says Nixon had notes and his familiar yellow legal pads. For the first time Nixon announced that Pat would be on the set with him, and explained that it appeared he would not get photocopies of his financial records from Price-Waterhouse in time to use them. Nixon said he did not know how he would end his broadcast, but "You'll know when I'm finished." All Nixon could suggest was that Rogers "feel" his closing line.

About 6:00 P.M. the Republican hierarchy lowered the boom. New York Governor Thomas Dewey called to tell Nixon he should announce his resignation at the end of the telecast without waiting for a popular response. Nixon was beside himself.[16] He was to go on the air in just thirty minutes.

Nixon rode to the El Capitan, met John Claar and the cameramen for the first time, and sat down in the library set. Rogers recalls someone putting a little pancake makeup on Nixon. Someone removed a vase of flowers from the set and Nixon went on the air at 6:30 P.M. Los Angeles time: "My fellow Americans. I come before you tonight as a candidate for the Vice Presidency and as a man whose honesty and integrity have been questioned." Nixon was seated behind a desk, a large boom microphone above him. The library consisted of a few books, one a dictionary. Nixon wore a light gray suit; he managed to look composed.[17]

He justified his slush fund by saying that others put wives on congressional payrolls and that Stevenson had his own slush fund. He read a legal opinion stating that in fact he was technically guilty of no financial wrongdoing. Then he offered a "complete financial history; everything I've earned; everything I've spent; everything I owe. . . . I'll have to start early." He made a reference to his wife's respectable "Republican cloth coat," a dig at Democratic scandals involving mink coats.

Then came the master stroke. Nixon claims he remembered how Franklin D. Roosevelt had blunted criticism in 1944 by joking about his dog Fala's unhappiness with press attacks.[18] Nixon momentarily covered his face with one hand, then said:

One other thing I probably should tell you, because if I don't they'll probably be saying this about me too. We did get something—a gift—after the election. A man down in Texas heard Pat on the radio mention the fact that our two youngsters would like to have a dog. And, believe it or not, the day before we left on this campaign trip we got a message from Union Station in Baltimore saying they had a package for us. We went down to get it. You know what it was.

It was a little cocker spaniel dog in a crate that he sent all the way from Texas. Black and white spotted. And our little girl—Trisha, the six-year-old, named it Checkers. And you know the kids love the dog and I just want to say this right now, that regardless of what they say about it, we're gonna keep it.

The deed was done, the broadcast scarely half over. Nixon turned to attacking corruption in Washington and read a letter from an admirer too young to vote who enclosed ten dollars from her monthly income of eighty-five dollars. Rejecting the advice of the party hierarchy, he refused to resign from the ticket. Instead Nixon announced he was "submitting to the Republican National Committee tonight through this television broadcast the decision which it is theirs to make." He urged viewers and listeners to "wire and write" but forgot to say where. As the broadcast ran overtime, Nixon's personal business card was superimposed over his face. He was cut off at the end of a sentence in a slow iris fade to black.

Rogers stayed in the control booth during the first twenty minutes of the broadcast, then squatted on the floor in front of Nixon's number-one camera to give the final signals. Nixon, according to Rogers, was so overcome with emotion he did not realize he was off the air, and walked directly into the camera, hitting his shoulder. "The number-one camerman, tears streaming down his own face, jumped around and steadied RN. Every technician was weeping at the conclusion of the telecast." Campaign aides Murray Chotiner and Jim Bassett had watched from the client's booth, and both rushed out to embrace Nixon. Rogers says he took a cab home, collapsed in the front yard, and was helped inside by friends. "I guess I had been up since something like Saturday morning straight through at that point."[19]

Eisenhower watched the address in Cleveland. Garry Wills is surely correct in his analysis of how Nixon had outflanked the campaign managers by making the Republican National Commitee the place to send those wires and letters. Two days later, Eisenhower and Nixon met publicly, and Ike assured Nixon, "You're my boy." But Nixon never forgot that he had been ordered to walk the plank on national television.[20]

Audience response to the broadcast was phenomenal. And because so many of the letters have survived and are carefully analyzed in *The Night Nixon Spoke*, it is impossible not to conclude that what present-day viewers find ridiculous, or unconvincing, really worked in 1952. The surviving letters to Republican party headquarters in Washington number more than 1 million signatures; telegrams and letters ran 350 to 1 in favor of Nixon. In a post-Watergate era it would be impossible to find an audience persuaded by Nixon's tactics. Viewers would side with those who cried "soap opera," or the sentiments contained in a hostile surviving letter:

> How stupid does Nixon think the people are? Puppy dog? Gad! I want to cast my vote for Ike, but will not be able to do so if that demagogue Nixon stays on the ticket. That was a cheap exhibition he performed and completely out of tune with Ike's fine crusade.[21]

Nixon emerged from the Checkers affair not only as vice-president of the United States but also as a self-avowed expert in the use of television. In March 1954, when he insisted that only one camera be used when he made a televised address, reporters praised his judgment. The *New York Times* television critic admiringly suggested that Nixon deserved a "Peabody prize all his own." Jack Gould noted that "the intrusive mixture of angle shots, close-ups and distant shots . . . is avoided," with no "theatrical busybody" interrupting the rapport between speaker and home audience. A year later, Nixon spoke in New York City to the Radio and Television Executives Society about how to be a successful television speaker. The *Times* story described Nixon as "widely regarded as an accomplished television artist." Nixon said that candidates should be prepared to spend as much money building an audience as they do on the air time itself. According to Nixon, he purposely put off the Checkers speech for two days to build suspense. He also indicated that an "intimate fireside technique" was best in political campaigning. Nixon particularly warned of how to avoid television problems: "Be sure the candidate is at his best, not worn down after a breathless day's campaigning." Nixon said he did not rehearse his speech in 1952 for fear of losing spontaneity, but he admitted that an "efficient 'off-the-cuff' appearance on television, creating the illusion of intimacy so desirable to win the viewers . . . entails many hours of preparatory work."[22]

The second of Richard Nixon's critical media experiences came eight years later. By 1960, political uses for television had been around for some time, but not everyone had gotten the word. The president of CBS News, Sig Mickelson, could still feel that newspapers dominated public thinking about politics: "I would also suggest," he told a group of radio and television executives, "that candidates not duck for cover at the sight of a tv camera, be it either film or electronic, in the mistaken belief that only the newspaper is able to purvey the news, but rather recognize that tv is a legitimate medium for the communication of the news."[23]

True, television was covering its third round of national conventions, but it was clear that Kennedy would get the Democratic nomination when the party met in Los Angeles on July 11, and nobody doubted Nixon would be selected when the Republicans met in the Chicago amphitheater two weeks later. *Advertising Age* reported that many viewers tired of watching democracy in action during the Republican convention. In Chicago itself *Wild Bill Hickok* and *Bugs Bunny* received a Trendex rating of 40.5 compared to 27 for the most-watched network coverage of the convention. A Detroit independent station found its audience up 236.6% over normal; one night its audience share was 47 percent as viewers avoided the convention.[24] Few sensed the excitement or uniqueness of watching the conventions for the first time.

Television was in its adolescence and, like real-life teenagers, had gotten into trouble. Revelations of the rigging of popular quiz shows had become public knowledge in 1959. NBC chairman of the board Robert Sarnoff discussed the impact. "It is now six months since the open season on television began with a vengeance," he reported. The charges—mediocrity, imbalance, violence, and overcommercialism—were "long-familiar." He claimed, "There is no firmer basis for those charges now than there has ever been, but those who press them are now armed with the cudgels represented by the quiz-show deceptions, and they are making the most of them." He went on to list a sudden rush of documentaries, operas, and assorted public service offerings that NBC was making available to the American people. The timing seemed a little too perfect.[25]

While the industry was trying to make amends for the quiz-show revelations, the 1960 campaign allowed television again to appear in the responsible role of assisting in democratic political decision making. Meanwhile Congress was at work trying to encourage greater participation in the political process. The Senate passed a resolution in 1960 suspending Section 315 of the Federal Communications Commission (FCC) Act, the "equal time" rule. The FCC had argued that equal time meant equal time for every presidential candidate, no matter how quixotic his crusade. In practice this meant, according to network logic, that no candidate could debate another, since television did not care to give free time to fifteen or sixteen people. Congress proposed lifting the equal time rule to give access only to the major party candidates. The networks wanted to see the suspension of Section 315, but opposed congressional action, lest it encourage the principle of federal regulation of television. *Broadcasting*, the industry organ, editorialized against S.3171, dubbing it the "free time-grab bill." CBS president Frank Stanton agreed, but sought to deflect criticism by promising to do voluntarily what the bill would make mandatory.

Stanton's voluntary plan did not appeal to congressional critics. On August 24, 1960, President Eisenhower signed into law a bill suspending Section 315 of the FCC Code (something successfully opposed by the networks in 1952 and 1956). The Socialist candidate, Eric Hass, protested: "Giving free TV time to the look-alike, talk-alike, act-alike major party candidates, while excluding the candidates of minor parties, is at war with the theory and intent of our constitutional democracy—the theory, that is, that the public should be acquainted with all sides of these vital issues, and, to this end, that there should be a 'free trade in ideas.'"[26]

As the campaign hit the home stretch, John Kennedy certainly had no clear majority. His extreme youth and his Roman Catholic religion were two strikes against him. Nixon, though he had his detractors, had the advantage of having been a public figure since 1948. His two terms as vice-president under a highly popular president made him seem a natural. True, there were more registered Democrats than Republicans, but many of the former felt little initial enthusiasm for their handsome, telegenic candidate.

It is a commonplace among campaigners that no front runner gives unnecessary exposure to a competitor. Why, then, did Nixon ever agree to a series of four hour-long debates carried by all three networks, debates that would be seen by a viewing audience of 75 million? Nixon, in *Six Crises*, offers the following explanation:

> Had I refused the challenge, I would have opened myself to the charge that I was afraid to defend the Administration's and my own record. Even more important, I would be declining to participate in a program which the majority of the American people, regardless of party, wanted to see.

In his *Memoirs*, this is amended slightly: "There was no way I could refuse to debate without having Kennedy and the media turn my refusal into a central campaign issue."[27] But these explanations ring false. Would not Nixon help his rival's cause more than his own by appearing side by side with him and conveying the image of two equally qualified candidates, especially when a major Republican campaign theme was to stress Nixon's greater leadership experience?

J. Leonard Reinsch, Kennedy's communications consultant, has a different explanation. He says that Kennedy made a poor impression in delivering his acceptance speech at the Los Angeles Coliseum in July. "Nixon watched this acceptance speech in the company of [William P.] Rogers," Reinsch claims, "and said 'I can take this man.' This reaction, plus all the publicity about his great ability as a debater, I think, made it possible for us to mousetrap him into the debate." Reinsch says this was a "crucial mistake" on Nixon's part.[28] Nixon, in *Six Crises*, claims he was at Camp David working on his own acceptance speech while the Democratic Convention was in progress. "I did not listen to any of the preliminary convention proceedings," he says, "except for a portion of Senator Frank Church's inept keynote address."[29] He then adds that Rogers drove up for the night, and they "were watching television together when the first news came over the air that Lyndon Johnson was to be Kennedy's running mate."[30] Nixon says nothing about hearing Kennedy's speech. There is no way to be certain which story is correct, but it is clear that Nixon went into the 1960 campaign considering himself a champion debater and a polished professional when it came to television performance. Had Nixon done to Kennedy what he did in debates with his hapless opponent Jerry Voorhis back in 1946, his gamble would be remembered as a stroke of political genius.

Events were to prove otherwise. Reinsch and William Wilson,

executive producer for the Kennedy campaign, represented the Democrats in tortured negotiations with four of Nixon's representatives: Under Secretary of the Treasury Fred C. Scribner, Nixon press secretary Herbert Klein, BBD&O's Carroll Newton (who had handled television clearances in the 1952 campaign), and Ted Rogers. Some twelve meetings were necessary to work out all sorts of questions about format, location, camera techniques, and the number of debates.[31]

The first debate—joint appearance might be a better term—took place in Chicago, Monday, September 26, 1960, at CBS station WBBM. The full hour was carried as a public service by all three networks. Close to half the entire population of the United States was watching. Howard K. Smith, then with CBS, served as moderator. Four reporters asked the questions: Robert Fleming, chief of ABC's Washington news bureau; Stuart Novins, moderator of *Face the Nation*; Charles Warren, chief of Mutual's Washington news bureau; and Sander Vanocur of NBC News. The broadcast, also heard over four radio networks, went on the air at 8:30 P.M. Central Daylight Time.

Howard K. Smith, seated at a desk, introduced the program: "Good evening. The television and radio stations of the United States and their affiliated stations are proud to provide facilities for a discussion of issues . . . restricted to internal or domestic American matters. And now for the opening statement by Senator John F. Kennedy."[32] Kennedy began talking while seated in his chair. Smith interrupted to ask him to move to his podium. Kennedy looked calm, self-assured, and rested. His eight-minute statement contained phrases he had rehearsed in countless speeches across the country: "I do not think we're doing enough, I am not satisfied as an American with the progress that we're making." He concluded by declaring, "It's time America started moving again."

Then it was Nixon's turn. Actually viewers saw a reaction shot of Nixon about seven minutes into Kennedy's opening remarks. Nixon also said things repeated countless times before and found himself supporting Kennedy's noncontroversial statements: "The things that Senator Kennedy has said many of us can agree with. . . . I subscribe completely to the spirit that Senator Kennedy has expressed tonight, the spirit that the United States should move ahead." He disagreed mostly with the suggestion that America had been standing still.[33]

And so it went. Nixon's opening eight-minute statement concluded, the four panelists introduced themselves, and Robert Fleming asked Kennedy whether he had leadership experience. Kennedy answered yes. In questions about farm surpluses both candidates came out in favor of the farmer, though Nixon claimed, "It's our responsibility to indemnify the farmer during that period that we get rid of the farmer uh—the surpluses."

The only loaded question came from NBC's Sander Vanocur, and it had less to do with leadership than trying to make Nixon look bad. "In his news conference on August 24," Vanocur began, "President Eisenhower was asked to give one example of a major idea of yours that he adopted. His reply was, and I'm quoting: 'If you give me a week I might think of one. I don't remember.'" Nixon's leg wiggled, and the perspiration stood out on his face, but his reply indicated he had given careful thought to how to answer this one: "Well, I would suggest, Mr. Vanocur, that uh—if you know the President, that was probably a facetious remark." He indicated that the concept of executive privilege did not permit a president to disclose who told him what, and Nixon added that a president should make his own major decisions. Then each candidate came out in favor of schools, education, and care for the aged, and each gave a three-minute summary extolling the virtues of progress. Howard K. Smith gamely concluded by saying, "This hour has gone by all too quickly." The networks were thanked for their time and facilities. The first debate was history.

Actually, the first debate had scarcely begun. Precisely because the campaign really was issueless and one had to choose between Tweedledee and Tweedledum, the role of the visual medium loomed large. Viewers could not arrive at a judgment about issues because the debate was not a debate at all—the candidates had made speeches to an enormous national audience.

In 1960 many still listened to the radio, one of them Harvard economist and close Kennedy aide John Kenneth Galbraith. He was in San Diego when Kennedy called to urge him to watch. "I heard you on radio in a Negro shoe shine parlor," Galbraith confided the next day, "and asked the proprietor how *he* liked it. He said, 'So help me God, ah'm digging up two from the graveyard for that boy.'" Those who listened to the first debate on the radio generally considered Nixon to have "won" it.[34]

Those who watched were aghast (or delighted, depending on their political affiliation). Kennedy, naturally telegenic, looked calm and professional. Particularly impressive was the attentive manner in which he listened to Nixon. Viewers saw Kennedy's response in what are known as reaction shots, as CBS producer-director Don Hewitt cut away from Nixon to show Kennedy's reaction. Kennedy appeared tanned and rested, he did not seem to perspire, and his black suit stood out dramatically from the gray set. Someone had coached Kennedy not to look as though anything Nixon said was having any impact on him.

Nixon looked terrible. He seemed to have completely forgotten one rule for successful television performance he had presented in New York City back in 1955—the rule about not scheduling a lot of tiring little speeches the day of a big television address. Nixon had been hospitalized in late August with a painful knee infection and during the first debate he obviously favored one leg. All could see that his knee still bothered him, but the wiggling leg suggested visually that he was ill at ease; the visual medium offered no data about the context of illness. Nixon had lost about ten pounds, enough so that his shirt appeared far too big for him around the collar. His campaign managers had scheduled an incredible number of appearances for him, including five stops in Chicago after he came by plane from Washington late on Sunday night, the twenty-fifth. Nixon did not get to bed until after one in the morning, and was up early to go address a hostile carpenters'-union meeting.

Nixon admits that he ignored the advice of his television adviser, Ted Rogers, about the need for professional makeup. Instead he let an aide apply a dime-store expedient, Max Factor "Lazy Shave," a white cream intended to cover five o'clock shadow. Nixon arrived wearing a light gray suit that blended into the color of the set. He had even received a GI-style haircut, which only added to the worries of his advisers. Rogers had lost out in a internal political power play to Herbert Klein and Carroll Newton, which meant he could not see Nixon before the debate. Klein admits Nixon received poor advice from his aides: "We saw so much of him that it was difficult to recognize how haggard he looked."[35]

Nixon looked wretched from the moment he walked into the studio. In his opening statement the perspiration was not yet apparent, but his beard showed through, his shirt did not fit, his suit was the wrong color, and he seemed acutely uneasy. He presented the image of one convinced he would lose. Ted Rogers claims that Nixon was more worn out and haggard when he made his Checkers speech, and that is probably true. But Nixon *looked* worse in the 1960 debate.

While the debate was in progress, another more furious debate took place in the director's control booth. Don Hewitt, producer-director of CBS's *Douglas Edwards with the News* back in 1948, and in charge of CBS coverage of the 1952 and 1956 conventions, was committed to making his medium visually interesting.[36] He considered it an article of faith that one camera focusing close up on a candidate's face as he talked could not possibly interest the viewer. He insisted on the use of selected reaction shots, at times of his own choosing, but controversy arose. Nixon, well aware of his problems with perspiration, asked for no reaction shots as he wiped his brow, and Ted Rogers wanted no reaction shots at all. On the other side, Kennedy's television adviser had no objections. CBS president Frank Stanton, in the studio during the first debate, finally settled the issue by instructing Hewitt to use the reaction shots.

Rogers insisted that Hewitt maliciously conspired with Stanton to ruin Nixon by selecting reaction shots in which Nixon appeared to be sweating out how he would reply to Kennedy's effective statements.[37] Rogers felt so enraged about the use of the reaction shots that he wrote a novel entitled *Face to Face*, in which a full-blown conspiracy theory is laid out. In the novel the thinly disguised CBS president (Fred Morgan of North American Broadcasting) works hand-in-glove with the Kennedy candidate (Joseph Green) to rig the debates and steal the election. Rogers wrote Nixon in September 1961 that he had been "ostracized" by CBS and that he was a martyr because he had blown the whistle on CBS's rigging of the first debate.[38]

The immensely valuable "Production Diary of the Debates" by Herbert Seltz and Richard Yoakam finds no evidence of conspiracy. True, the color of the set was wrong, and Stanton seemed more of a nuisance than a help with his on-the-spot artistic tips. But Seltz and Yoakam timed the number and duration of the notorious reaction shots and found that there were eleven for Kennedy for a total of 118 seconds out of an entire hour. For Nixon there were nine, totaling 85 seconds.[39]

A careful visual analysis of the entire broadcast should lay to rest the idea that Hewitt used reaction shots in some unfair manner to make Nixon look bad (something a partisan director obviously has the power

/. Nixon looks bad, but the image of him during his opening sta⸌ment looks just as bad as a reaction shot late in the broadcast, save for the perspiration. In this important sense, the argument over reaction shots was wide of the mark from the start.

Critics noted that the public became more aware of technical matters regarding television production in the aftermath of the first debate than ever before. Everyone associates excessive perspiration with guilt or fear. If perspiration is a problem, one solution lies with the thermostat in the building. The second debate in Washington involved an intense struggle between Nixon and Kennedy aides as to whether the studio would resemble Greenland's icy mountains or India's coral strand. Since 1960, voters—to say nothing of pundits—have devoted increasing attention to fine points of technique or image. The demand for a discussion of the so-called issues seems as far from fulfillment as ever. Nobody seemed to notice when Nixon offered to "get rid of the farmers" in the first 1960 debate, whereas in 1976 Gerald Ford lost a substantial degree of support by his momentary confusion about whether or not Poland had a democratic government.

Nixon's experiences in 1952 and 1960 provide an opportunity to trace the development of political television in the 1950s. In 1952 the popular vote rose some 65 percent over 1948, when Truman came from behind to defeat Thomas Dewey. Television executives insisted that television had made the campaign so interesting that voters turned out in record numbers. But careful investigation, particularly an important University of Miami study, failed to substantiate specific claims about the impact of television. The Miami study found that voter impressions had been formed by the time of the televised conventions, and that Eisenhower was certain of victory from that moment.[40] Television may have increased interest in the campaign, but there was no way of proving causality. One can only say that the conventions and campaign sold the virtues of political television to the consumer and the advertising potential of the mass medium to sponsors. Analyses of the impact of television in 1952 must take into account such Republican assets as a well-funded and shrewd campaign, a candidate who was a national war hero (with a smile that few could resist), enthusiasm for returning Republicans to power after twenty years of Democratic rule, worries about Truman's political scandals, and fears that Adlai Stevenson was "too intellectual." Public attention focused on the omnipresence of television and its potential, leaving estimates of actual impact to a later date. It is scarcely surprising that the newness of technological innovation is easier to gauge than its impact on more traditional devices for decision making.

The Checkers speech can be analyzed with more confidence. Nixon was in a bind, ordered by Eisenhower's aides to resign from the ticket, and with no time to mount a counteroffensive. He turned to television and his performance worked. In addition, this was the single most significant media event of the entire campaign. By a wide margin his speech drew more listeners and viewers than any speech by Eisenhower or Stevenson. Never before (or since) has a vice-presidential candidate proved such a potent vote-getter. Checkers demonstrated television's potential for intimate, direct, emotional communication at a stage of technical development when the very idea of coast-to-coast transmission still made headlines. In 1952 in all of Louisiana there was a single station on the air. The very day that the slush fund story broke, Oregon got its first television station. Only the large urban centers of the United States were television markets when the medium proved its power.

The primitive technical qualities of the Checkers speech bear close scrutiny; it is some sort of dinosaur out of television's prehistory. Ted Rogers used occasional reaction shots of Pat (he forgot to admit this when he attacked Don Hewitt during the first 1960 debate). The camera had to be laboriously cranked to pan the library set—a set seemingly out of someone's high-school prop collection. The accepted devices for political speeches had not yet been adapted to television. We see a flag, then Nixon's business card; the broadcast has to be cut when it runs over. It is akin to seeing a very early Western before such conventions as the barroom fight or the final shootout had come into being.

In 1960, political television was still an adolescent (it would reach its majority in the sophisticated commercials of the 1964 Lyndon Johnson–Barry Goldwater campaign). A majority of Americans owned television sets by 1960, but network news broadcasts were limited to fifteen minutes. Polls still indicated that Americans considered the newspaper their primary source of information. The first color news broadcast was still five years away.

Technically, the first debate left a lot to be desired. Studying the broadcast today, the set looks uninteresting in spite of Frank Stanton's love of sophisticated blacks and grays. The idea of shooting over the heads of the panelists so their haircuts loom in the foreground (especially when someone scratches his head in the middle of a question) reminds us that the forms of public affairs broadcasting were still in transition. The surviving television commercial spots employed by Kennedy and Nixon also seem to have a primitive quality, looking backward to Checkers rather than to the professional slickness of image advertising of a later day.

Nixon lost the first debate because of his visual image. In the aftermath of the closest election in American history, his appearance seemed a likely reason for his defeat. Franklin D. Roosevelt's political aide James Farley claimed, "Nixon never got up off the floor after the first debate."[41] Such assertions are not true. If Nixon's image in the first debate had been the only reason for casting one's vote, Kennedy would presumably have won by a landslide instead of just squeaking by. Kennedy's Roman Catholicism and his youth worried many voters; those who disliked Nixon had felt that way for years before the first debate. What television contributed was something, seemingly trivial, to ponder in an otherwise issueless campaign: visual image as a reason for supporting a candidate. The use of television as an image-building device for political candidates can be said to have begun in the postmortems of the 1960 Nixon defeat.

Nixon himself proved a quick study. In his 1968 presidential campaign, the "new Nixon" avoided unrehearsed debates; he looked and sounded like a different person, as Joe McGinniss reports in his entertaining but superficial *The Selling of the President 1968*.[42] Nixon captured many votes from persons horrified by the televised violence of the 1968 Democratic convention, to say nothing of Lyndon Johnson's unpopular Vietnam policies, but victory surely had much to do with effective television commercials and a campaign orchestrated for media coverage. Well-wishers hoped the new president really had matured.

Watergate proved Nixon's undoing. From June 17, 1972, until his resignation as president on August 8, 1974, Nixon often went on television to defend himself in the face of increasing public disbelief. Each television address fit conventions of how a president should look and sound, even Nixon's formal resignation speech. What does not fit the latter, however, is the emotional and tearful farewell speech to the

White House staff on the morning of August 9, 1974. Nixon's talk was rambling, terribly emotional, painful to watch. Nixon cried as he talked of his father: "I remember my old man. I think that they would have called him sort of a little man, common man." And his mother: "Yes, she will have no books written about her. But she was saint."[43]

What made a media professional break down completely in front of the American people? The farewell speech is a moment in which television covered the story as it happened. The truth Nixon could not bring himself to admit in his *Memoirs* is frozen on television videotape forever. No pancake makeup, the perspiration pouring from his face, actually crying, there was no hiding of emotions. Nixon stood humiliated before his favorite enemy, the news media, and admitted, to the extent he was capable, that he had failed to live up to what his mother expected of him. He now knew that history would remember him not as great, but as the first president to resign from office rather than face certain conviction for impeachable offenses.

We can agree with Nixon's own assessment, but we must say something more about the relationship of Nixon's political career to evolving political television. His campaigns span the entire history of candidate interest in the medium: Checkers as evidence of television's power of political persuasion; the 1960 debate as an instance of visual impressions being formed from minor, misleading considerations; 1968 as evidence of how to package an image candidate; and 1974 as a time of direct confession or personal purgation. Political television owes as much to Nixon for exploring the outer limits of the medium as Nixon does to television for making his political career possible.

NOTES

1. Louis Schirm to Richard Nixon, 27 February 1953, "TV in Campaigns" folder, Box 748, Series 320, Richard Nixon Pre-Presidential Papers, Federal Records and Archives Center, Laguna Niguel, CA (hereafter Series 320/PP/FRC-LN). I am grateful to Pat Anderson, Archivist, for help in making the Nixon materials available to me.

2. John Crosby, "TV and the 1953 Election," *American Magazine* 153 (April 1952): 21. For a brief overview of television news see Ted Nielsen, "A History of Network Television News," in Lawrence W. Lichty and Malachi C. Topping, eds., *American Broadcasting: A Source Book on the History of Radio and Television* (New York, 1975), p. 421-428. See also Erik Barnouw, *The Image Empire: A History of Broadcasting in the United States Vol. III—from 1953* (New York, 1970). Programs, and yearly network evening schedules, may be found in Alex McNeil, *Total Television: A Comprehensive Guide to Programming from 1948 to 1980* (Baltimore, 1980).

3. The Republicans met July 7-11; the Democrats, July 21-24, 1952. For a careful overview of television in the 1952 conventions see Charles A. H. Thomson, *Television and Presidental Politics: The Experience in 1952 and the Problems Ahead* (Washington, D.C., 1956), pp. 12-76.

4. CBS Press Release, 8 July, 10 July 1952, copies in Network Coverage folder, Box 368, TV-Radio Division, Democratic National Committee Papers, John F. Kennedy Library, Boston, Mass. (hereafter TRD/DNC/JFKL). For photographs of the new equipment see *Time*, 21 July 1952, p. 38; and *Life*, 21 July 1952, pp. 18-19.

5. Blake Hooper (irate viewer) to Kenneth Fry, 17 July 1952; John Olson to Dear Sirs, 15 July 1952, both in Box 367, TRD/DNC/JFKL.

6. Copy of program (including Door Card #2), Box 367; CBS Press Release, 12 July 1952, Box 368; both in TRD/DNC/JFKL.

7. Democratic Publicity Division, *How to Use Radio and Television, 1952*, p. 18, Box 372, TRD/DNC/JFKL; Edward A. Rogers, 1 April 1954, Television in Campaigns folder, Box 748, Series 320/PP/FRC-LN.

8. Rayburn quoted in CBS press release, 17 July 1952, Box 368, TRD/DNC/JFKL; Montgomery, "How to Make the Most of Your Regular Television Appearances," n.d.; Ken Adams, "Your Cameraman Looks at You," n.d.; both in Television in Campaigns folder, Box 748, Series 320/PP/FRC-LN.

9. Cited in Herbert R. Craig, "Distinctive Features of Radio-TV in the 1952 Presidential Campaign" (Master's thesis, University of Iowa, 1954), p. 71.

10. The Checkers broadcast was carried over 730 CBS and MBS radio stations for a Nielsen rating of 16.8 (7,367,000 homes); it was carried on 62 NBC and CBS television stations for a Nielsen rating of 20.8 (9,136,000 homes). The Republican Party spent $3.5 million for radio-TV campaigning; the Democrats $2.5 million. The Republican Party bought fifteen hours of television time; the Democrats nineteen hours, fifty minutes. The Republican strategy called for preempting popular programs; the Democrats bought time at less popular evening hours, hoping to build a regular viewing audience. Craig, "Distinctive Features," pp. 85, 89, 121-122, 130-132. Craig assembled an invaluable amount of statistical data and offers a detailed investigation of the uses of radio and television by both parties during the campaign. Also helpful is Malcolm D. Sillars, Jr., "An Analysis of Invention in the 1952 Campaign Addresses of Dwight D. Eisenhower and Adlai E. Stevenson" (Ph.D. diss., Iowa State University, 1955), pp. 129-130.

11. Garry Wills, *Nixon Agonistes: The Crisis of the Self-Made Man* (Boston, 1970), pp. 91-114; Richard M. Nixon, *Six Crises* (New York, 1968), pp. 77-138.

12. The nineteen-page Rogers memorandum concerning the Checkers speech and the first Kennedy-Nixon debate is with Ted Rogers to Nixon, 5 September 1961, Edward A. (Ted) Rogers folder, Box 652, Series 320/PP/FRC-LN. The folder contains Rogers's memoranda to Nixon, 1950-1962, and background material about Rogers.

13. Rogers memorandum, p. 2.

14. For a photograph of Lincoln, also used as a stand-in for Nixon in the second, third, and fourth 1960 televised debates, see Sidney Kraus, ed., *The Great Debates: Background—Perspective—Effects* (Gloucester, Mass., 1968), p. 88.

15. Rogers memorandum, p. 3.

16. Wills, *Nixon Agonistes*, pp. 105-106; Nixon, *Six Crises*, pp. 116-118.

17. For the text of the Checkers speech, see Robert W. O'Brien and Elizabeth J. Jones, *The Night Nixon Spoke: A Study of Political Effectiveness* (Los Alamitos, Calif., 1976), pp. 95-104. A kinescope on 16mm film of the speech can be rented from many places, from $15 to $100 (New Yorker Films). For an attractive price try Third World Newsreel, 160 5th Ave., Suite #911, New York, N.Y. 10010 (212-243-2310) or VCI Films, 6555 E. Skelly Dr., Tulsa, Okla. 74145 (918-583-2681). The vase of flowers was placed on the table in the middle of the set between Nixon and his wife.

18. Nixon, *Six Crises*, p. 109.

19. Rogers memorandum, p. 7.

20. Wills, *Nixon Agonistes*, pp. 107-114.

21. O'Brien and Jones, *Night Nixon Spoke*, p. 46.

22. Jack Gould, "How to Reduce Directorial Distractions? Use Single Camera, as Nixon Did," *New York Times*, 15 March 1954, copy with James Bassett to Nixon, 16 March 1954, Rogers folder, Box 652, Series 320/PP/FRC-LN; "Nixon Tells How to Win TV Friends," *New York Times*, 15 September 1955, p. 22.

23. Sig Mickelson, "Television and the Voter," Round Table Luncheon of Radio & Television Executives Society, New York City, 28 October 1959, p. 10, copy in Box 395, TRD/DNC/JFKL.

24. "Convention Was Just Ho Hum to Some TV Viewers," *Advertising Age*, 1 August 1960, copy in Box 394, TRD/DNC/JFKL.

25. Robert W. Sarnoff, "Broadcasting: Time for Reason," address to Academy of Television Arts and Sciences, New York City, 21 April 1960, copy in Equal Time folder, Box 364, TRD/DNC/JFKL. For an overview of the quiz scandals see Barnouw, *Image Empire*, pp. 122-129.

26. "Platforms and Platitudes," *Broadcasting*, 23 May 1960, p. 114; Frank Stanton, statement before the Subcommittee on Communications of the Senate Committee on Interstate and Foreign Commerce, 17 May 1960; Eric Hass, statement submitted to same committee, 19 May 1960, copies of both in Equal Time folder, Box 364, TRD/DNC/JFKL.

27. Nixon, *Six Crises*, p. 348; Nixon, *The Memoirs of Richard Nixon* (New York, 1978), p. 217. For an overview of the campaign, see Theodore White, *The Making of the President 1960* (New York, 1961).

28. Transcript, J. Leonard Reinsch, oral history interview, 5 January 1966, p. 10, JFK Oral History Program, JFKL.

29. The gratuitous reference to Church makes little sense unless one assumes Nixon had read White's *Making of the President 1960*, p. 214, where White quotes Nixon as saying Kennedy's acceptance speech was "'way over people's heads.'" See also Barnouw, *Image Empire*, p. 162.

30. Nixon, *Six Crises*, p. 336. In his *Memoirs* Nixon covers the 1960 campaign in a few pages, pp. 214-226; in *Six Crises* there are almost 150 pages, pp. 315-461.

31. Herbert A. Seltz and Richard D. Yoakam, "Production Diary of the Debates," in Kraus, *Great Debates*, p. 74. The Seltz and Yoakam essay, pp. 73-126, is essential to an understanding of all four debates.

32. For the text of the first debate see Kraus, *Great Debates*, pp. 348-368. One can rent a ¾-inch videotaped copy of the first debate from Allan Goodrich, Audiovisual Archives,

Kennedy Library, Columbia Point, Boston, Mass. 02125 (617-929-4530). The Kennedy Library also will sell videotaped copies of the 1960 Kennedy campaign spots and his address before the Greater Houston Ministerial Association.

33. Nixon received conflicting advice about whether to be tough on Kennedy and let people accuse him of dirty tricks, or to be gentlemanly. Eisenhower called Nixon on September 25, the day before the debate, and discussed strategy: "The Vice President said people thought he was somewhat of a debater, therefore he was, in the debates Monday night and after, going to play it in a low key. He was going to be gentlemanly, let Kennedy be the aggressor. He added that because of the religious angle, he felt he could not be too tough. The President agreed—said he would talk on the positive side if he were Nixon and not try to be too slick. . . . He suggested that Nixon show that he is knowledgeable, good humored, but that Nixon should not be too concerned about Kennedy looking bad." Telephone Calls September 1960 folder, Box 52, DDE Diary Series, Dwight D. Eisenhower: Papers as President, Eisenhower Library, Abeline, Kans.

34. Galbraith to Kennedy, 27 September 1960, TV Debates Correspondence folder, Box 51, JFK Pre-Presidential Papers, JFKL.

35. Nixon, *Memoirs*, pp. 218-219; Herbert G. Klein, *Making It Perfectly Clear* (Garden City, N.Y., 1980), p. 105; Rogers memorandum, p. 9.

36. Hewitt came to CBS television in 1948; he is currently producer of CBS's *60 Minutes*.

37. Rogers memorandum, p. 12: "I knew what the Director's [Hewitt] politics were, and sure enough, he took unflattering reaction shots of RN. Each time he did so, the JFK people in the control booth said, 'Let's have another one of those. Just as bad.'" Hewitt, in a memorandum prepared for Stanton and sent on to Nixon, admits that he and Rogers had quite an argument over reaction shots as early as a meeting in Washington on September 8: "I told Mr. Rogers . . . that to eliminate the reaction shot was 'cheating the audience' and that it was wholly natural for the viewer watching the discussion to want to see reaction from the other participant from time to time. I went on to make it very plain that I felt that a decision involving reaction shots was one that was proper for the director to make and that it was not open for discussion." Memorandum, Hewitt to Stanton, 5 October 1960, enclosed in Stanton to Nixon, 6 October 1960, CBS folder, Box 164, Series 320/PP/FRC-LN.

38. Ted Rogers, *Face to Face* (New York, 1962). On p. 240 Rogers goes into detail about his opposition to reaction shots. Rogers to Nixon, September 1, 1961, Rogers folder, Box 652, Series 320/PP/FRC-LN.

39. Seltz and Yoakum, "Production Diary," p. 96.

40. The Miami Study, Department of Marketing, Miami University, *The Influence of Television on the 1952 Elections* (Miami, Ohio, 1954), is discussed in Thomson, *Television and Presidential Politics*, pp. 55-57. For a published summary of the study distributed to industry executives, see *The Influence of Television on the 1952 Election*, Television in Campaigns folder, Box 748, Series 320/PP/FRC-LN.

41. Author's interview with Elmer Lower, Baton Rouge, La., 11 September 1980, p. 12.

42. Joe McGinniss, *The Selling of the President 1968* (New York, 1969).

43. Nixon, *Memoirs*, p. 1088. A videocassette in a number of formats of Nixon's

farewell speech (black and white) may be borrowed for a fee from the Vanderbilt Television News Archive, Joint University Libraries, Vanderbilt University, Nashville, Tenn. 37207 (615-322-2927). Most of Nixon's other presidential addresses relating to Watergate, and all of the network evening news coverage (plus many specials), may also be borrowed from Vanderbilt for very moderate fees.

9

Brian's Song: Television, Hollywood, and the Evolution of the Movie Made for Television

DOUGLAS GOMERY

 In November 1971 Richard Nixon reigned as president; the Vietnam War still needed to be unraveled; campus protesters still took to the streets; and Watergate lay in the future. What were Americans watching on television? *All in the Family* (CBS, Saturday, 8:00 P.M. EST) had surged to the number-one spot, far surpassing its closest competition: *The Flip Wilson Show* (NBC, Thursday, 8:00 P.M. EST), *Marcus Welby* (ABC, Tuesday, 10:00 P.M. EST) and *Gunsmoke* (CBS, Monday, 8:00 P.M. EST). Fifth in the overall ratings battle for that season (1971-1972) was ABC's *Movie of the Week* (Tuesday, 8:30-10:00 P.M. EST). Movies had always been popular on U.S. television, but this was the first series of movies made for television to break into the top ten. These movies easily surpassed a long-running detective series, *Hawaii Five-O* (CBS), and two short-lived offerings on NBC, *Sarge* (with George Kennedy) and *The Funny Side* (with Gene Kelly as host) on Tuesday night. On November 30 ABC presented a little-publicized TV movie, *Brian's Song*. That showing achieved a 32.9 rating and a 48 share, the highest for any TV movie up to that date. More importantly for the profit-seeking networks, *Brian's Song* ranked tenth for *any* movie presentation ever on television. With *The Wizard of Oz* accounting for five of the top ten to that November night, *Brian's Song* rose to join *The*

208

Birds, Bridge over the River Kwai, Ben-Hur, and *Born Free* to form TV's elite top-ten movies. Quite an honor for a film with no stars or publicity hype.[1]

But why? Here was a tale of friendship between two running backs who played for the Chicago Bears. Brian Piccolo was white, slow, and small. Gale Sayers was black, fast, and correctly built to become one of professional football's greatest runners. The film focused on their differences as people: Sayers quiet and introspective; Piccolo merry, effusive, ever the clown. Their friendship began at the Bears' training camp in 1965 and ended with Piccolo's death from cancer in 1970. At age twenty-six Piccolo left a wife and three daughters (the latter not seen in the film). Neither the film's undistinguished direction nor its open sentimentality seemed to diminish its popularity. The sum of the parts overcame any single drawback. This narrative situation, drawn from real events, seemed to have provoked—quite unexpectedly—a moment of memorable potency in the midst of the chaotic Vietnam-Nixon era.

The public's response to *Brian's Song* certainly caught television moguls by surprise. Quickly, awards and praise issued forth from all sides. *Brian's Song* won five Emmy awards, including outstanding single program for entertainment for the 1971-1972 television season. The Director's Guild honored Buzz Kulik. From nonindustry sources came a George Foster Peabody award for outstanding achievement in entertainment, and citations from *Black Sports Magazine,* the American Cancer Society, the National Conference of Christians and Jews, and the NAACP.[2] Even President Richard Nixon jumped on board. "Believe me," proclaimed America's thirty-seventh president, "*[Brian's Song]* was one of the great motion pictures I have seen."[3]

With *Brian's Song* the made-for-television motion picture came of age as an entertainment genre. Here we have a significant turning point in the history of United States television programming. Why did *Brian's Song* (and other movies specifically made for television) overtake Hollywood features in the ratings war of 1971? The answer takes us back to the origins of the American television industry, to the development of its business and programming practices. Most Americans are familiar with *The Late Show, The Early Show, Sunday Night at the Movies,* and other series that have turned television homes into cinema museums displaying the best (and worst) of Hollywood's creations. Nearly every one of the current "film generation" embraced the magic (and genius) of the

American cinema through television. And throughout this era the American television industry has prospered, becoming one of the more profitable of U.S. businesses. Consequently, we first of all need to examine the history and relations of two American businesses, one growing (television), one declining (theatrical motion pictures). Since we have precious little that qualifies as systematic history in this area, we should immediately begin to integrate the business history of television into a literature well synthesized by Alfred D. Chandler in his book *The Visible Hand: The Managerial Revolution in American Business*.[4]

The methods of business history alone cannot explain, however, the extraordinary popularity of *Brian's Song*. From a sociological perspective television movies seemed to serve the need for topical entertainment in an era of instability identical to Warner Bros.' social films of the Great Depression. But why *Brian's Song*? What intersection of ideological forces produced its unexpected overflow of popular interest? All television programs, not just news shows, deserve to be studied as indicators of significant shifts in dominant attitudes, beliefs, and values. Like motion pictures from earlier decades, popular television represents the merger of art and industry, a mass spectacle. Understanding how "hit" shows reflect and/or shape the dominant ideology is a difficult task. New work in film studies provides us with a start. Thus, this essay will address two fundamental problems of television and history (business history, and television and ideology) through the genre of movies made for television and one product in particular, *Brian's Song*.

On the surface, the historical relationship between the U.S. film and television industries seems clear enough: the leaders of the film industry unilaterally opposed any interchange with the television industry between 1945 and 1955. Only after the movies had clearly surrendered their mass audience to television did the movie moguls consent to deal with their poor visual cousin. Such claims portray the chieftains of the motion picture industry as narrow-minded dolts.[5] I argue they were not. On only one level did they refuse to do business with television. Until the mid-1950s the major Hollywood studios did withhold feature films from television presentation—but for quite sensible reasons. From 1945 to 1955 even the largest television networks could simply not afford rents competitive with even a declining theatrical box office. During that decade the chief operating officers of Hollywood's biggest concerns embraced (as it turned out incorrectly) the vast potential of revenues from theater and subscription television.

At first, Hollywood tried to purchase shares of major television properties. For example, Paramount Pictures owned parts of the Du-Mont network, KTLA (Los Angeles), a subscription television firm, and a theater television corporation. Fox also owned a subscription television concern. On the exhibition side the United Paramount Theater chain (900 theaters strong) acquired the American Broadcasting Corporation. For a variety of reasons, however (which would constitute another essay), the film industry never was able to gain enough power to challenge the radio, then television networks. All attempts at subscription and theater television during the 1950s proved unprofitable. But Hollywood was able to gain a foothold in the production end. As early as 1951 Columbia established a subsidiary, Screen Gems, to ~ro-duce filmed material for television. Within four years the major stud. plunged headfirst into production. Warner Bros., with *Cheyenne*, *77 Sunset Strip*, and *Maverick*, led the way. Soon this relationship proved so profitable that Hollywood stuck to the business of supplying programs, and/or studio space, while exhibitors turned to alternative investments.[6]

As this jockeying for power was taking place, feature film material was being shown on American television. Initially it came from abroad. In particular, the Ealing, Rank, and Korda organizations in Britain, which had never been able successfully to crack the U.S. market, supplied features as early as 1948. Undersized U.S. producers like Monogram and Republic came on board next. Although these two concerns and a dozen other competitors tendered more than four thousand titles, their cheap production values in Westerns (Gene Autry and Roy Rogers) and serials (Flash Gordon) only served to remind early television viewers of the vast storehouse of treasures still resting in the vaults of MGM and Paramount.[7]

To understand how and why the major Hollywood producers finally agreed to rent and/or sell their backtitles to television, we have to return to May 1948 when an eccentric millionaire, Howard Hughes, purchased controlling interest in the weakest of the major Hollywood companies, Radio Keith Orpheum (RKO). In five years Hughes ran RKO into the ground. Debts soared past $20 million; production fell by 50 percent; new activity neared a standstill. To appease minority stockholders, in 1954 Hughes purchased their shares for $23,489,478.16—in cash. (He wrote a personal check.) He then controlled a studio lot, stages, properties, films, and other assets. A year later Hughes sold the whole package to General Tire & Rubber Company for $25 million. At the time General Tire controlled WOR-TV in New York and desired the RKO features for its proposed *Million Dollar Movie* series. Since General Tire did not want to enter the film production business, it quickly rid itself of all nonfilmic physical property. The studio lot, for example, went to a former RKO employee, then television's number-one attraction, Lucille Ball, for her Desilu operation. It also peddled limited rights to 704 features and 1,100 shorts to C&C Television, Inc., for $15 million. Consequently, in July 1956 C&C auctioned rights to the RKO package to one station per television market for cash and/or "bartered" advertising spots. General Tire retained exclusive rights for WOR and other stations it owned. By July 1957, *Variety* estimated that C&C had grossed $25 million in eighty markets alone.[8]

Such profit figures impressed even the most recalcitrant movie mogul. Within the space of twenty-four months all the remaining major Hollywood corporations released their pre-1948 titles to television. For the first time a nationwide audience was able to confront a broad cross-section of American sound films, and rediscover two decades of Hollywood pleasure production. All the companies were able to tap a new source of needed revenue at the nadir of their transition into the post-television era. Columbia, a minor studio, moved first. In January 1956, it announced a deal to rent pre-1958 features.[9] As a result, in fiscal 1955—an otherwise dismal year—Columbia was able to achieve a record $5 million profit. Instantly this minor had become a major. Two months later, in March 1956, Warner Bros. sold its pre-1948 library of 850 features and 1,500 shorts to PRM, a Canadian-American investment company, for $21 million. Suddenly it could record a $15 million profit. Twentieth Century-Fox upped the ante. It licensed its pre-1948 features for $30 million (plus a percentage) to National Telefilm Associates. In August 1956, MGM topped the Fox figure. By distributing through a wholly owned subsidiary, on one day alone it completed contracts with CBS's owned-and-operated stations and seven other stations for more than $20 million, the largest single day's business in MGM's history. More came through additional contracts.

Paramount held out the longest because it had large investments in subscription television. In February 1958—nearly two years after the deals of RKO, Columbia, Warner Bros., Fox and MGM—Paramount sold, rather than leased, its pre-1948 library to MCA, then a talent agent. At the time the deal, worth $50 million, surpassed all others. But because Paramount *sold* rather than leased its library, MCA made out far better in the long run. By 1965, MCA had grossed more than $70 million and had not even tapped the network market. The excess profits MCA generated from leasing Paramount pre-1948 features enabled it to purchase Universal and join the ranks of giant media conglomerates.[10]

From 1955 on, pre-1948 feature films functioned as a mainstay of off-network schedules. The networks only booked feature films as specials, not regular programming. For example, during the 1956-1957 season CBS initiated its annual airing of *The Wizard of Oz*. By 1960 all three networks reasoned that *post*-1948 Hollywood features could generate high ratings if offered in prime time. Before that could begin, the studios had to settle with Hollywood craft unions on residual payments. In a precedent-setting action the Screen Actors Guild, led by Ronald Reagan, struck and won guaranteed amounts. Consequently, on September 23, 1961, NBC premiered *Saturday Night at the Movies* with *How to Marry a Millionaire*. The thirty-one titles shown in the series, fifteen in color, all were post-1950 Fox productions. All had their television premiere on *Saturday Night at the Movies*. Color films helped spur sales of RCA sets; then, as now, RCA owned NBC. Moreover, feature-length movies enabled NBC effectively to counterprogram proven hits on CBS (*Have Gun, Will Travel*; *Gunsmoke*) and ABC (*Lawrence Welk*). As was generally the case during the 1960s, ABC quickly imitated NBC's effort. A midseason replacement, *Sunday Night Movies*, commenced in April 1962. CBS, the ratings leader, did not feel the need to join in until September 1965. By then, the race was on. As early as the fall of 1968, the networks presented recent Hollywood feature films seven nights a week. By the 1970s, overlapping permitted ten separate "movie nights." In the long run, programming innovator NBC retained the greatest commitment to this particular programming form, probably because of continued corporate investment in colorcasting.[11]

This vast display of movie programming quickly depleted the stock of available first-run material. Although the total number of usable features had increased from three hundred in 1952 to more than ten thousand in 1964, growth then slowed to a trickle. Station managers began to wonder just how often they could repeat pre-1948 titles. The networks established a formula for post-1948 titles: show it twice on prime time and then release it into syndication. Not surprisingly, movie producers began to charge higher and higher fees for current theatrical product. Million-dollar price tags became commonplace. Soon network executives reasoned that costs had reached the point where it had become more profitable to produce and sell their own movies. Such a practice would reduce costs and provide a method for making pilot programs for projected series. Since at this time networks normally paid for part (or all) of the development of pilots, significant savings could be effected. And these made-for-TV features allowed the networks to test the rating power of proposed series in order better to forecast success.[12]

The first made-for-TV feature as part of a regular series was presented on Saturday, November 26, 1966, by NBC, *Fame Is the Name of the Game*.[13] This "World Premiere" resulted from NBC's contract with Universal to produce low-budget movies to be released first on television. These color films would, following network television airing, revert to Universal for domestic theatrical release (rare), and foreign theatrical and television release (common). In a short time the number of made-for-TV features increased rapidly. By the 1971-1972 season, when *Brian's Song* premiered, the networks had scheduled for the first time more made-for-TV features than theatrical products new to television. Again relative network power dictated who followed NBC's lead. In 1967 ABC reached an agreement with MGM for production of ninety-minute features. (NBC's television movies ran two hours.) Ratings leader CBS again trailed by two years.[14]

The rapid transformation to made-for-television movie programming took place because profits were higher than anyone expected. On the supply side a television movie cost on average $750,000, about equal to the cost of four showings of a popular theatrical release. On the demand side, TV movies quickly proved they could attract sizeable audiences, and even at times surpass blockbuster features. Not surprisingly top network movie rating choices have included *Gone With the Wind*, *Love Story*, *The Godfather*, and *Ben Hur*. More startling is the fact that *Ladies of the Night* (ABC, Sunday, January 16, 1977) vaulted to fifteenth place for all movies of any type ever shown on television. Others on the all-time top 100 list include *Helter Skelter*, *Night Stalker*, *A Case of Rape*, *Women in Chains*, and *Jesus of Nazareth*. The only repeat case in the top 100 has been *Brian's Song*. Moreover, this remarkable sports film achieved this honor in 1971 and 1972, when the made-for-TV publicity mill was only beginning to be set in motion. In general, ABC, which telecast *Brian's Song*, produced through its *Movie of the Week* the best ratings results. In 1971-1972, for example, ABC gathered thirteen of the top fifteen telefeature ratings of the season. Barry Diller, then head of ABC's movie programming, parlayed that position into the chairmanship of a major movie studio, Paramount Pictures.[15]

Brian's Song was an altogether typical made-for-television production. Producer Paul Junger Witt had a connection with ABC through *The Patridge Family* series, first aired in September 1970. He hired William Blinn to create a script from Gale Sayers's routine autobiography, *I Am Third*. Witt also secured Buzz Kulik, a veteran television director. Kulik, a football nut, knew the Sayers/Piccolo story from the sports pages, saw it in the tradition of Howard Hawks as a love story between two men. At first there was a problem of casting, since in Hollywood there were few young male black actors with experience. Billy Dee Williams, then thirty-three, had been kicking around Hollywood and Broadway since age seven. His fame from *Brian's Song* shot him into major roles in Hollywood feature films—*Lady Sings the Blues* (1972), *Mahogany* (1975), and *The Empire Strikes Back* (1980). The latter made him a household name. Indeed, *Brian's Song* advanced many of its contributors forward several significant steps in their careers. Producer Paul Junger Witt went on to form his own production company, which turned out the controversial ABC comedy *Soap*. William Blinn wrote part of *Roots*. Kulik amassed a string of important made-for-TV movie credits including *Babe* (1975), *The Lindbergh Kidnapping Case* (1976), and *Ziegfeld* (1978). Composer Michel Le Grand earned an Oscar for *Summer of '42* six months after *Brian's Song*'s premiere. Jack Warden (who played George Halas) was nominated for an Oscar as best supporting actor in *Shampoo* (1975) and *Heaven Can Wait* (1978). But it was James Caan who benefited most. In 1971 his career seemed at a standstill. *Brian's Song* thrust him into the spotlight; *The Godfather* (1972) made him a star. Since then he has remained a major box-office attraction. Here was an early case of a television movie helping create a theatrical movie star. James Caan has not appeared in a made-for-television movie since *Brian's Song*.[16]

Brian's Song cost about $400,000 to produce. The made-for-TV movie in the early 1970s had become what the B film was to Hollywood in earlier eras. Contending with restrictions on budgets, language and sex, ratings-minded networks, and a format demanding an opening "teaser" and six climatic "act curtains" before commercial breaks, creators had to work quickly and efficiently. The networks covered production costs in exchange for two runs. The producers then received 100 percent from syndication and worldwide theatrical rights. Production costs were kept to a minimum. Consequently, studio shooting constituted the bulk in most TV films. In *Brian's Song* the considerable use of NFL film highlights of actual Chicago Bears games reduced costs. Shooting schedules averaged eleven days. With the air date known in advance, all preproduction work was completed in less than two weeks. That time included script revisions, selection of locations and crew, and any hassles over casting the stars. No time was set aside for rehearsals. The script served as the director's bible—"Shoot as written," as in Hollywood in the 1930s. Lighting was one parameter that clearly suffered, for it required too much time to light elaborate shots; all Hollywood agreed that the TV movie was a form for the close-up. Postproduction necessitated yet another week or two. In fact that step was merely mechanical because so few additional takes were allowed, and only shots noted in the script were covered.[17]

If *Brian's Song* was a typical production, the public response was unprecedented. It proved to be the media phenomenon of late 1971 and early 1972, akin to *Love Story* of a year earlier. Columbia Pictures for the first time ever released the film to theaters after it was shown on television. This experiment was tried only in Chicago. Perhaps too many had seen it already on television; and against major Christmas releases, *Diamonds Are Forever* and *The French Connection*, this TV movie could not even hold its own. The most unexpected success came in ancillary areas. Books dealing with Brian Piccolo became bestsellers. The original Sayers autobiography had been issued by Viking in November 1970. After the film's success, sales took off. The publisher, caught short, had to double the copies in print within one month. Meantime *Brian Piccolo: A Short Season* by Jeannie Morris, wife of a Piccolo/Sayers teammate, was published by a small Chicago house to take advantage of the TV exposure. More than one hundred thousand copies were quickly sold, and Dell purchased the paperback rights for $175,000, a sizable sum even by today's inflated prices. The phonograph record industry was also caught short. Michel Legrand's orchestral version shot into the Top 100. Other artists quickly covered. Peter Duchin and Peter Nero produced versions for middle-of-the-road audiences; Hank Crawford created a soul version. This media blitz lasted only three months because the Hollywood publicity mill, caught unprepared, turned to other products. Yet the phenomenon has never completely died off. Throughout the 1970s *Brian's Song* has continued to be shown on television, in syndication, and in classrooms and other social gatherings in 16mm. Uncounted numbers have seen it; few do not know of its reputation.[18]

The *Brian's Song* phenomenon points up the fact that in twenty-five years, 1946 to 1971, movies on television had traversed through four unique stages. First, the Hollywood studios tried to withhold their best films, and pursue subscription and/or theater television. Then, needing the cash, they eventually agreed to sell and/or lease pre-1948 features and shorts to local stations. In 1961 the networks initiated stage three by beginning to broadcast post-1948 theatrical features in prime time. Such a strategy proved so successful that fees quickly escalated and inventories decreased to problematic levels. Thus in the late 1960s the networks began to commission their own films. These made-for-TV features proved to be so popular that they rivaled the ratings power of even the most expensive theatrical products. Miniseries, novels for television, and docudramas came next. The 1980s will initiate movies made for pay cable. In October 1981, Alan J. Hirschfield, chairman of 20th Century-Fox, announced a series of original pay-cable movies. Costing about one-third the price of an average theatrical feature, each would be shown first on pay cable, then on over-the-air network television. Next would come foreign theatrical release. Worldwide syndication would terminate the revenue cycle. That same month Home Box Office, a Time subsidiary, announced its first movie made for pay cable, *The Terry Fox Story*, the biography of another athlete who died young. And so the economic cycle continues.[19]

The made-for-TV movie has formed its own genre since 1966. This form seems to have fulfilled a particular cultural need: topical entertainment reaffirming basic values and beliefs. Here its function has resembled those Warner Bros.' features of the 1930s so often utilized by historians to understand transformations in ideas and beliefs during the Great Depression. During the 1930s Hollywood had to struggle in a moral and political straightjacket to produce acceptable social dramas like *I Am a Fugitive from a Chain Gang* (1932) and *Black Legion* (1936). Consider how historian Andrew Bergman described these "topicals":

> Throughout the thirties, the Warner studios produced a number of films which dealt explicitly with aspects of social and political life Hollywood usually shunned. . . . [These] remain, without exception, fascinating documents, demonstrating both a gritty feel for social realism, and a total inability to give any coherent reasons for social difficulties.[20]

A similar situation has existed for TV movies. Pressures from advertisers, the Moral Majority and the U.S. Congress have limited what networks would attempt to present. Yet every executive knew that bizarre, topical films could attract large audiences. Their problem became how to make controversial, noncontroversial TV movies—film that could titillate viewers without scandalizing them. Some public wrangling has always generated useful publicity. But too much could be disastrous. And always had to be a modicum of stress on the positive. So for every *Roots*, there were dozens of films like *Can You Hear the Laughter? The Story of Freddie Prinze*, and *Dawn: Portrait of a Teenage Runaway*. Topical products *Helter Skelter, Dallas Cowboy Cheerleaders, The Feminist and the Fuzz*, and *Raid on Entebbe* all reached the list of top-100 highest-rated films shown on American television during the 1970s. All emerged straight from the pages of a daily newspaper, *The National Enquirer, People*, and/or various features in broadcast journalism. Indeed TV-movie production schedules were so swift they could "scoop" theatrical fare. Some made-for-TV movies had completed their second runs before their more famous theatrical cousins had come to town.[21]

TV movies have excelled in telling small stories. Even in attempted extravaganzas or docudramas, the familiar elements of tight character development, the close-up, frequent interior shots, and repetitive dialogue help construct a particular form of narrative logic and style. As with Hollywood features from the 1930s, viewing could be interrupted and still be enjoyed because everyone was so familiar with the characteristics of the form. Film scholars David Bordwell and Kristin Thompson have described this mode as the classic narrative cinema. This formulation of storytelling on film depends on the assumption that action should result from individual characters acting as causal agents. Of course there can exist problems of nature and society. But these factors serve as catalysts or preconditions for narrative action. The story invariably centers on the difficulties of a small group of persons, their decisions, choices, and given character traits. So the hero or heroine has positive values and in the end wins (or loses gracefully). The villain has negative characteristics and fails in the end (or at least does not triumph). The plot moves on in a cause-effect chain as characters seek desired goals. When those figures with positive traits finally win out, we have the "happy ending."

In this classical narrative mode, according to Bordwell and Thompson, visual style is subordinated to a goal of effectively telling the story. So plot time omits all insignificant chunks in order to emphasize only the "important" events. The plot orders the story chronologically to tender the action most strikingly. If a character acts strangely, we soon learn why from (1) dialogue, (2) action, and/or (3) a flashback. Appointments, meetings, and "chance" encounters guarantee efficient character interaction. Motivation should be as clear and complete as possible. And all narrative puzzles must be closed at the finish. Leaving no loose ends, classical narrative films clearly seal up all questions or enigmas. We learn the fate of each major character, the answer to each mystery, and the outcome of each conflict.[22]

Although any subject is a potential candidate for classical narrative treatment, the more familiar the "story concept," the better chance it has to sell. Appropriately, for its *Movies-of-the-Week* ABC sought seventy-five-minute tales that could be comprehended in thirty seconds. In industry jargon, these were dubbed "concept films." And of course this meant that these narratives could effectively be promoted in thirty-second commercials. In fact network "concept testing" involved interviewing target audience members (twenty-five- to forty-year-old white, urban Americans): "Would you watch the story of such and such?" If the answer was yes, then the narrative concept was considered. Sex and violence were euphemized while "social realism" was zealously touted. So controversies surface predictably each year, to be quickly forgotten by the next season. For example, today few remember that NBC's *Born Innocent* kicked off the 1974-1975 season. That film, which chronicled the corruption of a teenager in prison, contained a graphic sequence depicting rape with a broom handle. Controversy was initiated; lawsuits were begun, ratings were high. And the studio developed a sequel, *Sara T.—Portrait of a Teenaged Alcoholic*. Indeed, for a time during the 1970s, treatments of rape and alcoholism provided the most popular controversial noncontroversial subjects.[23]

Brian's Song represents a classic narrative tale. *TV Guide* efficiently summarized its essential narrative traits:

> A drama that captures the warmth of deep friendship—and the horror of dying young. It's the true story of Chicago Bears running back Gale Sayers and his teammate Brian Piccolo, who died last year of cancer. Their training camp rivalries are tracecd and there's plenty of NFL footage, but football is incidental to the real story: a deeply moving account of the growing friendship between the Bears' first black and white roommates.[24]

Here, classic narrative cinema boils down the complex issue of race relations to competition between two individuals. Violence comes in an accepted form—professional football games. Sports fans, principally young urban males, already knew the ending. The concept of a friendship between men that is broken by death goes back to the origins of the American film industry. Indeed male "weepies" had been a staple of Hollywood's golden age. Consider *The Pride of the Yankees* (1942) or *Knute Rockne—All American* (1940). *Brian's Song* was a traditional story ripped from page three of 1970s sports pages.

Brian's Song's two central characters presented a vivid contrast. One was talented; the other tried hard. One was black; the other white. Football, as the *TV Guide* blurb indicated, simply served as a catalyst, a precondition for action. When both made the team and they became close friends, another enigma was needed. A clear villain emerged—cancer. But Brian Piccolo did not die in vain. Consider the final lines of voice-over narration in the film:

> But, when they [his friends and family] think of him, it's not how he died that they remember but rather how he lived. . . . How he did live . . .[25]

The lesson seems clear. Those who try hard and do their best in the face of adversity are life's true heroes. This is a "happy ending" in an otherwise very sad conclusion.

All techniques of camera work, editing, mise-en-scène, and sound were subordinated to the story. The plot, spreading over several football seasons, was easy to follow, since it always centered on the relationship between the two men. The film's structure, punctuated by five commercial breaks (two minutes each), conformed to an ABCC'B'A' structure. The opening (and closing) segment focuses on how the two men relate as they meet (and part). The contrast is vivid and striking. In the second and fifth segments we learn how each handles adversity. First Sayers helps Brian Piccolo simply make the team. Of course, All-American Sayers is assured of a place. Later Sayers learns to handle his friend's impending death, and the frustration of not being able to do anything about it. The two middle segments also mirror each other. First, Brian assists Gale with the rehabilitation of his knee injury; then Sayers tries to help Piccolo with his physical problems. This process of rhyming constitutes a classical cinematic ploy and unifies differences in the story elements. From beginning to end, *Brian's Song* ceaselessly repeats itself, making it easy to follow and fulfilling yet another characteristic of the classic narrative cinema.[26]

On the level of film genre *Brian's Song* sparked a resurgence of the sports biography. That category of narrative subjects had been important throughout the sound era. After *Brian's Song* came *Rocky* (1976), *Semi-Tough* (1977), *Slap Shot* (1977), and *Heaven Can Wait* (1978). In 1973 *Bang the Drum Slowly* earned sizeable box-office revenues. It too concerned a dying athlete (here a baseball player) befriended by a superior teammate.[27] Yet on the level of genre *Brian's Song*'s connections to the past were even more subtle than similarities in subject matter. Consider a long-standing character type film historian Russell Merritt has labeled "the bashful hero."[28] Since the 1930s one durable male figure has dominated American cinema. Whether essayed by Gary Cooper, Jimmy Stewart, or Henry Fonda, all moviegoers are familiar with the character of the easygoing, stalwart young fellow who was suddenly entrusted with great responsibility. Armed with homespun shrewdness and a laid-back, laconic attitude, he (never she) subsequently overcame formidable adversaries. He was likable, tall, lean, and soft-spoken. But when the situation demanded, he became eloquent in a simple, straightforward way. Fame seemed to seek him out. By any film's close he had emerged as the best at his calling. Success came to him, seemingly by chance.

The bashful hero was spawned in popular culture in the Progressive Era. The egalitarian philosophy of the Progressives precipitated as an article of faith the ineffable wisdom of the common man. Merritt locates its origins in the movies in a variety of genres created before World War I. The drawling cowboy, bashful in front of women yet stalwart in the face of danger; the rustic country boy; the shy but creative Chaplin tramp figure—all began in motion pictures made near the end of the Progressive Era. But this figure moved to the forefront in the 1930s with the emergence of sound films. Merritt points out the importance of the character this way:

> [The bashful hero] reassures us that we too could have enjoyed the same success in his shoes, if we only had the opportunity he had. His creators want to assure us that we are heroic, attractive people in our natural state.[29]

In an interesting twist *Brian's Song* cast a black man in the bashful hero role. Gale Sayers is the easygoing, quiet young man who possesses homespun shrewdness. But he changes. When the film opens we learn of Sayers's inability to speak before large audiences. Brian Piccolo must coach Sayers for a speech at a rookie-of-the-year award banquet. Yet when it becomes necessary Sayers can speak directly and to the point. Consider his terse but effective advice to Piccolo during their first training camp:

> Try it going to your left. They don't look for a right-handed guy to throw going to his left.[30]

All this changes when adversity strikes. Sayers takes charge. He *asks* to tell their Bear teammates of Piccolo's illness, and presents a moving speech "from the heart." Later at another banquet he informs the world of Brian's real courage in a touching address. Generally the bashful hero seems to be a gentle, nonagressive man. Yet he thrives on adversity, drawing on a seemingly unlimited pool of talent. He then easily moves others to tears and action. Gale Sayers in *Brian's Song* exemplifies this tradition with his new-found power of public address; as Merritt notes,

> the conversion scene itself, in which the hero converts skeptics into true believers, is a constant feature in films of this kind.[31]

Sayers moves the audience in the film (and at home in front of the television set) to tears by telling the world of the true courage of Brian Piccolo. And many seemed to respond, signaling the film's extraordinary success.

Yet the figure of the bashful hero cannot completely explain *Brian's Song*'s popularity. Simply put, why did it touch such a wellspring of public sentiment on that Tuesday late in November 1971? What intersection of special themes produced such an outpouring of interest and praise? In short, the film reconstituted a potent mix of popular mythic material during an era when many Americans seemed confused about fundamental conceptions of race, sex, and economics.[32] Specifically *Brian's Song* reworked three basic thematic concerns: (1) relations between blacks and whites, (2) the proper roles for women, and (3) the image and trappings of big business in the U.S. economy. The techniques of mythologization in *Brian's Song* function in subtle and complex ways, even as the film's form and style remain simple and direct.

What was this era like? Historians are still working on that question. But at present certain generalizations do seem clear. The "seething sixties" still formed a part of viewers' memories. Richard Nixon had been in power for two years, trying to unite the country around new goals: "To a crisis of spirit, we need an answer of the spirit." Yet questions of race, the proper way to end the Vietnam War, protest, and law and order refused to go away. Who should run corporate America? Weren't all large cities falling apart? And the youth were on drugs and practicing free love. Religion seemed under attack, replaced by the new morality. The 1960s did not end on January 1, 1970. Questions and doubt seemed to plague Americans up and through the Watergate affair in 1974.[33]

All these uncertainties had seemed more pressing in the 1960s. Why? Partly because from 1963 to 1969 the United States experienced one of its longest periods of sustained prosperity. The 1970s changed all that. Depending on which economist or government expert one listened to, a recession or depression overtook the U.S. economy in mid-1970. Whatever the label, the situation became grave very quickly. Unemployment, especially for minorities and youth, surged upward. The overexpanded war industries were especially hard hit, reflecting the winding down of the American involvement in Indochina. Educated middle-class technicians and engineers suddenly found themselves out of work and competing in a glutted job market. Moreover since 1893 the United States had enjoyed a generally favorable balance of trade with foreign nations. In 1971 the dollars paid for international debt exceeded imports, adding to the domestic economic woes. Times were not good when *Brian's Song* was presented, and Nixon had chosen to do little to alleviate hard times until the 1972 election drew closer.[34]

A few sectors of the economy did continue to prosper. One was professional sports. The American Football League (AFL) and the National Football League (NFL) had just merged. Leagues in hockey, basketball, and tennis were created and/or expanded. By 1975 there were more than three times the number of professional teams as there had been a decade earlier. Sports truly became a big business. It rewarded its star performers as well as or better than some of the larger industrial corporations did their top executives. Teams annually mined new-found wealth from television. Far more people watched professional athletes on television than could have crowded into all of America's stadiums. For example, more than 65 million—the largest number ever to see a sporting event up to that time—looked on in 1967 as the Green Bay Packers beat the Kansas City Chiefs in football's first Super Bowl. Just about the time *Brian's Song* aired, the mania about pro sports was reaching the peak of its growth cycle.[35]

Yet *Brian's Song* was far more than a motion picture taking advantage of a popular fad. As recent work in film theory has demonstrated, it is far more interesting to learn what's systematically left unsaid in classical Hollywood films than to continue to probe for more surface themes. That is, ideas and beliefs more often are dealt with through what is left out, "structured absences." Seemingly, marginal assumptions can tell us much about what people took for granted, their "lived relationships."[36] A complete analysis of *Brian's Song* would stretch far beyond the limits of this essay, but we can see in three specific ways how the film structured and simplified complex issues without ever directly "sending a message."

Race relations continued to be a festering issue in 1971. In October 1970, the U.S. Commission on Civil Rights reported "a major breakdown" in enforcement of civil rights. Public opinion polls showed that 78 percent of all Americans opposed the idea of busing schoolchildren to effect racial integration. And the North was rapidly replacing the South as the focus of violent confrontations over school integration.[37] In *Brian's Song* direct presentation of these contradictions was glossed over. How? By reducing the issue to the most personal level. Could two players competing for the same job get along? Recognize that these were special men. Sayers was an All-American, not an "uppity nigger." Here the use of the bashful hero mythos effectively stripped the Sayers figure of the threatening quality often associated with black men. He was portrayed not as loud, demanding, or assertive, but as quiet and shy, simply wanting to fit into the system. Subtler touches underscored Sayers as a nonthreatening black. He was very well dressed. He showed up at the Bears' training camp in a spiffy blue blazer and a well-trimmed Afro haircut. No wild clothes or exaggerated hairstyle for this character. He looked white, even "higher class" than Piccolo. Moreover he had a beautiful house in what was shown to be an all-white neighborhood. Sayers's wife had straightened her hair, and behaved appropriately "perky." She could be white too. Black children (suggesting the busing issue) were not seen, only referred to. In short, the Gale Sayers portrait fit conveniently into the superblack mold established by Sidney Poitier during the 1960s. He posed no problems. Once can almost hear viewers saying: "If only all blacks could be like him, then there would be no problems." Left unsaid is any consideration of the societal implications.[38]

Yet contradictions do exist. Consider the use of deep-focus photography. Here, with a wide-angle lens and placement of figures and decor, a motion picture director can create an image in depth. It is not as frequently used in television as in theatrical motion pictures because of video's limited screen size. But in a confined space, there do exist a number of possibilities for action on two levels, foreground and background. For example, near the end of *Brian's Song*, Gale Sayers calls Brian Piccolo for one last time. Behind Sayers, we see his new black roommate. It would have been easier to frame a shot with no roommate, so are we to believe that all other players at Sayers's position were black? (A rule was laid down early in the film that players should room together by position, hence Sayers and Piccolo.) But we know from elsewhere in the movie and the history of professional football that other whites were available. For example, Ralph Kurek, a white, was mentioned several times in the film as the man Piccolo had to "beat out" for the job. Are we then to assume that the interracial roommate scheme worked only for Piccolo and Sayers? That would surely not contribute to a happy ending. And such an interpretation undercuts the otherwise optimistic portrait of race relations in the movie.

If race relations were presented in a simple but not always straightforward fashion, so was the world of professional football. In 1971 professional football in the United States functioned as a prosperous, growing big business with enormous player salaries, well-organized unions, and million-dollar television contracts. But in *Brian's*

Song that world was categorically denied. Football was reduced to a simple game, with just coaches and players. For example, early in the film George Halas, owner and coach of the Chicago Bears, is shown as a single entrepreneur. He decorates his own office. Contract negotiations are done man to man, without high-priced lawyers. Players have no union or long-term contracts. Here is a world where all that counts is how one performs on the playing field. The best play; others warm the bench. *Brian's Song* omits all those characteristics sports fans have come to associate with professional football in its television era (post-1957). The George Halas figure states it directly in the film when he reminds Sayers that Piccolo cannot play:

> I've had a policy on this team from the very start—the best player plays, no exceptions. And right now Kurek is the best player.[39]

It's the outside world that is seen as unfair, either through racism (a societal problem) or cancer (a problem of nature). Cancer is the least fair because it is so random. There is no way one can compete against it. As such, cancer offers a counterweight to the film's portrayal of football.

Brian's Song portrays football as a Mom-and-Pop small-time business. But sometimes cracks show through. The producers made constant use of football replay films, some in slow motion, which visually reminded viewers of television's role in professional sports. Many sports contradictions are embodied in one character, JC. At first this black man seems to be a coach. He lectures the players about their playbooks; he instructs Gale Sayers on the difficulties of the new roommate policy. Quickly we sense he is merely a player, presumably the captain. (Knowledgeable football fans recognized the reference to J. C. Caroline, a famous Bears defensive halfback.) But soon he is replaced by the "true leader," Gale Sayers. It is the latter who tells the team and the world of Brian Piccolo's death. Indeed by the end of the film JC has become just "one of the guys." Certainly it was too radical an idea for JC to be a coach. All coaches were white. Gale Sayers was as close to becoming a leader as is possible for a black. As a bashful hero, he took on many of the characteristics of the white mythos. Even in this simple portrait of big business, whites ran things, and blacks worked for them. Like Jefferson Smith in Frank Capra's *Mr. Smith Goes to Washington* (1939), Sayers only assumes temporary power, and in the end the institution remains unchanged.

The least complex mythic portrait involves the role of women. Although women's-rights groups had made some progress by 1971, their victories had been small. Along with teenagers, women continued to be less trained, lower paid, and the last hired and first fired. In the world of *Brian's Song*, women became nearly invisible. This was a man's love story in which Sayers and Piccolo seem most comfortable together. So at the end Sayers held Piccolo's hand (we even got a close-up of that image), and comforted him while their wives, the only female characters in the film, stood off-screen. The film closed with Sayers, not Piccolo's wife, Joy, declaring his love. *Brian's Song* is a throwback to the buddy films so common in the 1930s and 1940s.

The two principle female characters, wives Joy Piccolo and Linda Sayers, have been reduced to flat stereotypes. They literally appear first in the film as two-dimensional black-and-white images, faded photographs tacked on the walls of their husbands' common dormitory room. As extensions of their husbands, they quickly become best friends. They sit together at football games. They giggle in unison at their husbands' jokes. When "real" help is needed (Gale learning a speech, or needing rehabilitation), it is Brian who helps him. Characteristically, in the end Joy and Linda break down, unable to handle the situation. Even Brian Piccolo, as sick as he is, must comfort his wife. In sum, women play limited and traditional roles in this modern "buddy" film. It is interesting to note that many traditional black groups like the NAACP and Urban League praised the film. At least blacks were visible on the screen. No woman's groups lauded *Brian's Song*. In no way can it be seen as a positive portrait of women.

In general, *Brian's Song* represented a major turning point in the economics of U.S. television by confirming the popularity of made-for-TV movies as an approved, respectable genre, and thus breaking the ground necessary for *Roots*, *Shogun*, and other original works for television. Analysis of this particular film offers interesting examples of how social and cultural forces in the United States during the Nixon era were reflected in the mass media. Through TV movies Hollywood was able to tackle social issues of race and sex in a controversial yet noncontroversial way.

NOTES

1. Cobbett S. Steinberg, *TV Facts* (New York: Facts on File, 1980), pp. 172, 181; Alex McNeil, *Total Television* (New York: Penguin, 1980), p. 31; Tim Brooks and Earle

Marsh, *The Complete Directory to Prime Time Network TV Shows, 1946-Present* (New York: Ballantine, 1979), pp. 419-420.

2. Other awards *Brian's Song* achieved include the following: Writers Guild of America Award; Golden Globe nomination; Golden Reel nomination; an "Eddie" nomination by the American Cinema Editors; National Conference of Christian and Jews Mass Media Brotherhood Award "For Outstanding Contributions to Better Human Relations and the Cause of Brotherhood"; Congressional Record commendation as "one of the truly moving television and screen achievements in recent years"; American Cancer Society Special Citation. As of 1981 all fines of the National Football League go to the Brian Piccolo Memorial Cancer Fund. See Craig T. Norback and Peter G. Norback, eds., *TV Guide Almanac* (New York: Ballantine, 1980), pp. 310-312.

3. *New York Times*, 28 January 1972, p. 91.

4. Alfred D. Chandler, *The Visible Hand: The Managerial Revolution in American Business* (Cambridge: Harvard University Press, 1977).

5. Gerald Mast, *A Short History of the Movies*, 3rd ed. (Indianapolis: Bobbs-Merrill, 1981), pp. 260-261; Robert Stanley, *The Celluloid Empire* (New York: Hastings House, 1978), pp. 126-127; Laurence Kardish, *Reel Plastic Magic* (Boston: Little, Brown, 1972), pp. 180-183.

6. Orton Hicks and Haven Falconer, MGM Television Survey: Interim Report, 29 April 1955, Dore Schary Collection, Wisconsin Center for Film and Theatre Research, Madison, Wisc., pp. 1-8; Charles Higham, *Hollywood at Sunset* (New York: Saturday Review Press, 1972), p. 149; Michael Conant, *Antitrust in the Motion Picture Industry* (Berkeley: University of California Press, 1960), pp. 109-110; Harvey J. Levin, *Broadcast Regulation and Joint Ownership of Media* (New York: New York University Press, 1960), pp. 62-63.

7. Hicks and Falconer, MGM Television Survey, pp. 8-11; Higham, *Sunset*, p. 107; *Broadcasting*, 17 January 1955, pp. 50-51; *Autry* v. *Republic Productions*, 213 F.2d 667 (1954), opinion; *Republic Productions* v. *Rogers*, 213 F.2d 662 (1954); Christopher H. Sterling and John M. Kitross, *Stay Tuned* (Belmont, Calif.: Wadsworth, 1978), pp. 345-346.

8. Hicks and Falconer, MGM Television Survey, Interim Report, pp. 14-25; *Broadcasting*, 23 April 1956, p. 96; Richard Austin Smith, *Corporations in Crisis* (Garden City, N.Y.: Doubleday, 1966), pp. 64-66; *Broadcasting*, 15 March 1954, p. 35; *Broadcasting*, 19 December 1955, p. 40; "Coup for Teleradio," *Time*, 16 January 1955, p. 86; *Variety*, 1 May 1957, p. 50; Conant, *Antitrust*, p. 132; Gertrude Jobes, *Motion Picture Empire* (Hamden, Conn.: Anchor Books, 1966), pp. 368-369; Donald L. Barlett and James B. Steele, *Empire* (New York: W. W. Norton, 1978), pp. 165-170, 210.

9. The preponderant number of titles were restricted to pre-1948 titles because of union agreements.

10. *Broadcasting*, 2 January 1956, p. 7; Bob Thomas, *King Cohn* (New York: Putnam, 1967), p. 262-287; *Broadcasting*, 23 April 1956, p. 96; *Broadcasting*, 27 August 1956, p. 68; *Broadcasting*, 21 May 1956, p. 52; *Broadcasting*, 5 November 1956, p. 48; Variety, 5 June 1957, p. 27; Broadcasting, 25 June 1956, p. 48; *Business Week*, 1 September 1956, p. 63; *Variety*, 6 March 1957, p. 25; *Forbes*, 15 December 1957, p. 31; *Forbes*, 15 November 1965, pp. 24-28; Stanley Brown, "That Old Villain TV Comes to the Rescue and Hollywood Rides Again," *Fortune*, November 1966, pp. 270-272.

11. Hollis Alpert, "Now the Earlier, Earlier Show," *New York Times Magazine*, 11

August 1963, p. 22; "Over the Rainbow," *Time*, 25 August 1967, p. 60; Robert Rich, "Post '48 Features," *Radio-Television Daily*, 29 July 1960, p. 27; *Forbes*, 1 August 1960, p. 23; "Saturday Night at the Movies," *TV Guide*, 23 September 1961, p. A-9; John B. Burns, "Feature Films on TV," *Radio-Television Daily*, 30 July 1962, p. 32; *Variety*, 24 September 1980, pp. 88–89; *Variety*, 21 June 1972, p. 34; *Variety*, 20 September 1978, pp. 48, 66; McNeil, *Total Television*, p. 851; Cobbett Steinberg, *Reel Facts* (New York: Random House, 1978), pp. 355-357; Brooks and March, *The Complete Directory*, pp. 416-420; Harry Castleman and Walter J. Podrazik, *Watching TV* (New York: McGraw-Hill, 1982), p. 149.

12. Martin Quigley, Jr., "11,325 Features for TV," *Motion Picture Herald*, 18 January 1967, p. 1; Neil Hickey, "The Day the Movies Run Out," *TV Guide*, 23 October 1965, pp. 6-9; Avra Fliegelman, ed., *TV Feature Film Source Book* 13 (Autumn 1972: 10-15; Walt Spencer, "Now Playing at Your Neighborhood Movie House: The Networks," *Television* SSV, no. 1 (January 1968), p. 49; Ryland A. Taylor, "Television Movie Audiences and Movie Awards: A Statistical Study," *Journal of Broadcasting* 18 (Spring 1974): 181-182.

13. Several sources list Universal's *See How They Run* telecast 7 October 1964 as the first movie made for television. The distinction between that work and *Fame Is the Name of the Game* is that the latter was the first TV movie broadcast as part of a regular series. *See How They Run*, *Scalplock* (1966), and *The Hanged Man* (1964) were more like filmed specials. See Alvin H. Marill, *Movies Made for Television* (Westport, Conn.: Arlington House, 1980), pp. 11-12, and Paul Michael and James Robert Parish, eds., *The American Movies Reference Book: The Sound Era* (Englewood Cliffs, N.J.: Prentice-Hall, 1969), p. 37.

14. Spencer, "Now Playing," p. 41; Henry Ehrlich, "Every Night at the Movies," *Look*, 7 September 1971, p. 63; Jack E. Nolan, "Films on TV," *Films in Review* 17 (December 1966): 655–657; *Variety*, 18 August 1971, p. 30; *Variety*, 14 June 1972, p. 29; *Broadcasting*, 15 January 1973, p. 37; Don Shirley, "Made-for-TV Movies: It's Coming of Age," *Washington Post*, 6 October 1974, pp. E:1-2; Douglas Stone, "TV Movies and How They Get That Way," *Journal of Popular Film and Television* 7 (1979): 147-149.

15. Dick Adler and Joseph Finnigan, "The Year America Stayed Home for the Movies," *TV Guide*, 20 May 1972, pp. 6-10; *Broadcasting*, 15 January 1973, p. 37; Roger Noll, Merton J. Peck, and John J. McGowan, *Economic Aspects of Television Regulation* (Washington, D.C.: The Brookings Institution, 1973), p. 67; Caroline Meyer, "The Rating Power of Network Movies," *Television*, 25 (March 1968): 56, 84; Jack E. Nolan, "Films on TV," *Films in Review* 24 (June-July 1973): 359; Caroline Meyer, "Series Movies: New Headache for Programmers," 25 (January, 1968): 44-60; Shirley, "Made-for-TV Movies," *Washington Post*, 6 October 1974, p. E:3; Herbert Gold, "Television's Little Dramas," *Harper's*, March 1977, pp. 88-89; *Broadcasting*, 25 September 1972, p. 61.

16. John W. Ravage, *Television: The Director's Viewpoint* (Boulder, Colo.: Westview Press, 1978), pp. 103-112; Ephraim Katz, *The Film Encyclopedia* (New York: Crowell, 1979), pp. 191, 708, 1208, 1236, 673; Les Brown, *The New York Times Encyclopedia of Television* (New York: Times Books, 1977), pp. 477, 43; Christopher Wicking and Tise Vahimagi, *The American Vein: Directors and Directions in Television* (New York: Dutton, 1979), pp. 27-28; Leslie Halliwell, *The Filmgoers Companion* (New York: Avon, 1977), pp. 248, 548, 430, 410, 750, 771, 119; Arleen Keylin and Christine Bent, *The New York Times at the Movies* (New York: Arno Press, 1979), p. 89; Marill, *Movies*, p. 348; *Variety*, 8 December 1971, p. 34.

17. Martin Kasindorf, "Movies Made for Television," *Action* 9 (January/February 1974): 13-15; Eileen Lois Becker, "The Network Television Decision Making Process: A Descriptive Examination of the Process Within the Framework of Prime Time Made-for-TV Movies" (Master's thesis, University of California-Los Angeles, 1976), pp. 19-56; *Variety*, 8 December 1971, p. 34; Gold, "Little Dramas," pp. 90-93; *Broadcasting*, 27 January 1975, p. 21; *Broadcasting*, 15 January 1973, p. 36; *Broadcasting*, 7 August 1972, pp. 23-25.

18. Kasendorf, "Movies," pp. 16-19; *New York Times*, 28 January 1972, p. 91; Gale Sayers with Al Silverman, *I Am Third* (New York: Viking, 1970); Jeannie Morris, *Brian Piccolo: A Short Season* (Chicago: Rand McNally, 1971); *Variety*, 15 December 1971, p. 29.

19. *Broadcasting*, 19 October 1981, p. 61.

20. Andrew Bergman, *We're in the Money: Depression America and Its Films* (New York: New York University Press, 1971).

21. Patrick McGilligan, "Movies Are Better Than Ever—On Television," *American Film* 5 (March 1980): 50-54; Becker, "Decision Making," pp. 41-54; Stone, "TV Movies," pp. 150-155; John M. Smith, "Making Do—Or Better? The American T.V. Movie," *Movie* 21 (Autumn 1975): 38-40; Bruce Cook, "Can Filmmakers Find Happiness on Television?" *AFI Report* 5 (Spring 1974): 38-40.

22. David Bordwell and Kristin Thompson, *Film Art: An Introduction* (Reading, Mass.: Addison-Wesley, 1979) pp. 50-59; Raymond Bellour, "To Analyze, to Segment," *Quarterly Review of Film Studies* 1 (August 1976): 331-354; Stephen Heath, "Film and System: Terms of Analysis," *Screen* 16 (Spring 1975); 7-77 and *Screen* (Summer 1975): 91-113.

23. Nancy Schwartz, "TV Movies," *Film Comment* 11 (March-April 1975): 36-39; Becker, "Decision Making," pp. 57-125; Gold, "Little Dramas," pp. 87-89; *Broadcasting*, 27 January 1975, p. 21; *Broadcasting*, 15 January 1973, pp. 40-45; Stone, "TV Movies," pp. 154-157; Smith, "Making Do," pp. 141-145; Cook, "Happiness," pp. 42-46.

24. *TV Guide*, 27 November 1971, p. A-55.

25. William Blinn, *Brian's Song: Screenplay* (New York: Bantam, 1972), pp. 118-119. All dialogue quotations were double-checked against a 16mm copy of the film.

26. Other elements also help unify the story and develop its important themes. Obvious to all must be the theme music. The leitmotif is directly associated with death and dying. More subtle but just as effective is a motif of meeting and gesture. First we see Brian and Gale greet each other very formally by reluctantly shaking hands. As they become close friends, they "slap hands," a gesture of black origin. At the end the two men gesture awkwardly. When Gale first comes to see Brian in the hospital, they must shake hands left-handed because of Brian's infirmity. In the death scene they clasp hands for the first time. (See the still at the beginning of this essay.) Here black and white are finally united, but only in death.

27. The theatrical film *Love Story* also influenced *Brian's Song*. Indeed young people dying through not fault of their own has been a popular narrative structure since the Romantic period. See also Steinberg, *TV Facts*, p. 334, and James Monaco, *American Film Now* (New York: Oxford University Press, 1979), pp. 7-10.

28. Russell L. Merritt, "The Bashful Hero in American Film of the Nineteen Forties," *Quarterly Journal of Speech* 61 (April 1975): 129-139.

29. Merritt, "Bashful Hero," p. 131.

30. Blinn, *Screenplay*, p. 25.

31. Merritt, "Bashful Hero," p. 134.

32. *Brian's Song's* narrative and genre elements proved so powerful no commentators seemed to notice the liberty the film took with the story (the intercut football sequences contain errors in matching of costume and color) and fact (Piccolo and Sayers were not very good friends off the field; racism continued in their private lives).

33. John M. Blum, Edmund S. Morgan, Willie Lee Rose, Arthur M. Schlesinger, Jr., Kenneth M. Stampp, and C. Vann Woodward, *The National Experience*, part 2 (New York: Harcourt Brace Jovanovich, 1973), pp. 758-792; Richard Hofstader, William Miller, Daniel Aaron, Winthrop D. Jordon, and Leon F. Litwack, *The United States*, 4th ed. (Englewood Cliffs, N.J.: Prentice-Hall, 1976), pp. 678-705; Samuel Eliot Morison, Henry Steele Commager, and William E. Leuchtenburg, *A Concise History of the American Republic* (New York: Oxford University Press, 1977), pp. 715-745; Richard D. Current, T. Harry Williams, and Frank Freidel, *American History*, 5th ed. (New York: Knopf, 1979), pp. 768-799.

34. Blum et al., *National Experience*, pp. 804-805; Hofstader et al., *United States*, pp. 708-709; Current et al., *American History*, pp. 817-818; Howard Zinn, *A People's History of the United States* (New York: Harper & Row, 1980), pp. 529-569.

35. Roger G. Noll, ed., *Government and the Sports Business* (Washington, D.C.: Brookings Institution, 1974), pp. 1–32, 275–324; Walter Adams, ed., *The Structure of American Industry*, 5th ed. (New York: Macmillan, 1977), pp. 365–400.

36. "John Ford's *Young Mr. Lincoln*" (a collective text by the editors of *Cahiers du Cinéma*), Screen 13 (Autumn 1972): 5-15; Nick Browne, "The Politics of Narrative Form: Capra's *Mr. Smith Goes to Washington*," *Wide Angle* 3 (19XX): 4-11.

37. Morison et al., *Concise History*, pp. 740-744; Jerome H. Skolnick and Elliott Currie, *Crisis in American Institutions* (Boston: Little, Brown, 1970), pp. 70-123; Hofstader et al., *United States*, pp. 707-708; Current et al., *American History*, pp. 816-817.

38. The use of other filmic parameters reinforced this picture of race relations. Consider, for example, the use of camera work that created the motif of running. Sayers and Piccolo seemed always to be paired in training camp spring tests. Who was faster? Of course, Sayers, the superhero, always won, with Piccolo struggling close behind. But here the continuous use of a telephoto lens, squashing spatial depth, linked the two together as they ran. In one lyrical moment, coupled with slow motion, we see the two race through the park "for a beer." With a telephoto lens and slow-motion photography, they seem to run as one. Even though these two athletes compete, they are united.

39. Blinn, *Screenplay*, p. 52.

10

Watergate, the Evening News, and the 1972 Election

LAWRENCE W. LICHTY

Five men wearing white gloves and carrying cameras were caught early today in the headquarters of the Democratic National Committee in Washington. They were caught by a nightwatchman. They did not resist arrest when the police showed up. They apparently were unarmed and nobody knows yet why they were there. The film in their cameras hadn't even been exposed. Anyway, they're being held.   —Garrick Utley
NBC Nightly News
June 17, 1972

. . . and guess what else he is, a consultant to President Richard Nixon's reelection campaign committee hired to install its security system. Police say McCord and his accomplices brought electronic listening devices with them. . . . But I don't think that's the last we're going to hear of this story.   —Garrick Utley
NBC Nightly News
June 18, 1972

No issue really dominated the campaign. Instead polls show that voters are concentrating on the men running for office, weighing that intangible quality—credibility.   —Walter Cronkite
CBS Evening News
November 6, 1972

I would only hope that in these next four years we can so conduct ourselves in this country and so meet our responsibilities in the world, in building peace in the world, that years from now people will look back to

the generation of the 1970s at how we have conducted ourselves and they will say, God bless America. Thank you very much. —Richard Nixon
Election night television address
November 7, 1972

Monday evening, June 19, 1972, the first weeknight after the break-in, the three network evening news programs—the *ABC Evening News, CBS Evening News with Walter Cronkite*, and *NBC Nightly News* (hereinafter often *AEN, CEN*, and *NNN*)—had filmed reports on the story. The top stories, however, were an airline pilots' strike and a meeting of Henry Kissinger with Le Duc Tho of the Democratic Republic of Vietnam (North).

What would later be called "Watergate" was overshadowed as an issue in the 1972 general election by the Vietnam war. On Monday, June 19, ABC anchor Howard K. Smith ended the *AEN* broadcast with a paean to the president's Vietnam policy, saying that in 1968 Mr. Nixon had said he had a plan "to end the Vietnam war without surrender," and the promise "apparently is being kept." Summarizing presidential trips to China and the USSR, the bombing of Hanoi, and the mining of the Haiphong harbor, Smith concluded:

> You may not like the Nixon plan—it's been extremely expensive in lives and time and money—but it is no longer possible honestly to deny that he had a plan, and it's a well-thought-out one if you accept his purposes.[1]

This led the trade newspaper *Variety* to report, "The love feast between Howard K. Smith of ABC News and the Nixon Administration is still in flower" since Smith was "making a strong argument for Nixon's credibility and seemingly for his reelection."[2]

Through the rest of June and all of July Watergate was not important news. There were the Democratic platform hearings, floods in Pennsylvania, and at the Democratic convention the nomination of George McGovern. When Martha Mitchell said that she was a political prisoner and that her husband, Attorney General John Mitchell, had been doing "dirty things," it was not taken very seriously.

More than any issue or other event, the selection of Thomas Eagleton would end the McGovern campaign before it had started. For a week rumors, then the admission, that Eagleton had undergone psychiatric treatment was the story—ending only when Eagleton stepped aside July 31. All this time, understandably, Nixon appeared "presidential," opening a new satellite ground station with a call to Golda Meir, vetoing a spending bill, and holding an impromptu press conference. The pattern of the campaign was set.

On August 9, Tom Pettit (NNN) noted (mostly in passing) that the attempt to bug the Democratic headquarters was a skeleton in the Nixon closet. On *AEN* Tom Jarriel said a plan to discredit the press during the campaign had been put on the shelf. On August 25 the supposed target of that plan, Dan Rather, stated on *CEN* that the shape of the coming campaign was now clear—a few carefully planned appearances by Mr. Nixon, reliance on the prestige of the office of the president, criticism directed at McGovern (but no mention of his name), the use of national defense as an issue, and a renewed attempt by the president to be warm and friendly and exude confidence. The goal, Rather argued, was to get the largest popular vote ever.

He was right. Nixon did.

Broadcasting and politics have been closely connected since the beginning of radio. One of the earliest broadcasts sent out election returns in 1916. Most historians use the first KDKA (Pittsburgh) November 1920 program of Harding-Cox election returns and the introduction of phonograph records as a convenient place to mark the "beginning" of broadcasting. The conventions and political speeches were broadcast in 1924. Since 1928 both parties have always spent more money for radio—then radio and TV—advertising than for any other media.

As early as 1925, scholars sought to describe broadcasting's ethereal programming. All such analysis has meant counting some unit of the content, and most early studies only reported the percent of programs in a week that were music, drama, or other program forms. Prior to and during World War II there was much development in the methodology of content analysis, particularly for the study of enemy broadcasts and propaganda. Other early studies focused on the "bias" or "slant" of radio news commentators. Studies of TV news in the 1950s focused on structure and production variables such as the use of photos, film, and other visuals. By 1960 there was much interest in TV news coverage of elections, particularly the Kennedy-Nixon "Great Debates."

Not infrequently, those doing content analysis sought to show that television news, for example, was "left" or "right" biased, and to "prove" it produced an empirical study. Thus, during the 1968 election writer Edith Efron sought to show that the three networks were "slanting" the news against Richard Nixon.[3] Scholarly reviewers found her method nonrigorous and not replicable. CBS paid for a replication of her study, and this second study concluded that candidate Hubert Humphrey had spoken more frequently of himself favorably while Nixon spoke more of other subjects, but that CBS did "not flagrantly favor one candidate over another." In fact the study showed that CBS had been ever so slightly "favorable" to Nixon.[4]

Controversy over the Efron book, a generally growing interest in TV news coverage, attacks on the press (especially on television—for example, the November 1969 speech by Vice-President Agnew), interest in coverage of civil rights and Vietnam, and an increasing number of young researchers in the area of mass communications were among factors contributing to the number of studies of the 1972 campaign. The growing availability and use of computers made it possible for such analyses to be more detailed and to be done more accurately and quickly.

Even after ten years, more studies were being done about the 1972 campaign than any other. At least eleven detailed content analysis studies conducted by university researchers—including this one— covered some aspect of the general election campaign. There were seven other studies that covered primaries, the conventions, the dropping of Eagleton as McGovern's running mate, and the reporting of election night.

The analysis that follows is based on a detailed review and categorization of all network evening news broadcasts from August 29 to November 7, 1972. All items about the election were coded, including those given by anchormen, reporter stories, and commentaries. As will be seen below, each item was coded as to subject matter, and several evaluations were made by coders. While this and nearly all other studies of news reporting use several measures of what is generally called "direction" rather than bias, other variables such as time, story order, and visuals were used to determine if either candidate was given more or different attention.[5]

TV News and the 1972 campaign. During the eleven weeks of the 1972 general campaign the three network evening news programs devoted more than a third of their total news to the presidential campaign. About one-quarter of this political time was given to McGovern as a candidate, and only about one-tenth to Nixon as a candidate. When those speaking on behalf of either candidate (for Nixon the "surrogates") were included, however, the total for the two candidates was almost exactly the same. On *CEN* and *NNN* Nixon received somewhat more coverage than McGovern because of the category "Nixon as President." There was very little coverage of state races, and almost no reporting of "other" candidates for president (see Table 1).

About four-fifths of the reporting time was by reporters and correspondents (film, live, and tape). The largest percentage of time taken by anchormen was on NBC—Chancellor had items of slightly longer average length. The ABC coverage was more visual, giving slightly more time to film and being less likely to have only a reporter ("talking head") reading a story live. There was more film on McGovern as he traveled about the country; more live coverage on Nixon—particularly by the White House correspondents. As the campaign developed, rather than shooting film, first CBS, then NBC and ABC began to make much wider use of portable video equipment (now variously called ENG for electronic news gathering, EJ for electronic journalism, and EFP for electronic field production).

As with other news, the "typical" anchorman story about McGovern or Nixon was about thirty seconds—twenty-five on ABC. Film stories by reporters averaged slightly over two minutes on NBC, slightly longer on ABC, and two and one-half minutes on CBS.[6]

In sum, there was a film report on McGovern on each of the networks almost every night—usually by those traveling with his campaign. There was a film or a live White House correspondent report on each network virtually every night, and there were often additional stories on Nixon's campaign.

There was no important variation in the amount of time given to the candidates during the eleven weeks of the campaign—although less time was given to Nixon early in the campaign and more time later,

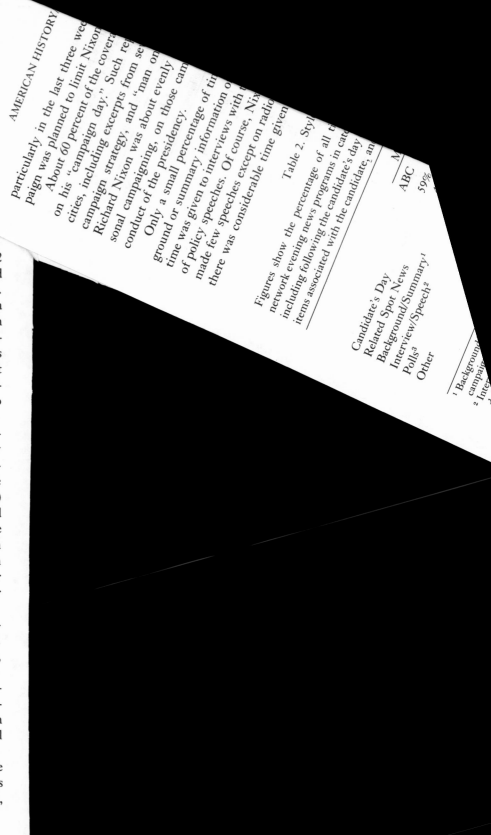

238

particularly in the last three weeks. The campaign was planned to limit Nixon
About 60 percent of the coverage on his "campaign day." Such reports cities, including excerpts from several campaign strategy, and "man on Richard Nixon was about evenly sonal campaigning, on those campaigns conduct of the presidency.

Only a small percentage of time ground or summary information of time was given to interviews with Nixon of policy speeches. Of course, Nixon made few speeches except on radio there was considerable time given

Table 2. Styl

Figures show the percentage of all the network evening news programs in categories including following the candidate's day items associated with the candidate, and

			M	ABC 59%
Candidate's Day				
Related Spot News				
Background/Summary[1]				
Interview/Speech[2]				
Polls[3]				
Other				

[1] Background
campaign
[2] Inter

with supporters of Nixon in other programming such as the regular Sunday "press conference" programs.

Most of the reporting of Nixon was by the regular White House reporters Tom Jarriel and Bill Gill for *AEN*, Dan Rather and Robert Pierpoint for *CEN*, and Richard Valeriani for *NNN*. Frank Reynolds (ABC) and Bruce Morton (CBS) did more reports on McGovern than did any other reporters for their respective networks. NBC divided most of the coverage of McGovern among Ron Nessen, John Dancy, and Catherine Mackin, who, under a new NBC plan, rotated in the assignment. These were certainly not the only reporters covering the candidates. In all, eight anchormen and twenty-five reporters covered the campaign during the eleven weeks.

On all three networks 5 percent of all stories were about polls and another 10 percent mentioned polls with no important differences among the networks. About one-fifth of all stories mentioned media as a part of the campaign. There were somewhat more of these on CBS than the other networks—just as there were more media stories about campaign practices in general on CBS.

More than half of all stories gave some information on one or more issues in the campaign—the largest percentage on CBS.

Vietnam was the issue given the most attention—18 percent of the time on all three networks. Watergate was second in importance—discussed here later—with nearly as much time. CBS gave more emphasis to government corruption and to welfare than the others and less to foreign policy. When the ranks of the time given to various issues is compared for the three networks, there are no important differences.

Television has been criticized in the past for not giving more attention to issues—and that charge was generally supported by the data here. Most coverage of Nixon and McGovern as candidates was a view of parades, crowds, and short speeches. Only CBS had special reports—three—that gave any significant reviews of candidates' stands on the issues. CBS also did special lengthy reports on three related campaign issues: the wheat deal (9/27), welfare (10/17), and two on Watergate (10/27 and 10/31).

Each evening much of the reporting of the candidate's day and the basic "hard" news about the campaign was very similar on all three networks. On a given day, about half of all the stories on Nixon and McGovern were essentially the same on all three networks. For just the categories of "candidate's day" and "related spot news" nearly 80 percent of the stories were the same on at least two networks each day.[9]

Several measures were used to detect direction bias in reporting or presentation of the candidates. While the differences were very slight, ABC was more likely than CBS or NBC to have stories about Nixon earlier in the order of political stories on each night's broadcast. CBS put stories about McGovern in the first or second position (among political stories) more frequently than either NBC or ABC—and had more stories about McGovern in these primary positions than about Nixon. Again, these differences were slight but consistent for stories about the candidate's day, campaign practices, related spot news, and for the total.

All stories containing statements—either actually shown on screen or attributed—judged favorable or unfavorable were coded as to the source of the statement. For all three networks there were more total negative (unfavorable) statements about both candidates compared with positive (favorable) statements. As would be expected, most favorable statements were from the candidate and his party, most negative items from the opposition. Comparing the ratio (percent of favorable to unfavorable) of these statements, CBS would appear to have given the most favorable treatment to Nixon, NBC the most favorable to McGovern. Comparing only statements by the network reporters or attributed to a network reporter, all three networks were more favorable to Nixon than McGovern—though CBS was the most "fair" in this category.

Two other judgments were made for each story to measure direction. After being screened, each story was coded as positive, neutral, or negative based on the question "given the *overall tone* of this report, was it more favorable or unfavorable toward the candidate?" For all three networks about 80 percent of all stories were judged to be neutral. ABC was slightly negative toward Nixon and McGovern. CBS and NBC were both slightly more negative then positive toward McGovern, and slightly more positive than negative toward Nixon.

Next we asked: was "the interpretation (if any) by the reporter more favorable or unfavorable toward the candidate?" In this case about 90 percent of all stories were judged neutral with no important difference among the networks for the two candidates. Both ABC and CBS were more negative than positive for both McGovern and Nixon. Interpreta-

Table 3. Favorable and Unfavorable Statements

Figurse show the number of stories that contained a favorable or unfavorable statement about McGovern or Nixon and whether the statement was actually seen, or only attributed. More than one of these categories could be coded for each story; the average was 1.5.

	ABC		CBS		NBC	
	McG	Nix	McG	Nix	McG	Nix
Favorable						
By Candidate	16	5	23	9	22	4
Attrib. to Candidate	14	4	14	10	15	10
By Same Party	12	20	18	20	15	17
Attrib. to Party	12	11	16	19	21	12
By Other Party	4	1	2	1	1	1
Attrib. to Other	1	3	2	2	2	6
Attrib. to Other	1	3	2	2	2	6
By Other People	6	15	8	8	9	8
Attrib. to Other	11	22	14	37	14	29
By Reporter	18	22	29	32	32	37
Attrib. to Reporter	1	—	3	2	2	1
Unfavorable						
By Candidate	2	—	—	—	1	—
Attrib. to Candidate	1	2	3	2	3	1
By Same Party	4	—	7	2	1	2
Attrib. to Party	11	—	15	1	6	4
By Other Party	21	47	28	50	18	51
Attrib. to Other	24	48	30	53	24	48
By Other People	6	6	9	9	12	11
Attrib. to Other	32	14	45	18	34	14
By Reporter	27	13	28	20	36	17
Attrib. to Reporter	1	—	2	—	2	3
Total Favorable	95	103	129	140	133	125
Total Unfavorable	129	130	167	155	137	151
Ratio Favorable to Unfavorable	.74	.79	.77	.90	.97	.82

tion by NBC reporters was more negative toward McGovern and very slightly more positive toward Nixon.

Taking these four measures together: all three networks were negative toward McGovern, ABC was negative toward Nixon, CBS was neutral toward Nixon, and NBC was the most positive toward Nixon. The most important conclusion, however, was that in the main the coverage was balanced between negative and positive evaluations of the candidates, and the great majority of the stories were judged to be neutral in direction and without evaluative reporter interpretation.

In conclusion, there was no clear-cut pattern of "direction" in favor of or critical of either candidate in the 1972 general election campaign as reported on the three network evening news broadcasts.[10] For the measurements used here ABC—often thought to be the most favored by the White House—was critical of Nixon on three of four measures but gave him better "position." CBS was more negative than positive to McGovern, but gave him better position; neutral to Nixon but gave him more time. NBC was negative toward McGovern on four of four measures, was positive to Nixon (3 to 4) and gave Nixon more time and better position. In all of these cases, however, the differences were small, and in general both candidates received fair and balanced coverage.

Further, looking at all the measures above for each indivudal reporter, no pattern of positive or negative direction emerges. Dan Rather, labeled as the correspondent most hated by the White House, was judged to have presented four "pro," one "anti," and 19 "neutral" reports about Nixon. Howard K. Smith, described as having a "love feast" with the White House during the primaries, was judged to have given two "pro," two "anti," and 19 neutral stories.

The different measures used here and the conclusions that can be drawn from them show the difficulty in putting to rest arguments of news bias. As noted above, the coverage of the 1972 campaign was studied intensively. Ten other detailed content analysis studies conducted by university researchers generally agreed that network news coverage did not deliberately favor Nixon or McGovern. According to Robert Frank's work, NBC gave more coverage to the Vietnam War while CBS covered more domestic news and gave more time to the Republicans, but that did not "demonstrate bias existing uniformly across all message dimensions." Robert Meadow says that McGovern got more coverage than Nixon as candidate, but when Nixon as president is considered the GOP got the most time. There were more negative statements about both parties and candidates, as reported by Dennis Lowery, although these were not from reporters but in quotations or in putting partisans on the air. Lowery does conclude that a study of the nonverbal part of the coverage revealed a pattern that can "be interpreted as pro-McGovern bias." In the largest and most detailed study, Richard Hofstetter says: "We can increase our confidence that partisan bias did *not* dominate network coverage of the 1972 presidential campaign."[11]

Watergate. With this general review of the campaign and an analysis of the network evening news coverage, we turn now to a more detailed discussion of the specific coverage of the Watergate matter during the general election.

Three issues were coded that together cover the major areas of the later Watergate hearings—(1) the break-in at Democratic National Headquarters and the subsequent trial of the case; (2) the so-called dirty tricks, particularly those of Don Segretti; and (3) the campaign funds said to be "secret" and those collected before the disclosure deadline.

CEN gave the most time to Watergate—especially the break-in; although *NNN* did just as many stories, they were not as long. Two-fifths of this extra time on CBS was in two long special reports.

Table 4. Time for Watergate Stories

Figures show the number of minutes and the percent of time of all election 1972 stories given to Watergate stories on the three network evening news programs, August 28, 1972, to November 7, 1972.

	ABC		CBS		NBC	
	Minutes	%	Minutes	%	Minutes	%
Break-in	41.5	8%	90.9	14%	46.4	9%
Dirty Tricks	25.3	5	29.1	4	30.0	6
Secret Funds	10.8	2	20.6	3	11.5	2
Total	77.6	15%	140.6	21%	88.1	17%
(N = Total number of reports)	(51)		(74)		(76)	

There were no important differences among the networks in the position, overall tone, or interpretation by the reporter for Watergate stories. *CEN* was slightly more likely to associate the Watergate break-in with Nixon's campaign, while *NNN* was more likely to "play" it as another story separate from the campaign. More than half the Watergate stories were on all three networks the same day, and three-fourths on at least two—the same duplication as for other political stories (see above). *NNN* had the most Watergate stories that were "exclusive"—not reported the same night on any other network evening news program; *AEN* had the fewest. The stories most likely to be covered by all three networks on the same day were in reaction to *Washington Post* stories leading to denials by GOP officials and stories tied to specific events with film.

Stories reported on all three networks the same evening include an October 25 press conference by Ronald Ziegler and Clark MacGregor (more details below), a new "bug" found at the Watergate building (September 14), the indictment of the seven (September 15), an assistant district attorney in Tennessee on the bugging (October 10), the fact that Stans was not indicted in Florida (October 20), and the Barker trial in Florida (November 1).

A majority of the statements (seen or attributed) coded as favorable or unfavorable in stories about Watergate were negative toward the Nixon campaign. The ratio of favorable to unfavorable statements about Nixon was about the same for the three networks—with more negative on *CEN* but a slightly higher ratio of unfavorable on *NNN*.

The overall tone and reporter interpretation of most Watergate stories were judged as neutral—but the percentage of time for negative stories was highest on *CEN*. While it can be argued that the "direction" of the *CEN* reporting was to be verified by subsequent events, it is still easy enough to see why the White House was often most critical of CBS. Most of the statements of criticism of Nixon in stories dealing with Watergate were from Democrats. While one-quarter of all stories having unfavorable statements about Nixon were Watergate stories, this did not constitute a large part of the campaign, nor was the story closely associated with candidate Nixon. In almost all cases, stories with accusations—by the *Washington Post* or by Democrats—were accompanied by a corresponding denial by GOP or White House officials. Richard Nixon never personally commented on or used the word "Watergate" on TV till much later.

Table 5. Watergate: Favorable/Unfavorable and Direction

Figures show the number of Watergate stories that contained a favorable or unfavorable statement about McGovern or Nixon, and the percent of stories judged to be positive, neutral, or negative in overall tone and reporter interpretation.

Statements	ABC	CBS	NBC
Favorable to McGovern	4	12	11
Unfavorable to McGovern	9	16	11
Favorable to Nixon	7	16	7
Unfavorable to Nixon	28	41	35
Overall Tone[1]			
Positive	—	11%	22%
Neutral	90%	77	80
Negative	10	21	18
Reporter Interpretation[1]			
Positive	—	—	—
Neutral	96%	89%	97%
Negative	4	11	3

[1] Percent of minutes.

One reason that McGovern's charges did not get more attention was that he was often upstaged by a well-planned Nixon campaign and an incumbent opponent who could make "news" almost at will. On August 28, 1972, at a press conference, McGovern asked for an investigation of GOP campaign funds; Stans replied that his procedures had been tight and accurate. But the most important story that day was the announcement by Melvin Laird that Nixon would end the draft.

On September 1, John Mitchell held a press conference denying he had anything to do with the break-in. On *CEN*, Daniel Schorr said Mitchell classified the press as the "Larry O'Brien press corps"—naming the head of the Democratic National Committee.

On September 13, the GOP filed a countersuit against the Democrats. David Brinkley commented that as a political issue the Watergate caper was falling flat. Repeating a familiar Brinkley theme, he said the public already believed in the low ethics of politicans.

On September 22, Nixon flew to the Texas-Mexico border for a "non-political" parade and a speech on drugs and "easy judges." Four days later there was a trip to New York to dedicate a museum for immigrants. There were some protesters, and Nixon said that he hoped the networks would not show only those six—referring to the protesters—but the other thousands. At this, on all three networks, a long shot showed the cheering Nixon supporters.

Probably the most controversial report of the 1972 campaign was by Catherine Mackin with Nixon in Los Angeles on September 28. She characterized the campaign as "for the most part, a series of speeches before closed audiences, invited guests only." Then she said:

> On defense spending and welfare reform, the two most controversial issues in this campaign, the two issues that are almost haunting George McGovern, there is a serious question of whether President Nixon is setting up straw men by leaving the very strong impression that McGovern is making certain proposals which in fact he is not.
>
> . . . On welfare the president accuses McGovern of wanting to give those on welfare more than those who work, which is not true.
>
> On tax reform the president says McGovern is calling for, quote, confiscation of wealth, unquote, which is not true.

At that, Ken Clawson, deputy director of communication in the White House, called Reuven Frank, then president of NBC News: "I was on the phone to Reuven Frank before the next spot came up. I said, in effect, this reporter had done a bad job journalistically."[12] Frank said he had not seen the report. After the campaign Mackin was sent to Los Angeles as a correspondent to, according to NBC, learn more about newsfilm, but David Halberstam said she was exiled because of criticism of this and other reports during the campaign. Later she moved to ABC News.

On October 3, the House Banking Committee, chaired by Rep. Wright Patman, voted not to hold hearings on Watergate and the campaign fund allegations until after the election. A week later, Sen. Edmund Muskie asked that the investigation be reopened, and the *Washington Post* said that there was a massive campaign of sabotage and a secret fund; Patman said he would reconvene his committee but failed to do so.

The earliest first-hand information on the Watergate caper was seen on CBS October 13 when Daniel Schorr interviewed Watergate collaborator Alfred Baldwin on a beach in Conneticut. Baldwin told Schorr:

Ah, my assignment initially was the monitoring of all conversation on the phone that was in the Democratic National Headquarters. . . . The conversations were transcribed . . . and then put on a log . . . and then these . . . turned over to Mr. McCord.

Schorr also reported that according to Baldwin, he was told by McCord that they were working for John Mitchell.

On October 16 and 17, Sam Donaldson (ABC) interviewed Lawrence Young of Los Angeles, who said that Donald Segretti worked for Dwight Chapin and did espionage against Democratic candidates. But the story just did not seem as important as stories that Nixon had made a surprise visit and speech to a meeting of POW families, and that McGovern had had trouble in Los Angeles with a fire marshal who tried to stop his speech.

On October 19, McGovern attacked Nixon on the spying and dirty tricks issue, but it was also the very day a Harris poll said that most Americans thought Watergate was not an important issue in the campaign.

The public attitude was reported on October 20 by Jim Kincaid in Columbus, Ohio—"the ABC city"—from which a number of reports on public opinion were filed. Four reactions were presented:

Well, it isn't much of a surprise . . . there are so many other things.

There's, I think, very little issue there as far as I've heard.

It seems like if you're . . . high-echelon political person that you can do this and nothing is said about it.

That's just the way our system operates.

Kincaid concluded that according to his sample one's political loyalties decided whether "Watergate was to be viewed with indignation, resignation or a wink."

On October 23, Daniel Schorr reported on CBS that the White House had quietly been investigating its own staff for links to Watergate. Schorr said that President Nixon had ordered John Dean to reopen the investigation and concluded:

It's believed that Dean inquiry was resumed after President Nixon was cautioned by acting FBI Director Patrick Gray that the agency had established more serious direct links to the White House than the president might know about. One presidential aide, asking not to be named, told CBS News, "Don't expect the president to admit anything before the election." But a lot of people in the White House are appalled at how far things got out of hand.

The series of Watergate reports in the *Washington Post* seemed to reach a preelection zenith on October 25, with the charges that Haldeman had controlled a secret fund for political spying. In separate press confrontations, the attorney for Hugh Sloan, Jr., said that Sloan denied that Haldeman had access to any secret fund, Ronald Ziegler attacked the newspaper (in a silent-film-only session) as printing hearsay and engaging in character assassination, and MacGregor said the *Post* was in close philosophic, strategic, and tactical "cooperation with the McGovernites." This prompted McGovern to charge, in the excerpt of a speech seen on *CEN* and *NEN*:

> No other American is so close to Richard Nixon as H. R. Haldeman. And I say that every American, whether he's a Republican, a Democrat, or an Independent, ought to be alarmed when the perversion of our political process, the wire tapping, the espionage, the sabotage, is traced right into the White House to the top man who sits day after day at the president's right hand.

AEN used an excerpt from a similar speech—apparently made earlier in the day—in which McGovern said: "It means that this whole ugly mess of corruption, of espionage, of sabotage, is now squarely traced right to the lap of Richard Nixon." That night there was a paid McGovern program on television—a speech about corruption—that had been taped two days earlier.

It later became clear why there was so much confusion in reporting Sloan's testimony to the grand jury. First, Sloan was one major source for much of Woodward and Bernstein's reporting in the *Washington Post* at this stage. Sloan told them that Haldeman knew of the secret fund, but had not told the grand jury—because, incredibly, they had not asked him.[13]

Then, on October 26, Radio Hanoi announced that a peace agreement had been reached, and at a press conference Henry Kissinger said: "We believe that peace is at hand. We believe that an agreement is within sight."

For the rest of the campaign there was little talk of Watergate. For a week, however, CBS had been planning more detailed coverage on Watergate. *CEN* had previously (September 27) presented a long (eleven minutes, twenty seconds) report on the wheat trade deal with Russia.

The first of two special reports on Watergate on *CEN* was broadcast October 27, with an introduction by Cronkite and reporting by Daniel Schorr and Joel Blocker. It ran fourteen minutes and forty seconds.[14] Such a long story is unprecedented—taking nearly two-thirds of the approximately twenty-three-minute "news hole" in the broadcast. It included a review of the break-in, the rebroadcast of part of the interview with Baldwin (September 13), and information on Segretti's activities. Cronkite concluded, "We at CBS News cannot, at this point, substantiate any Haldeman involvement." He also noted that the White House had not been willing to discuss publicly any of the specific allegations made by the nation's press (actually mostly the *Post*). For part of the report Cronkite stood away from his anchor desk in front of a visual showing the main characters and their interconnections. It was professional in tone and, some would say, effective television reporting. This same day *AEN* and *NNN* gave far more time than *CEN* to the peace settlement, which now did not seem so "at hand" (it came, of course, three months later).

A second long *CEN* report was broadcast on October 31. Running eight minutes and fifty-six seconds, it included Cronkite segments as well, with Daniel Schorr and Dan Rather.[16] Schorr said:

> We have concluded that a large secret fund was assembled in the Nixon campaign organization. Probably more than a million dollars. . . . It was a select little group who controlled the fund.

Cronkite said:

> What seems to emerge is a shadowy treasury paying for shadowy operations . . . divided between intelligence and operations projects, it seemed to resemble the CIA, from which so many of the participants came.

Dan Rather asked, "Is the president himself involved?" and concluded that if he did know it would have been through one of three men—Mitchell, Haldeman, or Chapin. He noted that the president's men kept issuing general denials: "They are depending upon that and silence to make the allegations go away."

This second report later caused more controversy. It apparently had first been scheduled to run October 30, but was delayed a day. Further, it was cut somewhat from an earlier length. Neither delay or shortening is unusual for TV news reports. In this case, however, it was alleged that changes were made in response to White House pressure, and CBS did acknowledge that Charles Colson had called to complain. William Paley, chairman and largest stockholder of CBS, and Richard Salant, then president of CBS News, acknowledged the call but stated that the reduction was based on sound and typical news judgment. Later Colson bragged to Daniel Schorr, saying, "We sure cut you down a bit." This review of all the Watergate coverage and the full record for veracity on the part of CBS News and the Nixon administration must give heavy weight to the version of CBS participants.

During the last week of the campaign, the war was the issue again, On the evening before the election, *CEN* gave a long review (eight minutes, forty seconds) of issues with excerpts from McGovern and Nixon, but Watergate was not mentioned as Walter Cronkite concluded: "No issue really dominated the campaign. Instead the polls show that voters are concentrating on the men running for office, weighing that intangible quality—credibility."

On election night Theodore White (CBS), discussing how people voted, said: "I think they were much more deeply disturbed by the access [accent?], the thrust of the McGovern campaign, particularly on defense and on amnesty, then they were stirred the other way by the Watergate scandal." Catherine Mackin (on NBC) concluded that McGovern got stuck in the public mind as representing "acid, amnesty, and abortion" and was hurt by the Eagleton affair. Theodore White concluded:

I think that the shadow on his victory is the Watergate affair, and I believe that a great many people very close to the president would like to have him move on that as one of the high priorities of his new administration.

Answering questions on CBS from Michele Clark and Schorr, Attorney General Richard Kliendienst said:

That matter has been investigated, there are indictments, and we're going to go to trial on those. So I think that the full course of justice and the prosecution of crime has to expend itself irrespective of an election.

To David Schoumacher (ABC), John Ehrlichman said: "They've

got a trial of the accused in that case, and that's probably the end of the story."

It was not the end but the beginning of the beginning. The twenty weeks from the break-in to the election were not very important in the history of Watergate. The break-in and the other revelations might have been important in the election—but they were not.

Television reported Watergate—during the election and after—the way it reported most other stories. It was best as a medium of presentation. At most it was a summary. There was less investigative reporting than some critics wanted. That came from Carl Bernstein, Bob Woodward, and many others in the print media. But it was television that would tell the nation and provide the small pictures of the experience. The story did not always come out right, but it came out.

What came to be called "The Watergate Affair" and the eventual resignation of President Nixon was a most unusual event in American history. While the important evidence came to light only after Mr. Nixon was reelected, much was suspected during the time covered in this analysis. These unusual events were covered by television and newspapers in very typical ways, for the most part. The reporting of the campaign in general and Watergate in particular was very similar on all three network evening newscasts. The most important aspect of this style was to give "balance." Thus, as with campaign arguments, each charge about Watergate was almost always neatly balanced with a statement of denial. Ziegler's statement that it was nothing but a "third-rate-burglary" will probably be the most remembered administration response.

Watergate, what was known of it during the campaign, was not an issue in the 1972 election. McGovern never had a chance after Eagleton—probably not much of a chance before. Much has been written to document the extent to which the *Washington Post* was most responsible for early and later reporting of the story. *Post* publisher Katherine Graham and executive editor Ben Bradlee would both later report that the extensive CBS coverage, described above, would be important in keeping attention on the story and specifically in getting other papers across the nation to carry the story. While that is interesting lore, it is not true so far as can be proved by a content analysis of a sample of such papers. It may be true, if only because those at the *Post* thought it so and acted accordingly.[17] The Watergate story, like much of journalism, emerged gradually and with many uncertainties. Much was written and spoken in the shorthand of news reporting citing various unnamed sources.

The "news" is commonplace and pervasive in our society. Many assume they know what is "there." Content analysis, properly and carefully done, can help with the valid and reliable study of news. Yet content analysis is often done for the wrong reasons—such as attempting to "prove bias" or promote a conclusion about the "effects" of media. Content analysis is a tool that can aid in the careful observation of what is reported. Analyses such as those noted here can provide a complete catalog of coverage to reveal trends and allow comparisons. With this information scholars can relate highlights of that coverage with more certainty and perspective. This can, then, show general themes in the coverage and provide hard data for comparisons across time.

NOTES

1. Unless otherwise noted, all quotes for evening news or other programs were transcribed from tapes by Lichty. Dates are the day reported on the evening news.

2. See "Howard K. Smith-Nixon-Agnew Axis," *Variety*, 28 June 1972. The text of the commentary in *Variety* differs slightly from the Lichty transcription.

3. Edith Efron, *The News Twisters* (Nash, 1971). Also see Edith Efron, with the assistance of Clythia Chambers, *How CBS Tried to Kill a Book* (Nash, 1972).

4. International Research Associates, "An Analysis of Thirty-Six Telecasts of 'The CBS Evening News with Walter Cronkite' Broadcast from September 16 to November 4, 1968," a report paid for and distributed by CBS, 1972; Robert L. Stevenson et. al., "Untwisting the News Twisters: A Replication of Efron's Study," *Journalism Quarterly*, Summer 1973. For other reviews of the 1968 campaign see: The American Institute for Political Communication, *Anatomy of a Crucial Election*, Washington, D.C., 1970.

Marvin Barrett ed., *Survey of Broadcast Journalism*, vol. 1, *1968–1969* (Grosset & Dunlap, 1969).

Marvin Barrett ed., *Survey of Broadcast Journalism*, vol. 2, *1969–1970* (Grosset & Dunlap, 1970).

Joe McGiniss, *The Selling of the President 1968* (Trident Press, 1969).

Harold Mendelsohn and Irving Crespi, *Polls, Television, and the New Politics* (Chandler, 1970).

Voters' Time Report of the Twentieth Century Fund Commission on Campaign Costs in the Electronic Era (The Twentieth Century Fund, 1969).

Paul H. Weaver, "Is Television News Biased?" *The Public Interest*, no. 26, Winter 1972.

John Whale, *The Half-Shut Eye: Television and Politics in Britain and America* (St. Martin's Press, 1969).

5. For more information on the methodology, and other information on the content analysis of TV news, see William Adams and Fay Schreibman, eds., *Television Network News: Issues in Content Research* (George Washington University, 1978; write Center for Telecommunications studies, GWU, Washington, D.C. 20052). Displayed there is a coding instrument similar to that used for the analysis reported here. This work also contains the most extensive review of related literature to date. All quotes and tabular material are based on an analysis of *ABC Evening News*, 1st feed, 6:00 P.M. ET Monday-Friday; *CBS Evening News*, 1st feed, 6:30 P.M. ET Monday-Saturday, and *CBS Sunday News*, 11:00 P.M. ET; and *NBC Nightly News*, 1st feed, 6:30 P.M. ET Monday-Sunday. Notes were kept by Lichty or Tim Larson. Tapes were recorded from Madison stations, except for the CBS Saturday, which was not carried in Madison, and several other Madison preemptions (for a telethon and paid political advertising—in these cases the recording was of Milwaukee or Rockford stations. No broadcasts were missed. Because of sports events, NBC Saturday and Sunday broadcasts were either not carried at all or were shorter than usual eleven times. Coding (from audiotape) was by Ray Carroll, Tim Larson, and Robert Kemper. Ray Carroll assisted with the analysis. Specifically, the proportion of news time devoted to election 1972 was: ABC 42.1 percent, CBS 44.1 percent, NBC 36.6 percent. This was a total of twenty-eight hours and fifteen minutes, or 1,076 stories by anchormen and reporters on the three networks.

Each film story, each item (separate story or subject matter) read by anchormen, and each commentary were coded as separate stories. Short (less than twenty seconds) live introductions by anchormen to film stories were counted as part of a reporter's live, film, or tape story if they were only an introduction; if anchormen gave different or additional information on a story or if the introduction was longer than twenty seconds, these were counted as anchormen stories. For a test of audio only versus audio and visual for such analysis see Richard A. Pride and Gary L. Wamsley, "Symbol Analysis of Network Coverage of Laos Incursion," *Journalism Quarterly* vol. 49 no. 4 (Winter 1972), p. 638.

6. For example, on ABC fewer than 3 percent of all reporter stories over one minute in length were live, compared with CBS, 15 percent, and NBC, 12 percent. "Reporters" was used to include anyone other than an anchorman who reports a story—usually introduced by the anchorman and ended with "(Reporter's name, Network)"; this includes those working for the network with more specific titles of correspondent, reporter, and occasionally other network personnel such as field producers or writers, and very rarely local reporters from affiliates.

7. For descriptions of this process see Timothy Crouse, *The Boys on the Bus* (Random House, 1973), particularly the chapter "Television," p. 139; and James M. Perry, *Us and Them* (Clarkson N. Potter, 1973).

8. Mr. Nixon made eleven campaign speeches broadcast on radio (ten were in the morning or afternoon, six were on Saturday or Sunday), but only one was also broadcast on TV in prime time.

9. This was tabulated only for Monday-Friday, when all three programs were on. Stories were coded as "duplicate" if they were essentially the same in subject matter and style.

10. For another review of network coverage in 1972, including some of this information, a detailed discussion of the importance of Watergate reporting later, and conclusions about this reporting and public opinion see: Gladys Engel Lang and Kurt Land, *The*

Battle for Public Opinion: The Press, the Presidency and the Polls During Watergate (New York: Columbia University Press, 1983)

A much more detailed analysis of this content might reveal more subtle differences using a technique such as evaluative assertion analysis. See, for example, Tae Guk Kim, "A Comparative Study of *Time* and *Newsweek* coverage of Buddhist Crisis of South Vietnam in 1963" (Master's thesis, Southern Illinois University, 1966). But such an analysis based on smaller units such as sentences or words would be very time consuming for such a large amount of content. Until such analyses are done and replicated, it would seem fair to conclude that most of the charges of bias in TV news must be attributed to the eye of the beholder.

11. These content analysis studies of the 1972 general election are:

Bert E. Bradley and Howard D. Doll, "A Study of the Objectivity of Television News Reporting of the 1972 Presidential Campaign" (mimeographed).

Edwin Diamond, *The Tin Kazoo: Television, Politics and News* (M.I.T. Press, 1975).

Dru Evarts and Guido H. Stemple III, "Coverage of the 1972 Campaign by TV, News Magazines and Major Newspapers," *Journalism Quarterly* 51 (Winter 1974).

Robert Shelby Frank, *Message Dimensions of Television News* (Lexington Books, 1973).

Robert S. Frank, "The 'Grammar of Film' in Television News," *Journalism Quarterly* 51 (Summer 1974).

Doris A. Graber, "Press and TV as Opinion Resources in Presidential Campaigns," *Public Opinion Quarterly* 40 (Fall 1976): 285–303.

Richard C. Hofstetter, *Bias in the News: A Study of Network Coverage of the 1972 Election Campaign* (Ohio State University Press, 1976).

Dennis T. Lowry, "Measures of Network News Bias in the 1972 Presidential Campaign," *Journalism Quarterly* 50 (Autumn 1973).

Robert G. Meadow, "Cross-Media Comparison of Coverage of the 1972 Presidential Campaign," *Journalism Quarterly* 50 (Autumn 1973).

Thomas E. Patterson and Robert D. McClure, *The Unseeing Eye: The Myth of Television Power in National Politics*. (Putnam, 1975).

For more information on the 1972 election, including several other content analyses, also see:

Alternative Educational Foundation, *Report on Network Treatment of the 1972 Democratic Presidential Candidates* (1972) (Primaries).

Marvin Barrett, ed., *The Politics of Broadcasting* (Thomas Y. Crowell, 1973).

Timothy Crouse, *The Boys on the Bus* (Random House, 1973).

Ernest W. Lefever, *TV and National Defense: An Analysis of CBS News, 1972–73* (Institute for American Strategy Press, 1974).

"Liberal Bias" as a Factor in Network Television News Reporting (The Institute for Political Communication, 1972).

Harold Mendelsohn and Gareet O'Keefe, *The People Choose a President: Influences of Voter Decision Making* (Praeger Special Studies, 1976).

Nixon Administration-Mass Media Relationship (The American Institute for Political Communication, 1974).

Robert Pepper, "An analysis of Presidential Primary Election Night Coverage," *Educational Broadcasting Review* 7 (June 1973) and "Election Night 1972: TV Network Coverage," *Journal of Broadcasting* 18 (Winter 1974).

James M. Perry, *Us and Them: How the Press Covered the 1972 Election* (Clarkson N. Potter, 1973).

12. Quoted in Aaron Latham, "The Reporter the President Hates," *New York*, 21 January 1974, p. 39; and see David Halberstam, *The Powers That Be* (Knopf, 1979), pp. 652–663.

13. This crucial point almost ended the *Washington Post*'s investigation of Watergate. See Bob Woodward and Carl Bernstein, *All the President's Men* (Simon & Schuster, 1974). This is an especially interesting segment in the movie version.

14. This report is fourteen minutes, forty seconds on the Vanderbilt TV Index videotape and on Lichty's audiotape, including information on the Patman report and contributions. Halberstam calls it "slightly more than 14 minutes" (*Atlantic Monthly*, February 1976), Whiteside refers to it as a "14-minute segment" (*The New Yorker*, 17 March 1975), and Crouse calls it "an astounding 14 minutes."

15. The impact of Cronkite standing away from the anchor desk is not known, but surely it is rare. Previously he had stood over table maps of Vietnam in reporting on the Vietnam war on *CEN* for the battles of Ia Drang Valley (November 1965) and Dak To (19 November 1967). In February 1968 he reported from Vietnam as well. Later Mideast (1973), Phnom Penh, and Saigon (1975) battles would be diagrammed at a chalk board. But this "involvement" by Cronkite in a story (and the wheat deal one) is without precedent (as noted). For the record, before becoming a regular on-air reporter for the evening news during the Korean war (when he reported from Washington), Cronkite prepared and gave regular chalk-talk briefings to then CBS anchor Douglas Edwards (in New York) on a closed circuit.

16. Halberstam says it "wound up 8 minutes," Whiteside says it "appeared in considerably shorter form," and Crouse says it was "six minutes" (see Gary Paul Gates, *Air Time: The Inside Story of CBS News*, Harper & Row, *1978*; and Halberstam, *Powers*, pp. 303–307); William S. Paley, *As It Happened* (Doubleday, 1970) and Richard Salant (letter), *Variety*, 4 December 1972 (reproduced in Paley), and Daniel Schorr, *Clearing the Air* (Berkeley Books, 1977), pp. 30–34.

17. Lichty and Ray Carroll in a separate investigation looked at the coverage of Watergate by a number of large and smaller newspapers before and after the *CEN* reports and found no increase in coverage. Similarly Lang and Lang report: "The CBS presentations were no doubt a real boost to a much harassed *Post* staff, but we could find no evidence that there was any significant change in the amount of press play given the Watergate story following the CBS special" (Lang and Lang, *Battle*).

11

The Selling of the Pentagon: Television Confronts the First Amendment

GARTH S. JOWETT

The First Amendment towers over these proceedings like a colossus and no espirit de corps and no tenderness of one member for another, should force us to topple over this monument to our liberties. . . . There may be no distinction between the right of a press reporter and a broadcaster. Otherwise the stream of news may be dried up. . . . I believe that we are embarked on a dangerous path and, what is more, we are doing it without any evidence of compelling need.
— Rep. Emmanuel Celler, July 1971[1]

We are concerned that the public be protected from deliberate staging and distortion of purportedly bona fide news.
— Rep. Harley O. Staggers, Chairman, Committee on Interstate and Foreign Commerce, April 1971.[2]

On Tuesday, February 23, 1971, during prime time, the CBS television network broadcast its documentary *The Selling of the Pentagon*; and while the controversial nature of the material presented was understood by the producers of the documentary, and a strong reaction was anticipated, the virulence and direction this reaction eventually assumed could not have been foreseen. For not only was the military-industrial establishment demonstrating the power it could mobilize to protect its own public image, but, more significantly, the congressional investigation that followed focused on the vital question of whether television news programming was to be accorded the same degree of protection that print journalism had traditionally received under the First Amendment to the Constitution. For this reason *The Selling of the Pentagon* as a historical document has a significance that transcends its content and gives this documentary a prominent place in the controversy concerning the juxtaposition of the right of free speech and the need to create controls to curb the supposed power of the mass media to shape the minds of the American public.[3]

One of the reasons that prevented CBS from foreseeing this particular reaction to the documentary was that the subject matter under scrutiny had been a part of the liberal political lexicon for many years, even predating President Eisenhower's warning farewell speech:

> In the councils of government, we must guard against the acquisition of unwarranted influence, whether sought or unsought, by the military-industrial complex. . . . We must never let the weight of this combination endanger our liberties or democratic process.[4]

The Vietnam War had been part of the nightly television sequence for more than eight years, and the reaction to draft resistance, marches in Washington, the Democratic presidential convention, and the radicalization of American society since the mid-1960s had combined to create a climate in which a substantial section of the American public (particulary those inclined to watch documentary television of this nature) were already predisposed toward a negative or at least suspicious view of the military-industrial complex. William L. O'Neill has noted, "One of the main side-effects of the Vietnam War was its tendency to discredit the military-industrial complex as a whole."[5]

The subject had also been debated in Congress, and had been extensively reviewed in a recent Twentieth Century Fund study, *The Military Establishment*, written by Adam Yarmolinsky.[6] Much of the groundwork for this CBS documentary, however, had been prepared by the junior senator from Arkansas, J. William Fulbright, who had first raised the subject in a series of four widely publicized speeches in the Senate in December 1969.[7] In November 1970, Fulbright published his book *The Pentagon Propaganda Machine*, and this formed the core around which the network constructed its version of the senator's ideas.[8] In an interview with the author, Richard S. Salant, president of CBS News at that time, noted that he originally suggested doing a show on government public-relations spending; undoubtedly influenced by the Fulbright book and other pertinent discussions, his production staff came up with the idea to concentrate on the Pentagon "propaganda machine" activities as an aspect of this problem. There was never any intent to focus deliberately on the U.S. military's behavior as an indirect attack on the Vietnam conflict.[9]

The documentary opens with a dramatic explosion caused by a rocket being fired by a jet plane, which streaks across the sky; this is followed by other explosions and shots of infantrymen running and firing rifles.[10] The narrator (Roger Mudd) says over this action that this is not Vietnam. Instead it is North Carolina, and what is going on is "an exercise in salesmanship—the selling of the Pentagon." The action shots conclude with a glimpse of civilians sitting in a reviewing stand being addressed by an officer who is explaining what they have just witnessed. The documentary immediately makes clear where it stands on the issue of such military displays, as Mudd's narration states that the free flow of information is essential to democracy, and that "misinformation, distortion, propaganda all interrupt that flow. They make it impossible for people to know what their government is doing, which, in a democracy, is crucial." The Pentagon estimated its public affairs budget at $30 million in 1971. In contrast, the narration cited the Twentieth Century Fund estimate that the real total was $190 million, exceeding by more than $40 million the combined total cost of all three networks[1] news coverage.

The documentary concentrated on three areas of activity to illustrate its theme: direct contacts with the public, Defense Department film, and the Pentagon's use of the media—the press and television. The opening showed Armed Forces Day in Fort Jackson, South Carolina, using dramatic footage of "firepower display," culminating in the last "mad minute" when all weapons are being fired simultaneously. After the demonstration children are allowed to handle the weapons, and there are several sequences of simulated gunplay:

First Child: All right, Jack, here's a cool tank.
Second Child: I'm going over to the other tank.
Third Child: Get off . . .
First Child: What are you doing?
Third Child: I'm going to shoot you.
Second Child: Ready . . . aim . . . fire!

There is a quick cut to an army colonel speaking from a podium.

This short excerpt from a lecture by Colonel John A. MacNeil proved to be one of the most controversial segments of the documentary, for what appeared on the program to be a verbatim, six-sentence passage from the talk was in fact a splicing of six separate statements taken out of sequence. The final statement was all the more devastating because the narration led into it by noting, "The Army has a regulation stating: 'Personnel should not speak on the foreign policy implication of U.S. involvement in Vietnam.'" MacNeil is then shown to be making the following statement:

1. Well, now we're coming to the heart of the problem—Vietnam. (55)
2. Now the Chinese have clearly and repeatedly stated that their land [Laos] is next on their list after Vietnam. (36)
3. If South Vietnam becomes Communist it will be difficult for Laos to exist. (48)
4. The same goes for Cambodia, and all the other countries of Southeast Asia. (48)
5. I think if the Communists were to win in South Vietnam, the record in the North—what happened in Tet of '68—makes it clear there would be a bloodbath in store for a lot of the population of the South. (73)
6. The United States is still going to remain an Asian power. (88)

The number in parentheses after each sentence indicates the page from the prepared text used by the colonel in delivering this speech to a group in Peoria, Illinois.[11]

Much of the later argument would be waged over the producer's right deliberately to create synthetic statements such as this, for in actual fact, sentences three and four were quotations MacNeil attributed to Premier Souvanna Phouma of Laos; this attribution was ommitted by the network. Thus MacNeil appeared to be contravening official military regulations by discussing policy. (In all fairness to the product, it does appear from a reading of the original MacNeil speech that he embraced Souvanna Phouma's remarks, and it is difficult to tell where Phouma left off and MacNeil began.)

The next scene involved displays of an Army Exhibit Unit in a St. Paul, Minnesota, shopping mall. Here again, the narration made it clear that despite army claims that it would not send out exhibits unless invited, the manager of the shopping mall indicates that this exhibit came about only after "a request" from the local recruiting sargeant with an indication that such exhibits were available.

The documentary illustrated its theme of the efforts to establish direct military contact with the public by showing the Air Force Thunderbirds, lecturing generals ("Tonight, like any other evening, there are between six and ten Pentagon speakers appearing in public"), and demonstrations of hand-to-hand combat by Green Berets to "about a thousand kids in New Jersey." (This last scene includes some rather unnerving shots of young children trying to copy what they have just seen by jumping on each other, kicking, or using karate chops.)[12] Civilian guided tours of key military installations were shown next, complete with grateful statements such as the following from those who had been privileged to witness the display of this nation's military power.

> Robert Greenhill: I think the message I would take back is that we have a first-class military organization led by first-class leaders and the people who carry the load on [sic] the enlisted men are some of the finest people that I've been privileged to see.

In dealing with the Pentagon's films, the documentary included several clips of films distributed for public showing, most of these featuring well-known movie and television personalities such as John Wayne, Robert Stack, James Cagney, and Jack Webb. Mudd's narration noted:

> On a policy level, the Pentagon says that it has discarded the rhetoric of confrontation . . . [but] . . . a Pentagon film often contains a map that seems to be bleeding. The blood turns out to be the spread of international communism. Interpretations of communism and assessments of Communist intent are significant themes in Defense Department films.

In particular, Jack Webb's film *Red Nightmare* (starring Jack Kelly of *Maverick* fame) is used to emphasize the Pentagon's belief that "one of the best ways to save Americans from a Red Nightmare that comes true is with films like these."

The third section of the documentary is given over to an anlysis of the Pentagon's relationship with the American media system. There are scenes from the Pentagon's daily press briefings, in which Deputy Assistant Secretary of Defense Jerry Friedheim is depicted fending off a series of questions with such statements as: "I just don't have anything I can give you on that. We'll pursue that question."

An interview with former public information officer Major Jack Tolbert, who noted that the Defense Department had many ways to get its story across "around, and over and under the media," serves to set the stage for the second controversial interview, this one with the man in charge of all Pentagon public relations, Assistant Secretary of Defense Daniel Henkin. Henkin was asked if he thought the press did a good job covering the Defense Department, and what purpose was served by the public displays of military equipment at state fairs and shopping centers.

Henkin, as required by his department, had his own tape recorder rolling at the time of the interview, and the transcript of the actual conversation between Mudd and Henkin reveals that answers were taken out of context. The significant question is whether these quotes were deliberately juxtaposed to make it appear as if the assistant secretary was, to quote Martin Mayer, "a weaseler and a fool."[13] Mayer goes on to suggest, "This episode clearly reveals a desire by the producers of the program that the man in charge of the Pentagon selling apparatus shall look bad on the home screen."[14] This interpretation was flatly denied by CBS. What caused writer-producer Peter Davis or his executive producer Perry Wolff to make the particular editing cuts they did is, of course, unknown; the results of their actions, however, caused a small earthquake in the broadcast industry.

The documentary continued its examination of Pentagon-media interaction with a review of taped television reports for home districts of congressional representatives, choosing deliberately to show a film of the new chairman of the House Armed Services Committee, F. Edward Hebert of Louisiana, interviewing a Green Beret major, who reports that "the support that the VC receives from the United States is the only thing that keeps them fighting." The question of deliberate "staging" of an event to gain effect was raised in an interview with Thomas DeMiter, a former Air Force Sergeant and cameraman, who told a story about his own exploits in which the Vietnamese troops were shown to be doing fighting actually done by U.S. forces. This issue was referred to Henkin, who noted, "There undoubtedly have been times when certain actions have been staged. I think this is true of all TV news coverage; after all, this interview here is being staged."[15]

The closing series of sequences dealt first with use of obfuscation in Army briefing sessions, and the development of a special language such as "protective reaction" or "selective ordnance" to mean the bombing of North Vietnam and napalm respectively. This was followed by a report by Tolbert about how a story on the air war over North Vietnam was deliberately "managed" for a CBS television crew to convey a sense of unity and satisfaction among Air Force personnel about the way the air war over North Vietnam was being fought. He noted that the military information arm had become so vast and so pervasive that by the sheer amount and variety of information it presented to the American public, it was able to influence public opinion. Tolbert's final comments symbolize much of what this documentary seemed to be trying to convey:

> I think this attitude [the military information arm] was able to develop allowed Vietnam to happen. Had we not been able to convince the American people prior to Vietnam that a military solution was a correct solution . . . we couldn't have had a Vietnam.

The documentary closed with a summation by Roger Mudd in which he noted:

"We have reported tonight only a fraction of the total public relations apparatus belonging to the Pentagon and supported by the taxpayers." Mudd also pointed out that President Nixon had sent a memorandum to executing agencies, criticizing what he called "self-serving and wasteful public relations efforts," and directing an end to "inappropriate promotional activities." The president specifically ordered a curtailment of "broadcast advertising, exhibits and films." Nevertheless, since the issuance of that memo, no specific programs had been deleted. The Pentagon informed CBS that there would be cuts in personnel, but not in activities. Roger Mudd closed the hour by noting that the next day would, as usual, see a full schedule of Defense Department public relations activities.

The documentary was on the air for only fourteen minutes when CBS received a telephone call attacking the program in its Washington office, and the caller accused Roger Mudd of being "an agent of a foreign power."[16] Even prior to the actual showing, on the basis of a report in the *New York Times*, Rep. F. Edward Hebert had denounced the program as "the most misleading and damaging attack on our people that I have ever heard of."[17] Thirty-seven minutes into the program, an Air Force colonel called in to object, and venting his wrath, proclaimed, "The next time I see Mudd I'm going to take the nose off his face."[18]

The response from the television critics was on the whole enthusiastic, but the reporters covering the Pentagon voiced disappointment that the show did not go far enough. The reporters' major concern was not with the amount of money being spent by the Pentagon for military public relations; just trying to get information was a much more frustrating problem, and this show had not really examined this aspect. One former Pentagon information officer confirmed this point when he noted: "The program simply didn't come to grips with the reality that Pentagon officials deliberately set out to misinform newsmen."[19]

The response to this documentary must be understood within the context of the administration-media relationship that had been established during Richard Nixon's first term in office.[20] In November 1969, Vice-President Spiro T. Agnew signaled what would be yet another period of confrontation between the administration and the nation's news media, when in his infamous Des Moines speech to the Midwest Regional Republican Committee he attacked television network news. He had called the network news officials "a little group of men . . . who decide what 40 to 50 million Americans will learn of the day's events" and who create views and opinions that "do not—and I repeat, not—represent the views of America."[21] Agnew's comments, carefully chosen and widely reported and debated, set the tone for the next five years, which, in a curious way, culminated in Watergate and Agnew's own dramatic demise as a powerful political spokesman.

The attack on *The Selling of the Pentagon* was by no means an isolated incident. Three times since 1968 a CBS documentary had been subjected to investigation by a House subcommittee; *Selling* was to be the fourth.[22] The most serious and most rancorous of these investigations had been that surrounding the show *CBS Reports: Hunger in America*, which had been aired in March 1970. This show had also been produced by Peter Davis, and among its many controversial sequences was one of a shriveled baby, supposedly dying of malnutrition in San Antonio, Texas. This had raised the ire of local and federal officials. Several members of Congress managed to persuade the FBI to detach two agents for their use and "sent them hounding down every person who had talked to or in any way assisted the producers of the show."[23] CBS had suffered a great deal of harassment over *Hunger*, despite the fact that the Federal Communications Commission (FCC) praised the network for the work done on the documentary.[24]

Hunger in America was a powerful exposé of how the United States Department of Agriculture was scuttling its own food-for-the-poor programs, with the encouragement of the congressional committees responsible for them. San Antonio civic leaders, who at this time were trying to entice visitors to Hemisphere, the world's fair the city was hosting, were incensed at the "dying baby" incident, and Rep. Henry Gonzalez of Texas for weeks afterward read into the *Congressional Record* speeches attacking the credibility of the show. In fact, the baby had died of complications following premature birth, but producer Martin Carr had insisted that hospital officials had stated that death was due to maternal malnutrition. (It is interesting to note that despite Secretary of Agriculture Orville L. Freeman's outcry, a congressional inquiry looked into these food programs, and Congress voted an additional $200 million to improve their implementation.)[25] A *New York Times* commentator noted that according to Agnew, "with Davis's hand in it, he wasn't a bit surprised to see CBS turning out another faked documentary."[26] There were similar attacks on the show by Herb Klein, the White House director of communications, Senator Robert Dole (R-Kans.), chairman of the Republican National Committee, and Secretary of Defense Melvin Laird. While these attacks were aimed at the overall depiction of military propaganda efforts, they had no legislative threats attached to them.

The real thrust of significant response came from two sources: Rep. F. Edward Hebert, chairman of the House Armed Services Committee, and Rep. Harley O. Staggers, chairman of the House Committee on Interstate and Foreign Commerce and of its Special Subcommittee on Investigations. These two individuals would set in motion over the next four-and-half months a sequence of events that would have far-reaching consequences, raising issues of vital importance concerning the legitimacy of the methods used by the mass media in the creation of documentaries, as well as the right of the government to obtain material used in the production process.

CBS was in a difficult position; the documentary itself was now the subject of intense interest for its content, but the methods by which the content had been created and presented was under attack fron influential members of Congress and the administration. On March 23, 1971, responding to the first of these issues, the network ran the documentary a second time, followed by twenty minutes of critical remarks by the vice president, Representative Hebert, and Secretary Laird, which were rebutted by CBS News president Richard Salant. This "postscript" was broadcast from 11:00 to 11:25 P.M. EST, and was once again moderated by Roger Mudd. In a filmed interview with Bob Schieffer, Hebert said of the documentary: "I think it was the most horrible thing I've seen in years. The most—the greatest disservice to the military I've ever seen on television, and I've seen some pretty bad stuff."[27] Hebert also took great exception to the clip used in *Selling* that showed him interviewing an ex-POW, claiming that it was obtained under the false representation that it was to be used in a POW documentary. (Salant countered this by quoting from a letter of permission from Hebert's press secretary, which stated, "Please feel free to use any portion of the film, as the Congressman has given his permission to do so." He also denied that the film had been obtained under false pretenses.)[28] On April 7, Representative Staggers caused subpoenas to be issued to CBS, demanding the record of the production of *The Selling of the Pentagon*, and also to NBC for the record of a proconservation documentary entitled *Say Goodbye* that had contained supposedly faked scenes of a polar bear being killed by rifle shots from a helicopter. The NBC subpoena was widely speculated to be a red herring to mask the true intent of the subcommittee—to punish CBS for *Selling*.

While NBC could very easily extricate itself by passing the subpoena along to the independent production company, David Wolper Productions, which complied without any constitutional questions, CBS was in a much more perilous predicament. It was hinted that the network's files contained material that could prove to be embarrassing to individuals such as Walter Cronkite, whose involvement in Pentagon propaganda films had given to be a difficult policy issue for the producers.[29] Also, many Pentagon informants had provided information on the basis of a guaranteed anonymity. On April 18, the network aired an entirely new show entitled *Perspective: The Selling of the Pentagon*. The show is of interest only in that its participants, Sen. J. William Fulbright, Adam Yarmolinsky, Brig. Gen. (Ret.) S.L.A. Marshall, and Arthur Sylvester, former assistant secretary of defense in the Kennedy and Johnson administrations, concentrated largely on the issue of Pentagon public relations spending, and very little on the presentation techniques of the documentary.[30]

The next move was up to CBS, and on the afternoon of April 20, on the occasion of the first executive session of the Special Subcommittee on Investigations for the hearings entitled "Subpoena Material Re Certain TV News Documentary Programs," the network responded through its deputy general counsel, John D. Appel.[31] Chairman Staggers had set the stage with his opening remarks:

> Our purpose is not to look into whether CBS has been biased against the Department of Defense. . . .
>
> The sole question under inquiry here is one which is clear, definite, and objectively ascertainable, that is, are the producers of television news documentary programs engaging in factually false and misleading filming and editing practices? . . . (P. 12)
>
> For my part, I am convinced that the American public has the right to know and understand the techniques and procedures which go into the production and presentation of the television news documentaries upon which they must rely for their knowledge of the great issues and controversies of the day. (P. 13)

CBS did not agree with Staggers on the question of the American public's "right to know," and Appel read a letter from Robert V. Evans, CBS vice-president and general counsel, which stated that CBS could not "conceive of any legitimate legislative purpose to which the materials could be relevant." In the interim the network had, however, voluntarily submitted the film and complete script of *The Selling of the Pentagon*, but refused to supply the outtakes, draft notes, payments to persons appearing, and other material that had been subpoenaed. CBS President Frank Stanton was already beginning to perceive the significance of the issues then taking shape when he took this stance. In a speech to stockholders in Los Angeles the next day, April 21, Stanton said that the issue "boils down to one central and vital question: Is this country going to continue to have a free press or is indirect censorship cynically masquerading as a 'federal standard' to be imposed upon it? The issue is as simple as that—and as crucial."[32]

The subcommittee, urged relentlessly on by its chairman, Representative Staggers, was clearly unsure of the legality of its case and the outcome of any confrontation that would involve a majority vote in the House. As F. Leslie Smith pointed out: "If the Court were to decide against the government and the Supreme Court were to uphold to the decision, the result would have been to proscribe the limits of Congressional inquiry. The Subcommittee certainly did not wish to risk this."[33] As an initial compromise, and in order to discover the strength of the CBS position, the subcommittee asked the network to submit a memorandum within ten days outlining the legal bases for its refusal to comply. In the interim, the subcommittee had obtained from the Pentagon the complete transcript of the Henkin/Mudd interview and the text of the MacNeil speech. Together with the available documentary footage from the Pentagon's files, this material constituted a large part of what the subcommittee was asking from CBS, and there was therefore no "compelling need" to continue to subpoena the outtakes. The subcommittee was, in essence, now able to judge for itself how CBS had edited the material in the making of the documentary.

The subcommittee received a further blow when, in late April, the FCC notified Staggers that the commission had decided against an official investigation of the complaints, despite the fact that the issues were "so substantial that they reach to the bedrock principles upon which our free and democratic society is founded." The commission cited its previous rulings on the *Hunger in America* and Democratic National Covention coverage cases, stating that, as in those cases, it lacked "extrinsic evidence or documents that on their face reflect deliberate distortion." Further, "It would be unwise and probably impossible for the Commission to lay down some precise line of factual accuracy—dependent always on journalistic judgement—across which broadcasters must not stray." The letter pointed out that any attempt to do so would be inconsistent with the First Amendment and the national committment to wide-open debate of public issues. CBS was not free from fault, however; the letter noted that the network had failed to address the criticisms expressed by Representative Staggers and others regarding the Henkin interview. The commission asserted, "Surely important issues are involved here, ones that every broadcast journalist should ponder most seriously."[34]

By this time the battle lines were being firmly drawn on First Amendment issues; forgotten in the increasingly strident statements issuing daily from a variety of sources was the theme of the documentary itself. The question of military public-relations activities were almost entirely ignored as the sides lined up to do battle on an issue that Richard Salant felt was "nothing more than whether free broadcast journalism can exist." Addressing a group of Boston University students, he went on to suggest that the Pentagon controversy represented "what may well be the most important, certainly the most far-reaching, First Amendment issue which has emerged in this century—the issue of how free journalism can exist in a context of licensing."[35] There was little doubt that CBS and the other networks were trying to convince the print media that they too stood to lose if Staggers's subcommittee had its way. CBS Broadcast Group president Richard W. Jencks, speaking to a meeting of the Association of American Publishers, noted that while broadcasters were regulated because of the need for allocating the broadcast spectrum, it was also true that the print media used government postal services; and yet "this has not prevented us from developing a robust legal tradition which has frustrated the government's efforts to supervise the contents of magazines."[36]

Probably because the stakes for future First Amendment interpretations were so high, the news media, with very few exceptions, lined up solidly with CBS against Staggers and his subcommittee. Dr. Frank Stanton, who was to become the symbol of the resistance to the subpoena, had told the CBS stockholders in his April 21 speech, "We will take every step necessary and open to us to resist this unwarranted action . . . and to keep broadcast journalism free of government surveillance. Too much is at stake for us to do less."[37] Stanton explicitly referred to the prestigious American Society of Newspaper Editors' resolution aligning the society with the television journalists; but there were many other organizations and individuals who supported the CBS position, including the Association of American Publishers, the American Newspaper Guild, and the National Academy of Television Arts and Sciences. The significance of the impending battle was not lost on the television community, and at the thirty-first annual Peabody awards, *The Selling of the Pentagon* was voted a special award in an obvious gesture of support, despite the fact that it had been broadcast too late to qualify officially for the 1971 ceremony. Several universities and the Emmy Committee also gave special awards to the documentary.

On April 30, Robert Evans wrote to Staggers that CBS remained "of the view that compliance with the subpoena would have a chilling effect on the ability of journalists at CBS and throughout the profession to report and interpret the news." He questioned the constitutional basis for the request of such a wide range of materials, and notified the subcommittee that "we respectfully decline to comply with the subpoena." This was not unexpected, but what was perhaps the most interesting aspect of Evans's letter was this statement:

> CBS recognizes that comments on "The Selling of the Pentagon" by other journalists have raised genuine issues as to the standards that ought to be applied in the editing of documentary broadcasts. While responsible journalists may reasonably differ concerning particular practices in particular cases, we do not intend to ignore those issues or to shrink from continuing self-examination of our standards and practices.[38]

The subcommittee had issued a new subpoena on May 26, which was "slightly redrafted" from the first one issued on April 7. The new subpoena made it clear that the subcommittee only wanted the unused parts of filmed or taped sequences which, after editing, got on the air. This new subpoena, returnable June 9, also requested the personal appearance of CBS president Frank Stanton. Even before seeing the new subpoena, Stanton stated that CBS would decline to give up any material on First Amendment grounds.[39]

The subcommittee met for the second time on May 12, at which time Assistant Secretary of Defense Henkin testified, and a deposition was read from Col. John A. MacNeil (MacNeil had in the interim filed a $6 million civil lawsuit against the network). Henkin provided detailed testimony as to how his interview had been edited; and he was characteristically fair with the network's right to cover the issue of military propaganda, refusing to speculate as to what point of view the show was trying to convey.[40]

On June 24, the subcommittee met for the third time; the star witness at these hearings was Dr. Frank Stanton, who began his testimony by stating that while he had great respect for Congress, he also had "a duty to uphold the freedom of the broadcast press against Congressional abridgement." It was the conflict between these duties that raised "a profound constitutional question going to the heart of the American democratic process."[41] Again, Stanton took the opportunity to point out the difference between print and broadcast journalism:

> There can be no doubt in anyone's mind that the First Amendment would bar this subpoena if directed at the editing of a newspaper report, a book, or a magazine article. . . . However, it is urged that, because broadcasters need governmental licenses while other media do not, the

First Amendment permits such an intrusion into the freedom of broad-cast journalism, although it admittedly forbids the identical intrusion into other press media. . . .

As broadcasters, it is our duty and responsibility in the public inter-est to resist any government action that threatens to transform a free and vigorous news medium into a controlled and timed one.[42]

Most of Stanton's testimony dealt with the usual CBS standards in dealing with the editing of interviews, as well as the circumstances surrounding the previous cases, when the network had consented to provide outtakes. (In 1969, CBS had provided outtakes of the 1968 Democratic Convention to the Commission on Violence; and also in 1969, the network had complied with a subpoena for a wide range of material dealing with "Project Nassau"—a planned documentary on an abortive invasion of Haiti.) Stanton was careful to point out that in these cases, the outtakes were made available for information, and not as a means of judging CBS's editing techniques. There was a most provocative interchange between Stanton and Representative Springer over the definition of "the press," with the congressman trying to prove, with the aid of a 1956 edition of *Webster's New Collegiate Dictionary*, that broadcasting was not part of "the press."[43] Stanton testified for more than four hours, and he was given a very rough interrogation by some members of the subcommittee. The basic thrust of Chairman Staggers and several other members was that this was not a First Amendment issue, but was, in fact, an investigation of deceit in which the public interest would be served by having all the footage shot by the network available for investigation. The hearing ended with Stanton maintain-ing his refusal to submit to the subcommittee's subpoena.

Four days later, on June 28, the subcommittee met in executive session and voted unanimously to refer the entire case to its parent Committee on Interstate and Foreign Commerce. It also voted to rec-ommend that CBS and Dr. Stanton be cited for contempt of Congress.

On June 13, 1971, as the increasingly dramatic *Selling of the Pentagon* case was moving toward its conclusion, there occurred one of those strange historical coincidences that make any attempt to establish caus-ality difficult. On that Sunday morning the *New York Times* published the first installment of what became known as the Pentagon Papers. For thirty-six hours the *Times* story went relatively unnoticed; but after the second installment on Monday the administration began to take action to have the publication of the papers stopped through court action. Moving rapidly through the courts, the Pentagon Papers case ended up in the Appellate Court on June 22; and on June 23 the case was decided against the government's position by a vote of seven to two. On June 24, the same day that Stanton gave his testimony, the Attorney General of the United States was appealing the case to the Supreme Court. Finally, on June 30, that court announced its six-to-three decision in favor of the unrestrained publication of the Pentagon Papers.[44]

It was against this background, on July 1, the day after the Supreme Court decision in the Pentagon Papers case, that the full committee, meeting in executive session, voted twenty-five to thirteen to report the matter of *The Selling of the Pentagon* to the House, with a recommendation that the network and Stanton be cited for contempt. Stanton could not help but notice the juxtaposition of the two decisions, one affecting print, the other the electronic media. He was quoted as saying: "This action is in disappointing contrast to the Supreme Court's ringing reaffirmation yesterday of the function of journalism in a free society."[45]

CBS had taken the somewhat unusual step of presenting to the subcommittee a memorandum entitled "CBS Operating Standards: News and Public Affairs" minutes before it had voted on June 29. This outlined policy regarding eight subjects: the filming of a news event, interviews and discussions, editing, prerecording and sound effects, film not made in the presence of a CBS correspondent, correspondent's signoff, payments to interviewees, and investigative reporting. Of most relevance to the *Selling* case was the passage in the section on editing that read:

> If the answer to an interview question . . . is derived, in part or in whole, from the answers to other questions, the broadcast will so indicate, either in lead-in narration, bridging narration lines during the interview, or appropriate audio lines."[46]

Clearly this procedure had not been followed in the Henkin interview or the MacNeil speech, and the subcommittee noted in a statement issued after its vote that these guidelines were similar to those issued after the infamous quiz scandals in 1959. The statement also pointed out that the techniques used in *Selling* constituted a deception on the American public far more serious than was the quiz case. William E.

Porter noted of the CBS memo: "In other words, although CBS had done nothing wrong, it had decided not to do it again."[47]

Staggers made his first bid for House support on July 8, with a floor speech and a letter to members of congress. In his floor speech Staggers urged the House to issue the contempt citation, warning that CBS's refusal to supply the outtakes could prevent enforcement of "any laws Congress might enact directed against calculated manipulation of the news."[48]

The issue came to a final vote on Tuesday, July 13, having also been debated the day before. The official 226-page committee report recommending the contempt citation to the House had taken the majority position that CBS was, in fact, a "public trustee" of the airwaves, and that the network had determined it was not answerable to the public's representatives. The debate on the issue was surprisingly heated, with Staggers continuing to insist that this was not a First Amendment matter.

The issue was finally decided when Commerce Committee member Hastings Keith (R-Mass.) introduced a motion to recommit the resolution to the committee. Keith's intentions were to have the committee report to the floor legislation that would more adequately express the intent of Congress and give authority to the FCC to move in a constitutional way that would require the networks to be as responsible for the fairness and honesty of their documentaries as for quiz shows and other programs. The House support for the motion to recommit seemed to gain favor as a way out of the impasse; a voice vote, however, seemed strongly opposed to the motion. When Keith requested a standing vote, 151 members supported the motion and 147 opposed it. Staggers requested a roll call vote, which resulted in 226 in favor, 181 opposed. Staggers commented: "The networks now control this Congress."[49] Stanton, as was to be expected, was extremely pleased by what he felt was "the decisive House vote."

Was the vote really decisive, or did the members of the House actually avoid the issue? The issues raised by the documentary were more complex than most people had originally thought they would be, and the level of emotion in the rhetoric from the floor of the Congress had risen as this fact became obvious. What had been proposed originally by Staggers's committee appeared to be punitive against the network, and its recommendations were not implementable under current

FCC regulations without incurring a lengthy court battle. Representative Keith followed through on his promises, and on July 15 he introduced legislation that would have prohibited broadcasters from staging an event or "juxtaposing or rearranging by editing" without indicating to the public that this had occurred. This proposed legislation never came to the floor. When pushed to make a decision that would have had far-reaching implications, Congress backed off, clearly not wishing at this time to deal with such complex problems.

The final outcome was a victory of sorts for CBS and broadcast journalism in general, for never in modern history had the House failed to sustain the vote of one of its committees to cite for contempt. As William E. Porter points out in his excellent analysis of these troubled years for the media:

> Titillating as the thought of Frank Stanton in jail might have been to some in the communications business, the whole industry rose with a roar of outrage. Of all the cries for freedom of expression during the Nixon years, this was the only one which provoked a widespread fighting response while there was still time for it to matter.[50]

The power of television as an instrument to inform had never been in doubt, and this perception of the medium was no doubt a major consideration in the clearly unwarranted ferocity with which Staggers set out after CBS. The personal role played by Staggers in this case is also worth considering, for he obviously did not fully comprehend the nature of the situation he was creating. He ill-advisedly sought a contempt citation for nondelivery of material that was readily available to his committee, and the Pandora's box of First Amendment issues he unwittingly opened every time he spoke doomed his case from the start.

The question of CBS's editing practices cannot be ignored. The subcommittee's entire thrust was aimed at what Representative Springer had termed "deceit bordering on fraud." Did CBS deliberately try to make Colonel MacNeil look like he was contravening Army regulations, or was it an honest mistake? Richard Salant still believes that the network performed a fair editing job, because "the selection of the relatively brief excerpts fairly represented the . . . [gist] . . . of what he was saying. And that is the essence of valid editing. . . . I do not think that what we did is significantly different from what a good newspaper reporter and editor would have done." Salant also claims that the Henkin interview was fairly representative, but that Henkin was trying to "wriggle out of a clear case of army staging by suggesting a situation which was *not* staging."[51] Frank Stanton pointed out in his testimony to the subcommittee: "The editing process is for the purpose of condensation, it is for the purpose of clarity and conciseness and it is done always by every journalist that I know fairly, objectively and in an effort to maintain the essence of what was said."[52] Clearly the practice of using cutaways to create a smoothly edited presentation was and is normal industry procedure. The problem with this particular show was that the content proved to be so volatile that the normal practice was being subjected to a level of scrutiny which made it appear that CBS was deliberately trying to deceive. There is no evidence to support such an accusation.

In the final analysis, *The Selling of the Pentagon* episode proved to be an embarrassment for the administration; both Richard Nixon and his adviser Herb Klein had disassociated themselves from the subpoena. The final result helped to define the independence of the broadcast media, but it also contributed to a general nervousness on the part of all the networks, CBS in particular. It is interesting to speculate what the House vote on the contempt citation might have been one year later, for in June 1972 the Supreme Court ruled in the Caldwell case that reporter privilege was not guaranteed by the First Amendment.[53] Richard Salant believes that the Caldwell case, which dealt with a reporter's refusal to divulge "sensitive sources," was quite a different issue. (It is interesting to note that a lengthy staff memorandum prepared for the subcommittee on the legal issues raised by the investigation of *Selling* suggested that the Caldwell decisions in the lower courts, which were in favor of retaining reporter's privilege, were "irrelevant and non-persuasive" in the CBS defense.)[54]

In many ways it was a pity that Congress did not take the opportunity to vote more decisively on the issue of electronic journalism when it had the chance. Now, more than eleven years after the *Selling* controversy, the questions raised about the methods used by television (and to a lesser extent radio) in covering the news are as volatile as ever. The electronic news media still operate under handicaps not faced by traditional print media in covering court cases, briefings, and other public events when cameras or tape recorders are limited or barred altogether. The FCC still exercises certain regulatory powers over the broadcast media that would not be tolerated by the print media, and while there now appears to be a strong shift toward deregulation of the broadcast industry by certain powers within the FCC, the outcome of this issue is unpredictable. Despite the potential for congressional interference, however, it does not appear likely that any administration is anxious to provoke an incident similar to that inspired by *The Selling of the Pentagon*. While the final resolution was legislatively inconclusive, the entire incident pointed out the dangerous vagueness of the First Amendment when applied to new technologies of communication.[55]

The Selling of the Pentagon was a milestone in the development of the television documentary, not so much for what it contained, but because it represented a clear statement that the networks could not be made to bend to government will simply because broadcasting was under some form of governmental control in the technological area. There was no evidence of a retreat; in fact CBS ran another hard-hitting documentary, *Justice in America*, just two months later (April 20, 1971). The documentaries on television have continued, as have the controversies. In many ways the reaction to some segments of CBS's *60 Minutes*, particularly in regard to editing of interviews, indicates that the issues raised by *Selling* have not been settled to anyone's satisfaction.[56] It is doubtful that they ever will.

What was forgotten in the First Amendment fight was the issue of military propaganda. The thematic content of the program became entirely incidental as the larger constitutional issue was being fought in Congress. *The Selling of the Pentagon* survives today as a primary artifact in the history of television—less for what it tells us about the American military establishment during the Vietnam years than for what it represents in the continuing judicial struggle to define and refine the meaning of the First Amendment.

NOTES

1. *Broadcasting*, 19 July 1971, p. 19.

2. *Hearings: Subpoenaed Material Re Certain TV News Documentary Programs*, 92d Cong., 2d Sess. (1970), Serial No. 92–16, p. 11.

3. There has long been a belief that the mass media have unlimited power to shape the thoughts of the mass public. This "direct-influence" theory has proven very difficult to eradicate and is responsible for a great deal of the inherent differences between the various mass media and those concerned with the moral and political welfare of society.

For more on this issue see the summaries in Melvin L. DeFleur and Sandra Ball-Rokeach, *Theories of Mass Communication*, 4th ed. (New York: Longman, 1982).

4. *Public Papers of the President: Dwight D. Eisenhower*, 1960–61, no. 421.

5. William L. O'Neill, *Coming Apart: An Informal History of America in the 1960's* (Chicago: Quadrangle Books, 1971), p. 408.

6. Adam Yarmolinsky, *The Military Establishment* (New York: Harper & Row, 1971).

7. The relationship of Fulbright's ideas on the military's public relations activities and the CBS documentary is extensively examined in Jimmie N. Rogers and Theodore Clevenger, Jr., "'The Selling of the Pentagon'; Was CBS the Fulbright Propaganda Machine?" *Quarterly Journal of Speech*, October 1971, pp. 266–273. Much of the following information on the Fulbright connection is taken from this source.

8. J. William Fulbright, *The Pentagon Propaganda Machine* (New York: Liveright, 1970).

9. Personal interview with Richard S. Salant, New York City, 12 December 1981.

10. The descriptions and dialogue are taken from the transcript in the *Congressional Record*, 26 February 1971, pp. 4103–4107, and from repeated viewing of the show.

11. The analysis of this sequence is taken from Reed J. Irvine, "The Selling of the Selling of the Pentagon," *National Review* 23 (August 10, 1971): 857–858.

12. "On April 9, 1971, the Pentagon announced that some excesses revealed by the documentary were being eliminated, including the glamorizing of judo and other hand-to-hand combat before young audiences" (Fred W. Friendly, "The Unselling of the Selling of the Pentagon," *Harper's* June 1971, p. 36).

13. Martin Mayer, *About Television* (New York: Harper & Row, 1972), p. 258.

14. Ibid., p. 259.

15. Henkin claimed later that the words "as one might say" were deliberately cut from this last sentence, and that this changed a statement into an accusation (see Friendly, "Unselling," p. 32).

16. "Unmasking the Pentagon," *Newsweek*, 8 March 1971, p. 74.

17. F. Leslie Smith, "CBS Reports: The Selling of the Pentagon," in *Mass News: Practices, Controversies, and Alternatives*, David J. Leroy and Christopher H. Sterling, eds. (Englewood Cliffs, N.J.: Prentice-Hall, 1973), p. 201.

18. *Newsweek*, 8 March 1971, p. 201.

19. Ibid.

20. The relationship of the Nixon administration with the news media had been widely covered. One of the best examinations of this topic is William E. Porter, *Assault on the Media* (Ann Arbor: The University of Michigan Press, 1976). Porter quotes Arthur Krock, the head of the Washington bureau of the *New York Times*, as noting of the Nixon-media relationship: "It's a congenital battle. They were born to fight each other like some warring tribes in Africa" (p. 7).

21. Address to the Midwest Regional Republican Committee Meeting, 13 November 1969; cited in *Congressional Record* 115 (1969):34043–34049, 34132–34134.

22. An excellent overview of the political history and context of this incident is found in F. Leslie Smith, "'Selling of the Pentagon' and the First Amendment," *Journalism History* (Spring 1975):2–5, 14.

23. Robert Sherrill, "The Happy Ending (Maybe) of 'The Selling of the Pentagon,'" *New York Times Magazine*, 16 May 1971, p. 79.

24. A detailed exposition of this controversy is found in *Hearings: Department of Agricultural Appropriations for 1970*, Part 5, 91st Cong., 1st sess. (1969).

25. See Charles M. Hammond, Jr., *The Image Decade: Television Documentary, 1965–1975* (New York: Hastings House, 1981), pp. 186–187.

26. Sherrill, "Happy Ending," p. 26.

27. Taken from the transcript of "The Selling of the Pentagon: A Postscript," CBS News, 23 March 1971, p. 1.

28. Ibid., p. 6.

29. Richard Salant stated in a letter to the author (21 December 1981) that there was no basis for these rumors. "Our refusal to turn over our notes and memoranda—a decision which Frank Stanton and I made—had absolutely nothing to do with the alleged fact that our files 'contained material which could prove to be embarrassing to individuals such as Walter Cronkite.' In fact, to this day, I do not know that there was such material. I doubt very much that there was, if for no other reason than that Walter was not, and is not, given to writing memos. When he's angry, he shouts: he doesn't write memos."

30. See transcript of "Perspective: The Selling of the Pentagon," CBS News, 18 April 1971.

31. The following section is extracted from the testimony found in *Hearings: Documentary Programs*.

32. "Face-off on the First Amendment," *Broadcasting*, 26 April 1971, p. 36.

33. Smith, "CBS Reports," p. 203.

34. *Broadcasting*, 3 May 1971, p. 18.

35. Ibid., p. 19.

36. Ibid., p. 20.

37. Ibid., 26 April 1971, p. 36.

38. The Evans letter is found in *Hearings: Documentary Programs*, pp. 154–156.

39. *Broadcasting*, 31 May 1971, p. 43.

40. Henkin revealed that *The Selling of the Pentagon* had been showed extensively to American service personnel overseas, until it had been withdrawn at the request of CBS (*Hearings: Documentary Programs*, pp. 35–36). According to Richard Salant, this was done at the request of CBS's lawyers once Colonel MacNeil filed his lawsuit (letter to author 19 May 1982).

41. *Hearings: Documentary Programs*, p. 71.

42. Ibid., pp. 73–74.

43. Stanton claims that he knew Springer before the committee hearings, and while they had once been friends, Springer had somewhat irrationally blamed CBS and Stanton for Richard Nixon having appeared in a negative fashion in the Kennedy-Nixon debates in 1960. Springer at one time refused to let Stanton visit him in his congressional office. (Personal interview with Frank Stanton, 19 January 1982).

44. The story of the Pentagon Papers is widely available. One of the best sources is Sanford J. Unger, *The Papers and the Papers* (New York: Dutton, 1972).

45. *Broadcasting*, 5 July 1971, p. 50.

46. Ibid., p. 52.

47. Porter, *Assault on the Media*, p. 122.

48. *Broadcasting*, 12 July 1971, p. 42.

49. Ibid., p. 17.

50. Porter, *Assault on the Media*, p. 113. Porter's comment about Frank Stanton in jail

is not as far-fetched as it sounds, for Stanton himself had strong visions of himself behind bars, and he was prepared to go, if necessary. Stanton claims that Attorney General John Mitchell informed him afterward that his department was preparing to send Stanton to jail the morning of the congressional debate (Stanton interview).

51. Letter from Salant.

52. *Hearings: Documentary Programs*, p. 109.

53. The Caldwell case involved reporter Earl Caldwell of the *New York Times*, who had been reporting on Black Panther organizations. He had been required to promise confidentiality to inside informants as a part of gaining access to information. When he refused to provide details of what he had seen and heard to a grand jury, he was cited for contempt. In the Supreme Court decision deciding this and other similar cases, Justice Byron White, writing the majority opinion, noted that reporter privilege was not guaranteed by the First Amendment. This decision set the stage for more than one dozen jailings of reporters in the next six months. The Supreme Court case was, in fact, three cases, which are collectively referred to as the *Branzburg* ruling (408 U.S. 655 [1972]).

54. Ibid., p. 340.

55. For an excellent overview of this complex issue see Richard S. Salant, "Broadcast Journalism and the First Amendment," paper delivered to the Simons Rock of Bard College Lecture Series on First Amendment Freedoms, 6 April 1982.

56. *60 Minutes* has often run into trouble. One case involved an attempt by the defendant to force the interviewer (Mike Wallace) and his producer (Barry Lando) to reveal their "state of mind" at the time that Wallace conducted an interview with Col. Anthony Herbert regarding Herbert's involvement with alleged war crimes during the Vietnam conflict. See Herbert Lando, 441 U.S. 153, 99 S.Ct. 1635 (1979). In another case, Greenberg v. CBS, 419 N.Y.S. 2d 988 (1979), the court found that Dr. Greenberg was not a "limited public figure," as the show had made him out to be in a segment dealing with the irresponsible dispensing of amphetamines. There have been many other complaints that investigatory television shows of this nature violate privacy, deliberately distort answers to questions, and generally try to inflame public opinion. Of course, newspapers and magazines have been criticized for many years for doing the same things; the perceived power of the broadcast medium, however, has made this issue much more volatile.

12

Roots: Docudrama and the Interpretation of History

LESLIE FISHBEIN

Roots was the sleeper of the 1976–1977 television season, surprising even its makers by its phenomenal critical and commercial success. An unusual risk, ABC's production of Alex Haley's 885-page opus represented the first time that a network actually made a movie based on a major unpublished book.[1] While blacks had gained visibility on television during the 1970s, their presence had been confined largely to situation comedies and variety shows rather than drama—with the notable exception of CBS's much-touted success with *The Autobiography of Miss Jane Pittman* (1973)—and *Roots'* makers had serious reservations about whether the public would accept a historical drama about slavery as seen from the vantage point of the slave. Advance sales of commercial spots in the miniseries were sold on the prediction of a relatively modest 30 share. Shortly before its airing date, program executive Fred Silverman rescheduled the show: instead of running on twelve successive weeks, it would run for eight consecutive nights, so that if it failed the agony would not be prolonged.[2]

Silverman's decision contributed to *Roots'* phenomenal success, but that decision itself derived from an odd blend of courage and caution. Producer Stan Margulies initially suggested the concept of a *Roots* week, but an ABC executive was fearful of the consequences of a low audience share the first night, so the idea was dropped for a year. "A year later," Margulies noted, "when we had completed production, and the big decision of how to show *Roots* came up again, this was raised, and to his credit Freddie Silverman, who was then head of the network, said, 'We've done something in making this that no one has ever done before. Let's show it in a way that no one has ever shown television before!'" In order to avoid losing the week in case of *Roots*' failure, Silverman kept strong programs like *Happy Days* and *Laverne and Shirley* and parceled *Roots* out in one- and two-hour segments; his innovative use of consecutive programming made television history.[3] Brandon Stoddard, then the executive in charge of ABC's novels for television, views Silverman's decision as simultaneously bold and circumspect: "It's certain that Fred's idea of scheduling it in one week was at the time very daring and innovative and theatrical and, I think, added a tremendous amount to the success of *Roots*—there's no question about it." Stoddard noted, however, the caution implicit in scheduling the series in January rather than in the more significant sweeps week in Febraury, a rating period in which network audience share is assessed as a means of calculating the attractiveness of each network to advertisers seeking a mass audience.[4]

Roots marked a dramatic shift in the nature of television programming, even though its ultimate format may have been a product of caution as much as daring. Although *Roots* already was in production when Silverman arrived at ABC from CBS, he was primarily responsible for radically altering the format of network programming by introducing limited miniseries in lieu of open-ended weekly series, by abandoning the rigid television season in a shift to real-time programming, and by deemphasizing the situation comedy and police/adventure series in favor of the drama of the television novel.[5] ABC's previous ratings success with Leon Uris's *QB VII* in 1975 and Irwin Shaw's *Rich Man, Poor Man* in 1976 had paved the way for *Roots* by demonstrating that the miniseries form pioneered by British television had genuine appeal for American audiences.[6] The miniseries format allowed television to achieve the thematic power and narrative sweep ordinarily reserved for film; in reviewing *Roots* as a successful competitor to the movies, film critic Pauline Kael remarked: "These longer narrative forms on TV enable actors to get into their characters and take hold of a viewer's imagination."[7]

The dramatic power of *Roots* sustained audience attention for eight consecutive nights, January 23–30, 1977. According to *Newsweek*, "A.C. Nielsen reported that a record 130 million Americans—representing 85 percent of all the TV-equipped homes—watched at least part of the twelve-hour miniseries. The final episode attracted a staggering 80 million viewers, surpassing NBC's screenings of *Gone With the Wind* and the eleven Super Bowls as the highest-rated TV show of all time."[8] All eight episodes ranked among the top thirteen programs of all time in terms of estimated average audience.[9] Despite the fact that *Roots'* cast was predominantly black and its villains largely white, none of the ABC affiliates north or south rejected *Roots*. In fact, more than twenty southern cities, all formerly citadels of segregation, declared the eight-day period of the telecast *Roots* week. More than 250 colleges and universities decided to offer courses based on the television program and the book.[10]

While even during production some critics of the series had feared that *Roots* would exacerbate racial tensions, if anything it served to promote racial harmony and understanding.[11] A handful of violent incidents did follow the broadcast. After a rape episode on *Roots*, black youths clashed with white youths in a parking lot of a Hot Springs, Arkansas, high school, leaving three students injured and eighteen arrested.[12] According to Kenneth K. Hur and John P. Robinson, "'Roots' was also blamed for racial disturbances at schools in Pennsylvania, Michigan and Mississippi, and for a siege in Cincinnati in which a man took hostages and demanded the return of his son he had abandoned 19 years previously."[13] But apart from these isolated instances of hostility, *Roots* seemed to have had a genuinely humanitarian influence on its audience. An informal survey of National Association for the Advancement of Colored People branch leaders in selected cities nationwide revealed highly positive local response; *Roots* was credited with reviving and strengthening the black-history offerings in schools and colleges, with enlightening whites about the black heritage, and with improving the quality of television programming.[14]

Various local surveys of black as well as white viewers indicated either that *Roots* had relatively little impact upon viewers' attitudes, since those most sympathetic to the plight of slavery were most likely to watch the programs in the first place, or that its effects were largely humanitarian. A Cleveland survey found that racially liberal whites viewed the programs in disproportionate numbers and were predisposed to be sympathetic to the shows' content; the data suggested that such liberals were most influenced by *Roots*' depiction of the hardships of slavery.[15] An investigation of the response of teenagers in metropolitan Cleveland similarly revealed that the racial attitudes of the teenagers rather than degree of viewing was the most accurate predictor of perceptions of the hardships of slavery; *Roots* had most impact on already liberal youths of both races.[16] A study of the racially heterogeneous southern community of Austin, Texas, a city with substantial representation of both nonwhites and Mexican-Americans, revealed a generally favorable impact of *Roots* upon its viewing audience. The white community in particular was overwhelmingly positive in its response: "They felt that the program was an accurate depiction of slavery, that the cruel and generally senseless whites depicted in the program were accurately portrayed, and they may have learned a great deal about the black culture and heritage that was previously 'missing.'"[17] A national telephone survey of 971 respondents revealed that although it was widely hypothesized that whites would react to *Roots* with increased tolerance and blacks with increased hatred or prejudice, in fact both black and white respondents overwhelmingly indicated sadness to have been their predominant reaction to the programs. *Roots* appears to have been a learning experience for both races, to have increased understanding of blacks, and to have fostered interracial communication.[18] A summary of research findings from five studies of the *Roots* phenomenon, including three mentioned above, indicates that *Roots* either reinforced audience preconceptions or that it "performed a prosocial, humanistic, and informational role for viewers."[19] At any rate, the series did nothing significant to exacerbate racial tensions and may well have eased them by fostering understanding and communication.

Roots' popular success was matched by the critical attention it received. The dramatization garnered an extraordinary thirty-seven Emmy nominations, far surpassing the record of twenty-three nominations of *Rich Man, Poor Man* the year before. The show actually received nine Emmys in fourteen categories, including that for "outstanding limited series."[20] It also was named "program of the year" at the Television Critics' Circle Awards.[21] *Roots*' author, Alex Haley, was himself deluged with honors, including a National Book Award and a special Pulitzer Prize.[22]

Roots' extraordinary popularity was the product of a combination of factors, some largely fortuitous and others the result of shrewd programming and marketing techniques. Published October 1, 1976, Alex Haley's book *Roots*, on which the series was based, became the nation's top best-seller within a month.[23] Prior to the book's appearance, its author estimated that as a result of his indefatigable lecturing during the previous six years, more than a million people had learned of his family history and of the book in which it had been reconstructed.[24] Actual publication transformed Haley into an instant public hero: "It was perhaps the first time in history a writer was so quickly elevated to this kind of 'celebrity.'"[25] But the ABC dramatization further fueled the demand for the hardcover edition, and sales hit a one-day peak of sixty-seven thousand on the third day of the TV series.[26] Haley's publisher, Doubleday, expected a favorable public response to the book, but initially the firm projected a first print run of fifty thousand copies. When Doubleday executives met with David Wolper, executive producer of the ABC series, and Brandon Stoddard, both men indicated that such a projection was ludicrously low, that Haley's material was far more powerful than the publisher realized. Nor did the Doubleday executives fully appreciate the degree to which the television version would be a twelve-hour commercial for their product.[27] Perhaps buoyed by Wolper's and Stoddard's optimism, Doubleday proved sufficiently confident of the book's success to risk a record first printing of a hard cover edition of two hundred thousand, which paid off royally once the series was televised; *Roots* remained on the best-seller list for months and sold more than a million copies at $12.50 during 1977.[82] Hence part of *Roots'* popularity as a television series was predicated upon the startling success of the book on which it was based.

Roots' success also may derive from the craftsmanship of its structure. The narrative structure of the miniseries is highly satisfying, combining the lure of end-of-episode teasers with thematic coherence within individual shows. Each show treats a single theme, an approach unique to *Roots* and to its sequel *Roots: The Next Generation*, and provides thematic resolution for the viewer by the end of the episode. While this thematic approach was employed far more blatantly in *Roots: The Next Generations* two years later, it is already present in *Roots*. For example, the first show deals with the pain and hardship slaveholding caused the whites engaged in the slave trade, a theme treated only marginally in later episodes.[29] We see the gradual corruption of a man of Puritan temperament, Captain Thomas Davies, a man of honor and steel determination, who succumbs to temptation and proves to be corruptible because he is willing to set aside his scruples to carry a cargo of slaves. Captain Davies initially merits our sympathy and respect. The script describes him as "a man who commanded by intelligence and preparation. . . . Any ship of which he's master is going to arrive on time and intact." Davies is a *naïf* regarding the means of torture employed to subdue the captured slaves; he takes refuge from the troubling world by reading the Bible, and he prefers to sail on the Sabbath to bless even this mercenary voyage—"Seems the Christian thing to do"—a decision that contrasts ironically with his distasteful inspection of the thumbscrews used to achieve compliance from the captured female slaves.

Davies regrets his decision to take command and confides his disenchantment in a letter to his wife, telling her how he rues his separation from his family, leaving unstated the moral degradation this venture has entailed, as first mate Slater enters with a terrified black girl brought to be a "belly-warmer" for the captain: "Little flesh to take the chill off them cold sheets. Didn't figure it'd be any problem to a highborn Christian man like you, sir." Although Davies insists that he does not approve of fornication, he longs for human warmth to allow him respite from his moral struggle, and he attempts to dissolve her terror, ironically introducing himself by his Christian name to the uncomprehending female and invoking heaven when he realizes that she does not understand him. Davies is ordinarily a righteous man who is corrupted by his participation in a mercenary, racist enterprise. The gradual progress of his corruption makes it seem inevitable, and we are meant both to pity him and to identify with him as a man buffeted by forces beyond his control. It is satisfying to unmask him as human and fallible even as we condemn his lapses from Christian morality.

Moreover, the narrative structure of *Roots* is surprisingly upbeat for a drama dealing with so grim a subject as slavery. With the exception of the sixth and seventh shows, which end ominously, each evening's viewing ends with a minor triumph or on a note of promise. *Roots* never sinks into despair regarding the fate of the slaves it portrays. After its harrowing scenes of the Middle Passage, the first show concludes with the exhortation of the Wrestler, a tribal leader, for the slaves to unite as one village, to learn each other's languages, so that they may destroy their enemies, ending with Kunta's voice repeating in incantatory rhythm: "We will live! We will live!"[30]

The second show ends similarly. The overseer Ames has ordered Kunta to be beaten until he submits to his slave name Toby. Fiddler ministers to the defeated Kunta, offering him solace, reassuring him of his African identity. Fiddler fondly soothes Kunta and consoles him: "There goin' to be another day! you hear me?—There gonna be another day."[31] The verbal promise is reinforced both visually and auditorially. The camera pulls back from the scene as Fiddler rocks Kunta in his arms, sponging his wrists, a Christological image made more emphatic by the cross formed by the fencing; as we see the final image of the plantation, we hear the drumbeats of Africa, a reminder that Kunta's African identity has not been effaced. The ending of the third show reinforces this theme. Kunta has been maimed by brutal slave-catchers, who amputated his foot; he has recovered his health due to the kindly ministrations of the main-house cook, Bell, who has taunted him into walking. Her pleasure at his accomplishment dims as Kunta reasserts his African identity: "Bell—I ain't no damn Toby! I Kunta Kinte, son of Omoro and Binta Kinte . . . A Mandinka fightin' man from the village of Juffure . . . and I'm gonna do better than walk. (*beat*) *Damnit! I'm gonna learn to run!*"[32] Kunta exults in his new-found strength, and his forward movement is our last image of him.

The triumphs are proof of human will, of the persistence of identity despite the obliterating impact of slavery. At the end of the fourth show, Kunta has opted to remain with Bell and their newborn daughter rather than follow the Drummer north to freedom. To reassure Bell, whose two children had been sold away from her after her first husband tried to escape, Kunta has given their daughter the Mandinka name of Kizzy to remind her that she has come from a special people and that she has a special destiny. The scene ends with the camera tightly focused on the baby Kizzy as we hear Kunta's voice: "Your name mean 'stay put'—but it don't mean 'stay a slave'—it won't *never* mean dat!!!"[33] Although this tiny creature cannot possibly comprehend her father's meaning, his words may serve to chart her future course; in her new life is the family's hope of redemption. In the fifth show the promise of Kizzy's name is betrayed as she is sold away from her parents because she aided her young beau Noah in his futile attempt to escape. Purchased by cockfighter Tom Moore, who rapes her the first night she is on his plantation, Kizzy recovers from her wounds by vowing vengeance against her oppressor. She grimly informs Malizy: "When I has my baby . . . he's gonna be a boy. (*beat*) And when that boys grows up, I promise you one thing . . . Massa Tom Lea is gonna get what he deserve . . ."[34] Kizzy's eyes glow with a hatred that will give her the sustenance her family no longer can provide.

The sixth and seventh shows end more ominously than the others, but they too bear witness to the small triumphs possible even in slavery. The sixth show was revised significantly for telecast, its penultimate and final scenes transposed. In the August 11, 1976, script by James Lee and William Blinn, the show ends as Kizzy takes revenge on the now-ancient Missy Anne, after the latter refuses her recognition, by surreptitiously spitting into her drinking cup before she hands it to her, small revenge for a betrayal of friendship, yet a minor victory that makes life worth living.[35] As actually telecast that scene precedes another in which Mrs. Moore asks her husband how Chicken George will react when he returns from England only to learn that his family has been sold off. Moore replies cynically: "He won't come back white, my dear . . . he'll still come back a nigger. (*then*) And, really, what's a nigger to do?" He takes up his drink and continues to stare emptily out the window.[36] The televised version reduces the significance of Kizzy's minor triumph and builds suspense regarding how Chicken George will seek to reunite his family and bring it to freedom.

The seventh show also juxtaposes triumph and ominous suspense. Tom has been forced to kill Jemmy Brent, a Confederate deserter caught trying to rape Tom's wife, Irene. In killing Brent, Tom has taken up his father's mantle. When Irene turns to Tom for guidance, "he draws himself up commandingly and suddenly we see the stamp of Chicken George on him, as never before—father and leader," as he tells her they will "bury him deep . . . and forget his name!" The episode actually ends, however, with Jemmy's brother Evan Brent, suspicious about Tom's battered face, menacing Tom: "You ain't seen the last of me . . ." as he jerks on his horse's bit and rides away. The camera focuses tightly on Tom: "His gaze is burning, fierce and unconquered. As he watches Brent go, a small flicker of triumph forms in his expression as we: FADE OUT."[37]

While the note of promise or minor triumph in the earlier shows is tempered by the bitter reality of slavery, by the end of the eighth show black/white power relationships have been altered significantly, and true optimism is possible. The final show concludes with a series of major triumphs: through a ruse of Chicken George, the family escapes from peonage; it moves to its own land in Tennessee and pays tribute to its African forebear, Kunta Kinte. Chicken George intones: "Hear me Kunta . . . Hear me, ol' African . . . you who was took from your father's house in chains . . . an' made a slave in a strange land . . . you who endured because you dreamed of bein' free . . . Hear me, African . . . the flesh of your flesh has come home to freedom . . . An' you is free at last . . . and so are we . . ." By invoking Kunta Kinte, this speech provides dramatic closure for the entire series. Its rhetoric echoes the famous "I Have a Dream" speech by Martin Luther King, Jr., in its final peroration. The show then telescopes the remainder of the family history even more drastically than Haley's own book and ends with the camera revealing the narrator of that history to be Haley himself, who tells of his obsessive search to learn of his family and its history, a search that took twelve years to complete and that resulted in a book called *Roots*.[38] At this point the show's optimism is complete: not only have Haley's ancestors achieved freedom and even prosperity, but Haley has done what blacks had only dreamed to be possible, he has traced his ancestry back to Africa; he has found his roots, and those roots have made him free.

In translating Haley's epic tale of slavery and emancipation to the television screen, *Newsweek* pointed out, "ABC could not resist applying the now standard, novels for television formula: lots of softcore sex, blood, sadism, greed, big-star cameos and end-of-episode teasers."[39] *Roots* represented the first time nude scenes would be shown on prime-time network television. The frontal nudity, however, was allowed only during the first four hours to preserve the authentic look of the Mandinka women in Africa and on the slave ship.[40] And ABC exerted a bizarre form of censorship to preserve decorum as it titillated its audience: "By the fine calibration of ABC's censors, no bared female breast could be larger than a size 32 or shown within 18 feet of the camera," *Newsweek* reported.[41] The episodes with sadistic appeal included the lashing of young Kunta Kinte to force him to accept the slave name Toby and the brutal amputation of his foot by depraved slave-catchers. Yet not all of the sex portrayed was sensationalistic. Haley's ancestors exhibited remarkable sexual restraint, with Kunta and Kizzy experiencing prolonged periods of volitional celibacy. As Brandon Stoddard has noted, however, *Roots* contained "some wonderfully erotic and sexually alive scenes with some of the black families."[42] But with the exception of Genelva's attempted seduction of Kunta, Haley's ancestors are sexually expressive only in love relationships with potential or actual mates. Their marriages are uniformly blessed with sexual fulfillment, with satisfaction lasting even into old age, as in the case of Matilda and Chicken George, so *Roots'* portrayal of sexuality also constitutes a paean to familial values.

Roots debunked the myth that white Americans would reject a black dramatic series of obvious social significance.[43] But the makers of *Roots* insured this success by deliberately catering to the white middle-class sensibility. *Roots* happened to be telecast during a record cold spell at a time when many people stayed home anyway on account of the gasoline crisis, and it profited from the fact that, anticipating little serious competition, the other networks had scheduled no strong counterprogramming.[44] While such extrinsic factors might account for a greater likelihood of tuning *Roots* in, they hardly explain *Roots'* ability not only to capture but to hold white attention over a period of time. The acting in *Roots* was of a higher quality than that found in much of the contemporary cinema, according to critic Pauline Kael,[45] so *Roots* provided gratis what films no longer could assure their paying public.

Since the decision was made to cast the hitherto unknown LeVar Burton as the key role of the young Kunta Kinte, ABC hedged that risk by selecting a star supporting cast for the University of Southern California drama student.[46] The choice of an unknown actor, requiring his introduction to the American audience, provided ABC with what Stoddard calls "a whole new layer of publicity and promotion." But, more important, "from a purely casting standpoint it was essential that Kunta Kinte be seen not as an actor being Kunta Kinte but this being Kunta Kinte, which is exactly what happened."[47] Since the public had no prior image of LeVar Burton, it became easier to suspend disbelief and to forget the fact that this young man was merely acting a role. To tempt whites into viewing, the rest of the cast was laden with familiar television actors. David Wolper, executive producer of the series, explicitly admitted the use of television stars to lure white viewers in particular: "You have got to remember that the audience, the TV audience, is mostly white, middle-class whites. That's why we picked Ed

Asner, Sandy Duncan, Lloyd Bridges, Chuck Connors, Lorne Greene, Cicely Tyson, Ben Vereen, and Leslie Uggams, all known TV actors. This was planned like this, because again here, we were trying to reach the maximum white audience."[48]

While Haley's book had devoted more than a fifth of its text to a richly detailed account of Kunta Kinte's life in Africa, the television miniseries extracts Kunta Kinte from Africa well before the first two-hour segment is over.[49] Brandon Stoddard, then a vice-president for novels for television at ABC, explained retrospectively why his gamble on *Roots* paid off so extravagantly in terms of its appeal to the parochial interests of its audience: "What seems to interest Americans most are Americans. A miniseries about the French Revolution wouldn't do it. In *Roots*, we got out of Africa as fast as we could. I kept yelling at everyone, 'Get him to Annapolis. I don't care how. Tell the boats to go faster, put on more sails.' I knew that as soon as we got Kunta Kinte to America we would be okay."[50] The African segment of *Roots* is an exotic, Edenic interlude, an excursion into an explicitly primitive world to which we, like Kunta Kinte, can never return; hence it poses no challenge to the social assumptions of white Americans.

Just as Alex Haley had subtitled his book *The Saga of an American Family*, so too did the miniseries aim at catholicity of appeal by advertising itself as "the triumph of an American family."[51] Critic Karl E. Meyer has noted that *Roots*, in fact, is a dramatic allegory comparable to a medieval morality play, being neither fact nor fiction, but a didactic popular entertainment.[52] As such it is concerned with Everyman, a figure representing the problems and limits of the human condition. Kunta Kinte and his heirs have a universal symbolic significance that overshadows their individual histories. Alex Haley argued that the universal appeal of *Roots* derived from the average American's yearning for a sense of heritage, from the equalizing effect of thinking about family, lineage, and ancestry, concerns shared by every person on earth.[53] This longing for rootedness transcended racial divisions. As James Monaco has noted, "Black Americans are not alone in their search for ethnic roots, and it seems likely that millions of white viewers were attracted as much by the saga of immigration and assimilation as by the racial politics."[54]

Although Haley's slave family was certainly atypical—Kunta Kinte came directly from Africa to American shores, a fate reserved for fewer than 6 percent of all slaves; his family had an exceptionally precise oral tradition; and Haley's ancestors were unusually privileged, both in Africa and in America—the television version of *Roots* consistently presented Haley's family as symbolic of all blacks.[55] Interviewed in his ancestral village of Juffure, Haley claimed that his authorial purpose had been more universal than personal: "I began to realize then that the biggest challenge I had was to try and write a book which, although [*sic*] was the story of my family would symbolically be in fact the saga of Black people in this country." For Haley, the family history of any American black would differ only in detail from that of any other; the fundamental outlines of their heritage remain identical.[56] Since historical details seem irrelevant to such archetypal experience, whites, too, could respond equally well to the search for roots. Haley argued: "What *Roots* gets at, in whatever its form, is that it touches the pulse of how alike we human beings all are when you get down to the bottom, beneath these man-imposed differences we set one between the other."[57] The television miniseries echoed Haley's approach: LeVar Burton was presented as "a young man everybody could identify with" rather than as "a true African of two hundred years ago," and *Roots* was mounted as "a drama *about* black people for everybody."[58]

The telecast created burgeoning interest in genealogy and in popular searches for ethnic and familial heritage. "Following the TV-special, letters to the National Archives, where Haley did genealogical research in census manuscripts, tripled, and applications to use the research facilities increased by 40 percent," one scholarly journal reported. Genealogy was absorbed into the university curriculum and inspired books on Jewish and black ethnicity.[59] Alex Haley even donated $100,000 of his royalty money to the Kinte Foundation to provide guidance but no financial aid for those engaged in genealogical research.[60] The interest in genealogy may well have eclipsed the concern with slavery for many viewers. Significantly, when Haley himself appeared on *The Tonight Show* following the broadcast of *Roots*, he did not want to discuss slavery or its evils, but instead appeared obsessed with genealogy and with the notion that blacks could be integrated into American society because they too had families.[61]

French theorist Ernest Renan once argued that an essential factor in the making of a nation was "to get one's history wrong," that new historical research that illuminated the deeds of violence upon which all political formations must be founded may pose a danger to national-ity.[62] *Roots* attempted to correct a political amnesia that had buried the horrors of slavery, but instead of threatening national self-image, *Roots* generated a search for personal heritage that transcended racial lines. In illuminating certain aspects of slavery—the victimization of blacks—it obscured others: the degree of their complicity and the degradation of character that might accompany powerlessness. ABC's promotional ma-terial for *Roots* emphasized the veracity of Haley's monumental re-search, explicitly billing the series as a nonfiction "ABC Novel for Television": "The epic narrative, an eloquent testimonial to the in-domitability of the human spirit, involved 12 years of research and writing during a half-million miles of travel across three continents."[62] Despite their claims to essential truth, Haley's *Roots* and the television series create a new mythology to replace the older one: if slavery never robbed Kunta Kinte's heirs of their essential dignity, how oppressive could the "peculiar institution" have been? It is a myth, the epic story of the African, that sustains them during all their trials and tribulations. And Haley and the makers of the miniseries use *Roots* to conjure with, to provide a viable mythology to enable a modern audience to find rootedness in a troubled world.

In an era of mass society in which the concept of the self-made person seems of only antiquarian value, *Roots* created a compelling symbolic alternative. *Roots*, and even more blatantly *Roots: The Next Generations*, may be viewed as success stories recounting the rise of Haley's family as it achieved not only freedom but respect, prosperity, and status within the community. *Roots* differs, however, from most examples of American fictional or filmic treatment of the success theme. There are very few American success stories with happy end-ings, perhaps reflecting a national ambivalence toward success that allows Americans to dissipate any guilt regarding their envy of success by noting the psychological price to be paid. Novels like Theodore Dreiser's *The Financier* and F. Scott Fitzgerald's *The Great Gatsby*, and films like *Citizen Kane* and *Mildred Pierce*, seem to imply that the acqui-sition of wealth and personal power precludes true happiness and ful-fillment. *Roots* breaks with this pattern, since in the culminating episode the family has achieved freedom and dignity on its own land in Tennes-see. In an essay on the rise of ethnic consciousness during the 1970s, James A. Hijiya has noted a significant shift in the American myth of success: "The fascination with the family and the ethnic group signals, I believe, a partial retreat from the traditional ideal of the self-made man. To an unaccustomed degree, Americans are conceiving themselves as products of groups."[64]

In *Roots* what makes the family "special" and, therefore, more worthy than its peers is its preservation of its ethnic heritage and its celebration of familial values. Chicken George returns from his triumphs as a cockfighter in England not to pursue personal success nor to achieve individual freedom but to win those accomplishments for his entire family. Because the family never forgets its roots not its obligations to its patriarch, it remains in Alamance County after the Emancipation until Chicken George returns and sets into motion the chain of events that will lead to its genuine freedom from the debt slavery accompanying Reconstruction. That ultimate success may be acceptable to an American audience because it fulfills certain essential criteria: the blacks were tricked out of their freedom by the duplicity of Senator Justin—hence they deserved a better fate; their success came through cooperation with a good white, Ol' George—hence black success is not necessarily linked to white deprivation; they deserved some reward for their uncompensated hard labor on the former Harvey plantation; and, most important, their success was familial rather than individual so that it avoided the corruption of the sin of pride. If success is not personal, it can be enjoyed without anguish, since it is not tainted with selfishness. Many American success stories, including those listed above, are bittersweet or tragic precisely because success entails the betrayal of familial values; by effacing the dichotomy between family and success, *Roots* offers a far more tantalizing promise than most other versions of the American Gospel of Success.

Roots also mythologized the African past. For example, Haley and the makers of *Roots* recreated Haley's ancestral village of Juffure as a primal Eden.[65] The African jungle in the dramatization appeared "as manicured as a suburban golf course."[66] In fact, Juffure was no isolated bucolic haven but rather the center of an active slave trade in which the villagers were complicit. Recent historical research by Philip D. Curtin places eighteenth-century Juffure in the center of one of the region's most thriving Afro-American trading networks. But Haley preferred to ignore Juffure's complicity in the violence and brutality of the slave trade and instead celebrated it as untouched by sordid reality.[67] In the year in which Kunta Kinte was captured, 1767, a commercial war was brewing between Ndanco Sono, the powerful king of Nomi, and the English who refused to pay tribute for navigating the Gambia River in pursuit of the slave trade. In reviewing Haley's book, historian Willie Lee Rose noted: "It is inconceivable at any time, but particularly under these circumstances, that two white men should have dared to come ashore in the vicinty of Juffure to capture Kunta Kinte, even in the company of two Africans, as Haley describes it." If such whites had appeared, the king would have exacted a terrible revenge by using his fleet of war canoes, each carrying forty or fifty men armed with muskets. According to Rose, Kunta's childhood was based on a myth of tribal innocence: "In fact history seems entirely suspended in the African section. No external events disturb the peaceful roots of Kunta Kinte's childhood."[68] Although Haley's prose portrait of Juffure had been subject to substantial historical criticism, it was recreated intact in the television miniseries. Haley ultimately admitted his intentional fictionalization of Juffure, which actually had far more contacts with whites than the village he described: "Blacks long have needed a hypothetical Eden like whites have."[69]

The portrait of slavery that appears in the televised version of *Roots* is laden with inaccuracies, including many that had been criticized after the publication of Haley's book. For example, Dr. Andrew Billingsley has noted that the manhood rites of the Mandinka took three or four years, not the several days depicted in the film.[70] John Reynolds is portrayed farming cotton in Spotsylvania County in an era in which the crop would have been tobacco.[71] Chicken George's fate makes little sense after he is taken to Britain for five years by a wealthy Englishman to train his fighting cocks: "Despite Lord Mansfield's 1771 ruling in the Somersett case, announcing that once a slave set foot on British soil he became free, Haley has George remain a slave to the British lord. Sent back to America in 1860, George continues a slave, even though he stops off in New York, where the personal liberty laws would certainly have guaranteed his freedom, and he returns docilely to the South to entreat his master for liberty."[72]

Subsequent to the telecast the genealogical foundations upon which *Roots* was based were challenged on several fronts. A British reporter with a reputation for integrity, Mark Ottaway, spent a week in Gambia studing Haley's factual claims.[73] Ottaway's investigation revealed that

Juffure in 1767 was hardly a "'combination of third-century Athens and Club Mediterranee with peripatetic philosophers afoot!'" but rather was a "white trading post surrounded by white civilization." Its inhabitants were not victims of the slave trade but collaborators in it, aiding whites in the capture of other Africans living farther up the river, hence the improbability of one of its residents being captured in 1767. Haley seems to have chosen 1767 as the year of Kunta Kinte's capture not on the basis of information obtained in Gambia but rather because it was the only year that would coincide with Haley's American research data. Kebba Fofana, whom Haley believed to be a griot who had preserved his family's oral tradition, was in fact not a member of that hereditary caste. A reckless playboy youth, Fofana had been a drummer (*jalli*), which in Mandinka can also mean griot, but he had received no formal training in the griot's complex art and learned his stories from listening to the village elders. There is strong evidence to indicate that Fofana knew in advance the nature of Haley's quest and sought to flatter his guest by reciting a narrative pleasing to him. Shortly before his death Fofana made a deposition of the tale he had told Haley for the Gambian Archives. The names of Kunta's father and brothers do not coincide with the names used in *Roots*. It seems highly improbable that any resident of Juffure could have been captured by slavers in 1767, since the British were allowed peaceful trade by the king of Barra on the condition that none of his subjects should ever be captured as a slave. The African evidence makes it likely that Fofana's Kunta Kinte was captured after 1829. Ottaway argued, "It is undoubtedly on the assumption of accuracy that the book's commercial success is founded"; while his investigation cast doubt on that accuracy, he conceded that the symbolic truth of *Roots* remained untarnished.[74]

More recently Professor Gary B. Mills of the University of Alabama and his wife, Elizabeth Shown Mills, a certified genealogist who specializes in the ethnic minorities of the South, have demonstrated the utter unreliability of Haley's pre-Civil War genealogical research. Crucial to Haley's narrative is the linkage of the identity of the captured Kunta Kinte to that of the American slave Toby. The Millses discovered that the "*Waller slave Toby appeared in six separate documents of record over a period of four years* preceding *the arrival of the* [*ship*] *Lord Ligonier*. Toby Waller was not Kunta Kinte.*" Strong circumstantial evidence indicates that "*Toby died prior to the draft of the 1782 tax roll—*

which was at least eight years prior to the birth of Kizzy, according to ROOTS." Nor is it possible to substantiate that Dr. William Waller ever owned a slave named Bell who had been callously sold away from her infants. Moreover, a "Deed of Gift" by William Waller of 1767 and additional county records indicate that the doctor's niece Ann was a fully adult married woman at the time Haley portrayed her as Kizzy's childhood playmate. A thorough study of the Waller documents filed in Spotsylvania County prior to 1810 and a continued study of family probate records filed through 1833 failed to uncover a single Waller slave by the name of Kizzy or by any of the other names Haley used to designate the Waller slaves. Nor does an analysis of country, state, and federal records substantiate Haley's portrait of the Lea family (renamed Moore for the television series). The only Thomas Lea in Caswell County, North Carolina, who was head of a houshold in 1806-1810 was far more affluent than the cockfighter pictured in *Roots*; Mrs. Lea was not barren and, in fact, bore at least two boys and two girls, with at least one son and one daughter surviving long enough to produce progeny of their own. The members of the Lea household do not correspond with Haley's account in *Roots*, nor could Tom Lea's economic disaster in the mid-1850s account for the dispatch of Chicken George to England in satisfaction of his debts, because Thomas Lea died between October 1844 and March 1845. In short, Haley appears to have misinterpreted or misrepresented the historical record in order to create a dramatic, stereotyped version of his family history, one with enormous popular and commercial appeal.[75]

Even the inaccuracies known at the time of the telecast were allowed to stand because the facts were far less significant than the myths *Roots* wished to generate. Haley himself conceded that *Roots* was not so much a work of history as a study in mythmaking. Haley called his methodology "faction": "All the major incidents are true, the details are as accurate as very heavy research can make them, the names and dates are real, but obviously when it comes to dialogue, and people's emotions and thoughts, I had to make things up. It's heightened history, or fiction based on real people's lives."[76] Haley's book, much like Harriet Beecher Stowe's *Uncle Tom's Cabin* (1851), is, as Meg Greenfield pointed out in *Newsweek*, "a work of historical imagination and re-creation," ultimately a powerful, provocative fiction.[77]

Subsequent events raised fundamental questions regarding Haley's authorial role in this research. In the wake of the success of the television miniseries, Alex Haley was barraged by a series of lawsuits charging him with plagiarism. While the court dismissed the charges of Dr. Margaret Walker Alexander that Haley had pilfered substantial portions of her 1966 epic novel *Jubilee*, Haley did agree to a half-million-dollar out-of-court settlement with Harold Courlander, who had charged him with plagiarizing several sizable segments of his 1967 novel *The African*. The trial illuminated the degree to which Haley had succeeded in creating an authorial persona that bore little relation to his actual experience as a writer. He denied ever having read either *Jubilee* or *The African*, an incredible omission for a writer who had spent a dozen years researching his family history. A scholarly journal asserted: "For him to have missed these books is almost akin to someone doing a book on the history of the Black church in America and knowing nothing of W. E. B. Du Bois and E. Franklin Frazier."[78] In testimony given at the trial Haley conceded that three brief passages in *Roots* had been derived from Courlander's novel. The plagiarism was depicted as inadvertent by Haley's lawyer, but his rationalization of it reveals a new side of Haley to his American audience: "Haley's counsel, George Berger of Phillips Nizer, said passages from 'The African' had probably been given to Haley during lecture tours while he was researching 'Roots,' when many of his listeners would volunteer material. The collected materials were subsequently culled by graduate students who did not identify their sources, Berger said."[79] This account contradicts Haley's repeated characterization of his twelve-year search as an arduous solitary one during which the author had to support himself with free-lance articles and lectures because any monetary return seemed so unlikely.[80] Clearly *Roots* was not simply the product of one man's quest and suffering as Haley had claimed in so many public forums, nor did it draw strictly upon his own family's authentic historical record.

The television dramatization had no more genuine respect for historical authenticity. For example, one of the most striking episodes in the televised *Roots*, the slave rebellion aboard the *Lord Ligonier*, did not occur in Haley's original version on account of seasickness and flux among the slaves.[81] There are numerous discrepancies between the miniseries and Haley's 1972 account in *The New York Times Magazine*. That account claims that the doctor, William Waller, was the one who named the African Toby after he had been maimed by slave-catchers, whereas the series has Kunta Kinte being beaten into submission less than a year after he has been acquired by the doctor's brother. In the *Times* version Kunta is captured while chopping wood to make himself a drum, whereas in the film he is making that drum, at his grandmother's request, for his younger brother Lamin. In the *Times* narrative Kunta Kinte is the eldest of four sons; perhaps to increase the pathos of his capture, he is given only one remaining brother in the film.[82] The character of Fiddler in the film has no historical basis; he is a composite of three characters in the book in order to provide continuity. David Wolper explicitly disparaged scholarly efforts to chide the film for its lack of historical accuracy: "Some critics complained because we showed a mountain peak in Henning, Tennessee, because that section of the country doesn't have mountains. Nobody cares; it is totally irrelevant. A film is not for reference, but for emotional impact to let you know how it was to live at a certain moment in time. *Roots* was supposed to let the viewing audience feel how it was to be a slave. If you're not moved by watching a film, then the film has failed."[83]

While the genealogy of *Roots* may have been flawed or even fictitious and many of the historical details inaccurate, both the book and the television miniseries provide a valuable corrective of traditional images of slavery. Certainly *Roots* effectively debunks many of the stereotypes of slave life propounded by historian Stanley M. Elkins in his seminal work *Slavery: A Problem in American Institutional and Intellectual Life* (1959). Elkins argues that the slave experience closely approximated the closed institutional framework of the Nazi concentration camp with the slaves forced to assume a strategy of accommodation via role playing in order to deal with their oppressors. Elkins claims that the role of Sambo, an infantile and utterly dependent creature, "docile but irresponsible, loyal but lazy, humble but chronically given to lying and stealing," was the most pervasive one assumed by American slaves. *Roots* argues that slaves had a remarkable ability to avoid this role, that the institution of slavery was neither coherent enough nor oppressive enough to coerce predominantly Sambolike behavior. Kunta Kinte never becomes servile despite repeated punishments, including mutilation, for his escape attempts; nor do any of his heirs identify with their owners as "good fathers"—Chicken George has to be restrained from killing his actual father when he realizes that he is no more than valuable chattel to the man. Elkins contends that slaves brought to North

America were so shocked by the effectiveness with which they were detached from their cultural background in Africa that they had no choice but to become infantile in the interests of physical and psychic survival. *Roots* shows that the African heritage was not obliterated with the first generation, that remnants of tribal culture might be transmitted even into modern times. Elkins argues that the slave child had no other viable father-image than that of the master, since the actual male parent was divested of any effective authority over the child. *Roots* presents Kunta Kinte, Chicken George, and Tom as patriarchal figures, able to command respect and to wield authority within the familial context. The miniseries makes it clear that the slave family was a viable counterweight to the oppressive nature of the "peculiar institution."[85]

In fact, *Roots* reflected the complexities of the slave experience revealed by modern historians who objected to Elkins's monolithic view of slavery. It recognized the persistence of African culture in slave society. As Lawrence W. Levine subsequently noted in *Black Culture and Black Consciousness: Afro–American Folk Thought From Slavery to Freedom* (1977):

> From the first African captives, through the years of slavery, and into the present century black Americans kept alive important strands of African consciousness and verbal art in their humor, songs, dance, speech, tales, games, folk beliefs, and aphorisms. They were able to do this because these areas of culture are often the most persistent, because whites tended not to interfere with many of these culture patterns which quickly became associated in the white mind with Negro inferiority or at least peculiar Negro racial traits, and because in a number of areas there were important cultural parallels and thus wide room for syncretism between Africans and Europeans.[85]

In *Roots* Kunta Kinte and his heirs are able to preserve vestiges of African language, folk beliefs, and customs, including the ritual of naming a newborn child by lifting it upward toward a full moon, a gesture of symbolic renewal of the link to Africa.

The willingness of modern historians to do "history from the bottom up," to take seriously as evidence slave narratives and other documents illuminating, even if indirectly, the vantage point of the slave, has revealed a hitherto undisclosed pattern of quotidian slave resistance to oppression. Gilbert Osofsky takes note of numerous slave narratives that demonstrate the slaves' "perpetual war to prevent debasement": "The powerful, the self-willed, those whose spirits could not be broken and who sometimes repulsed physically all attempts to whip them, presented the ultimate challenge to the mystique of the master caste."[86] Certainly both Kunta Kinte and Tom Moore fit this rebellious image, one that modern research demonstrates to be far more common than the Elkins model of slavery would assume.

While slave narratives were written from the perspective of those who successfully escaped the toils of slavery and thus may be biased toward expressing resistance and rebellion, the Slave Narrative Collection of the Federal Writers' Project of the Works Progress Administration, compiled during the years 1936–1938 as a result of more than two thousand interviews with former slaves, similarly debunks the Elkins thesis. The interviews reveal that the "peculiar institution" left "room for maneuver, for tactics and strategies, for blacks as well as for whites." The editor of these narratives, George P. Rawick, argues that it was the slave community, rather than the more tenuous institution of the slave's nuclear family, subject to dissolution at the master's whim, that was "the major adaptive process for the black man in America." The existence of the slave community insured that slaves did not suffer total domination by the master class; it enabled its members to alleviate the worst of their oppression and at times even to dominate their masters. Built out of materials from both their African past and their American present, "with the values and memories of Africa giving meaning and direction to the new creation," the slave community provided nurture for its members, who sought dignity and identity despite their physical subjugation.[87] In Roots the slave community is similarly portrayed as one largely supportive of its members, whether it be Bell inspiring the injured Toby to walk again or Kunta aiding the young Noah in his plan to flee North.

In fact, Roots reflects the historiographical insights of Herbert G. Gutman's The Black Family in Slavery and Freedom, 1750–1925 (1976). Relying heavily upon census manuscript materials, Gutman discovered that the prevailing stereotype of the tenuous nature of the slave family was erroneous: "Evidence of long marriages is found in all slave social settings in the decade preceding the Civil War." Despite the oppressive nature of slavery, Gutman argues, blacks were able to retain and develop familial and kinship ties that allowed them to "create and sustain a viable Afro-American culture." *Roots*, too, emphasizes the degree to which the family, based as it was on strong affectional ties and preserving remnants of the African heritage, allowed slaves to sustain dignity and identity despite generations of oppression by whites. In debunking the assertion of Daniel Patrick Moynihan that "it was by destroying the Negro family that white America broke the will of the Negro people," both Gutman's work and *Roots* have done a major service to black historiography, for they have demonstrated the essential role played by the black family in transmitting Afro-American culture across generations of enslavement.[88]

If historical details are of only peripheral interest, the series' true concern, much like Haley's, is with mythmaking. And the most potent myth that the television version has to offer is that of the family. It is ironic that Haley himself was a poor family man who had left home as a youth and subsequently was twice divorced.[89] Haley spent little time with his two children as they were growing up; he kept his family life so private that some of his oldest friends in Los Angeles did not know until Haley became a celebrity that he had grown children. Richard M. Levine has written of *Roots*' author: "Clearly, in Alex Haley, television has finally found a man whose insatiable nostalgia for the vanishing dream of the American family matches its own."[90]

The myth of the family may be a source of pride and dignity for its members, sustaining their morale despite adversity; but the family also was an institution that subverted slave efforts at escape and rebellion. The myth of the family perpetuates a nostalgic desire for self-reliance; it nourishes the belief that problems can be solved in small, decentralized units instead of preaching a wider scope for human interdependency. Historian Eric Foner has written of the constrictive effects of *Roots*' notion of the family:

> It is not simply that the narrow focus on the family inevitably precludes any attempt to portray the outside world and its institutions. To include these institutions would undermine the central theme of *Roots*—the ability of a family, through unity, self-reliance, and moral fortitude, to face and overcome adversity. Much like the Waltons confronting the depression, the family in *Roots* neither seeks nor requires outside help; individual or family effort is always sufficient.
>
> Here, I believe, lies one reason for the enormous success of *Roots* among whites as well as blacks. The emphasis on the virtues and self-

sufficiency of family life responds to a nostalgia for a time before divorce had become widespread, women had challenged their traditional homemaker role, and children had become rebellious, when the American family existed as a stable entity. Despite the black-nationalist veneer, in other words, the values of *Roots* are quintessentially American.[91]

Roots was acceptable to white audiences because of its essential conservatism; it unabashedly celebrated the family. Despite its own evidence to the contrary, *Roots* upheld the notion that the revolutionary spirit of the slaves was nurtured by the family unit. One film commentator has remarked, "Not for Alex Haley the more disturbing implications of William Styron's *The Confessions of Nat Turner*—that it was only when blacks were allowed to separate themselves from that family unit that their revolt became possible."[92] While for over a century historians and sociologists have debated the ravages to the black family wrought by slavery, Alex Haley may well have been the first to suggest that slavery may have made a positive contribution to family life.

But family life, in fact, can constrain freedom. The birth of Kizzy keeps Kunta Kinte from making a final attempt to escape to freedom. Although Kizzy had vowed to avenge her rape by Tom Moore by having her firstborn manchild kill him, Kizzy ultimately dissuades Chicken George from that course by revealing that "it'd be killing your own flesh and blood. He's your papa. You're his son." And even after emancipation the family decides to remain in North Carolina despite the depredations of the night riders, because George's wife Matilda refuses to let the family leave until her husband has returned: "We is a family and we is gonna stay a family." *Roots* fails to acknowledge that family and freedom may be mutually incompatible.[93] Nor does it ever question whether the family, as a product of hostility, may not crumble once prejudice and oppression are removed. The network may have championed *Roots* as "the triumph of an American family," but that triumph may have been purchased at the expense of freedom and social consciousness.

NOTES

The author would like to thank the Rutgers University Research Council for its fellowship support.

1. Harry F. Waters with Vern E. Smith, "One Man's Family," *Newsweek*, 21 June 1976, p. 73.

2. David L. Wolper with Quincy Troupe, *The Inside Story of T.V.'s "Roots"* (New York: Warner Books, 1978), pp. 50, 138; Richard M. Levine, "Roots and Branches," *New Times*, 4 September 1978, p. 54; James Monaco, "Roots and Angels: U.S. Television 1976–77," *Sight and Sound* 46 (Summer 1977):159.

3. Stan Margulies (producer), interview and discussion with Margulies and John Erman (director) in Arthur Knight's cinema class, University of Southern California, 15 February 1979. Film: *Roots: The Next Generations*, 1 reel, 7″, University of Southern California Special Collections. Also see Wolper with Troupe, *Inside Story*, pp. 136–139.

4. Telephone interview with Brandon Stoddard, vice-president for ABC Entertainment, Century City, California, 20 June 1981 (hereafter referred to as Stoddard interview).

5. Monaco, "Roots and Angels," p. 159.

6. Karl E. Meyer, "Rootless Mini-series," *Saturday Review*, 20 January 1979, p. 52.

7. Pauline Kael, "Where We Are Now," *The New Yorker*, 28 February 1977, p. 90.

8. Harry F. Waters with Bureau Reports, "After Haley's Comet," *Newsweek*, 14 February 1977, p. 97.

9. "Nielsen All-Time Top 25 Programs," *Nielsen Newscast*, no. 1, 1977, p. 6. Rankings based on reports through 17 April 1977.

10. Wolper with Troupe, *Inside Story*, p. 164; Les Brown, *The New York Times Encyclopedia of Television* (New York: Times Books, 1977), p. 369.

11. Stoddard interview.

12. Waters, "After Haley's Comet," pp. 97–98.

13. Kenneth K. Hur and John P. Robinson, "The Social Impact of 'Roots,'" *Journalism Quarterly* 55 (Spring 1978):19.

14. Gloster B. Current, "Cross-Country Survey on *Roots*—The Saga of Most Black Families in America," *The Crisis* 84 (May 1977):167–172.

15. Hur and Robinson, "Social Impact," pp. 20–24, 83.

16. K. Kyoon Hur, "The Impact of 'Roots' on Black and White Teenagers," *Journal of Broadcasting* 22 (Summer 1978):289–298.

17. Robert E. Balon, "The Impact of 'Roots' on a Racially Heterogeneous Southern Community: An Exploratory Study," *Journal of Broadcasting* 22 (Summer 1978):299–307. Quotation appears on p. 306.

18. John Howard, George Rothbart, and Lee Sloan, "The Response to 'Roots': A National Survey," *Journal of Broadcasting* 22 (Summer 1978):279–287.

19. Stuart H. Surlin, "'Roots' Research: A Summary of Findings," *Journal of Broadcasting* 22 (Summer 1978):309–320. Quotation appears on p. 319.

20. R. Kent Rasmussen, "'Roots'—A Growing Thicket of Controversy," *Los Angeles Times*, 24 April 1977, p. 5:1; Wolper with Troupe, *Inside Story*, p. 164.

21. Morna Murphy, "TV Critics Circle Picks 'Roots' as Program of Year, ABC Top Net," *Hollywood Reporter*, 13 April 1977.

22. Rasmussen, "Thicket of Controversy," p. 1; Hans J. Massaquoi, "Alex Haley in Juffure," *Ebony*, July 1977, p. 42.

23. "Why Alex Haley Is Suing Doubleday: An Outline of the Complaint," *Publishers Weekly*, 4 April 1977, p. 25.

24. "PW Interviews Alex Haley," *Publishers Weekly*, 6 September 1976, p. 9.

25. Wolper with Troupe, *Inside Story*, pp. 130–131.

26. "Why 'Roots' Hit Home," *Time*, 14 February 1977, p. 69.

27. Stoddard interview.

28. David A. Gerber, "Haley's *Roots* and Our Own: An Inquiry into the Nature of a Popular Phenomenon," *Journal of Ethnic Studies* 5 (Fall 1977):87.

29. Stoddard interview.

30. *Roots*, show #1, as telecast, by William Blinn and Ernest Kinoy, p. 6. Scripts of all the episodes of *Roots* were provided courtesy of David L. Wolper, David L. Wolper Productions, Warner Brothers Television, Burbank Studios, 4000 Warner Boulevard, Burbank, Calif., pp. 19, 89, 93–94. Quotation appears on p. 94.

31. *Roots*, *show* #2, as telecast, by William Blinn and Ernest Kinoy, p. 98.

32. *Roots*, show #3, teleplay by James Lee and William Blinn, 15 June 1976, 5th hour, p. 56.

33. *Roots*, show #4, by James Lee and William Blinn, 17 June 1976, 6th hour, p. 58.

34. *Roots*, show #5, by James Lee, second draft, 19 April 1976, 7th hour, p. 57. Note that rather than Tom Moore, in the script the name Tom Lea was actually used, as in Haley's book.

35. *Roots*, show #6, teleplay by James Lee and William Blinn, 11 August 1976, 8th hour, p. 51.

36. *Roots*, show VI, Part 2, 28 January 1977, Museum of Broadcasting, New York City. All the videotapes of *Roots*, *Roots One Year Later*, and *Roots: The Next Generations* were viewed courtesy of the Museum of Broadcasting.

37. *Roots*, show #7, by M. Charles Cohen, revised second draft, 30 August 1976, 10th hour, pp. 48, 50. For the last quotation the line in the actual telecast was: "You ain't seen the last of me, nigger" (*Roots*, Show VII, 29 January 1977, Museum of Broadcasting).

38. *Roots*, show #8, by M. Charles Cohen, final draft, revised final draft, 6 September 1976, pp. 100-101.

39. Harry F. Waters, "The Black Experience," *Newsweek*, 24 January 1977, p. 59.

40. Wolper with Troupe, *Inside Story*, pp. 73, 141.

41. Waters, "Black Experience," p. 59.

42. Stoddard interview.

43. Waters, "After Haley's Comet," p. 98.

44. "'Roots' Takes Hold in America," *Newsweek*, 7 February 1977, p. 26; Monaco, "Roots and Angels," p. 161.

45. Kael, "Where We Are Now," p. 90.

46. Waters, "One Man's Family," p. 73.

47. Stoddard interview.

48. Frank Rich, "A Super Sequel to Haley's Comet," *Time*, 19 February 1979. p. 87; Wolper with Troupe, *Inside Story*, pp. 62, 148.

49. Alex Haley, *Roots: The Saga of an American Family* (New York: Doubleday, 1976; reprint edition New York: Dell, 1977), pp. 11–166 out of 729 pages (all references to Haley's *Roots* will be to the mass market paperback edition, since that would be more widely available for classroom use); *Roots*, show #1, as telecast, by William Blinn and Ernest Kinoy, 27.

50. Wolper with Troupe, *Inside Story*, p. 44; Jean Vallely, "Brandon Stoddard Made a Monster Called *Roots*," *Esquire*, 13 February 1979, p. 76.

51. Haley, *Roots*, cover; Gerber, "Haley's *Roots*," p. 94.

52. Meyer, "Rootless Mini-Series," p. 52.

53. "Haley's Rx: Talk, Write, Reunite," *Time*, 14 February 1977, p. 72.

54. Monaco, "Roots and Angels," p. 161.

55. Gerber, "Haley's *Roots*," p. 90; David Herbert Donald, "Family Chronicle," *Commentary* 62 (December 1976):70–72; Harry F. Waters, "Back to 'Roots,'" *Newsweek*, 19 February 1979, p. 87.

56. Kalamu ya Salaam, "Alex Haley Root Man: A Black Genealogist," *Black Collegian*, November/December 1976, p. 32. Also see *Roots*, discussion between Alex Haley and Stan Marguilies, 1977, Pacifica Tape Library.

57. ya Salaam, "Root Man," p. 33.

58. Wolper with Troupe, *Inside Story*, pp. 81, 172.

59. Gerber, "Haley's *Roots*," pp. 87–88.

60. Lois Armstrong, "'Roots' Is Back with Brando and a Bumper Crop of Stars to Be," *People*, 26 February 1979, p. 59.

61. Stuart Byron, "Family Plot," *Film Comment* 13 (March-April 1977):31.

62. Ernest Renan, *What Is a Nation?* (1882), translated by Alfred Zimmen (London: Oxford University Press, 1939 ed.), cited in Ali A. Mazrui, "The End of America's Amnesia," *Africa Reports* 22 (May-June 1977):7–8.

63. "Roots,' Gripping 12-Hour, Multi-Part Story of an American Family, Traced from Its African Origins through 100 Years of Slave Life, Will Air on ABC Starting in 1977," press release of 14 June 1976, ABC Television Network Press Relations, 1330 Ave. of the Americas, New York, N.Y. 10019. Supplied courtesy of ABC public relations department.

64. James A. Hijiya,"Roots: Family and Ethnicity in the 1970's." *American Quarterly* 30 (Fall 1978):549.

65. Paul D. Zimmermann, "In Search of a Heritage," *Newsweek*, 27 September 1976, p. 94.

66. John J. O'Connor, "Strong 'Roots' Continues Black Odyssey," *New York Times*, 16 February 1979, p. C:1.

67. Gerber, "Haley's *Roots*," pp. 98–99; Rasmussen, "Thicket of Controversy," p. 1.

68. Willie Lee Rose, "An American Family," review of Alex Haley's *Roots*, *New York Review of Books*, (11 November 1976,) pp. 3–4.

69. Kenneth L. Woodward with Anthony Collins in London, "The Limits of 'Faction,'" *Newsweek*, 25 April 1977, p. 87.

70. Research cited in *"Roots* Grows into a Winner," *Time*, 7 February 1977, p. 96.

71. "Living with the 'Peculiar Institution,'" *Time*, 14 February 1977, p. 76.

72. Donald, "Family Chronicle," p. 73.

73. Woodward with Collins, "Limits of 'Faction,'" p. 87; Robert D. McFadden, "Some Points of 'Roots' Questioned; Haley Stands by Book as a Symbol," *New York Times*, 10 April 1977, pp. 1, 29.

74. Mark Ottaway, "Tangled Roots," *Sunday Times* (London), 10 April 1977, pp. 17, 21.

75. Gary B. Mills and Elizabeth Shown Mills, *"Roots* and the New 'Faction,'" *Virginia Magazine of History and Biography* 89 (January 1981): 7–13, 16–19, 24–26. Quotations appear on pp. 8 and 10 with italics in original.

76. Lewis H. Lapham, "The Black Man's Burden," *Harper's*, June 1977, pp. 15–16, 18; "PW Interviews," pp. 9, 10.

77. Meg Greenfield, "Uncle Tom's Roots," *Newsweek*, 14 February 1977, p. 100.

78. Herb Boyd, "Plagiarism and the *Roots* Suits," *First World: An International Journal of Black Thought* 2 (1979):32.

79. "Haley Settles Plagiarism Suit, Concedes Passages," *Publishers Weekly*, 25 December 1978, p. 22.

80. Haley, *Roots*, pp. 710–729; "PW Interviews," pp. 8–9, 12; Waters, "After Haley's Comet," p. 98.

81. Haley, *Roots*, pp. 184–207.

82. Alex Haley, "My Furthest Back Person—'The African,'" *New York Times Magazine*, 16 July 1972, pp. 13, 16.

83. Wolper with Troupe, *Inside Story*, pp. 150, 178.

84. This discussion of the Elkins thesis derives from Stanley M. Elkins, *Slavery: The Problem in American Institutional and Intellectual Life* (Chicago: University of Chicago Press, 1964); see especially pp. 82, 88, 128–130.

85. Lawrence W. Levine, *Black Culture and Black Consciousness: Afro–American Folk Thought from Slavery to Freedom* (New York: Oxofrd University Press, 1977). While this particular formulation of Levine's thesis was published after the appearance of *Roots* as a television miniseries, Levine's basic argument was readily accessible to historians in paper and article form.

86. Gilbert Osofsky, ed., *Puttin' on Ole Massa: The Slave Narratives of Henry Bibb, William Wells Brown, and Solomon Northrup* (New York: Harper & Row, Harper Torchbooks, 1969), p. 40.

87. George P. Rawick, ed.,*The American Slave*: A Composite Autobiography, vol. 1, *From Sundown to Sunup: The Making of the Black Community*; Contributions in Afro-American and African Studies, No. 11 (Westport, Conn.: Greenwood, 1972), pp. xv-xvii, 9–12.

88. Herbert G. Gutman, *The Black Family in Slavery and Freedom. 1750–1925* (New York: Pantheon, 1976), pp. xvii, 14, 327–360 *passim*. Quotations appear on pp. xvii, 14, 360.

89. Gerber, "Haley's *Roots*," p. 107; "View from the Whirlpool," *Time*, 19 February 1979, p. 88.

90. Levine, "Roots and Branches," p. 57.

91. Eric Foner, article in *Sevendays* (March 1977) reprinted in Wolper with Troupe, *Inside Story*, pp. 263–264.

92. Byron, "Family Plot," p. 31.

93. Levine, "Roots and Branches," p. 56.

13

The Guiding Light: Soap Opera as Economic Product and Cultural Document

ROBERT C. ALLEN

Soap opera? The very term has a pejorative connotation—as in, "That movie was nothing but a glorified soap opera." Viewed largely by women and relegated to the netherworld of daytime television, soap operas until recently have remained "hidden" from public and scholarly view, while reams of publicity and scholarly writing have been devoted to prime-time commercial television. As recently as 1972, Natan Katzman prefaced his analysis of soap opera content with the admission, "Despite the magnitude of the phenomenon, there has been no published research on television serials."[1]

Thanks in large measure to a broadening of the soap opera audience to include college students and a greater proportion of male viewers, soap operas have received considerably more attention both in the academic and general press since the mid-1970s. But this attention is still minuscule in light of the economic importance of soaps to the commercial broadcasting industry ($700 million in advertising revenue each year) and their audience appeal (10 million viewers daily).[2]

Focusing on one particular soap opera, *The Guiding Light*, this essay examines the role of the soap in the history of the commercial television industry and suggests a starting point for the study of soap operas as cultural phenomenon.

Each autumn the resources of the three major television networks are brought to bear on the new prime-time season. Program executives, advertisers, and stockholders anxiously await the "overnights" (Nielsen daily ratings data from selected cities) on shows to see which network "won" a particular time period. With hundreds of thousands of advertising dollars riding on each rating point, a hit series can mean millions in profits. As programming executives frequently discover, however, prime-time programming is a high-risk and high-cost undertaking—the "sure-fire" idea for a series, which the network spent millions to acquire, may disappear. The economic role of soap operas must be set against the turbulent, unpredictable, and risky nature of prime-time programming. By comparison, soap operas since the early 1950s have provided the three networks (particularly CBS and ABC) with a large and predictable profit base. While a single episode of a soap probably will never garner the prime-time ratings of *Roots*, *Dallas*, or the Super Bowl, far less must be spent to attract the soap audience. And, once a soap has established itself, the outlays for talent and production are almost sure to be recouped many times over.

What makes the soap opera so profitable is its ability to attract and hold what is, in advertising terms, a quality audience—women between the ages of eighteen and fifty-four. This group, particularly that portion of it under thirty-five, makes most of the American family's "soft"-goods purchases (consumable items as opposed to "durable" goods)—food, clothes, and, of course, cleaning products. This historical ability to sell products is evidenced by the fact that the soap opera is the only extant form of network television programming some of whose shows are still owned and produced by a sponsor and its advertising agency.[3] In prime time the television "series" brings audiences back week after week by presenting familiar characters in new, self-contained stories. The soap opera goes the series concept one better by presenting, on a daily basis, familiar characters in episodes that build one upon the other and in plot lines that can never (so long as the soap is on the air) be fully resolved.

Another reason soaps might be looked upon as the best solution yet devised to the networks' problem of the need for habitual viewing is that the costs of a soap opera are, relative to prime-time shows, low and, for the most part, predictable. As commentators have long pointed out, the soap opera world is an interior world. The mythical cities of

"Springfield" and "Port Charles" are constructions in the minds of viewers built upon what little the audience actually sees of these "typical" American metropolises. The hospital nurses' stations, lawyers' offices, restaurants, and executive suites that form the visual iconography of the soap opera world are the products of the economic need for locales that can be suggested by small sets erected cheek by jowl in one or two television studios. Keeping the number of these sets to a minimum and shooting on videotape rather than film helps keep the per-episode cost of a soap opera a fraction of that for a prime-time series.[4]

The development of self-contained, portable video recording equipment in the mid-1970s has enabled soap opera writers and producers to extend the landscape of the soap world to include such exotic exterior settings as Jamaica, Hong Kong, Bermuda, and the Canary Islands. Today characters are constantly flying off to these and other resorts—thanks to the assistance of national tourist boards, which provide transportation, production assistance, and sometimes even room and board for cast and crew in return for "plugs" added to the script and title credits. The cost to the production company for such location shoots is higher than that of shooting standard interior fare, but according to a *Guiding Light* producer, less than that of constructing even the most transparently bogus topical island sets in the studio.[5]

Over the more than three decades of televised soap operas, elaborate systems of production control and division of labor have been devised both to maintain production schedules and to keep production costs low. Scripts are turned out on an assembly-line basis, dictated by the need to produce five hours of new material each week. The show's head writer determines long-term story developments and provides a written summary of the action to occur in each episode. This outline is then turned over to associate writers, who fill in the dialogue to be spoken.

Production control and production economy are also exercised through contractual relationships between soap operas and their actors. An actor is under contract to a soap for a period of a year or more, during which time he/she is obligated to appear. Built into each contract, however, are thirteen or twenty-six-week renewal periods at the end of which the actor's contract can be terminated by the production company. If viewer response to a new character fails to come up to expectations or if a plot line falters, the story line, character, *and* actor can be disposed of quickly and economically. Within this system of labor relations lies a fundamental difference between soaps and prime-time shows—even the recently successful "serialized" prime-time offerings such as *Dallas* or *Flamingo Road*. The basis of the soap opera is the community of characters and their relationships rather than the actions of any one particular character. Hence soaps are not star-oriented as are many prime-time shows. Over the summer of 1980, *Dallas* star Larry Hagman (J. R. Ewing) used his summer-hiatus deathbed limbo and the resultant "Who shot J.R.?" media hype as a position from which to negotiate a substantial salary increase and financial participation in the profits of the show itself. No similar situation has or, in my opinion, ever could arise in daytime soaps. Whereas Hagman's agents successfully argued that without Hagman there would be no viable *Dallas*, no daytime star could exert such leverage. It is not just the serial format of soaps, with ample opportunities to dispose of recalcitrant actor/characters in narratively convenient ways, but the multiplot and multicharacter orientation of the soaps that put power in the hands of the production company rather than the actors.

The televised soap opera is, of course, a direct descendent of the radio soap. *The Guiding Light* began on radio in 1937. The popular literature usually traces the origins of the radio soap to an Ohio schoolteacher, Irna Phillips (the creator of *The Guiding Light*), who was hired by Chicago station WGN in 1930 to create a dramatic program for women. The success of that show, *Painted Dreams*, sparked interest among other stations, and by 1933 the networks picked up on the idea—or so we are told.[6] Irna Phillips certainly was a major force in the development of the soap opera in America (the creator of several radio soaps as well as *The Guiding Light* and *As the World Turns* for TV), but it is unnecessary (not to mention historically misleading) to cast one person as the mother of soap operas. The soaps developed in the early 1930s as radio first searched for ways to attract and hold a national audience, and then discovered the profits to be made from programming directed specifically toward women. When Phillips arrived in Chicago in 1930, radio as a mass-advertising medium was but a few years old. Already, however, both the serial form and the dramatic form had been used as a means of generating both audience and advertiser interest in radio—most notably in the case of *Amos 'n' Andy*, a serialized comedy with a national following of some 40 million.[7] The local and, later, network soap operas adapted the serialized dramatic form (used also in newspaper comic strips) to appeal to women by focusing on "female" concerns: the family, homemaking, romance, and perhaps most importantly, interpersonal relationships in general. As in television decades later, radio soap operas worked splendidly as an enticement to regular, habitual viewing.

The tremendous economic success of soap operas on both radio and television has made the form one of the most enduring and prolific in the history of American commercial broadcasting. Soap operas have been a daily part of network broadcasting since 1933, and one show, *The Guiding Light*, has run continuously since January 1937. Katzman found the number of minutes of soap opera programming to have risen steadily between 1952 and 1970, from approximately 60 minutes to 510 minutes (8.5 hours).[8] In the decade since his study, several half-hour soaps have expanded to one hour, and by 1981 the total minutes per day of soaps had reached 660 (11 hours). No prime-time programs can match the longevity of *Search for Tomorrow*, *As the World Turns*, or *The Guiding Light*, which together represent eighty-four years of continuous television programming). Nor can any prime-time programming form (situation comedy, talk show, variety, comedy variety, newsmagazine, action/adventure, etc.) match the soap opera quantitatively in terms of hours of programming per day, week, or year. At the time of this writing (late 1981) the twelve soap operas currently being broadcast generated fifty-five hours of programming each week, approximately twenty-eight hundred hours each year, or the equivalent of nearly two thousand ninety-minute feature films. In short, in terms of numbers of network broadcast hours per day the soap opera is and has been for years the predominant commercial television form, constituting at present 28 percent of the total network broadcast hours each weekday, 34 percent of the entertainment (nonnews) programming.

Finally, the soap opera's historical role in commercial broadcasting must be viewed in terms of the special relationship soaps enjoy with their viewers. Prime-time shows do develop strong viewer interest and loyalty, but none has engendered the long-term devotion that soaps have. In the case of some viewers, soap opera watching has been a part of their daily lives for decades, producing a relationship between soap and audience that Sari Thomas has characterized as "continuous intimacy."[9] When Pope John Paul II was wounded in Rome in May 1980, a St. Louis Television station reported to the Associated Press more than

100 calls from irate soap opera viewers complaining that their programs were being preempted by news coverage of an individual who, after all, "wasn't even an American." The loyalty of soap viewers combined with the size of the soap audience makes soap watching not a curious social anomaly, but a significant cultural phenomenon. In 1979, Arnold Becker, vice-president for research for CBS, estimated that 63 percent of all American women living in houses with television sets could be classified as soap opera viewers, making the audience for soaps 50 million persons. Over the summer of 1981, *General Hospital*, the highest-rated show in the history of daytime television, captured 14 million viewers daily.[10]

If soap viewing has been an important leisure activity for millions of Americans for decades, how can we get a handle on the social significance of soaps and soap opera viewing? What do soaps say about American society? That soaps might be important cultural documents has been recognized by scholars since the early 1940s, but studies of soap opera audiences have been relatively few. The predominant approach to the social meaning of soap operas has been content analysis—the quantitative analysis (counting) of various discrete categories of soap content. Scholars have tallied the number of marital infidelities, illegitimate births, alcoholics, criminal acts, and mental cases. Not surprisingly, scholars have been intrigued by what Natan Katzman has called the "almost reality" of soap operas: that fictional, parallel world that in so many ways seems to resemble the social world of the viewer, but that is also quite different from the world of the viewer's experience. Time in soap operas, unlike in prime-time shows, much more closely approximates real time. Characters on soaps do grow old, marry, bear children, and, sometimes, die. Their lives unfold over a period of years, if not decades. Bert Bauer, the character played by actress Charita Bauer on *The Guiding Light* for thirty years, has gone from feisty bride to consoling grandmother. Many of her viewers have, as she puts it, "grown old with her." But few viewers' lives can even begin to approach the traumatic eventfulness of most soap characters. Jo Anne Tate on *Search for Tomorrow* has been thrice widowed, tried for murder, kidnapped on the eve of her third marriage by her second husband (whom she believed dead), twice saved from murderers, stricken by psychosomatic blindness, and temporarily paralyzed by a gunshot wound—to name but some of her tribulations.

Most of the content analyses of soap operas have implicitly or explicitly presumed that soaps constitute a pseudoreality that can be measured against the "real" world. For example, in a study published in 1979, Cassata, Skill, and Boadu investigated "the occurence and distribution of health-related conditions in the soap opera world" and compared these health conditions to their statisical occurrence in the American population in general. They discovered that soap characters are more likely to suffer accidental death, murder, and mental illness and less likely to contract cancer than people in the "real" world.[11]

In 1981, two separate studies examined the depiction of sexual activity on soap operas. Each coded the variety and frequency of intimate acts and references. One of the studies even produced a rank ordering of soap operas in terms of sexiness—*General Hospital* "was clearly the 'sexiest' of the of the soap operas, with 16.00 incidents per hour." The authors of this study concluded, "Soap operas can be assumed to be presenting a distorted picture of sexual behavior in America. . . . A steady viewing diet of role models who engage in fornication and adultery may influence or cultivate viewers' attitudes and values concerning what is 'normal' and 'proper' in society."[12]

In her study of conversation topics and styles on soap operas, Marlene G. Fine found that, on the whole, soap opera characters discussed what we would expect them to discuss: romantic couples talked about marriage and romance; friends talked about friendship; co-workers talked about work; and strangers engaged in smalltalk. However, she concluded, soap opera conversations differed from those in "the world we live in" in several respects. Most importantly, perhaps, men and women soap opera characters talk to each other far more than do real-life working-class married couples.[13]

One of the most useful findings of soap opera content analysis comes from an ongoing study of television content conducted by George Gerbner and colleagues. In 1981 his research team reported in *New England Journal of Medicine*: "It may well be that daytime serials are the largest source of medical advice in the United States."[14]

Content analysis as a method has two serious shortcomings, however, when applied to soap operas. First, while it can tell us how the social world of the soap opera is similar to or different from certain aspects of empirical reality, it cannot tell us *why* soaps represent reality the way they do. Second, content analysis presumes that the manner by which soap opera audiences derive meaning from their viewing activity is both known and unproblematical. For purposes of quantitative analysis, events must be pulled out of their context in the soap opera world and isolated as discrete units of meaning. For his content analysis of soap operas, Katzman chose observers who had never seen the serial they were coding. Cassata, Sill, and Boadu did not even find it necessary to view the soap opera content they studied; rather they relied on plot descriptions provided in *Soap Opera Digest*.

The question arises: Does a sexual reference, heart attack, or illegitimate pregnancy "mean" the same when it is pulled out of its aesthetic context? Put another way, is reading a soap opera the same as reading a newspaper? I would argue that content analyses will continue to be of limited explanatory value until we have a better understanding of the aesthetic processes that lie behind soap operas' representations of social reality. Creation of meaning and aesthetic pleasure in the soap opera is a much more complex process than is generally recognized. In addition, what a soap opera means in a social sense is inextricably tied up with how it creates meaning for its viewers.

Let us consider how meaning is produced in a single episode of a soap opera—in this case the August 18, 1981, episode of *The Guiding Light*, an example chosen more or less at random. On the basis of the content summary of this episode (provided at the end of this chapter), several things stand out. First, except in the most superficial sense, there is very little meaning one can derive from this summary, or indeed from the actual episode itself, unless one has seen other episodes of *The Guiding Light*. Unless you catch the first episode of a new soap, you always join a soap's action *in medias res*. The meaning of the events in any one episode depends upon your knowledge of characters and events from previous ones.

This fact points to a fundamental problem in reading soap operas: what, for purposes of analysis, *is* a soap opera? This is a necessary question for two reasons: first, soap operas *do* create meaning differently than most other media forms, and second, if we desire to know the relationship between a phenomenon and its culture, we had better be able to define that phenomenon.

Clearly one episode of a soap opera cannot be said to "be" that soap any more than a page from the middle of a novel can be said to "be" that novel. But how can we define a soap? As a week's worth of episodes? A year's worth? Since any one episode of a soap is built on all the episodes that have preceded it—since soap operas accumulate meaning over time—then the only logical way to define a given soap opera is as the sum of all its episodes broadcast since its origination. Any more delimiting definition would of necessity be arbitrary. Hence with the soap opera we have a situation unique to broadcasting in which a program, *The Guiding Light*, for example, has taken shape over the course of thirty years (more than forty-five years if we include the years it was broadcast on radio). But even this definition has not completely solved the problem of specifying the nature of a soap opera. Whereas soaps do have a definite beginning (even if thirty or more years in the past), they have no endings. They are, in narrative terms, open—resistant to closure. The soap opera is unique among broadcast programs in this respect as well; it is the only form whose very nature precludes its having an ending. Even when soaps are taken off the air because of poor ratings (as was *Love of Life* in 1980), they do not wind up their subplots and leave everyone living happily ever after, but rather expire into a sort of eternal limbo of unresolution. Thus in the case of *The Guiding Light*, we have thirty years of a program that if broadcast sequentially would take more than a month of continuous viewing, twenty-four hours a day, to watch. But even at the end of this marathon screening, we could still not claim to have "seen" *The Guiding Light*, since during our sleepless month in the screening room another sixteen hours of the show would have been produced!

One way around this awkward definitional problem might be to attempt to discover the underlying principles of a given soap. Can we discern the vocabulary and grammar of the soap opera form that any episode or group of episodes uses to create meaning?

Some of these underlying principles can be extrapolated from the episode of *The Guiding Light* under consideration. Upon viewing this episode one is struck by the fact that so little "happens" in it in terms of plot development or, indeed, in terms of action of any kind. No time is spent establishing locales, there are no exterior shots, no character walks more than twenty paces in any given scene—we simply see characters talking to each other.

In terms of plot, the viewer learns very little from this episode. A few future plot lines are hinted at: what is the Springfield Investment Company and what is Ross's involvement in it? What secret does Henry Chamberlain not want his daughter to discover? Will Noela make good her threat of vengeance against Kelly and Morgan? But far less time is spent posing these questions than in elaborating on situations about which the viewer is already familiar: specifically, the Kelly/Morgan and Noela/Floyd weddings and the effect of Andy Norris's blackmail schemes on his mother and girl friend.

Further, there is in this episode a great deal of what we might call intraepisodic redundancy: the reiteration several times during the course of a single episode of information already known to the viewer. Redundancy between episodes (interepisodic redundancy) can be explained by the need to accommodate viewers who are unable to watch a particular soap every day and hence need to be reminded of events from previous episodes. The same reasoning cannot be used to explain intraepisodic redundancy, however.

If so little "happens" in a single episode of a soap, then what accounts for its daily appeal? Traditional narrative and dramatic critical approaches are of little use in answering this question, since soap operas are not "traditional" narrative or dramatic works. Applying the same critical standards to the soap opera that one would to the novel is inappropriate in that the soap opera lacks the climactic event and subsequent denouement that are defining features of the classic novel form. Traditional dramatic criticism still relies on Aristotelian notions of dramatic unity and structure that are ignored by the soap opera. If we turn, however, to semiotics (the scientific study of sign systems), we find an analytical approach capable of dealing with the peculiarities of the soap opera form.[15] Semiotics is the application of principles of structural linguistics to phenemona that are not, strictly speaking, linguistic: film, circus acts, table manners, wrestling matches, and television are among the sign systems that have been investigated by semioticians.

One of the fundamental discoveries of structural linguistics was that verbal languages are "arbitrary." The word *door*, for example, bears no natural or necessary resemblance to a real door; we might just as well substitute the word *cow* to stand for a door. *Door* takes on its meaning by virtue of its participation in a system of words. This system is one of similarity and difference, by which we are able to distinguish *door* from *boor*. Furthermore, verbal language is a "conventional" system, in that linguistic elements take on meaning because of their place in the system rather than through any natural or necessary relationships to something outside that system. We understand the meaning of *door* because in the English language it is conventional to refer to a large portal as a door. In other words, we participate in the "code" that is English. By knowing the lexical, grammatical, and syntactic codes of English, we can generate an infinite variety of word combinations from a finite number of letters and words.

Semiotics attempts to uncover the codes or generative principles that enable us to make sense of other cultural phenomena. We might ask, for example, "What are the codes that enable the viewer to understand and derive pleasure from soap operas?" A list of the codes of soap opeas would include (but would not be limited to):

1. *Video–cinematic codes*. This is the complex of codes of visual and auditory representation that television—and, by extension, the soap opera—has borrowed from Hollywood filmmaking style. It would include such devices as unobtrusive camera movements, "invisible" editing, and a naturalistic style of acting, among others—all designed to focus the viewer's attention on the story unfolding on the screen and away from the manner by which that story is being told.

2. *Codes of the soap opera form*. This set of codes is derived in large measure from the soap opera form itself; together these codes work to make the soap opera look and sound different from other forms of television. For example, in soap operas time and space are used differently than in other narrative forms of television. Time is prolonged rather than compressed. The spatial world of the soap opera is predominantly an interior one. Instead of a single, linear narrative drawn to a close within an hour, the soap opera features multiple, intersecting plot lines, each of which might last years. There is a great deal of redundancy in soap operas, both between episodes and within an individual episode.

3. *Textual codes*. Although the twelve soap operas currently being broadcast share all the above codes, each has its own distinguishing conventions that are easily recognized (although not as codes) by frequent viewers. The long-time soap viewer can immediately sense when something is "wrong" with his or her soap: a character is behaving in an uncharacteristic manner, for example. The frequent viewer can recognize not only appropriate and inappropriate behavior in a given character, but appropriate responses of a given character to another, based on the two characters' relationships in

the show's past. Characters in soap operas have memories, and relationships might well stretch back for a decade or more.

4. *Intertextual codes*. All cultural products exist within networks of other texts, to which they inevitably refer. The soap opera frequently includes references to other texts: a plot line "borrowed" from a popular novel or film, the appearance of a movie star or other show-business personality as him/herself. In each case a level of meaning is created by reference to another text or set of texts.

5. *Experiential codes*. Often in interpreting an action in a soap opera, the viewer will rely upon his or her own experience of the world. The viewer constantly compares soap opera actions with what "should" happen in such a situation—what is plausible, veristic, morally correct, etc., not in terms of the world of the soap but in terms of the viewer's own world of experience and values.

Let us return to the question, "If so little happens in a single episode of a soap, then what accounts for its daily appeal?" A further principle of semiotic analysis will enable us to deal with this question and, by doing so, to begin to see the complexity of the soap opera as a conveyor of meaning. All narrative works create meaning along two axes. The syntagmatic axis defines the temporal ordering of elements in the work (what follows what). The paradigmatic axis has to do with the arrangement of elements in terms of their similarity and difference (what goes with what), and would include relationships among characters. Hence if we read this episode of *The Guiding Light* syntagmatically, we find very little of importance. But there *is* a lot going on in this episode—not in the syntagmatic sense of cause-effect plot relationships, but paradigmatically in the system of correspondence and difference the scenes set up. Paradigmatically, this episode is "about" the relationship between two similar, anticipated events: the weddings of Floyd and Noela and of Kelly and Morgan. But while both weddings involve young, attractive, well-established characters, the regular viewer of *The Guiding Light* is immediately aware of the contrasts set up between the two events.

Kelly and Morgan's wedding will be the culmination of a relationship begun over a year ago, but thwarted for much of that time by the lies Noela told Morgan about Kelly. Morgan's belief, fostered by Noela, that Kelly had been unfaithful to her prompted Morgan to run away to Chicago, where she was nearly tricked into a life of drugs and prostitution. Noela's motive for this deceit was her desire to marry Kelly, whom, she believed, would become a wealthy doctor and boost her out of her family's working-class status. When she failed to entice Kelly into a romantic relationship, Noela tried to force him to marry her by making him believe that he had fathered her child one night when he was drunk. In reality, Floyd, with whom she had been carrying on a secret liaison for months, was the father and quite willing to marry Noela.

The difference—we might even say opposition—between the two weddings is established in this episode by the reactions of other members of *The Guiding Light* community upon learning of the two events. Most of the other characters had learned of Kelly and Morgan's wedding plans in previous episodes; only Carrie and Derek learn of the news in this one. Everyone, however, with the obvious exception of Noela, is delighted by the prospects of their marriage. A total of seven characters are informed of Floyd and Noela's wedding in this episode alone (Derek, Katy, Kelly, Morgan, Hilary, Ed, and Vanessa). Their reactions range from shock (Katy) to anger (Kelly, Morgan, Hilary), to consternation (Ed), to indifference (Vanessa). Only Derek can muster congratulations and he only because he is uninformed as to Noela's lies and failed scheme to trick Kelly.

This episode tells us that Kelly and Morgan's wedding will involve the entire community. The event will take place at idyllic Laurel Falls, where the two fell in love last summer. Thirty-seven members of Morgan's high-school graduating class (we are told twice) have volunteered to prepare the site. Mike Bauer will give the bride away. Ben McFarren loans the couple his rural retreat for their honeymoon. Ed Bauer has provided them with a place to live. Even Vanessa has already sent her wedding gift. Floyd and Noela, on the other hand, will be married in the office of a justice of the peace with only Noela's brother and mother and Floyd's sister Katy witnessing the event. Katy remarks sarcastically to Tony that she's glad *Floyd* will be allowed to attend.

But the system of similarity and difference created in this episode does not end here. As plans for Kelly and Morgan's wedding are being made in the living room, Katy stays in her bedroom recovering from the shock of the news that her boyfriend, Andy Norris, has been unmasked as the blackmailer who had been terrorizing the community for months. The eager planning is in ironic juxtaposition to the effects of the dissolution of a relationship Katy had hoped would lead to marriage. Also, Katy's plight is made implicitly to correspond to the possible future unhappiness of her brother, since both Andy and Noela have been untruthful and selfish in their romantic relationships.

In scene 2, Tony's reference to his girl friend Darlene serves to remind Noela and the viewer of the contrast between her family's view of marital relations and that she had held for herself. Tony remarks that while he was away the night before (preventing Noela from going through with an abortion), Darlene stayed behind at his apartment. When he returned at two in the morning he found her "on her hands and knees scrubbing the floor." Noela, whose mother runs a boarding house, desires above all else to be free from domestic drudgery. The life of social status, wealth, and leisure she had fantasized about with Kelly is not likely to materialize with Floyd, a hospital maintenance worker.

In scene 4, Jennifer, Morgan's mother, tells Ben of her other daughter Amanda's emotional response to the news of Morgan and Kelly's wedding. Amanda, who is married to but separated from Ben, has been emotionally distraught since she miscarried some months ago. She believes Ben left her for his first wife, Eve, and mistrusts all romantic relationships. To her the news of Kelly and Morgan's marriage is merely a reminder of her own painful experience with marriage.

In scene 1, Derek ask Hilary what she thinks of Kelly and Morgan's wedding plans. This question probably seems innocuous enough to the inexperienced viewer, but to regular viewers it is quite significant. They know that Hilary was once in love with Kelly, while he regarded her as only a friend. In fact, Hilary's residual feelings for Kelly have hampered the development of her relationship with Derek.

These are the most firmly established parallels and contrasts in this episode. But for the experienced viewer the paradigmatic network, of which the two weddings are but a part, extends much further. Because parentage, romance, marriage, and the dissolution of marriage are the foci of most plot lines in *The Guiding Light*, the first marriage (there will almost certainly be others for all of the four) of four young characters reverberates throughout almost the entire community, setting up implicitly or explicitly relationships between these weddings and the current marital/romantic status of other characters and reminding the experienced viewer of their past histories. At the time romance is being consummated for Kelly and Morgan, it is beginning for Ross and Carrie. Ross, the overly ambitious lawyer brother of Dr. Justin Marler, has recently become enamored of Carrie Todd, a new employee of Spaulding Enterprises. Carrie, who describes herself as "hopelessly romantic," has already had, as Ross puts it, "a profound effect" on curbing his less ethical tendencies. In this case, as in others in *The Guiding Light*, love is presented as a regenerating and transforming force. Ross and Carrie make mention of Alan Spaulding and Hope, his estranged wife. Ross comments that Alan, a sometimes selfish and materialistic business magnate, seems to have changed since his marriage to Hope Bauer, to which Carrie replies, "Love changes people."

There is also a budding romance between Ed Bauer and Vanessa Chamberlain. Separated from his wife, Rita, following Rita's affair with Alan Spaulding, Ed is connected with Kelly Morgan's wedding plans in that he is Kelly's godfather. Ed and Vanessa met when Vanessa was brought to Cedars Hospital after she had taken an overdose of sleeping pills in a pseudosuicide ploy to evoke the pity of Ross Marler, with whom she was infatuated. Thus, the wedding of Kelly and Morgan sets up an implicit comparison with Ed's own marital difficulties, while the parallels between Noela's romantic dissimulation and Vanessa's "secret" are obvious to the experienced viewer.

In short, even at the level of a single episode, meaning in a soap opera is created in large measure through the audience's familiarity with a complex network of character relationships and the history of this network as it recedes back toward the program's beginnings. The recognition of the paradigmatic complexity of the soap opera form is but a starting point in understanding the working of soap operas, but it does enable us to make a few generalizations—however preliminary—regarding the social meaning of soaps.

First and most obviously, the world of the soap opera is a social world—a world in which a character is defined in terms of his or her relationships with other members of the soap opera community. One reason it is difficult to describe what happened in a soap opera episode is not that soap opera plots are so convoluted but that each character has multiple, shifting identities *vis-à-vis* other characters. Ed Bauer is Vanessa's love interest, Rita's husband, Kelly's godfather, Bert's son, Mike's brother, and so on. The importance of any soap opera plot development is not so much its effect on a given character but the consequences of an event on romantic, familia, and other interpersonal relationships. There is no single protagonist with whose fate audience interest is ultimately bound. Even central characters of long standing have been eliminated from a soap (Adam Drake from *The Edge of Night* and Nancy Hughes from *As the World Turns*, to name but two) without doing noticeable damage to its audience acceptance. Individual characters might die, move away, be sent to jail, sink into comas, but the community survives; the functions played by departed characters are assumed by new ones. Hence it is not surprising that most current soap operas began as kinship sagas—*Ryan's Hope*, *The Guiding Light*, *As the World Turns*, *All My Children*, *Another World*, *Days of Our Lives*, *One Life to Live*. Particularly in the older, more established soap operas, family ties are of paramount importance. Romances, friendships, marriages might crumble over time, but ties of kinship can never be dissolved. In *The Guiding Light*, a new character's integration into the community is often marked by his or her joining a family (through marriage, usually), or through the establishment of a quasi-familial relationship between the new character and a family group. Kelly Nelson, a young medical student, was introduced into the show as the godson of longtime character Dr. Ed Bauer. Jennifer Richards and daughter Morgan entered *The Guiding Light* when their car crashed in Springfield. Morgan promptly took up temporary residence at the home of matriarch Bert Bauer while her mother recuperated in the hospital.

It would be simplistic to conclude on the basis of the above that soap operas function to reinforce the values of the nuclear family at a time of that unit's disintegration in the society as a whole. Few families in soap operas are themselves free from fragmentation—the single-parent family is the norm rather than the exception in the world of soap operas. One reason for this state of affairs is clearly narrative: were everyone in soaps happily married, the possible relationships among characters would be severely diminished. But the premium placed on kinship in soap operas does act as a socially conservative force—almost everything in the social world of the soap opera is mutable, except for the bond between mother and child, brother and sister.

Despite some plot lines dealing with working-class characters and interracial romances, the world of the soap opera is overwhelmingly white and middle class. The problem of including blacks and other racial groups in soaps is not one of working them into plot lines, but dealing with the paradigmatic consequences of their entry into the community of the soap opera world. These are three major types of relationships among soap opera characters: kinship, romance, and social (friend/enemy). As we have seen, much of the appeal of soap operas resides in the complexity and overlap of actual and potential relationships among these categories with regard to any particular character. Unless a particular soap were to embrace interracial marriage and parentage as a community norm, the admission of a nonwhite character into full membership in the soap community would be impossible. As yet this is a step no soap opera has been willing to take.

The middle-class orientation of all soaps is a frequently noted characteristic. To a degree this class focus is an attempt to make the soap opera world parallel that of the presumed viewer. The most frequently depicted work places in soap operas are hospitals, law firms, bars, restaurants, and the executive offices of business concerns. Physical labor, assembly lines, and factory work are almost totally absent. Blue-collar characters might inhabit the world of the soap, but the work they perform is almost never represented. But the middle-class work places of the soap opera world are also conditioned by narrative concerns. Because of the importance of interpersonal relationships in soaps, work places must allow for frequent contacts with other people and an opportunity to discuss matters not directly related to one's work—hence the prevalence of hospital nursing stations, waiting rooms, executive suites, and nightclubs. These are places where work is relatively unsupervised and does not require extended periods of close attention to mechanical detail. But much more socially significant, I believe, than the presence of certain middle-class and professional work settings is the total absence of the industrial work place from the world of the soap. Factory work and blue-collar employment in general have a negative social value in soaps, because these jobs are presumed to preclude the type of interpersonal contact upon which the soap opera community is based.

Despite the fact that a great deal happens in the lives of individual characters—multiple marriages, pregnancies, amnesia, temporary blindness, disabling accidents, and so forth—very little happens to alter the nature of the community. The soap opea community is a self-perpetuating and self-preserving system—a system little affected by the turbulence experienced by its individual members and fate of any one character. The naïve viewer might be dazzled by the implausible constant state of crisis experienced by individual characters, but the experienced viewer is watchful for the sometimes glacially slow but far more significant alterations in the network of character relationships that forms the very basis for the soap opera world.

CONTENTUAL SUMMARY
The Guiding Light
August 18, 1981

Scene 1

Setting: Hilary's apartment
Time: Early morning

Derek, Hilary's boyfriend, arrives, having returned from a business trip. They talk briefly about Andy Norris, his refusal to accept legal advice, and the effect of his arrest upon Katy.

Hilary tells Derek of Kelly and Morgan's wedding plans.

Kelly and Morgan arrive. The four talk of wedding plans. Trudy, Morgan's friend, has lined up thirty-seven volunteers to help plan the wedding.

Floyd arrives to tell Katy, his sister, the news of his impending marriage to Noela. He informs the four of his plans, revealing Noela to be the "mystery woman" in his life.

Scene 2

Setting: Bea Reardon's kitchen
Time: Breakfast

Bea tells Noela she is glad the latter did not go through with plans for an abortion. Tony, Noela's brother, enters and tells how his girl friend, Darlene, cleaned his apartment while he was out. Noela sarcastically notes that Tony probably regards that as a sign Darlene would make a good wife. There is talk of the wedding and of getting the marriage license so the ceremony can be conducted as soon as possible. Bea offers Noela the larger bedroom for her and Floyd.

Scene 3

Setting: Katy's bedroom
Time: Immediately following Scene 1

Floyd enters. Katy is depressed that everyone in the other room is talking of wedding plans. Floyds breaks the news of his plans to marry Noela. Katy is shocked.

Scene 4

Setting: Alan Spaulding's office
Time: Unspecified

Ben and Jennifer are discussing Amanda's seeing a new doctor. Jennifer says Amanda was upset at the news of Kelly and Morgan's wedding. Ben expresses suspicion regarding a company set up by Ross in Amanda's name, the Springfield Investment Co.

Carrie enters. Jennifer informs her of Morgan's wedding.

Jennifer leaves.

Carrie asks Ben why Philip, Alan's son, is living with Justin and Jackie. Ben tells her.

Ross enters. Ross inquires about Amanda's health.

Ben leaves.

Carrie is pleased that Ross is trying to control his dislike for Ben.

Scene 5

Setting: Fourth floor nurses's desk, Cedars Hospital
Time: Unspecified

Hilary, Kelly, and Morgan are talking about Floyd and Noela's wedding. Kelly says he feels awkward knowing that Noela tried to trick him into marrying her by claiming the baby fathered by Floyd was really his.

Kelly leaves.

Noela and Tony arrive on the elevator.

Scene 6

Setting: Same as Scene 5
Time: Same as Scene 5

Tony and Noela run into Kelly as he is about to get on the elevator. Noela walks away, and Tony asks that Kelly keep Noela's scheme a secret from Floyd. Kelly agrees to do so.

Floyd arrives on the elevator and walks over to where Noela is standing. He says he's been "walking on air" since Noela agreed to marry him.

Scene 7

Setting: Mike's office
Time: Unspecified

Mike and Derek discuss Morgan's wedding. Mike is to "give the bride away." Mike's secretary informs him that Henry Chamberlain is waiting to see him.

Mike asks Derek to check up on the Springfield Investment Co.

Scene 8

Setting: Alan Spaulding's office
Time: Unspecified

Ross is alone in the room making a telephone call to a stockholder of Spaulding Enterprises, offering to buy the person's stock. In the midst of his conversation there is a flashback to the previous evening when he dropped Carrie off at her apartment. In the flashback Carrie reminds Ross that ambition is not the most important thing in the world. After the flashback, Ross terminates his call before making an offer for the shares.

Scene 9

Setting: Mike's office
Time: Immediately following Scene 7

Henry expresses sympathy for Barbara, Andy Norris's mother, saying she reminds him of someone he was once very close to. He then says he wants to tell Mike of a confidential matter, which he doesn't want his daughter Vanessa to know. Henry asks Mike if he knows about Vanessa's faked suicide. Mike does. Henry says Vanessa is terrified that Mike's brother Ed will learn of the ruse.

Scene 10

Setting: Hospital
Time: Unspecified

Ed and Vanessa are talking. Morgan enters and talks about the wedding and the garage apartment behind Ed's house she and Kelly are to move into. Morgan leaves Ed and Vanessa, walking over to the nurses' station where Hilary is standing. Noela and Floyd walk by. Hilary tells Morgan not to get upset by Noela's presence. Floyd walks up to Ed and Vanessa and tells them of his marriage to Noela.

Scene 11

Setting: Alan's office
Time: Midday

Carrie and Ross are talking after lunch. Ross tells Carrie that her "philosophy" is having a profound effect on him. They talk of Alan and his separation from his wife, Hope. Ross says he believes Alan has changed since his marriage to Hope. Carrie expresses the opinion that "love changes people." Their conversation is interrupted by Vanessa, who asks where her father is. Ross and Carrie leave the room and Henry enters. Vanessa asks if Joe, the private investigator, has been able to come up with any damaging evidence about Diane's past. Henry says no. They talk of Stephanie Ryan, Henry's former secretary, who has recently died in Mexico. Henry tells Vanessa that Mike knows of her suicide fakery, but says Mike will not tell Ed.

Scene 12

Setting: Hospital
Time: Immediately following Scene 10

Ed, Kelly, and Hilary discuss Floyd and Noela's wedding and Kelly's plans. Floyd and Noela enter from the elevator. Floyd tells Noela that they can be married at the end of the week. Floyd leaves. Noela asks to speak with Kelly.

Scene 13

Setting: Same as Scene 12
Time: Immediately following Scene 12

Noela asks Kelly not to tell Floyd anything of her scheme. Kelly says he won't tell, but warns Noela to "stay away from Morgan and me." Kelly leaves; Noela, speaking to herself, says, "You're going to be sorry one day, Kelly; so will Morgan."

Scene 14

Setting: Elevator at hospital
Time: Immediately following Scene 13

Kelly tells Morgan not to worry about Noela: "She can't touch us now."

Scene 15

Setting: Katy's apartment
Time: Unspecified

Tony arrives to tell Katy of the wedding. Katy says she's going though a rough time. Tony tells Katy not to let Andy Norris get her down.

Scene 16

Setting: Derek's office
Time: Midday

Ross arrives to see Mike. Derek tells him he's in his office talking with Jennifer. Ross sits down to wait. Derek leaves for lunch.

Scene 17

Setting: Mike's office
Time: Immediately following Scene 16

Jennifer talks of Morgan's wedding, saying her own was not a very good example. She also asks Mike to check on Ross's involvement in the Springfield Investment Co. Cut to Ross listening outside the door.

NOTES

1. Nathan Katzman, "Television Soap Operas: What's Been Going On Anyway," *Public Opinion Quarterly* 36 (Summer 1972), p. 200.

2. "Television's Hottest Show," *Newsweek*, 28 September 1981, pp. 60–66.

3. Procter and Gamble currently own four soaps produced through their advertising agency, Compton Advertising.

4. For a fascinating examination of television programming in general, see Les Brown, *Televi$ion: The Business behind the Box* (New York: Harcourt Brace Jovanovich, 1971).

5. Interview with Michael Laibson, associate producer, *The Guiding Light*, 23 October 1981.

6. See Robert LaGuardia, *The Wonderful World of TV Soap Operas* (New York: Ballantine Books, 1974), pp. 58–65.

7. Erik Barnouw discusses *Amos 'n' Andy* in *A Tower in Babel* (New York: Oxford University Press, 1966), pp. 226-229.

8. Katzman, p. 201.

9. Sari Thomas, "The Relationship between Daytime Serials and Their Viewers" (Ph.D diss., University of Pennsylvania, 1977), p. 2.

10. Becker is quoted in Robert Lindsay, "Soap Operas: Men Are Tuning In," *New York Times*, 21 February 1979, p. 3:1; *Newsweek*, 28 September 1981, p. 60.

11. Mary B. Cassata, Thomas D. Skill, and Samuel Osei Boadu, "In Sickness and Health," *Journal of Communication* (Autumn 1979):73–80.

12. Dennis T. Lowery, Gail Love, and Malcolm Kirby, "Sex on the Soap Operas: Patterns of Intimacy," *Journal of Communication* (Spring 1981), pp. 90–96. See also Bradley S. Greenburg, Robert Abelman, and Kimberly Neuendorf, "Sex on the Soap Operas; Afternoon Delight," *Journal of Communication*, Spring 1981, pp. 83–89.

13. Marlene C. Fine, "Soap Opera Conversations: The Talk That Binds," *Journal of Communciation*, Spring 1981, pp. 97–107. Fine's work suggested that especially "lower-class couples" conversed less than their counterparts in the soaps.

14. George Gerbner, Larry Gross, Michael Morgan, Nancy Signorielli, "Health and Medicine on Television," *New England Journal of Medicine*, 8 October 1981, pp. 901–904.

15. See in particular Ronald Barthes, *S/Z* (New York: Hill & Wang, 1974); and Umberto Eco, *The Role of the Reader* (Bloomington: University of Indiana Press, 1979). The paradigmatic/syntagmatic axes of narratives are discussed in Charles F. Altman, "The American Film Musical: Paradigmatic Structure and Mediatory Function," *Wide Angle* 2 (November 1978):10–17.

14

Edward Kennedy and the Televised Personality in the 1980 Presidential Campaign

GREGORY W. BUSH

Facing both an overflow audience in Boston's historic Faneuil Hall and a flank of television cameras, Senator Edward Kennedy of Massachusetts announced his candidacy for the Democratic presidential nomination on November 7, 1979. Those watching the *ABC World News Tonight* broadcast that evening heard him say, "This country is not prepared to sound retreat. It is willing to advance. It is willing to make a stand, and so am I." This was classic military rhetoric written to attract followers to a political crusade. Correspondent Catherine Mackin commented that the announcement had been the "kind of high political drama that no other American family can match because it has nothing to do with the issues. It is just emotion. Even Senator Kennedy felt it; eyes filling up, swallowing hard, as he was announcing for president." Sure enough, pictures followed of the senator acting just as Mackin had observed.

Almost seven months later, shortly before the California primary, CBS correspondent Bruce Morton told viewers of the *Evening News* that the presidential primaries had started on a note of "uncertainty" and "excitement" but that things had changed. The roller discos were outdrawing the political rallies in California, he said, as skaters were shown racing around a rink.[1]

The excitement of the Kennedy-Carter race had dissolved long before the snows of winter, and the dramatic skills of the network producers were being tested in trying to maintain viewer's interest. By the time of the March 18 Illinois primary, which Kennedy lost by more than two to one, a top aide later related the pervasive view that the president held an "insurmountable lead that Kennedy under no conceivable set of circumstances would overtake before the convention." How had this deflation in political drama happened? What factors account for the fact that this scion of America's most prominent political family was now so easily derided as a loser after only six primaries had taken place?

A comprehensive study of this abrupt change in American politics would require an examination of a number of interrelated factors: the fluid quality of public opinion, foreign events such as the Iranian takeover of the American embassy and the Russian invasion of Afghanistan, the rising tide of conservatism in America, and the impact of political action committees are but a few. One of the factors accounting for the change in Kennedy's candidacy involved how he came across to television viewers, a matter of intense subjectivity. Television did make a difference in the outcome of the 1980 presidential campaign, contrary to what CBS television analyst Jeff Greenfield writes, because of the institutionalized collusion between the news process and the management of political campaigns in America.

Greenfield asserts that Kennedy was probably the greatest victim of the media in the campaign, but that "his troubles stemmed less from a bloodthirsty media and more from his own fundamental political failures, and from an accident of timing."[2] More than by his political failures, however, Kennedy's candidacy was fatally damaged by his own inability to acquiesce in, understand, or fully capitalize on the symbiotic relationship between television's perceived need to accentuate highly capsulized dramatic conflict and the professionalization of media image makers and campaign consultants. The Kennedy candidacy was "the last redoubt of the old politics," Sidney Blumenthal writes in his recent book, which delves into the "permanent campaign" syndrome of the television age.[3] A symbolic figure, Kennedy represented the transition from the older party system to the world of the thematic campaign aimed primarily at television audiences. In the 1980 campaign, he found that even the mythic power of the Kennedy name could not insulate him either from his own tarnished past or from the demands of a televised campaign.

Since the inception of television in the late 1940s, the formats of political telecasts, whether news programs, talk shows, or candidate advertisements, have favored an intimate atmosphere or one with dramatic conflict so that major party politicians, their agents, and journalists could engage the minds of their audiences. The pressure to condense the news was a parallel factor. Altogether there emerged a rationalized cynicism about the attention span of the average viewer-voter. "I could tell voters all they might want to know about a candidate's position on any issue in 30 seconds or less if I choose to do that," a prominent consultant boasted early in 1980.[4] "A person somehow has to get himself above the crowd" of his fellow office seekers, one network president explained.[5] It had become the commonplace political wisdom that to gain the attention of the TV audience most often required either practiced skills or special daring. Since the mid-1960s, political management firms have developed such sophisticated market research and effective television workshops for candidates that winning campaigns today often depend more on the skilled projection or avoidance of selected aspects of a candidates's personality than they do on "the issues." In well-funded, carefully managed contexts, through layer upon layer of what Daniel Boorstin has called pseudoevents, candidates are used through television to manipulate the otherwise alienated voter.[6] Likewise, in the relentless compulsion to condense images and impressions, television producers have found it easier (and cheaper) to focus on personalities. As political columnist David Broder writes, television has been compelled to "deal with political figures, not political institutions."[7] As a result, a talent for acting may be more valuable to a candidate than such political qualities as legislative acumen or the ability to compromise.

Several scholars have recently presented evidence that the use of personality as a cultural and political force predates television. At the turn of the twentieth century, American society was fast becoming what one historian has called a "culture of personality" in which a social role demanded of people as performing selves was supplanting the morally based role called for by the earlier "culture of character."[8] The capacity to emotionally arouse people through one's magnetic personality became a measure of self-worth and success in life. Theodore

Roosevelt functioned as an important link in extending this style into politics during his presidency. As one journalist noted in 1905, Roosevelt's "personality is a Program . . . for all parties whatever they believe."[9] Personality politics, in this sense, acted to deemphasize a belief in ideology itself and to undermine traditional political institutions.

Television's great impact on politics stems partly from its ability to magnify such personality factors. Political machines had been constructed on a variety of person-to-person relationships, depending on relatively stable populations and chains of command as well as candidates who depended on the organization to get out the vote. By 1960, however, former Eisenhower aide Emmet John Hughes would write that television "makes political life itself more fluid and more volatile. Men can surge or stumble with astonishing speed—either triumphing over obscurity or tripping over a hasty or graceless public word or gesture."[10] The burgeoning primary system aided personalities, not political parties.

Warnings were soon read about this developing obsession with the televised political personality. Perhaps the most alarmist scholarly critic was Dan Nimmo, who in his 1970 book *The Political Persuaders* posited:

> Elections are approached neither as conflicts between parties nor as confrontations of principle. They are viewed instead as contests of personalities and, even more basically, they offer a choice between the sophisticated engineers working on behalf of those personalities.[11]

Such observations found their way into the popular culture in such vehicles as *The Candidate* (1972), a movie in which a Senate candidate played by Robert Redford finds himself at a loss after winning his election and can only think to turn to his media consultant/campaign manager to ask: "What do I do now?"[12]

Becoming subjected to increasingly sophisticated TV marketing techniques, viewers often found themselves judging the viability of political personalities the way they judged television actors. They were becoming "connoisseurs of political drama," one critic noted in commenting on a TV speech given by President Carter in the summer of 1979.[13] The prototype of the increasingly sophisticated television watcher was the person to whom advertising man Tony Schwartz directed his famed "Daisy" spot for Lyndon Johnson in 1964. He envisioned the viewer who responded to a series of visual and auditory impressions designed to elicit purely emotional reactions to the traumatic possibility that an atomic holocaust could be brought on by an unstable political personality in the White House. Names or faces didn't even need to be mentioned. When candidates did appear as television personalities, the thematic quality of their performances seemed to reward the politician who could build from a theme and improvise through grand gesture.[14] Former Nixon press aide Herbert Klein notes in regard to televised political debates:

> We have been converted to watching and examining personalities rather than studying in depth the intelligence of answers given by candidates. Makeup, voice, personal chemistry, mannerisms, proneness to error, and audience charm become the important factors.[15]

Onto this emerging electronic stage, Edward Kennedy would lunge, a veteran politician soon to be deprived of his charismatic aura.

This article seeks to examine several specific aspects of television's impact on personality politics in the defeat of Edward Kennedy. First, his poor ability to project himself in one-on-one TV interviews (seen most explicitly in the program *Teddy* on *CBS Reports*) spread doubt about Kennedy's honesty and competence at a very early stage in the campaign. Second, by the time of the first primary, the network news had played a critical role in fostering a jingoistic politics of consensus that cast strong doubt about both the stability of Kennedy's personality and the patriotic quality of his character. Finally, evidence suggests that Kennedy's television advertising campaign had a significant effect in the primaries only after the Carter lead was insurmountable. I agree with Jeff Greenfield that the "real campaign"[16] was not fought entirely over television, but I would add that the specter of the televised personality had become symptomatic of America's denigrated view of the democratic ethos.

Teddy: The intimate perspective. One of the great ironies of Edward Kennedy's presidential candidacy in 1979–1980 was that even though he was one of America's preeminent celebrities, the youngest surviving brother of the country's most telegenic president (until 1981, that is), he remained so ineffective in using television. Able to give rousing speeches from a platform to crowds of admirers as his grandfather, Boston mayor John Fitzgerald, might have done, he projected himself as barely articulate in intimate conversations before the cameras. While his political skills were well respected and sufficient to get him elected to the Senate from Massachusetts on four occasions, he lacked communications skills.[17] The exposure of Kennedy's television weakness combined with voters' residual doubts about his character (based on the 1969 Chappaquiddick affair) severely damaged his candidacy even before he formally announced it. In this instance, a television program, an hour-long CBS interview aired November 4, 1979, acted as one important determinant of political perception to a relatively narrow audience of political journalists and potential recruits.

At age forty-seven and after seventeen years in the United States Senate, Kennedy had decided to run against incumbent president Jimmy Carter in the late summer of 1979. Carter's poor capacity for leadership on social issues and in foreign affairs, as well as his castigation of the American people for their materialistic values and narcissistic tendencies in a July 15 speech, had angered Kennedy. In addition, the brusque dismissal of five Carter cabinet secretaries and suggestions from TV commentators that Democratic officeholders who were up for reelection feared the public's response to Carter were additional factors in Kennedy's thinking[18] By July 29, Senator Henry Jackson of Washington state was heard on CBS saying that he had "never observed a political situation such as we face now from a Democratic Party standpoint where the opposition is as pervasive as it is to the president." Kennedy, he added, was the most viable alternative. Following Jackson's comments, actress Elizabeth Taylor was quoted by journalist Charles Osgood as having said that "she used to like Carter before he was president, but now thinks he's too wishy-washy." By late August, after the resignation of UN Ambassador Andrew Young, and after White House chief of staff Hamilton Jordan was accused of having taken cocaine at a fashionable New York discotheque, Carter's popularity was down to a 26 percent approval rating in the polls.[19]

As Carter's star seemed to be inexorably falling, the circumstances surrounding the death of Mary Jo Kopechne when Kennedy drove his car off a bridge at Chappaquiddick Island, and the memory of the earlier Kennedy assassinations were recurrent features associated with Edward Kennedy on the evening news. CBS did a tenth anniversary report on the Kopechne tragedy in July, producing a poll which seemed to indicate that memory of the incident might not be fatal to a possible

Kennedy candidacy.[20] In ghoulish competition as his candidacy was becoming more probable, all three networks decided to provide unprecedented coverage of Kennedy at all public gatherings so that they might be able to record any assassination attempt, were it to happen. One ABC News camera crew filming Kennedy through the primaries counted 2,150 appearances that it "shot."[21]

Chappaquiddick and any potential assassination attempt seemed to fade from the foreground briefly in early September, however, when *CBS Evening News* anchor Roger Mudd ran a lead item picking up newspaper reports indicating that Kennedy's wife and his mother were no longer opposed to his candidacy. "His direction is almost irreversible . . . he has cut off any retreat," Mudd said. After one reporter asserted that Kennedy was "less on the sidelines but not fully in the game," Bruce Morton told viewers, "The consensus among political professionals is that Edward Kennedy can have the Democratic presidential nomination any time he wants it." Using the often-featured poll results to buttress his case, Morton added, "Today's hint and wink is just more in a long-running act . . . but it was done skillfully, professionally, with maximum political impact, in the morning papers, in the evening news." Mudd ended the overall segment by revealing that Kennedy had reportedly given up eating ice cream to lose weight for the campaign. "Rest assured that if Edward Kennedy has given up eating ice cream," Mudd added knowingly, "he really is sure about the White House."[22]

The decision by Mudd, a veteran journalist at CBS, to lead the broadcast with the political story that day was undoubtedly reinforced by the research he had been doing on Kennedy for the prior few weeks. Back in June, Mudd had been asked by Robert Chandler, vice president for public affairs at CBS News, to do an hour-long *CBS Reports* broadcast on Kennedy.[23] Although widely thought to possess close associations with the Kennedys (Ethel Kennedy was a good friend of Mudd's wife), he was not personally close to the senator. He decided that he could approach any interviews professionally and "wouldn't have any problem asking any questions that ought to be asked."[24] Arrangements were made for several interviews with Kennedy—the finished show would be based on edited versions of two such sessions. A crew under producer Andrew Lack would film the senator on Cape Cod, on a family camping trip in Western Massachusetts, and in Washington. Mudd immersed himself in research on the Kennedy record at CBS headquarters in New York City. What he found out startled him. As he later told journalists Jack Germond and Jules Witcover:

> Generally speaking, most Americans' impression of him had been formed from minute-and-a-half clips on the evening news in which he was seen throwing a football or excoriating some corporate biggie in the [Senate] hearings. It was a very glamorous television image he had, but there had never been a sustained interview about him and his life and what he believed in. And we were determined that while we knew the hour would have to contain pictures of his family and an accounting of his glamorous life, we were determined that the bulk of the hour would be this interview.[25]

Apparently Kennedy agreed to talk with Mudd because he knew that CBS was going to do the program with or without his cooperation, and his refusal to speak for himself would be interpreted as an admission that he had something to hide.

The circumstances of the first meeting with Kennedy at his home on Squaw Island off Cape Cod are disputed. According to several of his aides, Kennedy thought they were there to take more pictures of him instead of to do a serious interview, but those at CBS felt the arrangements had been clear. What lends some credence to Kennedy's view is that his press secretary, Tom Southwick, who had been in favor of the senator's submission to the interviews in the first place, was not present. In fact no aides of Kennedy's were present, nor were any ground rules agreed upon in terms of the subjects to be covered.[26] Altogether, Kennedy was quite unprepared for the tough questioning that would follow on that overcast Saturday in late September.

The first part of the conversation on Squaw Island was taken up with general questions about how Kennedy defined Camelot, what it meant, and whether it was applicable to 1980. The physical danger and the political benefits of being a Kennedy were also discussed. According to Mudd, Kennedy seemed reasonably relaxed through all this, although "not terribly articulate." During a break in which the cameramen had to reload their machines, Mudd, Lack, and executive producer Howard Stringer shared their disappointment: "We were just not getting any good, vigorous, graphic kinds of words from him." After resuming the interview, Mudd asked about Kennedy's view of the press, and the senator acknowledged a "natural inquisitiveness of people about all aspects of [public] people's lives."[27]

Everything seemed to change in Kennedy's demeanor after Mudd asked abruptly, "What's the present state of your marriage, Senator?" The answer, slowly delivered and obviously painful, was as follows:

> Well, I think it's a . . . we've had some difficult times, but I think we have . . . we, I think, have been able to make some very good progress and it's . . . I would say that it's, it's, it's . . . delighted that we're able to, to share the time and the relationship that we, we do share.[28]

After several other questions related to the marriage, Mudd quickly jumped into the subject of Chappaquiddick. He was aware that the issue had been exhaustively recounted but felt that "there was no way we could do an hour on him without coming to grips with that issue." Mudd reasoned that the issue could no longer be considered as a personal one. "I regarded it as important as any of his votes in the Senate," Mudd said, adding, "It was a question of whether he told the truth or didn't tell the truth, and I thought that was basic to anybody's public candidacy."[29] Kennedy had said repeatedly that he would answer any questions about the "incident" (a word with almost clinical-sounding implications), but he volunteered nothing new, which irked the newsman, who was hoping for some new revelation. Mudd began to feel that Kennedy was "sort of defiant," challenging him time and again (Mudd counted nine times) to ask him questions about it: "Any question you want to ask me, ask me, because I'll answer it, as I have in the past." Mudd felt he was at a tactical disadvantage because he was in Kennedy's home and was interviewing a man who was physically imposing. It was a "sweaty moment for me. . . . I could back down and destroy myself professionally, and not be true to my calling." With Kennedy offering nothing new, other than referring to the inquest record, Mudd took on a prosecutorial role which, he must have been aware, made for more dynamic programming. He asked Kennedy why he had taken a right-hand turn off the paved road onto the dirt road "when all the signs led you to the left." Why hadn't the bumpy road alerted Kennedy that something was amiss? Still, nothing new came from Kennedy even after Mudd asked whether "anybody will ever fully believe your explanation." The interview ended with Mudd feeling it had been a "major, major disappointment."

> My view of him changed radically that day. For me it was almost a process of original discovery. It was as if I had been in a room that nobody else had ever been in. I knew that he tended to be inarticulate,

but when it was all over and particularly then with the second interview (two weeks later in Washington), it came to me that indeed we had a very revealing interview, and that professionally, for television anyhow, it was an original piece.[30]

The second interview, this time filmed in Washington with the senator surrounded by aides (off camera), showed Kennedy again "performing" poorly in the one-on-one format. He gave a broad and rather pointless response to a question Mudd asked about why he wanted to be president. In his own defense, Kennedy said that he was spending most of his time thinking about whether to run or not "and probably not as much time as I should have about how I'd spend the early days of the campaign, and developing and fashioning the kind of themes that I think probably would have aroused the most positive response."[31] Both Lack and Mudd, responding to criticism about the paucity of broadcast time detailing Kennedy's views on issues, claimed that when questions along this line were asked, the senator's answers weren't "coherent."[32]

The final *CBS Reports* special, based on the edited versions of the two interviews along with the visuals filmed by Lack and his camera crew, was devastating to Kennedy's candidacy. Although not a dramatic news event in the normal sense of the term, the interview became a major touchstone for reporters and political pundits seeking to explain Kennedy's campaign problems. He did come across as guarded, inarticulate, and unsure of why he wanted to be president. Mudd left the strong implication that he was not "truly his own man" but was a "captive of his bushy-tailed staff," a man who was "overly programmed," often moving through crowds "with what seems like a tape-recorded greeting." On the stump, Kennedy could be "dominating, masterful," while off the stump he could "be stilted, elliptical, and really doesn't want Americans to know him." Film shot in his Washington office showed Kennedy asking an aide about plans for his mother's special meeting with the Pope as well as his request from an aide for the first name of a Massachusetts congressman, a name with which one would have assumed he would be familiar.[33]

The most damaging part of the aired program was a dramatic reenactment, ten years later, of Kennedy's drive off the paved road onto the dirt road leading to the bridge at Chappaquiddick. With Mudd at the wheel, and a camera attached to the fender to approximate what the scene might have looked like from Kennedy' vantage point, viewers were made to feel the jarring sensation of the bumps on the unpaved road. The impression was left that Kennedy's plea of ignorance about the roads on the island was a lie.

While the goal of the program, Mudd had said, was to "report on the quality of his character, his performance in the Senate, and his conduct at Chappaquiddick," the edited version of the program added more excitement and drama than the relatively boring, if revealing, interviews would yield on their own. The introduction to the program traced the family history, their glamorous lives, and their conviviality. It included a black-and-white picture of the submerged Pontiac off Chappaquiddick Island in 1969 and a view of Kennedy leaving the Kopechne funeral. "His coming candidacy seems almost seductive," Mudd intoned, almost as a warning. As a documentary, instead of a live interview, *Teddy* exhibited how a narrator could present hints to viewers about what to look for in Kennedy's on-camera behavior.

The edited sequence of pictures suggests, further, that aside from Kennedy's inarticulate performance, he was the victim of a skewed contrast. The introductory segments—which included shots of Kennedy walking with his mother, having fun with his family during their camping trip, and visiting an amusement park—showed him surrounded by crowds of animated relatives and well wishers. The pace was fast. From there, the program shifted to the stark, grayish picture of the senator conversing with Mudd, alone, halting and without any visible emotion. The impression was created that Kennedy, on his own and without benefit of staff or family, would not be such an object of interest. Mudd's voice-over described how the "press seems to move with him like camp followers" and discussed his "extended family of celebrities," but implicitly viewers were asked how they had been taken in for so long by such a person.

Originally set to be telecast in mid-November, several weeks before Kennedy's expected announcement of candidacy, the program entitled *Teddy* was frantically rescheduled on the Sunday before his updated announcement of November 7. The "suspicion" lingers in Mudd's mind that the circumstances surrounding the change in Kennedy's schedule may have been related to an assessment of the damaging quality of the broadcast. CBS was in a bind because to comply with the "fairness doctrine" of the FCC it either had to air the broadcast before the announcement of candidacy or be prepared to offer equal time to the others in the race. The implication is that by updating his announcement, Kennedy could force CBS either to abandon the airing of the program or to bury it in a time slot where it could do little damage. In fact, despite the last-minute changes, the network devoted considerable attention to what it considered a high-quality documentary.[34]

Other television stations were in a similar quandary. NBC had aired an entire week of special segments (a total of twenty-seven minutes) on its evening news in October assessing Kennedy; ABC had done a *20/20* segment in late October that featured Tom Jarriel sharply questioning the senator about personal issues; and Metromedia station WNEW in New York City ran another hour-long documentary on Kennedy directly before Mudd's show. So aside from being a legitimate object of news analysis, it seemed inescapable that to local and national television stations, the aura surrounding a piece on Kennedy would have more audience appeal than attention focused on any other potential candidate. Full-page ads promoting the program in newspapers like the *New York Times* tended to underscore that Kennedy was a money-making commodity for television.[35]

A unique program, unprecedented in terms of the efforts devoted by one network to the coming candidacy of an aspirant to the White House, the audience for Teddy was noteworthy for its narrow casting rather than for its Nielsen ratings. The competition it was up against, the movies *MacArthur* and *Jaws*, clearly outdrew it; only 15 percent of the TV audience watched *Teddy*. But for journalists and political professionals, the program came as an important revelation that perhaps the Kennedy bubble was bursting.[36] Many had been aware that he could give rousing stump speeches and was a great raconteur in informal, off-camera settings, but the common wisdom was repeated for months, as Tom Pettit said later on NBC, that the interview "revealed an inability to thoroughly explain Chappaquiddick or anything."[37] The campaign was clearly off to a bad start, reflected in poor-quality campaign speeches as well as the damning television interviews. Kennedy himself told *Time* magazine in his own defense that "there is a problem moving from day-to-day life of a Senator, where you are involved in the details of legislation, to a campaign, where the expression of issues is quite different."[38] His staff tried to ease his plight by putting together thick briefing binders filled with concise answers to questions that might arise. The Carter camp, sensing that Kennedy would not be a good debater, within forty-eight hours of the showing of *Teddy* accepted the *Des Moines Register*'s offer to sponsor a debate.

Television news and the politics of consensus. As *Teddy* was being aired on November 4, Iranian students were seizing the American embassy in Tehran for the second time in less than a year. Television's coverage of the ensuing hostage crisis, as well as of the Soviet invasion of Afghanistan in late December, not only enhanced approval of Carter's performance as president, but aided significantly in kindling a jingoistic public response.[39] More conspicuously than print journalism, television news defused political criticism of the role of the Shah of Iran as well as Carter's decision to grant the Shah sanctuary in the United States. As foreign mobs were being pictured over television on a nightly basis, chanting slogans of defiance against the American government, Carter was the beneficiary of a perception expressed during World War I by Walter Lippmann, who said, "The sense of an enemy . . . almost obliterates personality and throws us back into a herd with animal loves and animal hates. . . . Danger requires us to be as 'one man' . . . as the fingers are welded into a clenched fist."[40] Carter's request that the nation speak with one voice in the conflict, aided by his "Rose Garden strategy," which feigned a withdrawal from active campaigning, had the effect of negating Kennedy's main issue (that of leadership) while subtly questioning the senator's patriotism. One example of TV's role in this reversal of political fortunes, which was to heap devastating scorn on Kennedy's candidacy, was the news highlighting of the KRON-TV interview the senator held in San Francisco in early December. A second example followed his "re-announcement speech" at Georgetown University in late January.

The flap over Kennedy's anti-Shah statement was stimulated by a provocative comment made by Republican candidate Ronald Reagan in the aisle of his campaign plane. Interviewed by NBC News on November 30, he wondered why the United States didn't grant political asylum to the Shah (who had been admitted to the United States only temporarily to seek medical treatment). This was not a subject that had previously been broached in public by other candidates, who were all trying to avoid any appearance of disunity over Carter's handling of the crisis. "I think the decision about when [the Shah] goes should be up to the Shah and his doctors, but I think that this country should make it plain that he is welcome to remain here," Reagan told the camera. After a reporter asked whether this meant permanent asylum, the former governor responded:

> Well, I don't know why not. You read those words on the base of the Statue of Liberty. We've got a history for being an asylum for political exiles. He certainly was as loyal an ally of this country as this country ever had.

Reagan was thus given air time, without being criticized, for making a statement that could be interpreted by Iranians as further proof of American approval of the Shah.

The following day, CBS News's Bob Shieffer reported a Kennedy statement that "the situation [in Iran] underlines that American fortunes should not be entrusted to regressive regimes that may become casualties at any moment." Clearly, the lines of a conflict over the disposition of the Shah were coming to a head. The political silence on Iran was being broken in terms of historical judgments about the role of th Shah, not about the Carter policy of demanding unconditional release of the hostages.

After a long day of campaigning on December 2, Kennedy found himself being interviewed by KRON reporter Rollin Post on a San Francisco talk show. Trying to elicit a novel or newsworthy statement from Kennedy about Iran, Post asked Kennedy for his reaction to Reagan's comment about the Shah. Tired and a little testy, Kennedy responded:

> The Shah had the reins of power and ran one of the most violent regimes in the history of mankind—in the form of terrorism and the basic and fundamental violations of human rights, in the most cruel circumstances to his own people.

How could the United States, Kennedy asked, justify taking into its own borders a man who "had stolen umpteen billions of dollars that he'd stolen from Iran"? Further, Kennedy wanted to know why this was being done when "Hispanics who are here legally" had to wait "nine years to bring their wife and children to this country."[41]

His remarks were soon extracted by a wire-service reporter and produced a firestorm of criticism. After reporting on the Iranian hostage crisis the next night, Walter Cronkite introduced the next segment as follows:

The Iran crisis today jumped into the middle of American politics. It happened when President Carter's leading rival . . . broke his month-long silence on the issue. Last night he roundly criticized the U.S. relationship with the deposed Shah.

Reporter Susan Spencer, one of a number of younger correspondents who were covering Kennedy and accentuating some of his campaign fluffs, said that in a month of campaigning Kennedy "has deflected hundreds of questions on Iran saying that it was inappropriate for him to comment as long as the hostages were held." Last night, she added, he "suddenly was more outspoken, saying that the Shah ran one of the most violent regimes in the history of mankind and react[ed] angrily to Ronald Reagan's suggestion that as an ally, the Shah should get permanent asylum." Close-ups of pieces of paper on which aides were scribbling notes seemed to lend an air of truth to Spencer's next statement that "distracted aides and speechwriters clustered near telephones to review his statement." The implication seemed plain that the actions of the aides all revolved around covering up for the mistake of their boss. The next day, Kennedy "clarified his position," Spencer noted in sarcastic tones, when he said that "support for the hostages does not mean support for the Shah." Spencer concluded her report by saying, "It's clear that when this crisis ends, what happened and why will become a major issue in the campaign."

Cronkite then related that there had been an "immediate chorus of reaction" against Kennedy's statement: "Top aides at the White House are convinced that Kennedy blundered by speaking out on Iran at this time and decided to draw attention to it." Robert Strauss was seen berating Kennedy as "ill advised and confused." Secretary of State Cyrus Vance, California governor Jerry Brown, and others all condemned him. No one came to Kennedy's defense on any of the evening news programs. On NBC's *Nightly News*, Senator Howard Baker said that if he were in Iran and "heard that statement from a presidential candidate and a member of the Senate, I think the first thing I would conclude is that the country's divided." Correspondent Tom Pettit said that the "establishment denounced Kennedy," giving as examples State Department spokesman Hodding Carter as well as the dramatic statement by Illinois congressman Henry Hyde, who suggested that the senator consider "registering for being a foreign agent." ABC's news show went one step further and presented an interview with the foreign minister of Iran, who said, "This is the kind of gesture which should be taken by the United States on the side of justice to expose the Shah." ABC correspondent Ann Compton made several references to the complete isolation that Kennedy was felt to occupy as a result of his statement. People in Washington "could scarcely believe that Kennedy would use such a gesture," she said at one point. Next came the negative comments by Hyde, Republican senator Ted Stevens, Robert Dole, and Robert Strauss. "Even Senator Kennedy's friends here in Congress who privately may agree with him say they feel uncomfortable, uneasy with his judgment on this issue."

Not only did the controversy linger in the TV news accounts, but it fit with the accumulated perception that Kennedy was an immature, overprotected, self-serving liberal who would use a delicate issue such as the Iranian hostage crisis to advance his personal political fortunes. He had taken a "big gamble in bringing it up," NBC's news program relayed to its audience on December 3. Three days later, ABC did a special report on the rule of the Shah in which Barry Sarafin reported that evidence did not "match Senator Kennedy's picture of it being one of the most violent in the history of mankind." One visual image reinforced by CBS on December 8 showed Kennedy addressing a group of Iowa farmers, but the focus was not on Kennedy; it was on one handmade sign that read: "Kennedy. Khomeni has your speech. Please call Iran." December 14 saw Catherine Mackin of ABC asserting that Kennedy's poor platform performances, his inexperienced staff, and his failure to articulate strong campaign themes were all "overwhelmed by [his] statement on the Shah. In short, Kennedy's campaign is the fifty-first Iranian hostage." While these comments were being heard, the screen showed Kennedy, alone and slightly befuddled, walking onto a talk show. The impression reinforced the idea that no respectable opinion makers supported his position, that as ABC then reported as historical truth on January 2, he had "blundered."

By January, after the Russian invasion of Afghanistan and Carter's call for a U.S. boycott of the Olympic Games and implementation of a grain embargo—both of which Kennedy opposed—Phil Jones reported that Kennedy had "gone more to handshaking and less talking."[42] Kennedy was thus made to appear to feel guilty for breaking the one-voice policy which, in fact, had most egregiously been done first by the politically unscathed Reagan.

Kennedy lost the important Iowa caucuses decisively (59 percent to 31 percent) on January 21, and within a week he made a major political speech at Georgetown University in which he redefined his candidacy, placing more emphasis on differences with President Carter over issues rather than over styles of leadership. Among other policies, he now advocated the immediate freeze on wages, prices, profits, and rents to help bring down soaring inflation, quick gasoline rationing to free the country from dependence on Middle Eastern oil, and opposition to the draft registration Carter had requested. In addition, he sought the creation of a United Nations commission to investigate Iranian grievances against the deposed Shah. He practiced the speech repeatedly and withdrew from interviews with the press over several days, which had the effect of building up interest in whether he was going to resign from the race.

Kennedy delivered an effective speech on January 28 to the Georgetown audience, a speech that, according to one print reporter, was "dripping with scorn and sarcasm for the first time in speaking of the President."[43] Yet television viewers could hardly have known that. The condensation of the speech's content as well as the prominence given the damning interpretation of it by the Carter forces sapped much of its potential impact.

Cronkite headlined the story on CBS by saying that Kennedy had "redefined his candidacy," accusing the president of crossing the threshold of Cold War Two. After some of Kennedy's newly emphasized positions were briefly noted, reporter Phil Jones again noted a sign in the crowd, this one held by a student instead of an Iowa farmer. It read: "Ted: Is the dream Sinking?" Kennedy, Jones said, was "fighting . . . but clearly a frustrated candidate." Before presenting several capsulized quotes from the speech, Jones introduced Kennedy by saying that he had "looked into a teleprompter and read a speech." Conservative columnist William Safire later wrote that the address had "revived the art of the political speech, which had been dormant for nearly a decade." The speech had been written, Safire continued, "by people with a feel for vivid prose; it was delivered with force and style; and it had meat for everyone to chew on."[44] But instead of presenting significant segments of the speech, CBS quickly turned to spotlight criticism of it.

Leslie Stahl, the White House correspondent, gave the "general themes of the response" from the Washington establishment: that it had been "politically opportunistic, demogogic, and hypocritical" and that it showed the senator to be a "hopeless liberal." Carter press secretary Jody Powell's reaction was printed on the screen: "one of the clear results of the Iowa caucuses has been to drive Kennedy to the left." Other nameless officials were said to have pointed to Kennedy's assertion that Carter was "overreacting" to the Afghanistan crisis as evidence of his "leftist tendencies." Other unnamed sources were saying that the senator had been "wishy-washy on the Olympics boycott" and were wondering, "What is he prepared to do to stand up to the Russians?" The last person that CBS viewers saw reacting to Kennedy's speech was Carter campaign spokesman Robert Strauss, who said his judgment was that "the country will little note nor long remember what he said."

There were variations in the coverage presented by the other two networks. ABC, which had had three camera crews covering the speech itself, showed the White House reaction to the speech even before it showed excerpts of Kennedy making it. NBC correspondant Chris Wallace did a piece before the speech mentioning that Kennedy was "laying claim to his birthright," that he had broken the truce on Iran and ever since had been 'timid" about discussing foreign policy, as old doubts resurfaced over Chappaquiddick and about his being a big spender on social programs. After Kennedy's Iowa defeat, Wallace said Kennedy had been "so desperate that he talked to administration officials before attacking it" and had rehearsed his speech on "a teleprompter."[45]

Following the network coverage of the Georgetown speech, print journalists of both liberal and conservative persuasion began to note the lack of fairness with which Kennedy was treated. Safire wrote, "The trend in wolf-pack journalism is to savage Mr. Kennedy while treating Mr. Carter's Rose Garden campaign with awe and reverence."[46] Fellow *New York Times* columnist Anthony Lewis agreed. What Americans were seeing was

> a revival of Presidentialism. Not even Vietnam and Watergate could altogether kill the romance of the Presidency. In dangerous times Americans like to look to the White House and see there a figure larger than life. When the Russians are threatening, it somehow becomes unpatriotic to treat the President as less than commanding in his wisdom or his resolution.

In contrast to the press's muted criticism of Carter, Lewis continued, the press has been zealous in its search for flaws in the Kennedy campaign. There have indeed been flaws, and the candidate has been responsible for most of his own troubles. But some reporters have seemed to be trying to show how hard-boiled they can be by scorning everything to do with the Senator.

Tom Shales of the *Washington Post* also castigated the networks for "playing get Teddy", adding that "we turn on the nightly news to find out how badly Teddy is doing today." Noting the CBS comment about Kennedy's use of a teleprompter, Lewis asked whether the network was "going to note every politician who uses a teleprompter from now on? How about broadcasters who use them?"[47]

The idea that there was a "pack instinct" in the coverage of Kennedy is significant. A whole series of personal dynamics were involved on the part of journalists who related similar impressions about the campaign, especially in the days before the first primary in New Hampshire on February 26. ABC and NBC used teams that comprised a senior correspondent paired with a junior correspondent; at CBS, correspondent Phil Jones was not enthusiastic about sharing his beat with Susan Spencer, the junior reporter, and Jed Duvall replaced him before New Hampshire. Network executives were aware of earlier criticism that the Kennedys always successfully cultivated the press by integrating them into the glamour of the campaign. Thus reporters who were relatively early in their careers had been picked to avoid an appearance of a pro-Kennedy bias.[48] One analyst has noted one aspect of the results—that many reporters felt pressured to perform under the more graphic demands of television.

> Editors had limited interest in objective accounts of what these young reporters were observing for the first time; they wanted something more sharply angled, judgmental but forced into the objective mode. They wanted to know whether Kennedy was failing or faltering, stumbling or mumbling, whether he would stand up to the pressure or quit.[49]

Another feature of the network coverage of Kennedy's Georgetown speech was that many of the economic issues he raised did not seem to lend themselves to dramatic treatment on television. TV wanted good visuals without "eyeball overload"[50] and consistently downplayed stories on the economy and other more or less abstract issues because they could not be visualized in dramatic enough fashion. After noting the minor focus placed on economic issues in the three presidential campaigns from 1968 to 1976, political scientist Doris Graber wrote in 1980: "Most people, though concerned, are unwilling to wrestle with a difficult subject that newspeople have not yet learned to simplify and dramatize. Rather than risk writing complex campaign stories that most of the audience would probably ignore, newspeople prefer to feature the horse-race glamour of campaign events."[51] But what Graber fails to mention is that television journalists, in conjunction with the aims of both corporate management and most American politicians over many years, had been using an endless avalanche of simplistic catch phrases to explain economic reality. That Kennedy's liberal economic positions were underplayed on television or tinged with the label of "leftist" and joined to his "weak" posture toward Soviet expansionism was no accident, nor was it a conscious conspiracy but a convenient collusion between the Carter camp and the structural demands of the medium. Like the contagion of diarrhea that plagued the occupants of the press bus following Kennedy, this "pack journalism" spread amid the contained atmosphere of the news business.[52]

From personality to protest movement: Television advertising and the changing focus of the Kennedy campaign. One prominent television consultant has said that television advertising is "the most reliable, the most effective, and the only one" of the three chief vehicles (the others being news and talk shows) "in which a candidate is able to say exactly what he or she wants to say in the words that he or she wants to use with a certainty of the delivery of the precise message that the candidate wants to deliver."[53] That advertising on television can give the only unfiltered view of a candidate many voters receive is the common wisdom of many media consultants. In the 1980 presidential campaign, the candidate with the highest national name recognition factor beside the president, Edward Kennedy, had perhaps the most poorly developed use of television advertising of any candidate. Not only did Kennedy project himself poorly through free media exposure on news and talk shows,[54] but he also possessed a severely limited appreciation of the use of paid attention engineering techniques on television. The changing style of his campaign advertising from a personalized orientation to a more general expression of a protest movement against the incumbent president gives significant evidence that the structural demands of American politics have created a norm of manipulation of the American public through television that is but dimly understood outside the confines of the political and media elite. The Kennedy campaign manifests how a candidate who originally had little appreciation and felt no need for the thematic use of television would be forced to accede to the dictates of the medium.

Although always surrounded by advisers, Kennedy had not needed to defer to media consultants in his past campaigns. They were a part of his campaigns but did not lead the parade. He had seldom faced significant electoral opposition in his Senate campaigns, and his commercials, put together by veteran Kennedy ad man Charles Guggenheim, were standard productions showing little change from those of the 1960s. "The image Kennedy projects is a function of what he believes far more than an assessment of what he thinks is palatable," his assistant Carl Wagner has said.[55] Late in the 1980 campaign, Kennedy himself acknowledged that his strident rhetoric, or "raising my voice on TV," as he termed it, was probably a factor in his sinking candidacy, but he told Elizabeth Drew that he wasn't "as concerned about those matters, nor have I given much thought to them. I'm sure I'll have a time in my life—but not now."[56]

He hadn't considered very seriously how to use television early in the campaign, concentrating more on organizational features of upcoming primaries coupled with policy concerns. Under the formal leadership of his brother-in-law Stephen Smith, the Kennedy campaign was organizationally fragmented, reflecting numerous layers of policy aides, family friends, and political loyalists. In November they solicited several media consultants. David Garth was approached. A prominent New York consultant, he had helped to elect the president of Venezuela, governors of New York, New Jersey, and Connecticut, and two mayors of New York. Yet Garth declined formally to join the campaign over Thanksgiving weekend, asserting afterwards:

> Their approach is from twenty years ago when reporters didn't ask questions. The Kennedy campaign just opened their doors and said we're doing business. You've got to have a strategy and a vision. They didn't understand media. And what's really shocking to me is that they didn't understand the modern use of polls. They still think in terms of getting Teddy moving around. But you don't have to stage a barnstorming tour. You have one press conference and one media event a day. What's amazing to me is that they were not prepared.[57]

Garth had unsuccessfully sought control of all media in the campaign in order to present thematically controlled images in an overall sequential strategy of marketing the candidate. The man who did become the chief media adviser at the beginning of the campaign was Herbert Schmertz, who took a six-week leave of absence from his job as vice president of public affairs of the Mobil Oil Corporation. Using the in-house expertise of Mobil's top ad man became a serious embarrassment when it became publicly known; Kennedy was a strong critic of the profits and power of the oil companies. NBC reported that Schmertz's appearance in the campaign was "curious," then quoted Jody Powell's comment that Schmertz might be "as successful with Edward Kennedy's image and credibility as he has been with the oil companies."[58] The whole episode, which also soon reverberated in radio commercials sponsored in New Hampshire by Governor Brown, made Kennedy's criticism of the oil companies appear rather ingenuous.[59]

Schmertz's place was eventually taken by Philip Bakes, a former counsel to the Civil Aeronautics Board, a man with no media experience. In actuality, however, there was no uniform media authority and no person traveling on a day-to-day basis with Kennedy, nobody who coordinated his statements to the perpetual barrage of news cameras and reporters. The campaign didn't hire a pollster until December 2, when Peter Hart and Associates of Washington was chosen.[60]

The Carter campaign had understood for months that Kennedy's weakness was Carter's strength; that traits such as honesty, decency, and trustworthiness, when accentuated in the president, would additionally act as an effective but subtle attack on Kennedy.[61] One Carter spot shown during the winter showed him seated at a table with his wife and daughter, Amy, saying, "I don't think there's any way you can separate the responsibilities of a husband and father and a basic human being from that of the president. What I do in the White House is to maintain a good family life, which I consider to be crucial to being a good president." An announcer added: "Husband. Father. President. He's done these three jobs with distinction." The contrast to the strained marital relations of Kennedy and his wife, Joan, would not be lost on many viewers. Another unsparing ad shows Carter addressing a town meeting as an announcer says:

You may not always agree with President Carter, but you'll never find yourself wondering if he's telling you the truth. It's hard to think of a more useful quality in any person who becomes President than telling you the simple truth. . . . President Carter. For the truth.[62]

Charles Guggenheim, who produced the early TV commercials for Kennedy, seemed frustrated in dealing with the Carter spots. "We really would have preferred to have focused on inflation and foreign policy," he complained in March, "but the polls show the voters feel two to one, that Carter is doing a poor job, yet they're voting two to one for him. I don't think there's any other conclusion that you can make, but that character is an issue."[63] Early Guggenheim commercials had shown Kennedy seated at a table with a flag behind him, telling several representative Americans such things as "It seems to me America means hope," followed by an announcer with the tag line "Commitment to a strong America."[64]

As the withering effect of the character issue was becoming obvious, new commercials were created as part of a tack labeled the "personalization campaign," which sought to work with viewers doubts about Chappaquiddick rather than ignoring them. The networks, in a number of instances in January, had relayed newspaper stories that renewed old charges doubting Kennedy's sworn testimony. The new tack, first unveiled by Kennedy himself in a *Meet the Press* interview in late November, was not prominently featured in advertisements, however, until late in January.[65] In an introduction to a paid rebroadcast of the Georgetown speech beamed at New Englanders, Kennedy told viewers that while he knew "many will never believe" his account of the events at Chappaquiddick, his version was the "only truth I can tell because that is the way it happened." He then asked to be judged by "the basic American standards of fairness."[66] A later five-minute Guggenheim commercial attempted to emphasize that Kennedy had risen above the tragedies which had beset him. Perhaps effective in softening the hatred of Kennedy in terms of Chappaquiddick, the commercials were too late in addressing the perception problem involving his personality.

Stunningly defeated in the early primaries—culminating in his 65 percent to 30 percent loss to Carter in Illinois–his campaign finances in serious trouble, Kennedy nevertheless decided to continue seriously to contest Carter in the March 25 primaries in New York and Connecticut, states that were hoped to be more sympathetic to his candidacy. Public perception of him remained extremely negative. But a number of events and shifts in public opinion were to collide with a change in Kennedy's advertising to allow him to win both states by shifting to a strongly negative campaign against the president. Part of the explanation involves a change in his media consultants; more importantly, the help that the Iranian crisis had given Carter was fast being eroded by a widening public view of a number of other issues and concerns.

New inflation and unemployment figures were released that proved that the country was in a definite recession period. Interest rates were climbing to 20 percent as the Federal Reserve Board was contracting the money supply. In addition, a switched vote by UN ambassador McDonald Henry created the unmistakable impression that Carter was antagonistic to Israel's interests while reconfirming earlier doubts about his administrative competence.

Another reason for the change in the direction of the campaign was more subtle and was ultimately reflected in television advertising. Carter had actually won the nomination, it was widely trumpeted to the public, because he had built a delegate lead that was insurmountable. According to Carter aide Robert Keefe,

"That changed the character of the Kennedy campaign from one of a viable campaign for the nomination to a protest movement against the president. That meant the issues were important and the personality wasn't."[67]

Kennedy's anti-Carter rhetoric was turning noticeably more pointed than it had been back in November as he now desperately sought to debate Carter on a broad range of issues.[68] Voter frustrations, however, could not easily be channeled into votes for Kennedy.

One man who picked up on voter anger and tried to make it work for Kennedy through television advertising was David Sawyer, a New Yorker with a dislike for Jimmy Carter's presidency. A rival of Garth, he had studied drama at Princeton University before making documentary films and starting his own media consulting firm in the early 1970s. Like Garth, Sawyer had sought control of all media in the Kennedy campaign in the fall after they had approached him. With the campaign in dire straits by March, he was finally given the go-ahead to produce some commercials for Kennedy at minimal cost. Sawyer reportedly later recouped by charging high fees for commercials he produced for Carter in the fall campaign.[69]

Nixon's 1968 campaign was the example Sawyer used to describe his belief that the communication of feelings by candidates was often a critical factor in a victory. He believed that Joe McGinniss's best-selling book, *The Selling of the President 1968*, was all wrong because it put forth the thesis that a bunch of Madison Avenue advertising executives "figured out how to hide the real Nixon and then packaged a campaign version of the candidate like a bar of soap and sold it to the public." Sawyer claimed that that was what the Nixon people "had tried to do" with a variety of artificial forums in which Haldeman had placed Nixon, but the real story of the 1968 election was the six-week loss of Nixon's 15 percent lead in the polls because Humphrey had stood up before the cameras and said, "Here I am; this is what I feel." The sophisticated voters had seen through the contrived Nixon personality, Sawyer felt.[70]

At the center of his theory was the belief that the "open personality" of a candidate was far more of a campaign asset that a closed one. Sawyer felt that Reagan was the classic example of a candidate who used the medium as an open person, just as Johnny Carson did. Both "were vulnerable as people, funny, but you can identify with them and feel comfortable with them. Kennedy was exactly the opposite."[71] Because Kennedy had been a public figure for so long, he had built up tremendous personal defenses, as do almost all politicians. Sawyer's usual technique with his clients was to help them recognize their defenses by taking them through a video workshop in which they answered questions before the cameras and then studied the videotape. Never allowed to see Kennedy alone, Sawyer wasn't pleased at having to vie for the senator's attention with policy advisers and political aides.[72]

Sawyer's research tools included using attitudinal polling, which was far more sophisticated than earlier polling that had simply asked whether a voter was in favor of a particular candidate. By 1980, as he told *New Yorker* columnist Michael Arlen in February, polls could "tell you not only the rough extent of somebody's Catholic problem but precisely what kind of people make up this problem, and why—what trade offs are involved." Such tools could be effective in "anticipating shifts in political attitudes" so that knowledgeable media people could orchestrate thematic shifts catered to voter opinion.

Another research technique of Sawyer's, focus groups, involved the selection of fifteen or twenty people on a "psychodemographic basis,"

who were placed in a room for a period of time under the guidance of trained moderators and asked "to speak their minds on a specific subject." Moderators often sought gut reactions to the personalities of candidates in relation to the political and social terrain. Sawyer's interpretation of the results of all the market research tools made the technique sound like an art form:

> In a political campaign it's practically impossible to persuade people who are dead set against a certain politician to vote for him. You can't advertise a politican as if he were Anacin. You know, the box and the name, the box and the name—all that repetition. People's feelings about politicians are too complex. But you can work with those feelings if you can find out what they are.[73]

Unable to use focus groups in the upcoming New York primary, however, because of a lack of time and money, Sawyer used polls and his organizational intuition, which picked up the great public anger at Carter. "We went bent for leather on one issue, Carter's incompetence (and the Jewish vote and the U.N. vote)," Sawyer related. The Kennedy camp was felt to be bereft of structure, strategy, or message. "We came in and it was very simple. We said, forget everything you've been doing."

In the next several days Sawyer proceeded to produce four ads that were put on the air in Kennedy's last-ditch effort. He later asserted, "The issue of the campaign had to be focused entirely on Carter in Washington and not Kennedy at Chappaquiddick."[74] Two of the ads featured actor Carroll O'Connor, who had played the Queens working-class bigot Archie Bunker on CBS for over ten years. Against a nondescript background in California, and addressing his "friends" on the other side of the television screen, O'Connor said that he had "seen some oddities offstage as well as on, but never anything odder than Jimmy Carter in the Democratic primary." Extraordinary scare tactics followed. For example, Carter "may give us a Depression which may make Hoover's look like prosperity. Our money . . . won't be worth the paper used to print it. We're looking at industrial layoffs and unemployment in all parts of the country . . . and Jimmy stays in Washington making warmhearted speeches."[75] The O'Connor ads, which were said to have been written by O'Connor himself, represented something radically different from the earlier Guggenheim commercials, one of which showed Ethel Kennedy on a tennis court, talking about the

senator's caring quality.[76] O'Connor's gruff, conservative manner, which was softened for the commercial to a perceptible degree, lent a credibility to the negative spots that the vague images of the earlier work did not. "Let's fight back" was the tag line of several of Sawyer's commercials, playing on the alienation and frustration felt by voters when confronted with Carter.

It was not the O'Connor spots, however, but the "Never Again" spot that represented the core of the Sawyer-Kennedy strategy in New York. This one showed a smiling Carter on the screen as an announcer related, "This man has led our country into the worst economic crisis since the depression. His broken promises cost New York a billion dollars a year. He betrayed Israel at the U.N., his latest foreign policy blunder." Then a picture of Kennedy came on screen and the announcer said, "This man has endured personal attacks in order to lead the fight for specific answers, like mandatory controls to stop inflation. Let's join Ted Kennedy and fight back against four years of failure." The audience was admonished "never again" to be exploited.[77]

Kennedy won the New York and Connecticut primaries. Although the impact of the commercials cannot be accurately judged, new life had been breathed into the campaign. Before the Pennsylvania primary, which was to take place on April 25, Sawyer used focus groups to "refine" the voter perceptions he had picked up before producing his New York spots. Anger against Carter had worn off somewhat, replaced by more of a blasé attitude, he felt. Two associations from the focus groups stuck out:

> People found it difficult to get really upset about Carter because he was like a nice grocery-store clerk who smiled when you walked in the door. The shelves weren't stocked, the prices were high, but you found it difficult to get mad at him because he was nice. The other figure which came out [of the focus groups] was that the nation was a ship of state; it was being tossed on stormy seas. Carter was standing on the bridge of the ship steering it in circles, getting nowhere. Kennedy was standing on the prow of the ship gesturing wildly into the darkness—"follow me, follow me." Under the circumstances, economic problems, etc., people preferred Carter in circles to Kennedy in distress.[78]

The spots for Pennsylvania reflected this. While still against Carter, they were softened somewhat. Instead of saying that Carter had "misled" the American people and created the "worst" economic crisis, the

Sawyer group portrayed Carter with his fingers crossed, an image of a weak and indecisive president. "When it came to inflation [an announcer intoned], his attitude was, 'I'll keep my fingers crossed.' Today we have 20 percent inflation. On housing, interest rates, even foreign affairs, his attitude was, 'I'll keep my fingers crossed.'"[79]

By the time of the California primary, when advertisements were beginning to descend on voters there from a number of groups backing ballot referenda as well as political candidates, focus groups had told Sawyer that the people in the state were not as willing to put up with failure as the rest of the country—that they had more of a success orientation, a can-do attitude. So aside from using the O'Connor spots, the fingers-crossed spot, and a man-in-the-street ad (with comments that included one man saying, "This nation is embarrassed by the leadership we've had"), Sawyer decided to try to project more of a positive picture for voters to associate with Kennedy, at least to bring his voice back. Although frustrated at the lack of time for proper buying of media time—a constant lament of media managers—Sawyer got together the "Apollo" spot, which soon was put on the air. Film of a rocket ascending into the sky was accompanied by the voice of an announcer asking whether the country had "lost the spirit that put man on the moon, the spirit that enabled us to solve the toughest problems and meet the greatest challenges. Or do you believe that spirit is still in us, that we have the greatest resources, technology, and minds of any country in the world, and that with strong leadership we can put those gifts to work and lift that spirit again? . . . Ted Kennedy, because we've got to do better." Perhaps reminding voters of the rhetoric and voice of John Kennedy, the commercial ended with Edward intoning, "This is the country that put footprints in the valleys of the moon, and I say that we can meet our challenges in the 1980s."[80] Using the symbol of the rocket—of lost hope for a new frontier, which his older brother had represented almost twenty years before—the commercial's matrix of power, energy, and imagination was designed to appeal to the achievement mentality believed to be so prevalent in California. According to the time buyer for the Kennedy campaign, Bill Murphy of Media Management in New York City, the budget was somewhat less in California than in New York because it was already conceded that Carter had won the race.[81] Kennedy's eventual victory in California was thus clearly of minimal value in the overall process. Moreover,

voter exhaustion with an extraordinarily extended and sustained political season was taxing the ingenuity of television journalists in their effort to find new angles to tell viewers about the rather stale horse race.

"A lot of people think this primary is for the birds," Bruce Morton told his CBS audience on the eve of the California primary. "A lot of them like birds better." A colorful parrot, "the latest fad here"—which could cost up to $10,000—appeared on the screen and repeated, "far out." The CBS report eventually concluded with a view of Morton, looking almost like a politician in a commercial with his coat thrown over his shoulder, walking along a Pacific beach and commenting sadly, "Californians have seen their election coming and they don't much care." The people in the largest state in the union obviously felt they possessed little meaningful choice, Morton intimated. What he didn't say, but what some viewers may have noticed, was that television would nonetheless still try to find something visually interesting to say.[82]

The campaign would continue until August, although at a greatly reduced pace after the final primaries. The Democratic Convention in New York produced no prolonged drama as it had in 1924, but from the perspective of one television critic it was all "soporific . . . a story without suspense, a highly touted battle that finally lacked villains or heroes."[83] Television, as well as the print media, speculated endlessly about whether Carter and Kennedy would clasp hands high in the victory salute following the president's inevitable acceptance speech. What actually did happen on the podium when the two appeared together would be the subject of numerous comments. While all this banality was going on, TV executives broadly hinted that such political conventions might well not be covered so extensively in the future because they made for uninteresting, costly, and unpopular programming.[84] Frequent speculation about Kennedy's candidacy in 1984 was aired, but that seemed tiresome as well.

Kennedy had formally begun his quest for the nomination in nonideological terms by using classic military rhetoric intended to rouse the faithful to him as a martial personality. He completed the campaign by using language that identified him with a broad, ill-defined movement, resonating to ideological references deep within the historical experience of the Democratic Paty. His final speech to the Democratic convention should have been his opening salvo. By many

accounts it was the most effective televised political address since the one given at the Republican convention in 1964 that started TV actor Ronald Reagan on his political career.

By 1980, amid a host of ambiguous assumptions concerning the legal status and the ethical norms of this new medium of mass persuasion, the televised personality had come of age and would secure the power of the presidency. Political conflicts fostered by television had come to appear petty and insignificant and had no doubt been partially responsible for the widely noted apathy of the electorate. Viewers were being encouraged to scoff at the antics of politicians through the illusory notion that the television camera allowed them to see behind the curtain of power.

WCBS-TV in New York City featured a piece on the dismantling of the interior political stage at Madison Square Garden after the convention.[85] One man, asked to contrast the 1976 convention with that of 1980, said, referring to the surrounding garbage, "This convention is heavier"—but the implication seemed plain to viewers that the whole production had been a waste. Tony Bennett was heard singing "The Party's Over" in the background. "It's time to wind up the masquerade," he intoned as viewers of television looked at a man sweeping up mounds of trash. What the story should at least have considered was that television bore considerable responsibility for this masquerade.

NOTES

1. *CBS Evening News*, 30 May 1980.

2. Jeff Greenfield, *The Real Campaign* (New York, 1982), p. 15.

3. Sidney Blumenthal, *The Permanent Campaign* (Boston, 1980), p. 260.

4. John Deardourff, chairman of Bailey, Deardourff and Associates, quoted in John Foley et al., *Nominating the President* (New York, 1980), p. 58.

5. Roone Arledge of ABC quoted on *Bill Moyers' Journal*, WNET, 17 September 1980.

6. Daniel Boorstin, *The Image* (New York, 1961); see especially chapter 2. See also Blumenthal, *Permanent Campaign*, pp. 28–35.

7. David Broder, "Of Presidents and Parties," *Wilson Quarterly*, Winter 1978, p. 110. Among the many others who have addressed this phenomenon are Herbert Gans, *Deciding What's News* (New York, 1979), pp. 61–63; Kurt and Gladys Lang, *Politics and Television* (Chicago, 1968), chapter 5; and Todd Gitlin, *The Whole World Is Watching* (Berkeley, 1980), p. 146.

8. Warren Susman, "Personality and the Making of Twentieth Century Culture," in *New Directions in American Intellectual History*, edited by John Higham and Paul Conkin

(Baltimore, 1979), pp. 212–226; John Cawelti, *Apostles of the Self-Made Man* (Chicago, 1965), pp. 171–183; Richard Sennett, *The Fall of Public Man* (New York, 1977), chapters 8, 11–14; Christopher Lasch, *The Culture of Narcissism* (New York, 1979), chapter 3. Lasch writes, "Success in our society has to be ratified by publicity . . . all politics has become a form of spectacle" (p. 117). See also Lee W. Huebner, "The Discovery of Propaganda" (Ph.D. diss., (Harvard, 1968), chapter 2; and T.J. Jackson Lears, *No Place of Grace* (New York, 1981), *passim*.

9. Gerald Stanley Lee quoted in *Mt. Tom*, December 1905, p. 218. See my forth-coming dissertation for Columbia University on the broad outlines of this question in the early twentieth century, "Lord of Attention: Gerald Stanley Lee and the Search for the Heroic Personality in the American Crowd."

10. Emmet John Hughes, "52,000,000 TV Sets: How Many Votes?" *New York Times*, 25 September 1960, p. 23, p. 189.

11. Dan Nimmo, *The Political Persuaders* (Englewood Cliffs, N.J., 1970), p. 197.

12. On the relationship between public relations and television in the Nixon White House see Jeb Stuart Magruder, *An American Life* (New York, 1975). On the Cadell memo given to Carter in December 1976, which detailed and argued for a White House stressing style over substance, see *New York Times*, 4 May 1977.

13. *Columbia Journalism Review*, September-October 1979, p. 24.

14. Robert Spero, *The Duping of the American Voter* (New York, 1980), pp. 83–85; Blumenthal, *Permanent Campaign*, p. 123. Tony Schwartz, a New York City television consultant, published *The Responsive Chord* in 1974 and concentrated on trying to explain how voters, not candidates, should be packaged. Voters should "feel a candidate" instead of actually seeing him, relating to the electronic medium, which made feelings surface most effectively. "The best political commercials are similar to Rorschach patterns. They do not tell the viewer anything. They surface his feelings and provide a context for him to express his feelings" (quoted in Blumenthal, *Permanent Campaign*, p. 125). In 1976, Schwartz worked for the candidacy of Jimmy Carter in the final stages of the presidential campaign. "Whether it's Coca-Cola [whose ads of warmth and fun he created] or Jimmy Carter, what we appeal to in the consumer or voter is an attitude. We don't try to convey a point of view, but a montage of images and sounds that leaves the viewer with a positive attitude towards the product regardless of his perspective." (Spero, the *American Voter*, p. 145). Not all practitioners agreed with Schwartz, but the effect in the 1976 race was to allow Jimmy Carter to represent all things to most voters.

15. Herbert Klein, *Making It Perfectly Clear* (New York, 1980), p. 438.

16. Jeff Greenfield, *The Real Campaign* (New York, 1982).

17. See Murray Levin, *Kennedy Campaigning* (Boston, 1966), for the 1962 campaign in Massachusetts.

18. For background material on Kennedy's life see James MacGregor Burns, *Edward Kennedy and the Camelot Legacy* (New York, 1976); Burton Hersh, *The Education of Edward Kennedy* (New York, 1980); and Max Lerner, *Ted and the Kennedy* Legend (New York, 1980). On Kennedy's decision to run, his aide Paul Kirk has said that the senator felt Carter's "Malaise" speech "violated the spirit of America, the things that he thought the American people wanted to do and feel about themselves" (quoted in Jonathan Moore, *Campaign for President*, p. 22.) See also Martin Shramm, "Carter," in Richard Harwood, ed., *The Pursuit of the Presidency* (New York, 1980), p. 100. According to a number of

sources, Kennedy's decision was also motivated by the intense pressure he felt, expressed privately, by fellow Democratic officeholders. The extraordinary attention of the press on his actions may also have been an important factor.

19. *CBS Evening News*, 24 August 1979, for poll results. Polls were becoming a pervasive part of television coverage of presidential politics in 1980. For example, see the network news programs for ABC, 3 and 30 July 1979; and for CBS, 7 and 17 July 1979. For network use of polls in 1976 see James David Barber, ed., *Race for the Presidency* (Englewood Cliffs, N.J., 1978), pp. 96–102.

20. *CBS Evening News*, 17 July 1979. Mudd introduced the program by wondering, "Who would have thought, ten years after Chappaquiddick and a presumably ruined political career, that Senator Edward Kennedy of Massachusetts would be, in the polls at least, the odds-on favorite among Democrats to be the presidential candidate?" During the program Reagan aide Lyn Nofziger asserted that Chappaquiddick "was a matter of . . . a man panicking in the clutch." With no independent polls taken by the Kennedy forces until December, it is probable that the network poll reinforced the idea to Kennedy and his staff that the 1969 incident could be containable in the minds of voters.

21. Personal interview with Pat O'Neil, ABC producer, 10 December 1981; personal interview with Jed Duvall, CBS correspondent, 11 December 1981; Harwood, *Pursuit*, p. 81.

22. *CBS Evening News*, 7 September 1979. If Kennedy thought that this kind of uncritical interest in his candidacy was going to continue, he only had to wait several days to find out otherwise. In an NBC news broadcast on September 13, Senator Howard Baker of Tennessee, an unannounced Republican candidate, said that it would be difficult to beat Ted Kennedy but that he was "just the man to do it," according to correspondent Tom Pettit. Baker had a "hunch" that "the country would quickly sort out the nostalgia from the facts and issues, that they would find that Senator Kennedy's record on a variety of issues was so far out of synchronization from what the country wants that it would produce a very favorable and successful result." "By that he means that Howard Baker would be the next president of the United States on issues only," Pettit editorialized. About Chappaquiddick, Baker's answer, Pettit said, was "carefully rehearsed . . . very carefully." Baker commented, "It would not be an issue by anything I do. I would never mention it, nor do I plan to or encourage anyone else to or condone anyone else doing it or permit it to the extent that I could contrive that, because I don't think it is a legitimate issue in the presidential contention. The incident is so collateral and indirect that it has no proper place in a presidential campaign." The broadcast ended with Pettit saying, "All the smart presidential candidates are wondering what issues might work against Kennedy. Back in 1960 the supersensitive issue was John Kennedy's Catholicism. During that campaign, Richard Nixon said that it should not be an issue . . . and it was." The story must have left an ominous reaction in the minds of many viewers. On one hand, by saying something publicly about the impropriety of discussing the "supersentitive issue" in the upcoming campaign, Baker elevated himself in front of the television cameras, appearing statesmanlike, fatherly, forgiving, and peaceful. But was Pettit trying to say that Baker wanted to bring up Chappaquiddick for a specific reason? Was he implying that Baker hypocritically wanted to defeat Kennedy by getting personal, even though formally denying the propriety of it? The implication was that the "smart" candidates would realize that it was an issue and get out front with it. The

unmentionable issue was very alive. Although Republican John Connally was soon to disagree with Baker, saying that he thought Chappaquiddick was indeed a legitimate issue, a more subtle approach soon surfaced, whereby an ostensible Carter slip of the tongue became a newsworthy crack at Kennedy. The president, while addressing a Kew Gardens, New York, town meeting, responded to a question about leadership by asserting that he had been a steady leader and that he hadn't "panicked in a crisis." Reporters immediately interpreted this as an indirect reference to Kennedy's acknowledged indefensible behavior after his car had driven off the Dyke Bridge in 1969. Kennedy was interviewed about it, then Carter sent a letter of apology to Kennedy for any possible misinterpretation that might have been taken from his remarks. It all stayed alive over television for several days and hinted at the acrimoniousness of the campaign that would follow. See the network news programs for CBS, 22 September 1979; for NBC, 22 and 26 September and 10 October 1979; and ABC, 26 September 1979.

23. Roger Mudd, in a telephone interview with this writer on 20 January 1982, claims that one of the reasons he was chosen was because he was thought to have better ties to the Kennedys than anyone else at CBS. He was given no specific instructions about how to handle the show. A former print and radio reporter for the *Richmond News Leader* and later radio station WTOP in Washington, Mudd came to CBS in spring 1961 and remained one of its chief political reporters until November 1980, when he joined NBC. See David Halberstam, *The Powers That Be* (New York, 1979), pp. 215, 593–595. Speculation existed that the tone of *Teddy* might have had an effect on CBS's subsequent decision to replace retiring anchor Walter Cronkite with Dan Rather instead of with Mudd. Mudd scoffs at such speculation as preposterous.

24. Jack Germond and Jules Witcover, *Blue Smoke and Mirrors* (New York, 1981), p. 56.

25. Ibid., p. 58.

26. Ibid., pp. 67–68.

27. Ibid., pp. 61–62.

28. *Teddy*, *CBS Reports*, 4 November 1979 (thanks to Sam Sauratt at CBS for providing me a copy of the broadcast); see also Harwood, *Pursuit*, p. 41.

29. Germond and Witcover, *Blue Smoke*, p. 65.

30. Ibid., pp. 65–67.

31. Ibid., p. 72.

32. Mudd telephone interview 20 January 1982, which confirms Witcover and Germond, *Blue Smoke*, p. 72.

33. *Teddy*.

34. Mudd telephone interview; see also Jeff Greenfield, *Real Campaign*, pp. 59–66.

35. ABC *20/20*, 1 November 1979. Jarriel said later that he was "going for box office" when he opened his interview with Kennedy by asking, "Senator Kennedy, you cheated in college, you panicked at Chappaquiddick. Do you have what it takes to be president of the United States?" Germond and Witcover, *Blue Smoke*, p. 76. See also Blair Clark, "Notes on a No Win Campaign," *Columbia Journalism Review*, September-October 1980, p. 38. Metromedia station WNEW in New York City also had a special on Kennedy from 9:00 to 10:00 on the evening of 4 November.

36. On the effect of *Teddy* on print journalism, see Greenfield, *Real Campaign*; *Time*, 12 November 1979, p. 76, and 19 November 1979, p. 36; *New York Times*, 15 November 1979.

37. *NBC Nightly News*, 3 June 1980.

38. *Time*, 17 December 1979, p. 27.

39. Ron Powers, *The Newscasters* (New York, 1980), p. 17; Edward Said, "Inside Islam," *Harper's*, January 1981, pp. 25–32. For the controversy on television and the Iranian hostage crisis see *New York Times*, 12 and 15 December 1980. For recent background revelations on the crisis see *New York Times*, 13 May 1981.

40. Walter Lippmann, *The Stakes of Diplomacy* (New York, 1915), pp. 35–36.

41. This and other newscasts quoted from videotape copies supplied by Vanderbilt University Television News Archives.

42. *CBS Evening News*, 9 January 1980.

43. *New York Times*, 29 January 1980, p. 1.

44. *New York Times*, 31 January 1980.

45. *NBC Nightly News*, 27 January 1980.

46. *New York Times*, 31 January 1980.

47. *New York Times*, 4 February 1980. Shales's comment is quoted in Lewis's column.

48. Personal interview with Jed Duvall of CBS, 11 December 1981.

49. Clark, "No Win Campaign," p. 40.

50. Personal interview with ABC producer Bob Siegenthaler, 10 December 1981 (see also Gans, *What's News*, p. 161); Edward Jay Epstein, *News from Nowhere* (New York, 1973).

51. Doris Graber, *Mass Media and Politics* (New York, 1980), p. 179. For the poor coverage of economic issues before the New Hampshire primary in particular and in the campaign in general see "Horsefeathers: The Media, the Campaign, and the Economic Crisis," *Columbia Journalism Review*, July/August 1980, pp. 41–46.

52. Duvall interview for the physiological contagion.

53. Deardourff quoted in Foley et al., *Nominating*, p. 58.

54. Correspondent Roger Sharp of WABC-TV in New York City related in a 16 December 1981 telephone interview that local TV stations would often give Kennedy four or five minutes on their local news shows because he was a big draw, whereas other candidates were given considerably less time. The length may have hurt Kennedy.

55. Quoted in Blumenthal, *Permanent Campaign*, p. 258.

56. *The New Yorker*, 23 June 1980, p. 65.

57. Quoted in Blumenthal, *Permanent Campaign*, pp. 262–263.

58. *NBC Nightly News*, 20 November 1979.

59. See *New York Times*, 6 November 1979, for the earlier dispute Mobil had with CBS over the reporting of its profits. Two radio commercials began to run on 5 December, to continue during December six to seven times a day on thirty stations, that showed Kennedy's link to Carter on the rising price of oil. One of the commercials dramatized a meeting of oil company executives in which the chairman is heard saying, "Gentlemen, it's time for U.S. oil companies to pick the next president," with several responding that they were for Kennedy, noting a 1976 vote that Kennedy supported to decontrol home heating oil. The commercial also noted the presence of Schmertz. "Forget what Kennedy is saying in public," a voice intoned. "One of our men, a vice-president of Mobil, is directing Kennedy's ad campaign" (Wayne Kint, *New York Times*, 6 December 1979). This kind of commercial would not only have outraged oil-starved New Hampshire voters but those liberal activists, so many of them sitting on the sidelines, who would be outraged by Kennedy's association with Schmertz.

60. Blumenthal, *Permanent Campaign*, p. 17; *New York Times*, 3 December 1979.

61. Martin Shramm, "Carter," p. 104.

62. *New York Times*, 16 March 1980.

63. Ibid.

64. The commercial was shown as part of Phil Jones's report on *CBS Evening News*, 9 January 1980.

65. Nicholas Lehmann, "Industry," p. 30. *New York Times*, 19 November 1979, reports on the *Meet the Press* interview. Garth reportedly coached him on the nature of his response.

66. Quoted in *New York Times*, 31 January 1980, p. 9.

67. Quoted in Jonathan Moore, *Campaign for President*, p. 74.

68. He was able to get on the evening news by using humor and a variety of techniques to get attention. See for instance his appearance following Carter (*CBS Evening News*, 1 February 1980), when he debated a tape recorder instead of being able to debate his real opponent, who left quickly before Kennedy's planned arrival.

69. See Germond and Witcover, *Blue Smoke*, p. 196, for details of the controversy.

70. Michael Arlen, "State of the Art," *The New Yorker*, 18 February 1980, p. 108.

71. Sawyer interview.

72. Ibid.

73. Michael Arlen, "State of the Art," p. 112.

74. Sawyer interview.

75. "Spokesman" spot 3/19 from Sawyer and Associates.

76. Unidentified Guggenheim commercial.

77. "Smiling Carter" 3/19/79 produced.

78. Interview with associate of David Sawyer, 15 December 1981.

79. "Fingers Crossed" spot from Sawyer and Associates.

80. "Apollo" spot from Sawyer and Associates.

81. Telephone interview with Bill Murphy, a time buyer with Media Management in New York City, 21 December 1982.

82. *CBS Evening News*, 30 May 1980. For evidence of media overload on voters see *Advertising Age*, 2 June 1980, p. 1.

83. Tony Schwartz, *New York Times*, 13 August 1980, p. C:28.

84. *Broadcasting*, 18 August 1980, p. 24.

85. WCBS-TV local news, 6:00 P.M. August 1980.

Chronology

The introductory essay to this volume identifies four approaches through which scholars might productively utilize television as artifact in the study of American history and culture. The following selective and impressionistic chronology is not intended to be a comprehensive outline of the history of American television. Rather, it is meant to illustrate some of the events and developments that relate to one or more of those four avenues of study:

1. television news and documentary as primary evidence for historical events
2. television as social and cultural history
3. the history of television as an art form industry
4. docudrama and historical documentary as interpreters of history.

1873   Englishmen Joseph May and Willoughby Smith discover that the element selenium will create a small electric current in response to light shined upon it.

1883   In Germany Paul Nipkow develops mechanical scanning disc capable of scanning and transmitting an image.

1923   First use of networking in radio as programs are aired simultaneously in different cities, an important precedent for TV.

Charles Francis Jenkins gives first public demonstration of mechanical television in the United States, a wireless transmission from Washington to Philadelphia of a still picture of President Harding.

Russian immigrant Dr. Vladimir Zworykin, working for Westinghouse (and later for RCA), develops the iconoscope, the first electronic scanning device.

David Sarnoff reports to the NBC board of directors: "I believe that television, which is the technical name for seeing as well as hearing by radio, will come to pass in due course."

1926 (September 9) RCA creates the National Broadcasting Company, retaining 50 percent of the stock.

1928 (September 11) *The Queens Messenger*, a TV melodrama, is broadcast over a GE station in Schenectady, N.Y., one of several experimental stations broadcasting test patterns and irregular programming to a few hundred sets.

William Paley, young heir to a cigar-company fortune, buys CBS.

Federal Radio Commission, licenser prior to the FCC, notes that "such benefit as is derived by advertisers must be incidental and entirely secondary to the interest of the public."

1930 (March) Broadcasting ratings begin when a group of national radio advertisers form an organization, Cooperative Analysis of Broadcasting.

Philo T. Farnsworth develops an electronic image-dissecting device and a new scanning system. Together, Farnsworth's and Zworykin's developments far outclass earlier mechanical devices.

1933 FDR's first fireside chat on nationwide radio.

1934 Communications Act establishes the Federal Communications Commission and many of the basic regulations that govern the industry today.

1935   The Nielsen ratings begin, with the use of "Audimeters" in sample radio audiences.

1938   (Christmas) At least five companies already have television sets on the market, although there are no standards established and programming is still available only on an irregular experimental basis.

1939   (April 30) Franklin D. Roosevelt becomes the first president to appear on television at the opening of the New York World's Fair.

   (May 17) The first baseball game is telecast between Princeton and Columbia at Baker Field in New York.

1940   (March 30) FCC grants RCA permission to begin "limited commercial television," but warns public that TV sets bought now might not meet future standards.

1941   (July 1) Regular commercial broadcasting is authorized to begin by the FCC. Both CBS's and NBC's New York City stations convert from experimental to commercial status.

   NBC, founded in 1927 and operated until this time as two radio networks, the Red and the Blue, is required to sell off the Blue Network, which becomes the basis of ABC.

1942   Commercial development of television is halted by World War II. In New York City only the DuMont station maintains limited programming throughout the war.

1946   (November) Premier issue of *Sponsor*, a journal designed specifically for broadcast industry, tells potential broadcast sponsors, "Censorship is integral to the central purpose of creating good will."

1947   *Meet the Press*, a long time-radio broadcast, makes its television debut.

1948   (September 29) As new stations are formed, frequency problems become so acute that the FCC declares a freeze on the assignment of all new channels. In 1952, when freeze is lifted, commercial VHF stations are limited to twelve channels.

(October 3) The National Football League is the first professional sports organization to allow regular broadcasts, initially on ABC.

U.S. vs. *Paramount*. The Supreme Court orders a "divorcement" of theater holdings from production and distribution of films, thus seriously harming the power of the big Hollywood studios.

1949   (May 5) *Crusade in Europe* is shown on ABC. Time-Life Inc. produces this first of many documentary series for TV that address the subject of World War II.

(May) Milton Berle appears on the cover of both *Time* and *Newsweek*.

Television sets make their first appearance in a Sears, Roebuck catalog. Price: $149.95.

CATV, first precedent for what is now cable TV, develops in areas of Pennsylvania and Oregon where geographical factors limit access to broadcast signals.

1950   (June 22) *Red Channels* is published. A "newsletter of facts to combat communism," it names personalities in the entertainment business who are "reported" to have Communist leanings.

(August 19) ABC becomes the first TV network to begin Saturday morning programming for children with *Animal Clinic* and *Acrobat Ranch*.

By this year, 3.9 million households (9 percent of the total) have television sets. Within ten years 45.8 million households (87.1 percent) will possess at least one set.

This year also finds $200 million expended on television advertising by American business, 3 percent of all the money spent on ads. By 1960 the total rises to $1.6 billion (13.6 percent) and 1970 sees $10.2 billion spent (20.5 percent).

1951 (March 14) Opening of televised Senate hearings on organized crime. In ensuing weeks, Senator Estes Kefauver is seen by millions of Americans and is considered a presidential candidate.

(April 26) Kurt and Gladys Lang and a team of thirty-one University of Chicago sociologists engage in the first large-scale analysis of a major news event. Their subject is the MacArthur Day Parade in Chicago, which followed the general's dismissal from involvement in the Korean War. Their findings cast strong doubt on the reality TV presented to its viewers.

Amos 'n' Andy comes to CBS television.

1952 (January 14) NBC launches the *Today Show* at 7:00 A.M.

(June 30) *The Guiding Light* begins on CBS-TV.

(July) First telecast over a national hookup of the Democratic and Republican conventions in their entirety to upwards of 50 million people.

(September 23) Richard Nixon's "Checkers" Speech.

(Fall) NBC produces *Victory at Sea*.

One hundred and eight stations are on the air.

Emmy Awards name Bishop Fulton J. Sheen as the "most outstanding television personality."

1953 (January 20) Eisenhower's presidential inauguration is the first to be covered live by television.

(February 1) *You Are There* with Walter Cronkite premieres on CBS-TV.

(May 24) *Marty* is shown.

(June 2) In puzzled awe, Americans watch the coronation of Queen Elizabeth.

(October 20) *See It Now* airs *The Case of Milo Radulovich #0589839*.

Twenty-five percent of motion picture theaters are closed. Only drive-in theaters continue to expand.

Eighty percent of network shows are done live before television cameras at the time of televising.

Policies laid down for the *Ray Bolger Show* by the sponsor, Sherwin-Williams Paint Company, include this injunction: "Do-it-yourself activity around the home by the husband or wife should never be ridiculed or made to appear difficult."

1954   (March 9) *See It Now*'s *Report on Senator McCarthy*.

(April 22-June 17) Army-McCarthy hearings.

(October 27) *Disneyland* premieres. Program is keyed to the four divisions of a planned California amusement park of the same name: Adventureland, Frontierland, Fantasyland, and Tomorrowland.

(November 27) What began a year before as a local New York City program with Steve Allen goes network as *The Tonight Show*.

(December 15) *Disneyland* begins the first of a three-part series, "Davy Crockett," that begins a consumer fad with children all over America wearing coonskin caps and Davy Crockett outfits.

A new series of Senate hearings into the causes of juvenile delinquency frequently relates the involvement of TV in the development of children's habits.

Warner Brothers' movie studio breaks precedent and signs a contract with ABC to produce *Cheyenne*, a Western, the first of numerous profitable series.

1955   (November 15) Original scheduled air date for *Nightmare in Red*. Actual broadcast does not take place until December due to sponsor pressure.

Mutual Broadcasting buys RKO Pictures, not for its studio facilities but for its film library. For years thereafter the films are shown on WOR-TV's *Million Dollar Movie*.

Queen for a Day premieres on ABC, hosted by Jack Bailey. For more than a decade this is one of America's most popular daytime shows. Life's downtrodden compete to see who can make the audience pity them most.

1956   (January) Columbia Pictures is the first of the studios to rent its pre-1958 feature films to television. Within two years the other major studios have followed suit.

(April 14) Ampex Corporation demonstrates the first prototype video recorder to CBS affiliates gathered for a convention in Chicago. Ultimately videotape will completely replace the earlier kinescope form of recording.

(June 5) Milton Berle's show is dropped by NBC.

The first closed-circuit fund-raising political dinner, "Salute to Eisenhower," is held simultaneously in fifty-two cities, netting the Republicans $5 million.

(October) The second production of CBS's *Playhouse 90* is *Requiem for a Heavyweight*, starring Jack Palance and Keenan Wynn.

Armed Forces Radio and Television Service has twenty television stations, each receiving seventy hours of filmed network programming per week and gaining large foreign audiences.

NBC replaces John Cameron Swayze's news anchor job with the team of Chet Huntley and David Brinkley.

John Henry Faulk sues CBS after it fires him for allegations of his links to communism. Edward R. Murrow sends Faulk a check for $7,500 so that he can retain the famed attorney Louis Nizer as his counsel. The courts awarded Faulk $3.5 million in 1962.

1957   (September 24) To quell mob violence and protect school integration, Eisenhower sends troops to Little Rock, Arkansas. TV cameras follow.

(October 4) TV spreads the news of the Russian launch of Sputnik.

American Bandstand begins broadcasting from Philadelphia on weekdays.

Krushchev appears on the CBS series *Face the Nation* from his Moscow office.

1958   (October 2) The *Playhouse 90* production of *Days of Wine and Roses* is shown. Like *Marty* (1953), it later becomes a film.

(November 23) Ronald Reagan appears in a Thanksgiving special on *GE Theater*, *A Turkey for the President*.

(Fall) *$64,000 Question* is canceled in the midst of scandal, but not before it gives away more than $2 million and twenty-nine Cadillacs.

CBS cancels *See It Now*.

1959   (April) Fidel Castro appears on *Meet the Press* only months before his takeover of Cuba.

(July) On camera, touring Vice-President Nixon and Premier Krushchev "debate" each other over a kitchen display in a Moscow exhibition.

(October) The Television Information Office, sponsored by stations and networks, is formed to give the public a positive attitude toward TV.

(November 2) Columbia University professor Mark Van Doren admits fraud before a congressional subcommittee in relation to the quiz show scandals.

Bonanza (NBC) is the first series regularly broadcast in color.

A typical hour-long variety show costs more than $100,000 to produce.

1960   (April) ABC's show about gangsters, *The Untouchables*, gains first place in the Arbitron ratings, even though, according to Erik Barnouw, it was "probably the most violent show on television."

(September 26) First Kennedy-Nixon debate.

(November) Election night coverage reaches 92 percent of homes and is the third-most-watched special event in history.

(Thanksgiving Day) *Harvest of Shame* is broadcast by CBS, documenting the plight of migrant farm workers.

Five hundred fifteen commercial TV stations and forty-four noncommercial stations are broadcasting.

The Flintstones becomes the first prime-time animated cartoon show. Otherwise, Saturday morning is almost exclusively the province of cartoons and advertising aimed at their young viewers.

Ted Bates & Company, advertising agency, issues a statement of policy regarding use of tobacco products on *Bourbon Street Beat*, a series sponsored by Brown and Williamson Tobacco Corporation. It states: "Cigarettes should not be ground out violently in an ash tray or stamped out underfoot."

1961 (January 19) FCC authorizes AT&T and Bell Labs to develop and maintain Telstar. Within a year they have inaugurated transatlantic satellite relays.

(May 9) Newton Minow, new chairman of the FCC, blasts television as a "vast wasteland" in a speech that shocks broadcasters.

James Hagerty, former press secretary in Eisenhower White House, becomes vice-president of ABC.

1962 (February) Lietenant Colonel John Glenn, Jr., becomes the first American to orbit the earth. His blast-off and recovery are given extensive TV coverage.

(October 1) Johnny Carson begins his long stint as host of *The Tonight Show*.

(October 22) President Kennedy uses television to present an ultimatum to Krushchev for the removal of missiles from Cuba.

(December) *The Tunnel* (NBC) documentary dramatizes the escape of fifty-nine East Berliners through a 450-foot tunnel under the Berlin Wall.

As an effort to compensate for the bad public image produced by the quiz-show scandals, more hours of documentary programming are placed on TV than in any season before or since (253 hours).

Douglas Edwards is replaced by Walter Cronkite on the *CBS Evening News*.

Jacqueline Kennedy's *Tour of the White House* on CBS is highly publicized and adds to the glamorous image of the Kennedy family.

1963 (January 1) Newly manufactured TV sets are required to receive UHF as well as VHF stations.

(March) Prominent folk singers (Joan Baez, Bob Dylan among them) announce a boycott against ABC's *Hootenanny* for refusing to use either Pete Seeger or the Weavers because of blacklisting.

(April) *CBS Reports* recognizes the existence of a new public interest in the environment with its broadcast *The Silent Spring of Rachel Carson*, based upon that author's best-selling book.

(September 2) *CBS Evening News* expands from fifteen to thirty minutes. NBC follows with a similar expansion within one week.

(September 2) NBC broadcasts a three-hour program on problems involving civil rights.

(November 10) A one-hour NBC special introduces American audiences to the BBC's satirical blast at current newsmakers, *That Was the Week That Was*. Soon an American version would be hosted by David Frost.

(November 22-25) Assasination and funeral of President Kennedy rivets the attention of the nation to television as no previous event, reaching 96 percent of households. Coverage of the Oswald murder on November 24 also featured the use of instant replay, a technique that would soon be widely used in sports telecasts.

John Henry Faulk publishes *Fear on Trial*, documenting the damage done to one man's reputation and indirectly to the TV industry as a whole by McCarthyism in the media.

The House Commerce Committee investigates broadcast ratings services, during which widespread irregularities are uncovered. Thereafter improvements in audience analysis techniques are instituted.

1964   (February 9) The Beatles appear on the *Ed Sullivan Show*.

(February) Betty Friedan, author of *The Feminine Mystique*, takes to the pages of *TV Guide* to accuse TV of creating "millions of mindless, passive housewives who lead empty lives."

During the first three months of the year, seven episodes of the *Beverly Hillbillies* are to rank among the thirty most-watched programs from 1960 to 1977.

(July 13) Republican convention opens with 1,308 regular delegates outnumbered by the 1,825 accredited representatives of the three television networks.

(August 7) TV news makes passing reference to approval of the Gulf of Tonkin resolution in Congress.

(November) *Profiles in Courage* is broadcast. Based on the book by John F. Kennedy, the series dramatizes personalities in American history who risked their lives and reputations for unpopular causes.

(Fall) "Daisy Ad": Democratic Party ad man and television consultant Tony Schwartz creates a controversial political commercial implying that Senator Goldwater's finger would be hot on the nuclear button.

(Fall) Ronald Reagan's television speech supporting Senator Goldwater for president is well received by a number of wealthy California businessmen, who begin efforts to launch Reagan's own political career.

1965   (August 11–16) Blacks riot in the Watts area of Los Angeles. Sensational shots of rampaging mobs are taken from a KTLA helicopter and broadcast nationwide.

(August) CBS newsman Morley Safer reports the burning of a Vietnamese village by American troops, while viewers see film that backs up his description.

(October) Nam June Paik, Korean-born composer and video artist, predicts, "As collage technique replaced oil paint, the cathode ray tube will replace canvas." In 1970 he invents the video synthesizer.

(November 9) Power failure blacks out New York City and parts of eight Northeastern states. Without TV to watch, couples find other things to do, and nine months later maternity wards are overflowing.

The Federal Trade Commission orders the makers of Geritol to cease claiming that their product will cure "tired blood" resulting from iron deficiencies.

1966 (February) Fred Friendly resigns from CBS News after the network's unwillingness to televise live the Fulbright hearings on U.S. involvement in Vietnam.

(September 12) The Monkees begin a two-year run on NBC. A totally media-created pop singing group, the show wins an Emmy as Outstanding Comedy Series.

Noxema Shave Cream ad campaigns: "Take it off. Take it all off."

1967 (January 15) Superbowl I.

(November 7) President Lyndon Johnson signs the Public Broadcasting Act, which establishes the Corporation for Public Broadcasting.

FCC requires countercommercials for cigarette ads.

Michigan governor George Romney, the front runner for the Republican presidential nomination, claims before the camera that he was "brainwashed" by U.S. officials during his earlier visit to Vietnam. This statement is said to have destroyed his hopes for election victory.

Rockefeller Foundation funds television artists-in-residence programs at WGBH in Boston and KQED in San Francisco.

1968   (January 31) NBC News, rushing to scoop other networks, airs unedited footage of Vietcong "sappers" who had attacked the U.S. embassy in Saigon.

(February 2) "Rough Justice on a Saigon Street": In front of two American TV crews, General Loan, chief of South Vietnamese police, executes a Vietcong terrorist with a bullet in the head.

(February 25) Pete Seeger appears on *The Smothers Brothers Comedy Hour* and is allowed to sing his antiwar song "Waist Deep in the Big Muddy," which had been deleted by CBS censors from a show earlier that season.

(February 27) Walter Cronkite, in a half-hour special from Vietnam, concludes, "It seems now more certain than ever that the bloody experience of Vietnam is to end in a stalemate." According to David Halberstam, President Johnson decides not to run again, thinking that "if he had lost Walter Cronkite he had lost Mr. Average Citizen." Later scholars disagree.

(April 4) Martin Luther King, Jr., is assassinated. His funeral, attended by several hundred thousand people, is telecast around the world.

(May 21) *Hunger in America* is aired on CBS.

(June 5) Viewers who watched the results of the California presidential primary are shocked to see Robert Kennedy stricken by an assassin's bullet.

(August 5) Vanderbilt University Television News Archive begins to tape the evening news of the three major networks.

(August) "The Whole World Is Watching": TV is widely criticized for playing up demonstrations and violence in the streets outside the Democratic convention in Chicago.

Action for Children's Television is formed to foster better TV programming for children.

The McHugh-Hoffman firm of news consultants get their first chance at reorganizing a major TV station, WABC-TV in New York City, inaugurating greater emphasis on the personalities of television newscasters.

Richard Nixon is seen in a *Laugh-In* cameo appearance repeating the popular phrase, "Sock it to me!"

Julia premieres, starring Diahann Carroll as a registered nurse. This is the first show in sixteen years to have a black woman play the central role.

1969   (May) In the Red Lion case, the U.S. Supreme Court upholds the right of the FCC to enact a Fairness Doctrine and reaffirms the importance of the public interest under the Communications Act of 1934.

(July 20) Apollo 11 moon landing is watched by 94 percent of all homes reached by TV and is the second-most-popular TV special event.

The Howard Wise Gallery in New York City is the first to show the work of independent video artists in an exhibit entitled "TV as Creative Medium."

(Fall) Public television airs *Sesame Street*, which had been formulated by the Children's Television Workshop with Ford and Carnegie foundation and U.S. Office of Education funding.

The impossible happens. The New York Mets win the World Series against Baltimore, four games to one.

(November 13) Vice-President Spiro Agnew accuses "a small group of men" in TV news of controlling the images that 40 to 50 million Americans receive of the day's events.

(December 17) Tiny Tim stops his falsetto singing of "Tip-Toe through the Tulips" long enough to pledge his marriage vows to Miss Vicki on *The Tonight Show*.

Marcus Welby, M.D. premieres on ABC. Robert Young, the show's kindly physician, had earlier been the star of *Father Knows Best*. By the late 1970s Young capitalizes on his fatherly-professional image in coffee commercials, warning about the dangers of caffeine.

Joe McGinniss's *The Selling of the President, 1968* becomes a best seller, focusing attention on the manipulation of the public and the isolation of Nixon that resulted from his reliance on TV experts during the election campaign.

1970   NBC broadcasts another *Bob Hope Christmas Show*. This one ranks in the top ten shows of all time.

(September 19) *The Mary Tyler Moore Show* debuts. This situation comedy, based on the operation of a TV newsroom, creates characters that are able to spin off their own shows, *Lou Grant*, *Phyllis*, and *Rhoda*.

(Fall) With major funding from Mobil Oil, *Masterpiece Theater* begins to broadcast BBC-produced historical dramas over PBS on a regular basis.

(Fall) *Civilization* series, narrated by art historian Kenneth Clark, airs on PBS.

Congress bans cigarette advertising on television.

1971   (January 12) The first episode of *All in the Family* disclaims: "The program you are about to see . . . seeks to throw a humorous spotlight on our frailties, prejudices, and concerns. By making them a source of laughter we hope to show—in a mature fashion—just how absurd they are."

(February 23) CBS broadcasts *The Selling of the Pentagon*.

(April 7) Congressman Harley Staggers, chairman of the House Committee on Interstate and Foreign Commerce, issues subpoenas to CBS demanding the record of production of *The Selling of the Pentagon*.

(May 2–5) TV watches as antiwar demonstrators march on Washington, D.C.; 13,400 are arrested.

(November 30) *Brian's Song* is aired.

(December) U.S. Surgeon General's office issues report, "Television and Growing Up: The Impact of Televised Violence."

1972   (February 21–28) Followed by television cameras, President Richard Nixon visits China.

(June 17) Watergate break-in.

(July 8–9) Democratic Party stages eighteen-and-a-half-hour telethon to raise funds to help cut its debts before the 1972 campaign.

(July) Catherine Mackin becomes the first female network TV floor reporter at a national political convention.

(September 27) *CBS Evening News* devotes an unprecedented eleven-minute segment in reporting "who benefited from the grain deal" with the Russians.

(September) TV camera crews in Munich to film the Olympics wind up covering Arab terrorists' invasion of Olympic Village and murder of eleven Israeli athletes.

(September 14) "Good Night John Boy": *The Waltons*, a family drama of rural life in the Great Depression, premieres.

(October 26) National Security Adviser Henry Kissinger uses TV to proclaim that "peace is at hand" in the Vietnam conflict.

(October 27) *CBS Evening News* devotes over fourteen minutes to an overall analysis of the Watergate break-in and subsequent revelations concerning it, as well as the 1972 presidential campaign. Still, the Watergate issues have little impact on the outcome of the election.

(November 14) Premiere of Alistair Cooke's *America*, a thirteen-episode "personal history" of the United States.

(December 9) *TV Guide* becomes the fourth magazine in publishing history to carry more than $100 million in annual advertising revenue.

David Wolper's *Surrender at Appomatox* is broadcast, a production "filmed as if a newsreel camera had actually captured the final days of the Civil War."

The Tonight Show moves from New York City to Los Angeles.

Home Box Office (HBO) announces the beginning of service in Wilkes-Barre, Pa.

The FTC encourages an end to "brand X comparisons" in TV advertising. Within four years brand-name comparisons are included in 25 percent of prime-time ads.

1973   (February) PBS begins its broadcasts of *An American Family*, tracing the daily lives of the Loud family of Santa Barbara. Unlike TV's typical fantasy view of family life, this realistic documentary shows a family coming apart at the seams.

(March) The National News Council is established by Twentieth Century Fund to monitor complaints about unfair news coverage.

(May 4) On *Steambath* (PBS), a *Hollywood Television Theater* production, Valerie Perrine becomes the first woman to bare her breasts on American network TV.

(May 9) On national TV, Nixon announces resignation of key aides, H.R. Haldeman and John Ehrlichman and the firing of John Dean. He admits responsibility, but not blame, for Watergate.

(June) CBS voluntarily drops its "instant analysis" of Nixon administration speeches. Procedure reinstalled several weeks later.

(September 20) Howard Cosell hosts a "battle of the sexes" as tennis stars Billie Jean King and Bobby Riggs face $100,000 winner-take-all challenge in Houston Astrodome.

(October 1973-March 1974) Huge lines at gas pumps mark the beginning of the "energy crisis." Television news is criticized for failing to explain adequately the complicated nature of the international economic, political, and technological problems. The Crisis peaks again in 1978-1979.

TV cameras are present as Senate Watergate Committee hearings focus on the growing scandal.

Twenty percent of CBS local affiliates refuse to carry repeat showing of Norman Lear's *Maude* episode dealing with Maude's decision to have an abortion. This same year, CBS is forced to postpone telecast of antiwar play *Sticks and Bones* in response to "an unprecedented level of affiliate defections." Showing would have coincided with return of American POWs.

1974   (January) CBS airs *The Autobiography of Miss Jane Pittman* with Cicely Tyson, who portrays a proud black woman in four stages of her life.

(Summer) The House Judiciary Committee hearings on the Nixon impeachment are covered live on national television.

(August 9) Nixon resigns and makes an emotional departing speech before the cameras. One month later President Ford grants Nixon a complete pardon.

(September) NBC correspondent Ron Nessen becomes the White House press secretary.

ABC breaks tradition by naming Ann Compton to be the first female full-time network White House correspondent.

A Roper poll indicates that for the first time a majority of Americans are relying more on television than on newspapers for their news.

PBS presents *Upstairs, Downstairs*.

ITT aggressively promotes a series of children's programs, entitled *The Big Blue Marble*, in an attempt to defuse public criticism for its involvement in political corruption.

Responding to crusades by Action for Children's Television, the National Association of Broadcasters adopts amendments to its television code ordering an end to selling by program hosts and shortening the time for commercials on children's programs.

The National Citizens Committee for Broadcasting, under the leadership of ex-FCC Commissioner Nicholas Johnson, moves to Washington, starts a magazine (*Access*), and begins to pressure broadcasters on behalf of various public interest groups.

1975 (April 29) All three networks present extended reports on the fall of Saigon.

(September 1) *Gunsmoke* goes off the air, symbolizing the waning popularity of the Western series.

(September 30) CBS airs a two-hour docudrama, *Fear on Trial*, about its own mistreatment of John Henry Faulk twenty years before.

NBC begins a sixty-second news summary in prime time called *Update*.

1976 (January 11–12) ABC presents *Eleanor and Franklin*, based on the biography of the Roosevelts by Joseph Lash.

(January 20) After winning the Iowa caucuses, candidate Jimmy Carter appears in New York City on all three network morning news shows.

(April) NBC *Today Show* host Barbara Walters resigns and joins ABC as cohost of its Evening news with a five-year contract for $1 million a year.

(September 5) All sponsors except one withdraw from the CBS documentary *The Guns of Autumn* after 20,000 letters are sent by the National Rifle Association protesting the program.

(September 23) Gerald Ford becomes the first U.S. president to submit to a television debate with his opponent for reelection. Under pressure, Ford leaves the impression that he is unaware that the Polish people are dominated by the Soviets.

(November 11) "I'm mad as hell and I'm not going to take it any more": Paddy Chayevsky's movie *Network* opens in New York.

(November) The two parts of the movie *Gone With the Wind* wind up being the third- and fourth-most-watched programs in broadcasting history, gaining a rating of over 47 percent of TV households.

The National Endowment of the Humanities supports thirteen episodes of the *Adams Chronicles*, a history of the prominent family, in recognition of the U.S. bicentennial.

The development of a new computer chip provides the technological breakthrough necessary to stimulate a boom in video games. Atari, a small company founded in 1972, is soon to become a household word.

The *MacNeil-Lehrer Report* begins its in-depth news analysis on PBS.

CBS/Broadcast Group exceeds $1 billion in sales for the first time, producing $215 million in pretax profit.

1977 (January 23–30) Over an eight-day peiod, *Roots* is telecast by ABC. Episode eight is watched by 51.1 percent of all homes reached by television and is the second-most-watched entertainment program in TV history.

(February 6) *Tail Gunner Joe*, a docudrama, chronicles the reach for national prominence by Senator Joseph McCarthy.

(May 4) After nearly three years of seclusion, former president Nixon appears in the first of five interviews with David Frost.

(June 1) Roone Arledge, president of ABC Sports, becomes president of ABC News as well.

The Best of Families is broadcast, tracing the lives of three families in New York City during the period of 1880–1900.

TV Guide, with a weekly circulation of 20 million, is the nation's most popular magazine.

Columbia University professor Charles Frankel hosts a series, *In Pursuit of Liberty* (PBS), which explores important questions involving American freedoms.

The QUBE system, introduced on an experimental basis in Columbus, Ohio, by Warner Amex, allows interactive viewer response through the same cable that delivers the programming.

1978   (April) Four nights of *Holocaust* draw nearly 120 million viewers and personalize for them the experience of a Jewish family in Nazi Germany.

(November 18) A TV news correspondent and cameramen are killed along with Representative Leo Ryan at the Jonestown, Guyana, airport. Nearby, the religious followers of Jim Jones are encouraged to commit mass suicide.

(December 15) "DiscoVision," the first video disk player, is marketed.

1979   (January 30) The Carnegie Commission on the Future of Public Broadcasting releases a report calling for a new structure for public TV and for a commitment by the federal government to a larger, more independent, and better financed noncommercial system.

(February 25) The *New York Times* reports that "newly disclosed White House telecommunications policy office documents for 1969–74 indicate that the Nixon administration tried to control Public Broadcasting, purge it of commentators hostile to the President and to reorganize it to serve administration aims."

(March 28) TV news coverage of the incident at the Three Mile Island nuclear plant and of subsequent events satisfies neither critics nor proponents of nuclear energy.

(July 15) President Jimmy Carter uses TV to scold the American people for their material preoccupations and to observe that a "national malaise" exists.

(November 4) *Teddy* is aired by *CBS Reports*. Under intense questioning by newsman Roger Mudd, Edward M. Kennedy is noticeably uncomfortable. Across the world, Iranian students are taking over the American embassy.

(November 8) ABC News preempts regular programming at 11:30 P.M. ET for the first of a series relating to the Iranian crisis. Called *America Held Hostage*, the program later proves there is an audience for late-night news programs.

Sony announces its intention to market satellite dish antennas for less than $350.

1980 (Spring) Roger Sharp, ABC local New York reporter, is given an exclusive interview with President Carter, who swears not to provide the Arabs with spare parts for fighter planes. This ultimate example of "narrowcasting" is intended for one man, New York mayor Ed Koch, who insisted Carter go on the public record with this before he would campaign for the president among Jewish voters in the Florida primary.

(June 1) Ted Turner's Cable News Network begins twenty-four-hour programming.

(July 6) Pope John Paul II warns against the growing manipulation of the human mind by radio and television.

(August) Edward Kennedy upstages the winner of the Democratic convention, Jimmy Carter, with an unusually effective televised speech.

(September 9) The FCC creates "secondary stations," a new classification for low-powered local television stations.

(September) *Shogun* is broadcast. This five part miniseries dramatizes James Clavell's novel about an English navigator in sixteenth-century Japan.

(November) NBC takes a full-page ad in the *New York Times* to brag of its early projections of the Republican election victory. The computer-aided projections of all three networks are the target of widespread criticism.

(November) Fundamentalist preachers are given wide credit for having used television and direct mail techniques in aiding the election of TV actor Ronald Reagan to the presidency.

(November) The climactic episode of the popular evening drama *Dallas*, "*Who Shot J.R.?*" reaches into 53.3 percent of American homes and becomes, up to that time, the most-watched entertainment program in history.

1981 (January 26) The Supreme Court rules 8–0 that states are free to allow TV cameras in courtrooms.

(January) The House of Representatives allows TV cameras to record its floor proceedings. The Senate fails to follow suit.

(March 6) Walter Cronkite retires after nearly twenty years as anchor of the *CBS Evening News*, "the most trusted personality in America."

(March 26) Carol Burnett wins a $1.6 million libel suit against the *National Enquirer*.

(March 30) John W. Hinckly attempts the assassination of Ronald Reagan. The networks preempt regular programming to cover breaking events. The death of press secretary James Brady is erroneously reported.

(May 14) "Does the TV Camera Distort Reality?" Mobil Oil Corporation buys one-quarter of the *New York Times* op-ed page and criticizes the networks for their negative reporting about corporations.

(July 23) The *Washington Star*, a 128-year-old daily newspaper in the nation's capitol, ceases publication.

(July 29) An estimated 700 million view the wedding in England of Prince Charles and Lady Diana.

(July 31) Vladimir Zworykin, developer of the iconoscope, celebrates his ninety-second birthday.

Thirteen-week strike by the Screen Writers Guild of America wins it a share in profits from pay TV and sale of its products for home videocassettes.

"Television: Corporate America's Game," a major study conducted by three national unions, is critical of images of labor presented by the three networks in news and entertainment programming. *Lou Grant* is the one program that is highly praised.

Deep cutbacks in the Corporation for Public Broadcasting are announced by the newly installed Reagan administration.

1982 (April 10) On *Saturday Night Live*, Eddie Murphy asks viewers to telephone in their votes on whether or not "Larry the Lobster" should be boiled alive on coast-to-coast television; 426,000 people respond, spending 50¢ each to dial a 900-code telephone number. Larry lives.

(September) The *Blue and the Gray*, a week-long miniseries, dramatizes the Civil War. One plot line follows an aide to Lincoln blessed with powers of ESP. Needless to say, he gets to Ford's Theater too late.

(Fall) Pro football strike sends networks scurrying to fill weekend air time. Football widows rejoice.

Lou Grant is canceled by CBS. Ed Asner, the show's star, claims it is due to pressure on sponsors and the network from people who disapprove of his liberal politics.

Fred Silverman leaves his post as president of NBC. Prior to this job, Silverman had held key programming positions at ABC and CBS.

Sony introduces its "Watchman" pocket-sized television, which sells for about $350.

1983 (January 8) National Public Radio reports that ABC's insurance coverage for the 1984 Olympics includes a provision that would make up any financial loss incurred by the network if audience ratings should fall too low.

Notes on Contributors

John E. O'Connor, associate professor of history at New Jersey Institute of Technology, is also co-chairman of the Columbia University Seminar on Cinema and Interdisciplinary Interpretation and co-editor of the quarterly journal *Film & History*. He is co-editor of the companion to this volume, *American History/American Film: Interpreting the Hollywood Image* (Ungar, 1979). His other publications include: *William Paterson: Lawyer and Statesman, 1745–1806* (1979); *The Hollywood Indian* (1980); *I Am A Fugitive From A Chain Gang* (1981); and, for the Rockefeller Foundation, *Film & The Humanities* (1977).

Erik Barnouw is professor emeritus of dramatic arts, Columbia University. He is the author of ten books, including *Tube of Plenty: The Evolution of American Television* (1975), *The Sponsor: Notes on a Modern Potentate* (1978), and the three-volume *History of Broadcasting in the United States*. *The Image Empire* (1970), the third of those volumes, was awarded the Bancroft Prize in American History. Barnouw is also producer of films, such as *Hiroshima-Nagasaki, August 1945* (1970). He served as chief of the motion picture, broadcasting, and recorded sound division of the Library of Congress until his retirement in 1981.

Robert C. Allen is assistant professor in the department of radio, television, and motion pictures at the University of North Carolina-Chapel Hill. He is the co-author (with Douglas Gomery) of *Film History: Theory and Practice* (Addison-Wesley) and has published articles on film history, broadcasting, and popular culture in such journals as *Cinema Journal*, *Sight and Sound*, *Film & History*, and *Wide Angle*. He is currently at work on a book about soap operas.

Gregory Bush teaches history at New Jersey Institute of Technology and is assistant editor of *Film & History*. He is presently involved in several book projects focusing on the early history of advertising and public relations and on the concept of the crowd in American culture.

Thomas Cripps is professor of history and coordinator of the graduate program in popular culture at Morgan State University. He is the author/editor of several books, including *Slow Fade to Black: The Negro in American Film 1900–1942* (1977), *Black Film as Genre* (1978), *The Green Pastures* (1979), and *Afro-Americans in Film: A Bibliography* with Alma Taliaferro Cripps (forthcoming). In addition he has produced an award-winning film and more than fifty articles, two of which have won the George P. Hammond Prize and the Charles Thomson Prize.

David Culbert is associate professor of history at Louisiana State University, Baton Rouge, He is author of *News for Everyman: Radio and Foreign Affairs in Thirties America* (1976) and editor of *Mission to Moscow* (1980). Culbert is also coproducer (with Peter C. Rollins) of the film *Television's Vietnam: The Impact of Visual Images* (1982).

Leslie Fishbein is associate professor of American studies at Rutgers University. She has previously taught at Hunter College, Harvard, Occidental College, Rice University, and Simmons College. Her articles on film have appeared in *Film & History* and *American Quarterly*. Her book *Rebels in Bohemia: The Radicals of the Masses, 1911–1917* (1982) is published by North Carolina University Press.

Douglas Gomery is associate professor of communication arts and theater at the University of Maryland, where he teaches courses in radio, television, and film. His articles on media history have appeared in *Screen* (U.K.), *Yale French Studies*, *Cinema Journal*, *Film & History*, *Wide Angle*, and others. He is editor of *High Sierra* (1979) and coauthor (with Robert C. Allen) of *Film History: Theory and Practice*, forthcoming from Addison-Wesley.

Kenneth Hey is associate professor of film and chairman of the department of film at Brooklyn College (CUNY). He has special interests in music, art history, and theater history and has published in such journals as *American Quarterly*, *Film & History*, and *Popular Music and Society*. He is currently finishing a book on the interaction between cultural values and the Hollywood film industry.

Robert F. Horowitz, assistant professor of history at Rutgers University, Camden, is the author of *The Great Impeacher: A Political Biography of James M. Ashley* (1979). Horowitz has also published articles and reviews in such journals as *Ohio History* and *Film & History*. At present he is at work on a book about television docudramas and historical documentaries.

Garth S. Jowett is professor and director of the School of Communication at the University of Houston. He is author of *Film: The Democratic Art* (1976), *Movies as Mass Communication* (with James Linton), and numerous chapters in books and articles in scholarly journals. Jowett is also editor of the Arno Press series *Dissertations on Film* and *Aspects of Film*.

Daniel J. Leab, professor of history at Seton Hall University, is also the editor of *Labor History*, the secretary-treasurer of the Society for Cinema Studies, and cochairman of the Columbia University Seminar on Cinema and Interdisciplinary Interpretation. His publications include numerous articles. His books include *A Union of Individuals: The Formation of the American Newspaper Guild* (1970) and *From Sambo to Superspade: The Black Experience in Motion Pictures* (1975). He is the editor of the forthcoming *Labor History Reader*, to be published by the University of Illinois Press.

Lawrence Lichty is professor of communication arts and theater at the University of Maryland. He is author (with Malachi Topping) of *American Broadcasting: A Sourcebook on the History of Radio and Television*. Lichty is also director of research for *The Vietnam Project*, a major television series in production at WGBH-TV in Boston.

Peter C. Rollins is associate professor of English at Oklahoma State University. He is author of *Benjamin Lee Whorf: Transcendental Linguist* (1980) and numerous articles on film, television, and American culture. His film *Will Rogers' 1920's* (1977) won a CINE Golden Eagle Award. With David Culbert he has recently completed a new film, *Television's Vietnam: The Impact of Visual Images*. Rollins is president of the national Popular Culture Association.

Bert Spector, a Ph.D. in American history, is a research associate in the Harvard University Graduate School of Business Administration. His interest in the Smothers Brothers grew out of his dissertation on Pete Seeger. He has published articles on social and political history in *Antioch Review* and the *Journal of American Culture* and is correctly completing a book on human resource management.

Arthur F. Wertheim teaches history at California Polytechnic State University at San Luis Obispo. He has written two books, *The New York Little Rennaisance: Iconoclasm, Modernism, and Nationalism in American Culture, 1908–1917* (1976) and *Radio Comedy* (1979). At present he is at work on a volume about television comedy, and in 1983 he will publish *American Popular Culture in Historical Perspective: A Bibliography*.

Guide to Archival and Manuscript Sources for the Study of Television

Before a truly comprehensive and critical historical analysis of television is possible, there must be convenient access by scholars to relevant archival sources. In recent years a few such archival collections have opened up. Several of the most significant are listed below, both those dedicated to the preservation of the programs themselves in kinescope or videotape form and those devoted to collecting related manuscripts, oral history, and other materials.

Audiovisual Archives

At present there are five major research centers through which scholars can study a wide variety of historical television programs. In each case facilities are very busy, and reservations must be made before you arrive.

1) The Museum of Broadcasting
   One E. 53rd St.
   New York, N.Y. 10052

   The *Catalog to the Radio and Television Collection of the Museum of Broadcasting* (1979) is available from the Museum for $5. More than 6,000 classic and representative television programs are available for viewing on site. There is also a small library of relevant books and periodicals.

2) ATAS/UCLA Television Archive
   University of California, Los Angeles
   Melnitz Hall, Room 1438
   Los Angeles, Calif. 90024

This is an extensive collection of more than 20,000 tapes and programs covering almost every area of the history of television broadcasting. For example, in addition to thousands of entertainment, drama, and comedy shows, there are commercials, political speeches (such as a score of John F. Kennedy's campaign addresses from the 1960 camapaign and even TV spots from his 1952 Senate race in Massachusetts). There is a comprehensive catalog and index, *The ATAS/UCLA Television Archive Catalog*, published in 1981. All viewing must be done on site.

3) Library of Congress
   Motion Picture, Broadcasting, and
      Recorded Sound Division
   Washington, D.C. 20540

By far the largest part of this collection is made up of prints that producers have deposited with the government at the time of their application for copyright. Such submissions were spotty and irregular in the early years of television, but the collection from the early 1970s through the present is especially strong. Although there is no separate published index, television entries are listed in the published *Catalog of Copyright Entries, Motion Pictures 1950–1969*, available from the Government Printing Office. There are semiannual supplements also available. All research must be done on site.

4) Vanderbilt University Television News Archive
   Vanderbilt University Libraries
   Nashville, Tenn. 37203

Since August 5, 1968, this archive has been videotaping the three networks' evening news broadcasts, preserving them and making them available for scholarship. Unlike almost all other audiovisual archives, Vanderbilt will lend copies of videotaped news programs to teachers and researchers. There is a fee for the preparation of such tapes for loan (currently $30 for each 60 minutes directly copied and $60 for each 60 minutes compiled to order from different newscasts, plus a postage and handling fee). It is possible to design exactly the compilation of broadcasts you need by using the *Television News Index and Abstracts* published monthly by the archive. Annual subscriptions are available for $60.

5) Wisconsin Center for Film & Theater Research
   6039 Vilas Communications Hall
   University of Wisconsin
   Madison, Wis. 53706

The archive contains a television collection of about 3,500 titles in addition to its extensive film collection. The archive is housed in the State Historical Society of Wisconsin on the Madison campus.

Other audiovisual materials for studying the history of television are available in smaller collections in a variety of places. At the School of Journalism and Mass Communications at the University of Georgia, for example, there is the George Foster Peabody Collection of programs that have been submitted over the years as entrants in the annual Peabody competition. A similar collection of news and public affairs programs is to be found at Columbia University in the archives of the Alfred I. duPont Awards in Broadcast Journalism. More television news materials are available at the Television News Study Center at George Washington University and at the National Archives. Although intended to serve in-house researchers and those who seek to purchase footage for independent productions, each of the major networks also maintains an archive; use by scholarly researchers in severely limited, approved only on a case-by-case basis, and likely to involve considerable fees. As noted above, archival access to television materials has only begun to grow in the past decade; any researchers interested in doing their own serious work should look far and wide for collections that may contain relevant materials. Although somewhat sketchy in its coverage, some guidance can be found in FIAF's *International Directory of Film and TV Documentation Sources*, available from the Department of Film at the Museum of Modern Art in New York City.

Manuscript Archives

As with the audiovisual materials, collections of manuscripts, screenplays, oral history, and other materials relating to research in the history of television have only recently become available. At present there are three places in the country where comprehensive collections exist.

1) University of California-Los Angeles
   Theater Arts Library
   Research Library
   Los Angeles, Calif. 90024

   University of California-Los Angeles
   Special Collections Department
   Research Library
   Los Angeles, Calif. 90024

There are extensive collections in both these divisions of the university research library. Partly because of its proximity and varied associations with the Hollywood community, dozens of industry personalities have deposited their papers here. Some collections are rich with correspondence, and others consist primarily of script materials in mimeographed form. But even in the latter case such material can allow the comparison of various stages in the evolution of final scripts.

2) University of Southern California
   Special Collections
   Doheny Library
   Los Angeles, Calif. 90007

As with UCLA, here researchers will find extensive collections of papers deposited by industry personalities from in front of and behind the scenes. USC has in addition the very rich Warner Brothers Collection of corporate records on almost every aspect of that company's film and television production history.

3) Wisconsin Center for Film & Theater Research
   6039 Vilas Communications Hall
   University of Wisconsin
   Madison, Wis. 53706

This collection, housed in the Historical Society of Wisconsin building, represents perhaps the richest collection of both corporate and personal papers dealing with news and public affairs. Because of the very active journalism school at Wisconsin, many broadcast journalists have entrusted their papers and materials there. A published catalog is available from the center, *Collections of the Mass Communications History Center and the Wisconsin Center for Film & Theater Research*.

As noted above in describing the availability of audiovisual materials, this should be taken as the beginning rather than the end of the search for archival materials. Although manuscript materials relating to television are only beginning to find their way to the archives, new collections are opening every month. The three locations listed above maintain the most comprehensive television-related collections, but researchers should keep track of new materials which are added regularly to the collections of other archives across the country. One might pay especially close attention to those archives that have specialized in collecting motion picture material in the past. These include, for example, The Library and Museum of the Performing Arts of the New York Public Library (at Lincoln Center), and the Museum of Modern Art in New York; the Margaret Herrick Library of the Academy of Motion Picture Arts and Sciences and the Charles K. Feldman Library of the American Film Institute, both in Los Angeles. Farther afield are The Brigham Young University Library in Provo, Utah and the University of Wyoming at Laramie. The Museum of Broadcasting in New York has plans to begin collecting the papers of people in the business. The personal papers of other industry professionals are likely to find their way to the archives of various universities with which individuals have maintained a special relationship. Such collections already exist at Boston University, Syracuse University and Brown University, to name a few. Also significant are the papers of individuals or organizations (such as the political parties and the NAACP noted by authors in this book) which had a special concern about television. As they become available, the records of various federal agencies responsible for the regulation of television (the Federal Trade Commission for TV advertising, for example) should provide interesting new insights as well. As the sources for the critical historical study of television gradually open up in the decades to come they will provide exciting opportunities for scholarship.

In addition to the traditional finding aids for manuscript collections, there is one special guide to film and broadcasting materials which, while limited to the west coast and already somewhat dated, can still be of considerable help: Linda Mehr, *Moving Pictures, Television and Radio: A Union Catalog of Manuscripts and Special Collections in the Western United States* (G.K. Hall: Boston, 1977).

Bibliography

Daniel J. Leab

Despite the fact that television is an extremely visual medium, a considerable amount of printed material has been produced since the medium worked its way into the American conciousness in the years immediately after the end of World War II. Some of this material is valuable, some of it is useful, some of it is provocative, and most of it is interesting.

The following representative bibliography makes no pretense to completeness nor even to comprehensiveness; it is a selection whose operative description is representative. The items mentioned represent a wide range of types of what I consider useful material. Included here are books (both fan-oriented trivia and more substantial technical tomes), scholarly monographs and angry essays, biographies and autobiographies, reports and articles from both learned journals and less esoteric vehicles.

This bibliography offers what I hope are an abundant number of clues to what has been done and what is available as well as to additional sources of information and enlightenment. Herman Melville once wrote, "To produce a mighty book, you must choose a mighty theme. No great and enduring volume can ever be written on the flea." There are those who would compare TV to the flea, and they may be right, but even if TV is a flea it has proved to have a mighty bite. One may argue that much of what has been written on the effect of that bite is not enduring, but it is there. And I hope that you will find the following books (and other printed material) if not enduring, at least useful and informative.

Anyone interested in the history of American television must begin with

Erik Barnouw's award-winning multivolume *History of Broadcasting in the United States*: vol. 1, to 1933, *A Tower of Babel*; vol. 2, to 1953, *The Golden Web*; vol. 3, from 1953, *The Image Empire* (New York: 1966, 1968, 1970). A very useful condensation and updating is his *Tube of Plenty: The Evolution of American Television* (New York, 1975). Less comprehensive but not to be ignored is his *The Sponsor: Notes on an American Potentate* (New York, 1978).

Since Barnouw's work first appeared, it has served as a source (both acknowledged and not) for many of the published works on the development of TV. One work that represents considerable original research, and also takes issue with some of Barnouw's conclusions, is Joseph H. Udelson, *The Great Television Race: A History of American Television 1925–1941* (University, Ala., 1982). Also of interest for his approach and for the material he utilizes is Laurence Bergreen, *Look Now, Pay Later: The Rise of Network Broadcasting* (Garden City, N.Y., 1980).

Somewhat dated but still very useful as a source is Lawrence W. Lichty and Malachi C. Topping, editors, *American Broadcasting: A Source Book on the History of Radio and Television*, which has an eclectic series of selections (New York, 1975).

What appears on the screen has been dealt with in a variety of ways. *Television: The First Fifty Years* (New York, 1977) is an Abrams Artbook, and as such is an attractive coffee-table tome with marvelous pictures (many in color) and occasionally trenchant commentary by its author, media critic Jeff Greenfield. Less glamorous is Harry Castleman and Walter J. Podrazik, *Watching TV: Four Decades of American Television* (New York, 1982), a season-by-season review of prime time offerings intelligently presented. Arthur Shulman and Roger Youman, *How Sweet It Was: Television—a Pictorial Commentary with 1435 Photographs* (New York, 1966) is just what its subtitle says. Max Wilk, *The Golden Age of Television: Notes from the Survivors* (New York, 1976) substitutes anecdotes for pictures but is also lighthearted in its approach. More detailed but equally fan-oriented are Richard Meyers, *TV Detectives* (La Jolla, Calif., 1981), Rick Mitz, *The Great TV Sitcom Book* (New York, 1980), Jeff Rovin, *The Great Television Series* (New York, 1977), Gary Gerani with Paul H. Schulman, *Fantastic Television: A Pictorial History of Sci-Fi, the Unusual, and the Fantastic from Captain Video to the Star Trek Phenomenon and Beyond . . .* (New York, 1977). Fascinating but mindless is Bart Andrews with Brad Dunning, *The Worst TV Shows Ever: Those TV Turkeys We Will Never Forget . . . (No Matter How Hard We Try)* (New York, 1980.

There are a number of trivia-oriented books that can be of use to scholars and other serious students of TV; among these works are Tim Brooks and Earle Marsh, *The Complete Directory to Prime Time Network TV Shows, 1946-Present* (revised and enlarged, New York, 1981); Les Brown, *The New York Times*

Encyclopedia of Television (New York, 1982); Leslie Halliwell, *Halliwell's Teleguide* (London & New York, 1979), thumbnail descriptions of Anglo-American TV shows and personalities; Vincent Terrace, *Television 1970–1980* (San Diego, Calif., 1981) which list story lines, casts, and production credits for more than fifteen hundred TV shows. Somewhat more substantial is Christopher Wicking and Tise Vahimagi, *The American Vein: Directors and Directions in Television* (London, 1979), which attempts to apply the auteurist theory to TV directors in the United States.

There are a variety of sources dealing with individual shows or series. Perhaps the best and most entertaining, if also frightening, view of the creation (or in this instance the noncreation) of a TV series is Merle Miller and Evan Rhodes, *Only You, Dick Daring, or How to Write One Television Script and Make $50,000,000* (New York, 1964). Less humorous but also much less acid are E.J. Kahn, Jr., "Profile: Sixty Minutes, Parts I and II," *The New Yorker*, July 19, 26, 1982; Stephen E. Whitfield and Gene Roddenberry, *The Making of Star Trek: What It Is—How It Happened—How It Works!* (New York, 1968); Robert Metz, *The Today Show* (Chicago, 1977); Terry Galandy, *Tonight!* (New York, 1974); Robert Metz, *The Tonight Show* (Chicago, 1980); Larry Ceplair, "Great Shows: You Are There," *Emmy: The Magazine of the Academy of Television Arts and Sciences*, January/February 1982; Ted Sennett, *Your Show of Shows: The Story of Television's Most Celebrated Variety Program Starring Sid Ceasar and Imogene Coca* (New York, 1977); Chris Rodley, "Degree Absolute: The Production, Destruction, and Afterlife of *The Prisoner*," *Prime Time: The Television Magazine*, March-May 1982. A model study of a long-running series is Marc Scott Zigree, *The Twilight Zone Companion* (New York, 1982), which is much, much more than just a fan item.

Quite often it is possible to learn a great deal about an individual show or series from the material sent out by the networks or the producers, for this material in some cases goes far beyond being a mere press kit. Thus there are such diverse objects as the "Curriculum Guide" for the 1975 PBS series *The Adams Chronicles* (which included an intelligent historical essay by David Rothman of Columbia University's history department); the richly illustrated hardback that contains the text of Ronald Ribman's *The Final War of Olly Winter*, the production inaugurating the 1967 *CBS Playhouse* series; and the specially created book brought forth jointly by ABC and McGraw-Hill announcing the nontheatrical distribution in part form of the special four-hour telecast in 1967 on Africa.

More traditional are such books as *60 Minutes Verbatim: Who said What to Whom: The Complete Text of 114 Stories with Mike Wallace, Morley Safer, Dan Rather, and Harry Reasoner* (New York, 1980), and Edward R. Murrow and Fred

398 BIBLIOGRAPHY

W. Friendly, *See It Now: A Selection in Text and Pictures* (New York, 1955), as well as the special issue of *Educational Broadcasting Review* (Winter 1971–1972) devoted to "The Selling of the Pentagon Papers."

There are also, of course, shows and series that result in a spate of works, many of them serious. *Sesame Street* was such a program. Among the works it provoked were Thomas D. Cook, et al., *Sesame Street Revisited* (New York, 1975), which raised questions about the program's intended impact: Gerald S. Lesser, *Children and Television: Lessons from Sesame Street* (New York, 1974), which details how the show operated and what its goals were; and Richard M. Polsky, *Getting to Sesame Street: Origins of the Children's Television Workshop* (New York, 1974), which relates the background to the creation of the program. Of great interest is D. Cater and S. Strickland, *TV Violence and the Child: The Evolution and Fate of the Surgeon General's Report* (New York, 1975).

Although much of television's prime-time programming is meretricious and/or banal, the medium has a rich heritage of noteworthy plays, and a considerable number of these have been published. Individual authors include Paddy Chayefsky, *Television Plays* (New York, 1955) and Reginald Rose, *Six Television Plays* (New York, 1956). A first-rate anthology is Richard Averson and David Manning White, editors, *Electronic Drama: Television Plays of the Sixties* (Boston, 1970). Also first rate is William I. Kaufman, editor, *Great Television Plays* (New York, 1969), which by 1981 had gone through fifteen printings. Kaufman also edited the various volumes of *The Best Television Plays of the Year* (New York, 1950-1954), which is worthwhile not only for the text of the plays but also for the comments of the directors and for the staging instructions. Irving Settel also provides these instructions in his *Top TV Shows of the Year: Complete Scripts of the Best Television Programs* for the 1954–1955 season (New York, 1955); he includes not only entertainment shows but also such news and public affairs programs as *Meet the Press* and the *See It Now* show on Senator McCarthy.

Commentary about these programs, if not always cordial, was not restrained. Some of the best critics have had their work collected and published. Among them are Michael J. Arlen, *The Living Room War* (New York, 1969) and *The View from Highway 1* (New York, 1976); John Crosby, *Out of the Blue* (New York, 1952); and Tom Shales, *On the Air!* (New York, 1982). In *Open to Criticism* (Boston, 1971), Robert Lewis Shayon not only reprints some of his perceptive critiques but also, with the advantage of hindsight, comments on them.

The impact of television on American society has occasioned commentary from various quarters during the past quarter-century, Arthur Asa Berger, a prolific commentator on American culture, in *The TV-Guided American* (New York, 1976) describes what in his opinion various TV programs "tell us about ourselves." TV producer/media teacher Marc Eliot, in his *American Television:*

The Official Art of the Artificial, Style and Tactics in Networks Prime Time (New York, 1981), tries (not always successfully) to deal with thirty-five years of TV shows in prime time and to comment meaningfully on many of them. *The TV Ritual: Worship at the Video Altar* by theologian Gregor T. Goethals (Boston, 1981) is a not-always-successful attempt to deal with the "symbolic power of television" as icon and as ritual. *How to Talk Back to Your Television Set* (Boston, 1970) was published while its author Nicholas Johnson was still a maverick FCC commissioner and represents his then-iconoclastic view of how America's airwaves should be governed. Successful TV producers Richard Levinson and William Link have produced a fascinating insider's account in *Stay Tuned* (New York, 1981), which deals with the production of shows for prime-time television; this book is readable and discerning. One of the best books ever written about the medium is Martin Mayer's *About Television* (New York, 1972), which deals with all aspects of the industry intelligently and critically. Typical of the many books critical of the impact and programming of American television is Harold Mehling, *The Great Time-Killer* (Cleveland, 1962). Horace Newcomb, *TV: The Most Popular Art* (Garden City, N.Y., 1974) and Stan Opotowsky, *TV: The Big Picture* (New York, 1961), are intelligent surveys in their time of the pros and cons of TV. A first-rate collection of essays about television by a perceptive scholar is Robert Sklar, *Prime-Time America: Life on and behind the Television Screen* (New York, 1980). Less funny, less well written, but still useful is *Seven Glorious Days, Seven Fun-Filled Nights* by Charles Sopkin (New York, 1968), which is an account of simultaneously watching six New York City TV channels around the clock. Ben Stein, *The View from Sunset Boulevard: America as Brought to You by the People Who Make Television* (New York, 1979), raises some important questions about the social values of those in charge of prime time and their possible distortion of the meaning of America. "What Is TV Doing to America?" in the August 2, 1982, issue of *U.S. News & World Report* doesn't answer the question successfully, but it does summarize the most important arguments about the current impact of TV on American social values.

These differing responses are also to be found in the various anthologies that have been published over the years. The following, all of which contain at least some outstanding material, are just a sample of the diverse works that have been published: A. William Bluem and Roger Manvell, editors, *Television, the Creative Experience: A Survey of Anglo-American Progress* (New York, 1967); Barry G. Cole, editor, *Television: Selections from TV Guide Magazine* (New York, 1970); Douglas Davis and Allison Simmons, editors, *The New Television: A Public/Private Art* (Cambridge, Mass., 1978); Judy Fireman, editor, *TV Book: The Ultimate Television Book* (New York, 1977); Jay S. Harris, editor, *TV Guide: The First 25 Years* (New York, 1978); Carl Lowe, editor, *Television and American Culture* (New York, 1981); Horace Newcomb, editor, *Television: The Critical View*, second edition (New York, 1979); *The Eighth Art: 23 Views of Television*

Today (New York, 1962); Gaye Tuchman, editor, *The TV Establishment: Programming for Power and Profit* (Engelwood Cliffs, N.J., 1974).

There are many accounts about the people involved in the world of TV, then and now, but few of these biographies or autobiographies are substantial. Most are puff jobs or are spawned via the tape recorder for gullible fans. Among the many such works are Jackie Cooper, *Please Don't Shoot My Dog: The Autobiography of Jackie Cooper* (New York, 1981), Phil Donahue, *Donahue: My Own Story* (New York, 1979), Mike Douglas, *Mike Douglas: My Story* (New York, 1978), Virginia Graham, *If I Made It, So Can You* (New York, 1978), Merv Griffin, *Merv* (New York, 1980), Gil Noble, *Black Is the Color of My TV Tube* (Secaucus, N.J., 1981).

Of more substance are Kenneth Tynan, "Heeeeere's Johnny: A Profile of Johnny Carson," *The New Yorker*, February 20, 1978; Larry Ceplair, "Fred Coe: Forgotten Genius," *Emmy: The Magazine of the Academy of Television Arts & Sciences*, July/August 1982; George Everson, *The Story of Television: The Life of Philo Farnsworth* (New York, 1949); Peter Goldmark, *Maverick Inventor: My Turbulent Years at CBS* (New York, 1973); Alexander Kendrick, *Prime Time: The Life of Edward R. Murrow* (Boston, 1969); William Paley, *As It Happened: A Memior* (Garden City, N.Y., 1969); Eugene Lyons, *David Sarnoff: An American Biography* (New York, 1966); Sally Bedell, *Up the Tube: Prime Time and the Silverman Years* (New York, 1981); Michael David Harris, *Always on Sunday: Ed Sullivan—an Inside View* (New York, 1968).

For understandable reasons perhaps the most thoughtful and incisive commentary is to be found in that material dealing with TV news. Fred W. Friendly, *Due to Circumstances Beyond Our Control . . .* (New York, 1967) is an angry and extremely readable memoir by a former head of CBS News who quit over a decision by the network to rerun for the fifth time an *I Love Lucy* show rather than to broadcast hearings of a Senate committee dealing with vital national interests. Harry J. Skornia, *Television and the News: A Critical Appraisal* (Palo Alto, Calif., 1968) is a dispassionate overview of the handling of news by TV and of what the author finds to be the medium's shortcomings. *The Half Shut Eye: Television and Politics in Britain and America* by James Whale (London, 1969) is a comparative study that finds shortcomings in political coverage both in the United States and the U.K. Edward W. Chester judiciously views the impact that media changes have made on American politics in *Radio, Television and American Politics* (New York, 1969); the book has an extremely useful bibliography. A veteran media news practioner, William Small, raises in his book *To Kill a Messenger: Television News and the Real World* (New York, 1970) serious questions about the viewer's response to the issues raised by TV broadcasters in public affairs programming. More restrained is Sig Mickelson, also a veteran of the broadcast world, in his *The Electronic Mirror: Politics in an Age of Television* (New York, 1972). But little restraint marks Edward Jay Epstein's provocative study *News from Nowhere: Television and the News* (New York, 1973), which finds that a variety of social and commercial factors determine what kind of news is presented and that this presentation may be seen as only one version and not necessarily the most correct one. The vital impact of television on the American body politic is entertainingly questioned by Edwin Diamond in his sassy *The Tin Kazoo: Television, Politics and the News* (Cambridge, Mass., 1975). A much more sober and detailed study is *Deciding What's News: A Study of CBS Evening News, NBC Nightly News, Newsweek & Time* by Herbert Gans (New York, 1979); the author tries with considerable success to discern why the United States is portrayed as it is by those branches of the media he is dealing with. *Media Unbound: The Impact of Television Journalism on the Public* (Boston, 1982), by Stephen Lesher is a vigorous "warts and all" portrait of contemporary TV journalism that ultimately comes down in favor of what is being done.

There are many aspects to television's handling of news. There is, of course, a show-business aspect, as is cleverly demonstrated by Ron Powers in his *The Newscasters* (New York, 1978), which deals with "the news business as show business." Because of the excitement intrinsic to the subject as well as its obvious importance, disparate sources have dealt intensely and intelligently with the subject of TV news. Great Britain's Open University has dealt in a comparative fashion with the subject as demonstrated by the materials on "Television and Politics" for the third-level course Mass Communications and Society (1977), which ape a case study of a subject in the United States as well as across the Atlantic Ocean. Media critic Robert Sam Anson published his article "Behind the Lines in the Network News War" in *Playboy*, September 1982. At the opposite end of the spectrum are the articles to be found in *Fortune* such as resident guru Max Ways's analysis, "What's Wrong with News? It Isn't New Enough" (October 1969) and Sheldon Zalanick's report on "The Rich Risky Business of TV News" (May 1969).

Of considerable importance to anyone interested in this subject are the reports that have been published periodically since 1969 surveying the field of broadcast journalism—the Alfred I. duPont/Columbia University Survey, mostly edited solo or in tandem by Marvin Barrett, is a detailed overview of what's happening, undertaken with some verve and presented with a fine eye to what will be of interest. Since the end of World War II, CBS has generally dominated the news arena, and a fine overview of that network's operations in this area is to be found in *Air Time: The Inside Story of CBS News* by Gary Paul Gates (New York, 1978). The network's operations are not without their detractors, however. Edith Efron's *The News Twisters* (Los Angeles, 1971) was less than kind to the network's news operations, and the next year, with the assistance of Clytia Chambers, Efron wrote about what she described as *The Campaign by CBS to Kill The News Twisters* (New York, 1972). Joseph Keeley's *The Left Leaning Antenna: Political Bias in Television* (New Rochelle, N.Y., 1971) was much more vociferous and broad based in its charges about the overly liberal slant of all the networks' news departments.

Documentary deals with various historical treatments of what has happened and what is happening. A first-rate introduction to the subject is A. William Bluem, *Documentary in American Television: Form, Function, Method* (New York, 1965). Less successful is the follow-up by Charles Montgomery Hammond, Jr., *The Image Decade: Television Documentary, 1965–1975* (New York, 1981), although it is an adequate survey. A worthwhile puff job is the booklet distributed by NBC News, *The Invention of the Television Documentary: NBC News, 1950–1975* (New York, 1975). David G. Yellin, *Special: Fred Freed and the Television Documentary* (New York, 1973) is an outstanding study of the medium, the subject, and the man. That documentary on TV can take various forms is often overlooked—and a valuable treatment of one of the less-well-publicized forms is Stanley Field, *The Mini-Documentary: Serializing the News* (Blue Ridge Summit, Pa., 1975).

Sports is one of the major features of television, and a good introduction to the impact of sport upon television is William O. Johnson, Jr., *Superspectator and the Electric Lilliputians* (Boston, 1971). There is also a special section of the *Washington Journalism Review* (June 1980) on the TV sports explosion, which raises some diverse lines of inquiry in articles ranging from cost escalation to the quality of broadcasters.

Commercials are also a major feature of television. A nostalgic view of that genre is Lincoln Diamant, *Television's Classic Commercials: The Golden Years, 1948–1958* (New York, 1971). That same author has also penned *The Anatomy of a Television Commercial: The Story of Eastman Kodak's "Yesterdays"* (New York, 1970), a perceptive and sophisticated account of the making of a classic, award-winning commercial. A somewhat dated but enjoyable work is Robert L. Foreman, *An Ad Man Ad-libs TV* (New York, 1957). More recent is Paul Stevens, *I Can Sell You Anything: How I Made Your Favorite TV Commercials with Minimum Truth and Maximum Consequence* (New York, 1972). The quality of these commercials as regards children is devastatingly revealed in Charles Winnick, et al., *Children's Television Commercials: A Content Analysis* (New York, 1973). See also Jonathan Price, *The Best Thing on TV: Commercials* (New York, 1978).

Various scholars have examined various aspects of television and done well utilizing the tools of their trade. An early but still viable study is Leo Bogart, *The Age of Television: A Study of the Viewing Habits and the Impact of Television on American Life* (New York, 1956). Also dated but somewhat more sophisticated is Gary A. Steiner, *The People Look at Television: A Study of Audience Attitudes* (New York, 1963), which is a report of a study undertaken by the Bureau of Applied Social Research, Columbia University. Dealing solely with minors is Wilbur Schramm, Jack Lyle, and Edwin B. Parker, *Television in the Lives of Our Children*

(Stanford, Calif., 1961). Less jargony and less statistics-oriented but equally ominous is Marie Winn, *The Plug-In Drug* (New York, 1977).

On the business behind the scenes see Les Brown, *Television: The Business behind the Box* (New York, 1971). More readable than most of the works dedicated to treating the economic aspects of television are Roger G. Noll, Merton J. Peck, and John J. McGowan, *Economic Aspects of Television Regulation* (Washington, D.C., 1973), a Brookings Institution study, and Harvey J. Levin, *Fact and Fancy in Television Regulation: An Economic Study of Policy Alternatives* (New York, 1980), whose view of the future is so bleak. So too is The Network Project, *Directory of the Networks* (New York, 1973) in its implications on who and what controls American broadcasting. A more rosy-hued view is to be found in the special issue of *Television Magazine* (August 1964) entitled "The Many Worlds of Local TV," which is a fine rundown in pictures and text of what's being done "out there." *Inside ABC: American Broadcasting Company's Rise to Power* by Sterling Quinlan (New York, 1979), despite its tough-talking introduction, deals very gingerly with the network and provides no more than a colorfully written travel guide to the fringes of the company. Only a bit more informative, but much better presented, is *CBS: Reflections in a Bloodshot Eye* by Robert Metz (Chicago, 1975). A useful view of the network at the end of the 1940s is CBS, *Closeup: A Picture of the Men and Methods That Make CBS Television* (New York, 1949), which is an unpretentious picture book with a minimum of text. CBS has for some time been of interest to those who write about corporate America, so it is possible to find sound articles about the company in a variety of magazines such as *Fortune*, including such articles as Peter Bernstein, "CBS Fights to Regain the Title" (January 29, 1979), and Stratford P. Sherman, "CBS Places Its Bets on the Future" (August 9, 1982). A somewhat bemused view of television's future is to be found in Stuart M. DeLuca, *Television's Transformation: The Next 25 Years* (San Diego, Calif., 1980), which touches on both the technical and the economic future of the industry. A perceptive treatment of just one aspect of that future is Richard Adler and Walter S. Baer, *The Electronic Box Office: Humanities and Arts on the Cable* (New York, 1974). More hard-headed and informative is the survey of cable television to be found in *Industry Viewpoint*, February 1981; this issue of a report issued by Donaldson, Lufkin & Jenrette is intelligently devoted to the business state of the art at the end of 1980.

Television has also been thoroughly dealt with in various works dealing with the media in the United States. Typical of the textbooks that attempt to place television as a medium within the history of the American media is Don R. Pember, *Mass Media in America* (2nd ed., Chicago, 1977). The very prolific John Tebbel has also taken a stab at this kind of interpretation in *The Media in America* (New York, 1974). A well-written and engagingly contentious work is *The Communications Revolution: A History of Mass Media in the United States* (New

York, 1982). Very colorful, very erratic, and very fascinating is David Halberstam, *The Powers That Be* (New York, 1979), which deals with what are described as the "kings of the media," including CBS, and assays how they got the top and what they do to stay there. Equally provocative but much more broadly oriented is David L. Paletz and Robert M. Entman, *Media, Power, Politics* (New York, 1981), which concentrates on media manipulation. *Who Owns the Media?* edited by Benjamin M. Compaine (New York, 1979), deals frighteningly with the "concentration of ownership in the Mass Communications Industry" and includes two thorough chapters on television and radio broadcasting and on cable and pay television. The international impact of American television is discussed with some care and vitality in William H. Read, *America's Mass Media Merchants* (Baltimore, 1976), and Jeremy Tunstall, *The Media Are American* (London, 1977).

Various branches of government have expressed a concern with television programming. Among the more interesting results are the following reports of congressional hearings: House Committee on Interstate and Foreign Commerce hearings, *Investigation of Radio and Television Programs*, 82nd Congress, 2nd session, 1952; hearings before the subcommittee on communications, *Sex and Violence on TV*, 94th Congress, 2nd session, 1976; report of the subcommittee on communications, *Sex and Violence on TV*, 95th Congress, 1st session, 1977; Senate Committee on the Judiciary, hearings before the subcommittee to investigate juvenile delinquency, *Juvenile Delinquency*, parts 10 and 16, jointly titled *Effects on Young People of Violence and Crime Portrayed on Television*, 87th Congress, 1st and 2nd sessions, 1961–1962, 88th Congress, 2nd session, 1964. Also hearings before the Select Committee on Aging, 95th Congress, 1st session, 1977, *Aging Stereotyping and Television*. Considerable impact was made by the surgeon general's Scientific Advisory Committee on Television and Social Behavior with its report *Television and Growing Up: The Impact of Televised Violence* (1971). Another agency whose reports are of interest is the U.S. Commission on Civil Rights, which issued *Window Dressing on the Set: Women and Minorities in Television* (1917) and *Window Dressing on the Set: An Update* (1979). All three reports are published by the U.S. Government Printing Office in Washington, D.C. For the Department of Health and Human Services (National Institute of Mental Health) there has been issued a two-volume update on the previous report, *Television and Behavior*, edited by David Pearl et al., and published by the department in 1982.

An unusual and extremely interesting collection of "addresses and papers on the Future of the New Art and Its Recent Technical Developments" are the volumes issued by the RCA Institute's Technical Press (New York City), the first volume of which appeared in 1936; subsequent volumes were published in 1937, 1946, and 1947. While the majority of the articles deal with technical subjects such as transmission and reception, also included are more accessible topics, such as David Sarnoff's views on the future of television broadcasting.

Blacklisting, which must not be overlooked as a factor in the history of television, is dealt with at some length or mentioned in passing in many of the previously cited books and articles. There are two works that should be cited separately, however. One is a document of infamy: *Red Channels* (New York, 1950), compiled by the editors of the anti-Communist newsletter *Counterattack*, which, along with the various updates emanating from diverse groups, served as a who's who for those doing the blacklisting. John Cogley, *Report on Blacklisting: II. Radio-Television* (New York, 1956) is a restrained but vital exposé of what was happening. John Henry Faulk, *Fear on Trial* (New York, 1964) is the engrossing story of the ordeal of one man whose court case helped to break the blacklist, but whose once-bright career was never resurrected.

Rental Sources for Productions Discussed

Almost all the television productions discussed in this book are available for classroom rental as outlined below.

A special arrangement has been made with the Vanderbilt Television News Archive whereby teachers or researchers who wish to study the essays printed here side by side with the relevant news footage may borrow compilations of videotape that are keyed directly to the articles. See below for details.

As of this writing, the only two productions discussed in this book for which no video rental materials are available are *The Guiding Light* and *The Smothers Brothers Comedy Hour*. For access to new materials as they become available, watch for new editions of the industry-wide guide published by the National Video Clearing House, 100 Lafayette Dr., Syosset, N.Y. 11719, under the title *Video Sourcebook*. The rental sources below represent information in the 1982 edition.

See It Now

Several broadcasts, including the *Report on Senator McCarthy*, can be rented from the CBS Publishing Group, 600 Third Ave., New York, N.Y. 10016.

Amos 'n' Andy

Videocassettes of approximately twenty broadcasts are available from Shokus Video, Box 434, Van Nuys, Calif. 91409.

Milton Berle

Several programs of the *Texaco Star Theater* are available on videotape from Shokus Video (see above) and from Video Dimensions, 110 E. 23rd St., Suite 603, New York, N.Y. 10010.

You Are There

These programs were widely distributed in 16mm at the time of their production and are still available from several university film rental libraries such as those at Pennsylvania State University and Syracuse University.

Marty

The television production is available from Video Images/Reel Images, 495 Monroe Turnpike, Monroe, Conn. 06468.

Nightmare in Red

This production, like others of the *Project 20* series, is widely available in 16mm. For purchase contact McGraw-Hill Films, 1221 Ave. of the Americas, New York, N.Y. 10020.

"Checkers"

Richard Nixon's speech is widely available in 16mm. Contact, for example, New Yorker Films, 43 W. 61st St., New York, N.Y. 10023.

Brian's Song

The TV-movie is distributed in 16mm and in various video formats by Learning Corporation of America, 1350 Ave. of the Americas, New York, N.Y. 10019.

Watergate and the 1972 Elections

The television news footage discussed in Lawrence Lichty's essay can be borrowed from the Vanderbilt University Television News Archive, Vanderbilt University Libraries, Nashville, Tenn. 37203. A special compilation of the news stories discussed in Lichty's article has been prepared. Request the *American History/American Television* "Watergate Compilation." There is a fee of $30 plus shipping and, although you may use the tape for several months, it must be returned.

The Selling of the Pentagon

This documentary is widely available for rental in 16mm. For purchase contact Carousel Films, 1501 Broadway, New York, N.Y. 10036.

Roots

The entire series is available in 16mm and various video formats from Films Incorporated, 1144 Wilmette Ave., Wilmette, Ill. 60091.

Edward Kennedy and the 1980 Presidential Campaign

The television news footage discussed in Gregory Bush's essay can be borrowed from the Vanderbilt University Television News Archive (see above). A special compilation of the news stories discussed in Bush's article has been prepared. Request the *American History/American Television* "Kennedy Compilation." There is a fee of $30 plus shipping and, although you may use the tape for several months, it must be returned.